Native Place, City, and Nation

Native Place, City, and Nation

Regional Networks and Identities
in Shanghai, 1853–1937

Bryna Goodman

UNIVERSITY OF CALIFORNIA PRESS

Berkeley / Los Angeles / London

University of California Press
Berkeley and Los Angeles, California

University of California Press, Ltd.
London, England

Library of Congress Cataloging-in-Publication Data

Goodman, Bryna, 1955–
    Native place, city, and nation: regional networks and identities in
Shanghai, 1853–1937 / Bryna Goodman.
        p.   cm.
    Includes bibliographical references and index.
    ISBN 0-520-08917-0 (alk. paper)
    1. Shanghai (China) — Social life and customs. 2. Social networks —
China — Shanghai — History — 19th century. 3. Social networks —
China — Shanghai — History — 20th century. 4. Rural-urban migra-
tion — China — Shanghai — History — 19th century. 5. Rural-urban mi-
gration — China — Shanghai — History — 20th century. I. Title.
DS796S25G66   1995
951'.132035 — dc20   94-24416

Printed in the United States of America
9 8 7 6 5 4 3 2 1

for my parents

Contents

LIST OF ILLUSTRATIONS   ix

ACKNOWLEDGMENTS   xi

1
Introduction: The Moral Excellence of Loving the Group   I

2
Foreign Imperialism, Immigration and Disorder: Opium War
Aftermath and the Small Sword Uprising of 1853   47

3
Community, Hierarchy and Authority: Elites and Non-elites in
the Making of Native-Place Culture during the Late Qing   84

4
Expansive Practices: Charity, Modern Enterprise, the City
and the State   119

5
Native-Place Associations, Foreign Authority and Early
Popular Nationalism   147

6
The Native Place and the Nation: Anti-Imperialist and
Republican Revolutionary Mobilization   176

7
"Modern Spirit," Institutional Change and the Effects of
Warlord Government: Associations in the Early Republic   217

8
The Native Place and the State: Nationalism, State Building
and Public Maneuvering   258

9
Conclusion: Culture, Modernity and the Sources of National
Identity   305

APPENDIX
Population Growth in the International Settlement, 1910–30   315

GLOSSARY   317

BIBLIOGRAPHY   325

INDEX   349

Illustrations

TABLES

1
Guangdong Associations in Shanghai (1919)   238

2
Zhejiang Associations in Shanghai   239

MAPS

1
Major provinces of China supplying immigrants to Shanghai   3

2
Shanghai in the mid-nineteenth century: a Chinese view   51

3
Shanghai in the mid-nineteenth century: a Western view   52

4
Shanghai in 1880   148

5
The development of the French and International settlements   149

FIGURES

1
Yamen architecture   19

2
Huiguan architecture   20–21

3
Ningbo participants in Parade of the Shanghai International
Settlement   30–31

4
Yulanpenhui   94–95

5
Huiguan opera   108–9

6
French destruction of the Siming Gongsuo wall, 1898   166–67

7
Yu Xiaqing and his Shanghai residence   200

8
The Ningbo Tongxianghui on Tibet Road   227

9
The Pudong Tongxianghui   279

Acknowledgments

My greatest intellectual debt is to my advisors at Stanford University, Harold Kahn and Lyman Van Slyke, who guided me through a dissertation on this topic and whose careful readings and insightful criticisms challenged and inspired me over the course of many revisions. They created a rare atmosphere of intellectual collaboration at Stanford and set high standards for teaching, scholarship and integrity.

I would also like to thank Carol Benedict, Prasenjit Duara, Joseph Esherick, Christian Henriot, Wendy Larson and two anonymous readers for the press, each of whom provided detailed, thoughtful and provocative readings of my full manuscript, substantially enriching its quality. Susan Mann helped guide my initial formulation of my topic and provided insightful suggestions at various points along the way. During a postdoctoral year at the University of California at Berkeley I benefited from the presence of Frederic Wakeman and Yeh Wen-hsin, who took time to read and comment on my work and who challenged me with the breadth of their own work on Shanghai and related topics. Cynthia Brokaw, Andrew Char, Paul Katz, William Rowe and Ernst Schwintzer each read portions of the manuscript and provided insightful comments and suggestions. I am grateful for the generosity of each of these readers, with whose help I have avoided some of the pitfalls of earlier versions.

My initial research in China was greatly facilitated by my Fudan advisors, Professors Huang Meizhen and Yang Liqiang. They also opened their homes to me and introduced me to the special foods of their native places, in Fujian and Guangdong provinces. Zhang Jishun and Zhu Hong, of the Center for Research on Shanghai, together with Huang Meizhen, smoothed arrangements during a subsequent research trip in 1991, as did the staff of the Foreign Affairs Office at the Shanghai Academy of Social Sciences. I would also like to thank the staffs of the Shanghai Municipal Archives, the Shanghai Municipal Library and the Shanghai Museum of History. Fan I-chun, Yao Ping and Zhao Xiaojian spent long hours helping me interpret elusive documents. Fu Po-shek, Hamashita Takeshi, Luo Suwen, Ted Huters and Jeff Wasserstrom alerted me to sources of which I had been unaware. Dorothy Ko kindly hosted me and helped to orient me during a research trip to Tokyo. Colleagues in the History Department of the University of Oregon provided encouragement and made me more vigilant in my choice of words.

Tom Gold and the staff of the Center for Chinese Studies provided a stimulating environment for writing during my 1990–91 postdoctoral fellowship. I would like to thank the organizers of the 1988 International Symposium on Shanghai History, as well as the Center for Research on Shanghai, for two subsequent conference invitations which provided a forum for discussing my findings with colleagues in the People's Republic of China. The Committee on Scholarly Communication with the PRC (CSCPRC) and the University of Oregon provided funding to attend these conferences. I am also indebted to Christian Henriot and the staff of the Institut d'Asie Orientale in Lyon for their many kindnesses in hosting me during fall 1993 and providing a conducive intellectual climate for my final book revisions.

My research in China was made possible through a CSCPRC grant, funded by the U.S. Department of Education. I would like also to acknowledge funding from the Oregon Humanities Council and a Reed College Vollum Award, both of which permitted me to spend time on research and writing. I am grateful to Sheila Levine at the University of California Press for her support and interest in the manuscript, to Laura Driussi for her patient editorial assistance and to Sarah K. Myers for her meticulous copyediting. My friends Jeff and Rosemarie Ostler provided much-needed help with my manuscript preparation at the last minute. Finally, I would like to thank my husband, Peter Edberg, for editorial and computer assistance and many other contributions which cannot all be detailed here.

CHAPTER ONE

Introduction

The Moral Excellence of Loving the Group

Shanghai is a hybrid place which mixes together people from all over
China. The numbers of outsiders surpass those of natives.
Accordingly, people from each locality establish native-place
associations [huiguan] *to maintain their connections with each other.*
The Ningbo people are the most numerous, and they have established
the Siming Gongsuo. The Guangdong people are second in number,
and they have established the Guang-Zhao burial ground and the
Chao-Hui Huiguan. In addition to these, the people from Hunan,
Hubei, Quanzhou, Zhangzhou, Zhejiang, Shaoxing, Wuxi,
Huizhou, Jiangning, Jinhua, Jiangsu, Jiangxi and other places have
each established huiguan. *As for people from localities which have not*
established huiguan, *they have meetings of fellow-provincials every*
month. This is for the purpose of uniting native place sentiment. . . .
Among the people of our country, there are none who do not love to
combine in groups. Thus fellow-provincials all establish huiguan.
And people of the same trade all establish gongsuo. . . . *From this it*
is possible to know that Chinese people have the moral excellence of
loving the group.

— Li Weiqing, *Shanghai xiangtuzhi*
(Shanghai local gazetteer), 1907

You remarked to me that the Chinese, being actuated by a common
feeling, none of them would be willing to come forward [as witness
against a fellow Chinese]. . . . You entirely ignore the circumstance
that the Chinese people have never been influenced by any common
feeling. Further, in the [street], people from every part of China
are mixed together, owing to which, no one cares for the
sorrows and ills of another *[emphasis added]*.

— Daotai Wu Xu to British Consul (Great Britain, Public
Record Office, FO 228.274, 1859)

This study explores social practices and rituals related to *xiangyi*, also called *xiangqing* and *ziyi*, Chinese expressions for the sentiment that binds people from the same native place. This sentiment, and the social institutions which expressed it, profoundly shaped the nature and development of modern Chinese urban society. The two quotations which begin this chapter suggest twin aspects of urban social organization and behavior that correspond to native-place sentiment. The account in the 1907 Shanghai gazetteer describes organization by native place as a necessary, natural, specifically Chinese and indeed "morally excellent" response to the dangers posed by urban admixture and anomie. Daotai Intendant Wu Xu's description of the city under his jurisdiction indicates a possible drawback to the "moral excellence" of native-place sentiment, suggesting that, when individuals from different native-place groups mixed together on a city street, they felt no common identity as Chinese.[1] The chapters which follow address these themes — the prominence of native-place sentiment and organization in Chinese cities and the influence of such ideas and social formations on city life, social order and urban and national identity.

The study is based on Shanghai and covers nearly a century, from the opening of the city to foreign trade in 1843 to the establishment of Guomindang dominance in the Nanjing decade (1927–37). Throughout this period immigrant groups from other areas of China dominated Shanghai's rapidly expanding urban population, which more than quadrupled in the nineteenth century (see Map 1). Shanghai's population in 1800 was between one-quarter and one-third million. By 1910 it was 1.3 million. It doubled again by 1927, to 2.6 million. Throughout the late nineteenth and early twentieth centuries, immigrants comprised at least 75 percent of the total figure. Some of these immigrants came to Shanghai to explore economic opportunities; others came in waves to flee war and famine in their native place.

Combining forces to meet the imperatives of their new urban surroundings, these immigrants formed native-place associations, *huiguan* and *tongxianghui*. Such associations and the sentiments which engendered them were formative elements of Shanghai's urban environment

---

1. Daotai Wu's comment here is somewhat disingenuous, for he was attempting to deflect British concerns that the Chinese residents of the settlement could mobilize effectively together in anti-British behavior. In this instance, the Daotai clearly found it useful to suggest that the logic of local native-place identity impeded national identity as Chinese.

Map 1. Major provinces of China supplying immigrants to Shanghai

throughout the late Qing and early Republican periods. Social, economic and political organization along lines of regional identity shaped the development of the city.

Such prominence and continuity of native-place sentiment and organization was possible because of the flexibility, adaptability and utility of native-place ideas to forces of economic, social and political change in the city. The numbers of associations and their shifting forms and practices demonstrate these traits of persistence and change, familiarity and changing meaning, which make native-place sentiment a crucial arena for understanding the texture of modern change in the city.

Shanghai, though notable in this regard, was certainly not unique. Immigrant Chinese population groups characterized and even dominated nearly all expanding commercial areas in China during this period.[2] Immigration itself does not distinguish Chinese cities from their European and American counterparts.[3] Nonetheless, the degree of cultivation and elaboration of native-place identities and native-place organizations, and the power and duration of these sentiments and institutions, are peculiar to Chinese cities.

The Idea of Native Place

Identity and Connection with the Native Place. The Chinese language contains a variety of expressions for the concept of native place. Terms such as *jiguan, sangzi, laojia, yuanji,* and *guxiang,* which abound in Chinese records and literature, translate variously as birthplace, hometown, native place and ancestral home. The concept of native place was a critical component of personal identity in traditional China, and geographic origin was generally the first matter of inquiry among strangers, the first characteristic recorded about a person (after name and pseudonyms), and the first fact to be ascertained regarding individuals coming before the law.[4]

For immigrants who sought a living in Shanghai, native-place identity expressed both spiritual linkage to the place where their ancestors

2. See Chang Peng, "Distribution of Provincial Merchant Groups in China" (Ph.D. diss., University of Washington, 1958); Mark Elvin and G. William Skinner, eds., *The Chinese City between Two Worlds* (Stanford, Calif., 1974); G. W. Skinner, ed., *The City in Late Imperial China* (Stanford, Calif., 1977); G. W. Skinner, "Mobility Strategies in Late Imperial China: A Regional Systems Analysis," in *Regional Analysis,* ed. Carol A. Smith (New York, 1976), vol. 1, 327–64; William Rowe, *Hankow: Commerce and Society in a Chinese City, 1796–1889* (Stanford, Calif., 1984). Nonetheless, immigration was particularly dramatic in Shanghai because it was a relatively small city prior to 1840 and because it experienced extremely rapid growth after 1860.

3. Recent studies of urban labor and social movements in the United States have stressed the importance of immigration and ethnicity. See, for example, Joseph Barton, *Peasants and Strangers: Italians, Rumanians and Slovaks in an American City, 1890–1950* (Cambridge, Mass., 1975); Eric L. Hirsch, *Urban Revolt: Ethnic Politics in the Nineteenth-Century Chicago Labor Movement* (Berkeley, Calif., 1990); Richard B. Stott, *Workers in the Metropolis: Class, Ethnicity and Youth in Antebellum New York City* (Ithaca, N.Y., 1990); Judith Smith, *Family Connections: A History of Italian and Jewish Immigrant Lives in Providence, Rhode Island, 1900–1940* (Albany, N.Y., 1985); John Bodnar, *Workers' World: Kinship, Community and Protest in an Industrial Society, 1900–1940* (Baltimore, Md., 1982). For a study of the cultural meaning of local identity at both the regional and the national levels in Germany, see Celia Applegate, *A Nation of Provincials: The German Idea of Heimat* (Berkeley, Calif., 1990).

4. See G. William Skinner, "Introduction: Urban Social Structure in Ch'ing China," in Skinner, *The City in Late Imperial China,* 538–48; Skinner, "Mobility Strategies"; Ho

were buried and living ties to family members and community. These ties were most frequently economic as well as sentimental, for local communities assisted and sponsored individual sojourners, viewing them as economic investments for the community. Both religious and economic practices depended on the assumption that the traveler's identity would not change along with his place of residence, that changes of residence were only temporary, and the traveler would return to his native place regularly on ritual occasions, and finally, upon his death.[5] These beliefs were not altered by a residence that lasted several generations. Children of immigrants who were born in places of "temporary residence" similarly did not acquire a new native-place identity but instead inherited the native place of their fathers or grandfathers. In practice, insofar as possible, immigrants returned home for marriage, mourning, retirement and burial. Moreover, throughout their period away, they sent money back to their native place, expressing their family and geographic loyalties in flows of remittance.

Because of these patterns of belief and practice, urban immigration

---

Ping-ti, *Zhongguo huiguan shilun* (On the history of Landsmannschaften in China) (Taipei, 1966); Rowe, *Hankow: Commerce and Society*, 213–51. Numerous popular expressions describe attachment to the native place, such as *hun gui gutu* (the soul returns to the native place); *rong gui guxiang* (to retire in glory to one's native place); *luoye gui gen* (falling leaves return to the roots); *jiu shi guxiangde hao; yue shi guxiangde yuan* (wine is better from one's native place; the moon is rounder in the native place). The term *youzi* refers not just to a wanderer but to one who is separated from his native place. Separation from one's native place is also a prominent theme in classical Chinese poetry. Meng Jiao's poem, "Youzi Yin" (Sigh of a wanderer), is understood to express the sojourning condition and the ties binding the sojourner to his native place:

> The thread in the hand of the loving mother
> Is woven into the sojourning son's garments.
> Before he leaves she makes her stitches double
> Fearing he will be long in returning.
> However deep his gratitude, how can he ever
> Repay a debt that will bind him always?
> Adapted from Liu Shih Shun, ed. and trans.,
> *One Hundred and One Chinese Poems, with
> English Translations and Preface* (Hong
> Kong, 1967), 72–73.

5. See Skinner, "Introduction," 538. This normative viewpoint was expressed in terms of male sojourners. Men dominated sojourning communities in late-nineteenth-century Shanghai. Sojourning merchants at the head of large families kept most, if not all, of their family members in their native place. While women sojourners did exist, notably as prostitutes in nineteenth-century Shanghai and as prostitutes and factory workers in the twentieth century, the imperatives for linkage to their native place were weaker, owing to the fact that women married out of their families and were not buried in their natal villages and, moreover, to women's customary exclusion from public activity.

in China was perceived as sojourning and did not involve a fundamental change of identity. Immigrant communities in Shanghai referred to themselves as "Ningbo sojourners in Shanghai" (*lü Hu Ningboren*) or "Guangdong lodgers in Shanghai" (*yü Hu Guangdongren*). These labels stress the fundamental nature of native-place identity, even as they recognize the sojourners' location in Shanghai. The labels also suggest the hybrid nature of sojourners' identities: while linked to both Shanghai and their native places, once sojourning, they were not purely of their native place, nor could they simply adopt their locational identity (Shanghai).

For individual sojourners the maintenance of elaborate ties with their native place was an ideal which could only be fully achieved by the wealthy.[6] Nonetheless, all but the most impoverished sojourners tried regularly to visit their homes, even when their villages were distant. This included members of secret societies and criminal gangs. Reporting on the January plunder of a pawnshop by a Guangdong gang as well as attacks on wealthy households in the Shanghai suburb of Gaoqiao (on the east bank of the Huangpu River), the *North China Herald* of January 23, 1858, noted that this was the season when Cantonese were about to return to their native province for the Chinese new year, "the Scoundrels thereby laying in a stock of clothing and money for their new year dissipations and absconding with impunity."

It was most critical for sojourners to return to their native place for burial. Chinese death ritual required that the dead be buried in ancestral soil and that tablets for the deceased be installed in the family altar, so that their spirits could enjoy the comforts of home and the sacrifices and solicitude of later generations.[7] Nonetheless, the cost of shipping a coffin safely home could be prohibitive. To avert the tragedy of burial away from native soil, native-place associations assisted less able fellow-provincials in achieving the goal of home burial. The associations also

---

6. Skinner ("Introduction," 545) suggests that failed sojourners were among those buried in paupers' graves, dying an "anonymous and ignominious urban death." Nonetheless, "pauper burial grounds" (*yimu*) were maintained by a number of native-place associations, in addition to their regular cemeteries and coffin repositories, so that impoverished sojourners could receive a burial connecting their spirit to their native place. Chaozhou and Ningbo *huiguan* meeting notes suggest that corpses were only retained by the Tongren Fuyuantang (a major Shanghai charitable institution) when native place could not be determined (or when a native-place association did not claim the corpse).

7. See C. K. Yang, *Religion in Chinese Society* (Berkeley, Calif., 1970), 39–40; James Watson and Evelyn Rawski, eds., *Death Ritual in Late Imperial and Modern China* (Berkeley, Calif., 1988).

established graveyards in Shanghai for sojourning fellow-provincials entirely lacking in means. Many of these burials were considered temporary, pending shipment home. Similarly, buildings were erected in Shanghai for the temporary storage of coffins until they could be shipped back to the native place, and funds were collected within the native-place community to assist with building expenses. Foreign travelers in China in the late nineteenth and early twentieth centuries frequently observed the shipment of corpses in heavy, hermetically sealed coffins, expressing adherence to the ideal in practice. Large-scale temporary storage of coffins, contact with cemeteries in the native place, coordination of transportation, and the underwriting of coffin transportation expenses were continual and important areas of *huiguan* activity.[8]

Separation and Suffering. The act of sojourning stimulated both the cultivation of native-place sentiment and linkage among fellow-provincials. Mutual ties developed and intensified as fellow-countrymen traveled beyond their native place, leaving the special way of speaking and the unique forms of dried tofu or sweet cakes of their village; passing through neighboring counties with still comprehensible dialects and recognizable dishes; and arriving finally in strange places where words were unfamiliar and palatable food was difficult to find. Both the *tongxiang* (fellow-provincial) bond and the nostalgic re-creation of the native place were sojourner responses to separation from the native place and the hardship that such separation was perceived to entail.

The suffering that sojourning entailed was a frequently evoked literary theme. Few literate Chinese would not have been familiar with Li Bai's famous poem:

The moon shines on my bed brightly
So that I mistake it for frost on the ground.

8. For example, see J. J. M. de Groot, *The Religious System of China,* vol. 3 (Taipei, 1892–1910), 838; "Notice of the Siming Gongsuo," *Shenbao* (hereafter referred to as SB), March 14, 1912. Rowe (*Hankow: Commerce and Society,* 265) suggests that in Hankou there was little evidence of the shipment of coffins. There is no doubt regarding Shanghai ("Siming gongsuo yi'anlu" [Meeting notes of the Siming Gongsuo], 1915–39, manuscript, Shanghai Municipal Archives [hereafter referred to as SGY]; "Chaozhou huiguan yi'an beicha" [Meeting notes of the Chaozhou Huiguan], 1913–39, manuscript, Shanghai Municipal Archives [hereafter referred to as CHYB]; see also SB, March 14, 1912).

I gaze at the moonlight with head lifted;
Now my head droops and I think of my native place.[9]

Immigrants separated from their native place were not merely nostalgic, they believed they suffered physically and spiritually from the separation. In a letter to the Shanghai newspaper, *Shenbao,* the Xiangshan writer "Rong Yangfu" (a pseudonym) defended the integrity of people from his native place in the province of Guangdong, who had been maligned in a previous article. He began by describing the richness of Xiangshan intellectual traditions, evidenced by the famous Huang and Zheng families which had produced eighteen generations of Xiangshan scholars. Then, in order to account for the existence of disreputable Xiangshan prostitutes in Shanghai, he argued that because of their separation from their native place, the moral character of these individuals had deteriorated and they were no longer really Xiangshan people. They may have been born in Xiangshan, but they had become impure in the polluting atmosphere of Shanghai: "How is it that none speak the Xiangshan dialect? The reason is that they were kidnapped young from Xiangshan to serve in Shanghai in these despicable professions. Moreover, when they came to this foreign place they drank the water and ate the food, and their language changed. Their hearts also changed."[10]

For Rong and his audience, native-place identity derived as much from the food and water of the native place as from the culture and dialect — in fact, the intake of foreign food resulted in linguistic and even spiritual destruction. In the sojourning condition, native-place identity was invoked less as a birthright than as a delicate plant which demanded constant cultivation.

Expressions of the importance of connection with the native place for the living were mirrored in the spiritual realm. There were two types of *huiguan: yang huiguan,* for the living; and *yin huiguan,* for the dead. Serving the dead in the manner that *yang huiguan* served the living, *yin huiguan* were built in burial grounds where they housed coffins, comforting and uniting the sojourning souls.[11]

Even gods who were away from their native place were believed to

9. "Thoughts on a Quiet Night" (*Jing ye xiang*), adapted from Liu Shih Shun, *One Hundred and One Chinese Poems,* 20–21.

10. SB, January 17, 1874. "Rong Yangfu" is the composite of three surnames.

11. The term *yin huiguan* has sometimes been misunderstood to refer simply to the building constructed by the *huiguan* to house coffins. The larger ritual function is apparent from records of *yin huiguan* construction in CHYB, December 1923; January 1924.

suffer. In cities outside Fujian, figures of the Fujianese goddess Tianhou (Empress of Heaven) were carried to the local Fujian *huiguan* to be ritually reunited with their native soil.[12]

Sojourners' Constructions of Native-Place Community. Huiguan were nodal points in a system of formal and informal native-place coalitions which marked the urban landscape, and they are therefore a major focus of this study. Because they bore native-place labels, brought together sojourners in various activities and represented the "face" of different native-place communities, they were crucial sites for the construction of a positive idea of native-place identity and community for their sojourning populations. This development of community relied on financial resources and networks of influence in the city, resources which motivated the development of patron-client ties connecting poorer sojourners to a sojourning elite. Groups without the means to construct native-place associations tended to have weaker identification with fellow sojourners in Shanghai and weaker notions of native-place identity.

Sojourners established *huiguan* to create a supportive home environment in an alien city as well as to symbolically assert the importance of their sojourning community.[13] Formal association began with the construction of a temple for local gods and burial-grounds or coffin repositories for sojourners. Through their connection with religious life and critical ritual moments in the lives of sojourners, associations maintained native-place ties and sentiment over long periods in foreign environments, contributing to the organization of trade and safeguarding native-place business or trade interests. These associations played a formative role in organizing what might be called the "raw materials" of native-place sentiment—dialect and the local practices people brought with them into the city—and reformulating them into an urban representation of native-place community.

Native-place sentiment and organization in the sojourning community worked in the manner of a large kin organization. The number of

---

12. Zhang Xiuhua, "Wo he Tianhou gong" (My experiences with the Temple of the Empress of Heaven), *Tianjin wenshi ziliao xuanji* (Selected materials on Tianjin history and culture) 19 (March 1982):190.

13. The native place itself provided no such supportive environment but, rather, one fraught with strife and competition. The nature of native-place community was transformed by sojourning. See James Cole, *Shaohsing: Competition and Cooperation in Nineteenth-Century China* (Tucson, Ariz., 1986).

actual kin sojourning in a city could rarely be large enough to constitute a powerful organizational base. The *tongxiang* tie had the advantage of encompassing a significantly larger group, subsuming within it kin ties.[14] *Huiguan* directors consciously reinforced the linkages between their associations and actual organized lineages through the institution of the worship of deceased *huiguan* directors. The spirit tablets of these former directors (*xiandong shenwei*) served the role of *huiguan* ancestral tablets.[15]

Although sojourners at most levels of society coalesced into native-place groups, only communities with sufficient capital could undertake the construction of the large buildings and burial complexes that characterized fully developed native-place associations. Within each city, the native place was reconstituted according to the size and stature of the sojourning urban community. If sojourners from one province were sufficiently numerous and wealthy, they formed several prefectural-level (sometimes even county-level) associations. Where sojourners were more scarce, they formed provincial-level associations and even associations of people from adjacent provinces. Thus, for instance, a person in Shanghai from Huilai county, in Chaozhou prefecture (Guangdong), belonged to the Chao-Hui Huiguan (representing the two counties of Chaoyang and Huilai), one of several associations serving the relatively large population of Chaozhou sojourners. In Suzhou, by contrast, as the Guangdong community grew smaller over the course of the nineteenth century, the originally separate Chaozhou association merged with the Liangguang association, which represented the two provinces of Guangdong and Guangxi.

The variability of association names and degrees of territorial inclusiveness in different cities has led some scholars to question the real importance of the native-place idea in social organization.[16] Evidence from Shanghai of contact among associations in different cities representing overlapping native-place areas suggests that, in fact, such flexibility was an active tactic facilitating the maintenance of native-place

14. Skinner, "Introduction," 541.

15. According to meeting notes of the Siming Gongsuo, after one hundred years directors had "spirit niches" (*shenkan*) built for them in the Gongsuo's Tudi (earth god) temple, which were worshipped on the Chinese New Year, "in return for their service" (SGY, July 1919).

16. Gary Hamilton, "Nineteenth Century Chinese Merchant Associations: Conspiracy or Combination?" *Ch'ing-shi wen-t'i* 3 (December 1977):60–62; Rowe, *Hankow: Commerce and Society*, 263.

communities. Although it is certain that native-place associations re-flected practical as well as sentimental imperatives, it would be a mistake to imagine that sentiment (as opposed to instrumentality) was second-ary in the nature and activities of these associations. First, there were definite limits to the flexibility of the concept. Although the native-place unit could expand to encompass adjacent prefectures and even prov-inces, it was normally unthinkable that northerners and southerners, for instance, or people from nonadjacent provinces would organize to-gether in a single *huiguan*. Second, study of the broad compass of asso-ciational activity (as opposed to a limited functionalist view which sees native-place ties as tools of economic self-interest) makes clear an inex-tricable interweaving of religious practice, economics, taste, habit, and other cultural meanings. Finally, and most important, it is critical to recognize that (however flexible the native-place idea was in practice) communities in the city nonetheless constructed themselves symboli-cally in reference to a unit of place, a "placeness" which provided a basis not simply for individual identity but also for connections among people. The impulse to organize on the basis of place is epitomized by the Pudong Tongxianghui, a native-place association in Shanghai formed by local people who were not actually sojourners.

The construction of organized communities and institutions of fellow-provincials meant that the native-place identity of sojourners linked them not only to their native place but also to their reconstituted native-place community in Shanghai. This resulted in a kind of doubling of gestures. The wealthy maintained face in both communities, funding charitable works among fellow-sojourners in Shanghai and for fellow-provincials at home. Similarly, birthdays and other celebrations were held in both places. Upon his father's sixtieth birthday, for instance, the wealthy Xiangshan businessman Xu Run demonstrated his filial piety by constructing congratulatory "longevity halls" (*shoutang*) in both Shang-hai and Xiangshan. Thus an understanding of the nature of native-place sentiment in Shanghai must comprehend the re-creation of the native-place community in Shanghai.[17]

Because Shanghai *huiguan* often established regular communication with *huiguan* in other cities representing the same native place, it is also possible to speak of the creation (despite the apparent contradiction) of a third, interurban, level of native-place community on the national

17. Xu Run, *Xu Yüzhai zixu nianpu* (Chronological autobiography of Xu Run) (Shanghai, 1927), 25.

level. This seemingly paradoxical creation of national communities out of native-place ties was a critical element in the modern transformations of native-place community. Although the grouping together of fellow-provincials segmented cities internally, it also resulted in the transcendence of urban borders, integrating urban centers into larger interurban networks of fellow-provincials. Sojourning Guangdong merchants in Shanghai were in close touch with sojourning fellow-provincials in other ports where they maintained business interests. In several cases, stronger and wealthier Shanghai *huiguan* directed the activities of smaller and weaker ones. The Shanghai Chaozhou Huiguan, for instance, often directed the affairs of the Suzhou Chaozhou Huiguan. The Siming Gongsuo, or Ningbo Huiguan, maintained close contact with Ningbo groups in other cities and oversaw and coordinated activities on a multiport scale.

The potentially national scope of native-place communities is confirmed by the example of the Hu She, an association formed by sojourners from Huzhou (Zhejiang). The Hu She was explicitly established in 1924 on a national basis, with its central headquarters in Shanghai and branch offices in Nanjing, Wuhan, Suzhou and Jiaxing, among other cities. The existence of formally and informally constituted national sojourning networks highlights the paradox of "local" native-place ties as they functioned historically. Although it might be imagined that native-place sentiment was necessarily localistic and parochial, the existence of multiple levels of native-place community meant that in practice the horizons of native-place sentiment could range from the provincialism of the native place, to more cosmopolitan Shanghai urban awareness, to deep involvement in national issues.[18]

The Native Place and China. Although Chinese commentators understood native-place sentiment to be natural, they also described it as virtuous and "morally excellent," as illustrated by the quotation which begins this chapter. The virtue of native-place sentiment lay

18. CHYB; SGY; *Hu She dishisanjie sheyuan dahui tekan* (Special issue on the 13th general members' meeting of the Huzhou association) (Shanghai, 1937); Chen Lizhi, *Hu She cangsang lu* (Records of the vicissitudes of the Hu She) (Taipei, 1969). In her compelling study of Zhejiang elites, Mary Backus Rankin describes interprovincial networks of Zhejiang sojourners centered on Shanghai; see *Elite Activism and Political Transformation in China: Zhejiang Province, 1865–1911* (Stanford, Calif., 1986), 268–73. The degree to which individual sojourners participated in national communities would depend both on the individual's place within the sojourning community (elite or non-elite) and on the commercial or political reach of the particular native-place community in question.

in its groundedness in a larger political ideology which deepened the rationale for native-place ties and gave them broader and extralocal significance. Love for the native place was virtuous because it helped to constitute and strengthen the larger political polity of China. Native-place sentiment was vulnerable (as suggested by the second quotation) if it was not attached to this larger ideal. Therefore the leaders of native-place organizations in the nineteenth century legitimized their associations not through appeals to nature or to utility but through reference to Chinese identity.

For most of the nineteenth century the ideological connection between native-place identity and Chinese identity was grounded in quasi-Confucian ideas of concentric circles of cultural and territorial identity. This rationale for the establishment of native-place associations is reflected in a statement of the origin of the Shanghai Guang-Zhao Huiguan (Guangzhou and Zhaoqing prefectures, Guangdong):

China is made up of prefectures and counties and these are made up of native villages, [and the people of each] make a concerted effort to cooperate, providing mutual help and protection. This gives solidarity to village, prefecture and province and orders the country. Since [ancient agrarian harmony deteriorated], merchants have increasingly sojourned in distant places, living with people not from their native village, county or prefecture, and they have different senses of native-place feeling. Thus people from the same village, county and prefecture gather together in other areas, making them like their own native place. This is the reason for the establishment of *huiguan*. This is the ancestors' way of expressing affection for later generations. Shanghai is first under heaven for commerce, and the gentry and officials of our two Guangdong prefectures of Guangzhou and Zhaoqing are more numerous here than merchants from other places. [Therefore we established a *huiguan*.][19]

Such statements, which resembled in structure the concentric logic of the Confucian text "The Great Learning" (*Daxue*), also served strategic purposes, defusing threats both from the state and from hostile locals in Shanghai who would view the establishment of an outsiders' *huiguan* with suspicion. Given the hostility of the Qing state toward private associations, this statement, like others of its type, invoked Confucian values as a means of providing legitimacy to the organization by linking local

19. "Shanghai Guang-Zhao huiguan yuanqi" (The origin of the Shanghai Guang-Zhao Huiguan) (Tongzhi period [1862–1874]; hand-copied document, courtesy of Du Li, Shanghai Museum). My interpretation of this quotation has benefited from discussions with Joseph Esherick and Ernst Schwintzer.

solidarity to the order of the polity (leaving the commercial advantages of association unstated). Similarly, such statements stressed a common orthodoxy which could be shared by people from different places, helping to dispel perceptions that sojourners were utterly foreign. In this regard, native-place associations brought with them into the city a language of common Chinese identity, even as they served as powerful markers of cultural difference among different Chinese groups.

The Chinese elites, reformers, and community leaders who articulated ideological connections between the native place and the larger political entity of China would, over time, abandon their invocation of Confucian values and take on the rhetoric of modern Chinese nationalism. In the process, their use of native-place sentiment and organizations would both reflect and help to define the urban development of Chinese nationalism.

Native-Place Divisions in Shanghai:
The Surface of City Life

In late-nineteenth-century Shanghai more than half the population was made up of immigrants from other areas of China, and distinctions along lines of regional identity were reflected everywhere in city life. Language separated immigrant groups, as did varying ethnic traditions, differences in the organization of daily life and preferences in the choice of marriage partners. There were also regional divisions in urban geography, religious expression, the organization of trade, education and welfare, and even the organization of social control and social unrest.

Regional groups were not just distinct but unequal. Native-place identities helped structure socioeconomic and to some extent gender hierarchies in the city. These hierarchies corresponded to the economic power of different sojourning groups. At the peak of regional and occupational hierarchies were people from Zhejiang, Guangdong and southern Jiangsu province. The stature of a given sojourner community depended on the power of its elites, because workers (in terms of sheer numbers) dominated nearly all sojourning communities. Immediately after the opening of Shanghai as a treaty port, Guangdong merchants rose quickly through involvement in foreign trade. By the 1860s, despite Guangdong and Jiangsu competition, Zhejiang sojourners dominated the critical banking, shipping, and silk sectors. Considerably lower in the Shanghai native-place hierarchy were people from Shandong, Hubei, and northern Jiangsu (Subei), regional communities with weak elites and whose non-elite members were often unskilled laborers in Shanghai. As Emily Honig points out, the appellation *Subei ren* "was a metaphor for low class." Even today Subei people are avoided as marriage partners by Shanghainese.[20]

Language was the first marker of native-place differences, separating new immigrants from other residents in the city. Even after generations of common residence in the city, distinct and frequently mutually unintelligible dialects made communication among different immigrant groups uncomfortable at best and often impossible. According to a description published in 1917,

Shanghai is a mixed-up place of people from many regions, the languages are numerous and jumbled and cannot be carefully enumerated. We can generally divide them into categories: 1) Guangdong speech—foreigners came north from Guangdong to Shanghai, therefore Guangdong people are powerful. 2) Ningbo speech—Ningbo borders the sea and opened relatively early; Ningbo people also came to Shanghai first. 3) Jiangsu people's speech—the hosts. 4) Northern speech—wealthy merchants, traders and actors from Beijing, Tianjin, Shandong, Shaanxi. . . . 5) Shanghai local speech . . . [but] aside from the areas south and west of the city wall where there are pure locals, speech has continually changed and so-called Shanghai vernacular is usually a mixture of Ningbo and Suzhou speech; not the same as before the opening of the treaty port.[21]

As late as 1932, the Shanghai writer and astute social observer Mao Dun commented on the lack of a functioning common language among working people in Shanghai. After conducting an investigation among Shanghai workers to see how people from different places communicated with each other, he concluded that after eighty years of immigration into the city, Shanghai had no common language. He found instead

20. See for example, Yuen-sang Leung, "Regional Rivalry in Mid-Nineteenth Century Shanghai: Cantonese vs. Ningbo Men," *Ch'ing-shih wen-t'i* 8 (December 1982):29–50; Rankin, *Elite Activism*, 85; Emily Honig, "The Politics of Prejudice: Subei People in Republican-Era Shanghai," *Modern China* (hereafter referred to as MC) 15 (July 1989):243–74; Emily Honig, *Creating Chinese Ethnicity: Subei People in Shanghai, 1850–1980* (New Haven, Conn., 1992), 4.

21. Yao Gonghe, *Shanghai xianhua* (Shanghai idle talk) (Shanghai, 1917; Shanghai Guji Chubanshe reprint Shanghai, 1989), 19. An account of the languages of Shanghai written in nearly identical language may be found in Xu Ke, *Qing bai lei chao* (Qing unofficial writings) (Shanghai, 1916; Shangwu yinshuguan reprint Taipei, 1983), 43:24.

a minimum of three emerging types of "common speech." The first type
used Shanghai local dialect as a basis, with an admixture of elements of
Guangdong, Northern Jiangsu (Jiangbei) and Shandong dialects. The
second used Jiangbei dialect as a basis, with liberal additions of Shanghai and Shandong phrases. The third was a kind of Shanghai-accented
northern speech, with similar admixtures from other dialects. The
"common language" used in any given location depended on which native-place group predominated. For people who spoke other native dialects, he observed, this meant that any communication in the "common
language" would be necessarily crude and limited in vocabulary.[22]

People from different parts of China tended to live in different neighborhoods, or "small cultural enclosures," in the description of a recent
study of Shanghai popular culture.[23] Ningbo people in Shanghai lived
in the northern part of the Chinese city and in the French Concession.
Guangdong people lived in the southern part and southern suburbs of
the Chinese city, and in several distinct neighborhoods in the International Settlement. Jiangxi people were concentrated in Zhabei, to the
north and west of the International Settlement. Poor immigrants from
northern Jiangsu settled first in shack districts along the banks of the
Huangpu and in growing tenement areas, especially in Zhabei, that
were referred to as "Jiangbei villages."[24]

These residential divisions were complex and often overlapping, reflecting different areas of settlement for workers, as opposed to wealthy
sojourners or resulting from different immigrant waves. Although the

22. Mao Dun, "Wenti zhong de dazhong wenyi" (Problems for art and literature for
the masses), originally published in *Wenxue yuebao* (Literature monthly) 1 (July 1932),
reprinted in *Zhongguo xiandai wenxue shi cankao ziliao* (Research materials for the history
of modern Chinese literature) (Beijing, 1959), 335–37. Jiangbei refers to the area of Jiangsu
province north of the Yangzi. For the definition of Jiangbei in Shanghai, see Honig, *Creating Chinese Ethnicity*, chap. 2.

23. Zheng Tuyou, "Chongtu, bingcun, jiaorong, chuangxin: Shanghai minsu de xingcheng yu tedian" (Conflict, coexistence, mixture and new creation: The formation and
characteristics of Shanghai popular culture), in *Shanghai minsu yanjiu* (Research on
Shanghai customs), *Zhongguo minjian wenhua* (Chinese popular culture), ed. Shanghai
minjian wenyijia xiehui (Shanghai popular culture committee), vol. 3 (Shanghai, 1991), 9.

24. Because the entire native-place community did not live together, neighborhood
divisions were not neat. Different trades were located in different areas; workers often
lived around the enterprises employing them; new immigrants often lived in areas other
than those in which older residents lived. This complexity did not mean that different
groups blended in a neighborhood; rather, the city was made up of many small groups,
parts of larger native-place communities. See Leung, "Regional Rivalry," 30–33; interview
with Shen Yinxian, who cared for the gods in the Jiangxi Huiguan until the Cultural
Revolution, Shanghai, October 1983; Honig, *Creating Chinese Ethnicity*, 45.

intricacies of residential divisions and subdivisions make them difficult to trace on a map, they were present in the minds and daily experiences of Shanghai residents. Newspapers commonly referred to areas such as Hongkou as Cantonese, or, similarly, to "the Fukien part of the suburbs." Specific roads were identified by the native place of their inhabitants. According to Zhan Xiaoci, son of the Quan-Zhang Huiguan director, Zhan Ronghui, sojourners from the Minnan dialect area of southern Fujian lived around Yong'an Road and East Jinling Road. In the words of Hu Xianghan, whose description of Shanghai neighborhoods was published in 1930, North Sichuan, Wuchang, Chongming and Tiantong roads were "just like Guangdong"; Yanghang Road, outside the small east gate of the Chinese city, was "just like Fujian." Prior to the renaming of many streets in the Communist era, a number of Shanghai street names were named for native-place associations which built them or were located on them, or for their Guangdong, Fujian or Ningbo sojourner inhabitants.[25]

Because of residential overlap and the needs of trade, people from different native areas might do business together at the same teahouse. Nonetheless, the regional types—to the extent of body shapes and sartorial differences—were easy to distinguish, even for the foreign observer: "An experienced eye readily detects in the crowd that peoples the teashop, the visitors from the different cities which have dealings with Shanghai and the man who is at home. We see Soochow men, Shantung men in their warm hoods, both contrasting with the spruce Cantonese or the man from Hangkow or Kiukiang."[26]

Shanghai architecture, like Shanghai street names and neighborhoods, reflected the influence of different native-place groups and the presence of native-place associations. As Shanghai housing strained to accommodate the growing population, there was widespread construction of simple adjacent houses along Shanghai alleyways (*lilong*). Among the several types of *lilong* housing were the "Guangdong-style

25. *North China Herald* (hereafter referred to as NCH), August 17, 1850; interview with Zhan Xiaoci, Quanzhou, Fujian, March 19, 1984; Hu Xianghan, *Shanghai xiaozhi* (Little Shanghai gazetteer) (Shanghai, 1930; Shanghai guji chubanshe reprint, Shanghai, 1989), p. 51; Xue Liyong, *Shanghai diming luming shiqu* (Shanghai place-name and street-name anecdotes) (Shanghai, 1990), 140–48. The passages in Hu are cited in Zheng Tuyou, "Chongtu," 9, and in Elizabeth Perry, *Shanghai on Strike: The Politics of Chinese Labor* (Stanford, Calif., 1993), 17. Regional differentiation of neighborhoods persists, to a degree. Ningbo people are particularly numerous in the southern part of the old city; Zhabei continues to be the residence for many people from Subei.

26. NCH, February 8, 1872.

residences" (*Guangshi fangwu*), relatively simple two-story buildings which grouped three to four residences together in an entryway. Such homes were concentrated in the Hongkou area (an area known for its Guangdong population), where they housed workers, peddlers, and other low-income people.[27]

The continuous construction and renewal of buildings housing native-place and trade associations provided visible reminders both of the permanence of regional organization within the city and the unequal power of specific regional groups. In post–Opium War Shanghai and in many other cities, the headquarters of wealthy associations were the most imposing buildings in the city, encrusted with gold-painted carvings, often with wood or special construction materials brought from the native place. British visitors to Shanghai in the 1850s found the larger *huiguan* more impressive than Chinese government offices. In contrast, weaker sojourner groups often lacked the funding to establish even rudimentary buildings. Subei sojourners, for example, had no association hall in the nineteenth century and therefore lacked a crucial symbol and organizational unit for developing identity and community.[28]

Although the care employed in the construction of *huiguan* distinguished them from the unenthusiastically built government offices, they resembled these offices in both architectural form and function. Self-conscious expressions of the wealth and power of their communities, the grandeur of these buildings and their formal resemblance to the county and circuit *yamen* expressed also their function as governing centers for their sojourning populations. The architecture of the city attested to what Van der Sprenkel described as two loci of government in Chinese cities, the official (stemming from the *yamen*), and the unofficial (stemming from associations like *huiguan*).[29]

Huiguan buildings incorporated the great walls, gates, multiple courtyards, halls, side offices and gardens of the official *yamen* style, and

27. Chen Congzhou and Zhang Ming, eds., *Shanghai jindai jianzhu shigao* (Draft history of modern Shanghai architecture) (Shanghai, 1988), 161–63.

28. *General Description of Shanghae and Its Environs* (Shanghai, 1850) provides the following explanation for the poor appearance of public buildings: "The reason is that when . . . offices [of the Shanghai magistrate and Daotai] have to be erected, an order is issued to the people to build . . . and as the officials are seldom or ever favorites, the people do as little for them as they possibly can. Hence they procure the smallest sized timber and the most fragile materials, so as to run up sheds of a given size in the cheapest manner."

29. On the lack of a positive self-definition of Subei native-place identity, see Honig, *Creating Chinese Ethnicity*, 28–35. See also Sybille Van der Sprenkel, "Urban Social Control," in Skinner, *The City in Late Imperial China*, 609–32.

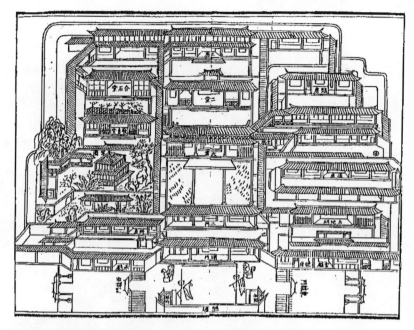

Figure 1. *Yamen* architecture. Source: *Tongzhi Shanghai xianzhi* (Tongzhi-reign Shanghai county gazetteer) Shanghai, 1871.

also features of temples, notably altars for their local gods and stages for theatrical productions (see Figures 1 and 2). In this composite architectural form they embodied both secular and spiritual authority for their communities.

The spatial and architectural effects of regional communities did not function only to divide the city. Although residential patterns and architecture marked native-place differences in the city, the fact of immigration and the presence of small Guangdong, Ningbo, Fujian and Jiangxi areas in the city in a sense made Shanghai into a miniature of all of China. Even as immigrant groups maintained their own customs in the city, their common presence concretized the diversity of China in one locality, making the larger polity more conceivable. *Huiguan* buildings, mostly grouped together around the old city and the eastern commercial areas, suggested not simply difference but also — in their common form — a certain Chinese universality. Although the ornaments and furnishings of different *huiguan* reflected the tastes and materials of their native places, there is a certain irony in the fact that (for all their regional specificity in function and culture) in architectural form all *huiguan* were

structurally similar. In this sense, once again, *huiguan* present the curi-
ous paradox of containing both provincial and universal aspects.

Native-place identity was frequently worked out on the streets, on
the docks and in factories, where tensions emerged among economically
competing groups. People from different regional backgrounds were often involved in fights. Native-place ties also organized or subdivided
Shanghai gangs. Guangdong gangsters backed up Guangdong merchants on the street. The Subei gangsters Jin Jiuling and Gu Zhuxuan
recruited followers through the native-place association they directed.[30]

30. For a discussion of regional divisions in gangs, see Wu Zude, "Jiu Shanghai banghui xisu tezheng" (Characteristics of old Shanghai gang culture), in Shanghai minjian
wenyijia xiehui, *Shanghai minsu yanjiu,* vol. 3, 80–85.

新 寧 會 館

Figure 2.
Huiguan architecture.
Source: *Huitu Shanghai
zazhi* (Shanghai pictorial
miscellany) Shanghai,
1905.

Major social conflicts could also reflect native-place community and organization. There were, for instance, two major "Ningbo Cemetery Riots" when, in 1874 and 1898, the French attempted to build a road through a Ningbo burial ground. In the Revolution of 1911 as well as in the great nationalist social movements of the twentieth century, the May Fourth Movement and the May Thirtieth Movement, native-place associations were responsible for the mobilization of their fellow-provincials.

Similarly, native-place divisions were critical to social control. Both Chinese and foreign authorities held native-place associations responsible for the actions of their fellow-provincials. Chinese and foreign courts also routinely referred cases back to fellow-provincial associations. The severity of punishments meted out in Chinese courts could also vary according to the native place of the offender. A foreign observer noted in 1868, for instance, that "the heavy bamboo is only used on very bad Characters or Cantonese."[31]

Distinctive native-place cultures were reproduced through a variety of social institutions and practices. Education was frequently organized by native-place groups, a practice which reinforced and perpetuated differences in dialect and custom. Guangdong children went to Guangdong schools; Ningbo children went to Ningbo schools; Fujianese attended school at the Quan-Zhang Huiguan (Quanzhou and Zhangzhou prefectures).

Native-place identity was vigorously defined through cuisine, an enormously significant area of cultural articulation in China. Chinese guides to Shanghai written in the late Qing and Republican period abound in descriptions of regional cuisines and characterizations of the types of people who ate each sort of food. Restaurant location and the relative importance in Shanghai of a regional cuisine depended on the prominence of sojourners from that area. The principles underlying the distribution of Shanghai restaurants are explained by Wang Dingjiu, editor of a 1937 guide entitled *The Key to Shanghai* (*Shanghai menjing*), in a section entitled, "Key to Eating":

Shanghai commercial power has always been divided between two major groups, Ningbo and Guangdong. . . . Although the power of Guangdong people is not as widespread as that of Ningbo people, their strength is still considerable. The three famous department stores, Yong'an, Xianshi and Xinxin, all are headquarters of Guangdong merchants. Thus the Guangdong restaurant trade, in recent years, has become extremely well developed. . . .

Because Anhui people are most numerous among the clerks in the Shanghai pawnshop trade, on the streets where there are pawnshops there will always be one or two Anhui restaurants to serve the appetites of their *tongxiang*. Thus [the existence of Anhui restaurants] is in direct proportion to the existence of pawnshops. . . .

There are many Ningbo people sojourning in Shanghai and they are extremely powerful . . . [but] the taste of Ningbo food is not congenial to most people. Therefore, aside from Ningbo and Shaoxing customers, people from other areas don't welcome it.[32]

---

31. NCH, October 3, 1868. This article goes on to observe a "notable . . . difference [in the manner in] which the punishment is carried out on Cantonese and Northerners; the former catching it awfully."

32. Wang Dingjiu, "Chi de menjing," in *Shanghai menjing* (The key to Shanghai) (Shanghai, 1937), 7–26.

Rather than cultivate cosmopolitanism, most Shanghai residents preferred when possible to eat their own native-place cuisine. By the 1930s Shanghai guidebooks encouraged the development of somewhat more experimental tastes, and observers reported that Guangdong food (and occasionally Sichuan food) had become fashionable. This was achieved, apparently, only with strenuous promotion on the part of entrepreneurial chefs who wooed local palates. According to one account, although Guangdong restaurants were physically attractive, most Shanghai residents found them too expensive and, moreover, could not understand the ornate food names on their menus, with their references to "phoenix claws," "tigers," "dragons" and "sea dogs." Beginning in the 1920s the Guangdong Xinya restaurant on Nanjing Road added to its menu sauteed shrimp, a popular Jiangsu dish, thereby luring Jiangsu people inside. Although guidebooks admitted that Cantonese food tasted good and could be enjoyed even by non-Cantonese, this was not the case for other regional cuisines. Anhui restaurants, for example, languished economically because they were unable to attract a large clientele. Not only was Ningbo cuisine feared by nonnatives, but those who walked unaware into the restaurant of another regional group risked poor treatment: "If you try Ningbo food make sure you go with a Ningbo person. The price will be less expensive and the quality better. If you go as an outsider they will cheat you."[33]

Native-place tastes and affectations were equally pronounced in the "flower world" and "willow lane." The lore of Shanghai prostitution suggests regional recruitment and organization, with different euphemisms, prices and practices associated with prostitutes from different regions. Wang Dingjiu introduces Shanghai brothels in much the same manner as his account of Shanghai restaurants:

Shanghai is a great marketplace . . . and it is also a marketplace of sex. The many brothels are convenient for travelers and stimulate the market. Thus prostitution and commerce are intimately related. . . . Since there are so many sojourning Ningbo merchants in Shanghai, Ningbo "temple disciples" [euphemism for prostitutes] have a special position in the prostitute world. . . . When non-Ningbo people hear the speech of Ningbo girls they get gooseflesh and shiver. But they suit Ningbo appetites. Thus the customers of Ningbo prostitutes are mainly their own *tongxiang*.[34]

33. Quotation from Wang Dingjiu, "Chi," 26. Other sources are Hu Xianghan, *Shanghai xiaozhi*, 39–41; Zheng Tuyou, "Chongtu," 17–18.
34. Wang Dingjiu, section titled "Piao de menjing," 1, 34.

Prostitutes were ranked imaginatively in a native-place hierarchy. According to a guide to Shanghai, Suzhou women dominated the most expensive grade of prostitutes, called *chang-san.* Suzhou women were also considered most beautiful. The next rank of Suzhou prostitutes were called *yao-er.* Ningbo prostitutes, whose quality and ranking were between the two levels of Suzhou brothels, were called *er-san.* Prostitutes from Guangdong were divided into two categories, a high-class "Guangdong prostitute" (*yueji*) and the lower class "salt-water sisters" (*xianshuimei*). These latter were unique in that they catered exclusively to foreigners. Each regional group brought its own local brothel tradition. Ningbo prostitutes wore different clothes and served different delicacies than did Guangdong prostitutes. Although higher-priced prostitutes of different groups all sang pieces from Beijing opera, they specialized in the songs and opera of their native place.[35]

The example of prostitution points to the importance of native-place identities as a classificatory scheme in the minds of Chinese urban residents. As Christian Henriot has demonstrated, in contrast to the insistence of Shanghai writers on the existence of a strict regional hierarchy, the regional organization of prostitution was an ideal which was only partially maintained in practice. Economic conditions and recruitment channels were such that the largest number of prostitutes came from places near Shanghai. The numbers of Cantonese and Ningbo prostitutes were small compared with the size of their communities. Because of widespread recognition of the beauty of Suzhou women (and perhaps because exoticism was an asset in the realm of sexual desire) Shanghai elites showed more cosmopolitan tastes in this area, patronizing the higher-class Suzhou prostitutes, whether or not the clients themselves were from Suzhou. Such cosmopolitanism could nonetheless reinforce native-place distinctions, real and fictional.

35. Ibid., 33–39; Qian Shengke, "Jinü zhi hei mu" (Dark secrets of prostitutes), in *Shanghai hei mu bian* (Compilation of Shanghai's dark secrets) (Shanghai, 1917), 1–24; "Piaojie zhinan" (Guide to prostitutes), *Shanghai youlan zhinan* (Guide to visiting Shanghai) (Shanghai, 1919), 1–51; Chen Boxi, ed., *Shanghai yishi daguan* (Anecdotal survey of Shanghai) (Shanghai, 1924), vol. 3, 79–100; Renate Scherer, "Das System der chinesichen Prostitution dargestellt am Beispiel Shanghais in der Zeit von 1840 bis 1949" (Ph.D. diss., Free University of Berlin, 1981), 97–99, 116, 134–35; 146; Gail Hershatter, "The Hierarchy of Shanghai Prostitution, 1870–1949," MC 15 (October 1989):463–98; Gail Hershatter, *Shanghai Prostitution: Sex, Gender and Modernity* (tentative title, forthcoming). The names *chang-san* and *yao-er,* derived from mah-jongg tiles, referred to a scale of prices.

Non-Suzhou women cultivated Suzhou accents in order to command higher prices.[36]

Theater, like cuisine and like "the flower world," reflected different regional styles and aesthetics. The existence of different regional operas in the city—Anhui, Suzhou, Guangdong, Shaoxing, and Beijing styles, to name a few—and the location of many opera performances in *huiguan* suggest not a common theatrical experience but a divided one. Open-air performances did not exclude nonnatives and were surely enjoyed by many urban residents who were simply attracted to the excitement. But insofar as native-place communities sponsored performances of their regional operas, these performances reflected the "face" of specific native-place groups in the city.

Urban religious practices also marked group boundaries, dividing the Chinese urban residents of Shanghai into separate communities. Different native-place groups identified with different deities, different locations for religious observances and somewhat different festival calendars. Even when different communities shared gods, they commonly had different temples. For example, sojourners from coastal, seafaring areas, especially along China's southeast coast, worshipped the goddess Tianhou. People from the adjacent southeastern provinces of Guangdong and Fujian could come together for an occasional large-scale procession for Tianhou, but normal Tianhou worship was regionally subdivided: "Each Shanghai *huiguan* has built a Tianhou altar for worship and burning incense. Her birthday is on the 23rd day of the third lunar month. [For several days at this time] each *huiguan* has opera performances. . . . But the Jiangxi Huiguan only has a celebration [in the eighth lunar month], since Jiangxi is a linen-producing region. In the spring the merchants are in the production area buying goods. They wait until the market is slack, and use this time for [their devotion to] the god."[37]

In addition to worship of particular, regionally identified gods and regionally identified calendars, Chinese urban religious practice in

36. See Henriot's definitive study, "La prostitution à Shanghai aux XIXe–XXe siècles (1849–1958)," 3 vols. (Thèse d'Etat, Paris, Ecole des Hautes Etudes en Sciences Sociales, 1992).

37. Yao Gonghe, *Shanghai xianhua*, 22–23. Tianhou, a goddess known as a protector of fishermen, was worshipped along the southeast coast of China, particularly in Fujian and Guangdong but also in Zhejiang. See James Watson, "Standardizing the Gods: The Promotion of T'ien Hou (Empress of Heaven) Along the South China Coast, 960–1960," in *Popular Culture in Late Imperial China*, ed. David Johnson, Andrew Nathan and Evelyn Rawski (Berkeley, Calif., 1985), 292–324.

Shanghai involved the differential practice of common festivals and a common calendar. All Chinese in Shanghai observed the common holidays of the Chinese lunar calendar—among these the Chinese New Year, Qingming (the day of sweeping graves), and Duanwu (summer solstice). But how the holidays were celebrated—what individuals did, ate, or said on such occasions—varied according to local customs. For example, native-place tastes resulted in different styles of *zongzi* (leaf-wrapped steamed rice delicacies eaten at the time of the Duanwu holiday). Zhejiang-style *zongzi* are small and contain meat or red beans in addition to rice. Guangdong *zongzi* (considered faulty by Zhejiang and Jiangsu natives) are larger and contain a wider variety of stuffings mixed together—salted duck egg, yellow beans, sausage or chicken. Even today these local differences are a matter of regional pride and a means of emphasizing regional identity.

Qingming, the day on which families ritually swept their ancestral graves, could only have served to reinforce geographic differences. Native Shanghainese and people from areas close to Shanghai traveled to their family burial grounds in the outskirts of the city or in nearby villages. Sojourners from distant areas were drawn instead to their native-place cemeteries and coffin repositories in Shanghai.

The practices of everyday life in Shanghai suggest a number of observations about the possible ideas of identity and community available to Shanghai residents. It is important to consider and distinguish three obvious levels of territorial identity: native-place, urban (Shanghai), and national (Chinese) identity.[38] Most obviously, dialects, religious observances, culinary differences, and the presence of *huiguan,* native-place schools and other institutions in the city provided the sources and practices which defined native-place identity in the city. This potential basis for individual self-definition and collective community was experienced in the context of other, larger, bases for community and self-definition.

In addition to marking native-place identity, the quotidian habits of Shanghai residents provided sources for feelings of common Chinese identity. This becomes very clear in the context of holiday customs. Although differential New Year or Qingming practices heightened aware-

---

38. For a stimulating review and reconceptualization of theoretical debates regarding the sources for and nature of ethnic and national identities, see Prasenjit Duara, "De-Constructing the Chinese Nation," *Australian Journal of Chinese Affairs* 30 (July 1993):1–26.

[handwritten: but did this make them feel a national identity?]

ness of distinctive regional identities, the common lunar calendar entailed the simultaneous celebration by all Chinese residents, sojourners
and nonsojourners alike, elites and non-elites, of important festivals at
intervals in the year. The obvious observance of common holidays by
Chinese residents — contrasted with the equally obvious nonobservance
of these holidays by the foreign residents in the city — highlighted a
shared Chinese identity. Although it might be argued that the ideological connections between sojourner communities and China were elite
constructions not shared by non-elite sojourners, daily religious practices provided an obvious source for non-elite constructions of common
Chinese identity.

The question of a specifically Shanghai identity is more difficult.[39] As *[handwritten: urban?]*
suggested earlier, the act of sojourning and the location of sojourners in
Shanghai were crucial in providing sources for Chinese identity, both
because sojourners moved beyond their localities and confronted a
"China in miniature" in Shanghai's diverse Chinese population and because in Shanghai sojourners confronted foreign concessions and foreigners in a semicolonial framework. Residence in Shanghai brought
Chinese into daily contact with foreigners and with the indignities of
foreign privilege and foreign jurisdiction over Chinese soil. Because of
these features of the city, and although the urban location was crucial,
the subdivision of Chinese residents into native-place groups and the
semicolonial context (which created a greater and more absolute division between Chinese and foreigners) worked together to minimize the
development or expression of a common cosmopolitan, specifically urban, Shanghai identity among sojourners.

Aside from common residence in the city, it is difficult to pinpoint
specifically urban practices which might provide a basis for the formation of Shanghai identity, prior to the development of a Shanghai municipal government in 1927. Although customary religious observances
at times took place on a citywide scale, these celebrations did not convey
a specifically urban meaning. The locations of specific festivals in *hui-*

39. Location and periodization of the development of specifically Shanghai identity is
a matter of some debate. For a summary of pertinent issues, see Frederic Wakeman and
Wen-hsin Yeh, "Introduction," in *Shanghai Sojourners,* ed. Frederic Wakeman and Wen-
hsin Yeh (Berkeley, Calif., 1992), 1–14. For studies which assume (with varying degrees of
emphasis) that shared urban identity is a crucial development in a modernization process
that necessarily transcends local particularisms, see Rowe, *Hankow: Commerce and Society;*
William Rowe, *Hankow: Conflict and Community in a Chinese City, 1796–1895* (Stanford, Calif., 1989).

guan, in native-place cemeteries, or in temples associated with specific regional groups divided Shanghai space into local territories for ritual purposes. The varied regional opera performances in the city reflected the lack of a common urban cultural style.[40] Although the foreign municipal councils of the concession areas busily constructed municipal edifices—monuments, grand avenues and government buildings—there were no competing Chinese municipal spaces—city halls or public squares—to spatially represent Shanghai identity.[41] Sojourner associations did not take part in the Shanghai city-god procession. Processions expressing specifically municipal consciousness originated in Shanghai with the foreign-concession governments and their habits of public military drilling and fire-brigade parades. These foreign demonstrations of prowess in municipal government were tied to the nationalistic sentiments of the foreign powers; each used its municipal accomplishments in Shanghai to demonstrate the superior institutions of its nation.

The presence of such displays of national power, manifested through municipal institutions, had a crucial catalyzing effect on Shanghai's Chinese residents. Their response was self-defensive participation in these foreign parades and institutions, as a matter of Chinese identity and national pride (see Figure 3). Such participation, and such expressions of Chinese identity in the last decades of the Qing, occurred in the context of organization by native-place and (occasionally) trade group. Although such moments reinforce the coexistence of native-place and Chinese identity, they do not provide evidence for common Shanghai identity.

40. An opera style specific to Shanghai did not develop until the mid-Republican period. Shenqu (Shanghai song), recognized by the 1920s, developed gradually from an amalgamation of Jiangsu and Zhejiang styles. Mature Shanghai opera, Huju, was formalized only in the 1930s. Even in the 1930s the solidification of a Shanghai style was not a spontaneous cultural development but, rather, the result of the new municipal government's efforts to organize culture through the creation of a Municipal Shanghai Opera Research society. See Gu Tinglong, *Shanghai fengwu zhi* (Shanghai landscape gazetteer) (Shanghai, 1982), 270–71; Luo Suwen, "Cong xiqu yanchu zai jindai Shanghai de qubian kan dushi jumin de yule xiaofei ji shenmei qingqu" (Looking at urban residents' entertainment consumption and tastes through opera performance trends in modern Shanghai) (paper presented at the University of California, Berkeley, March 7, 1992). Scholarly and commercial elites from different native-place groups found common enjoyment in the *kun* and *jing* (Suzhou and Beijing) operas, which played at the expensive commercial theaters that appeared in late-nineteenth-century Shanghai. Such elite cosmopolitanism (or connoisseurship) was a *Chinese* cosmopolitanism, not a demonstration of specifically *Shanghai* culture or identity.

41. For a discussion of the contrasting spatial and architectural features of Chinese and European cities, see F. W. Mote, "The Transformation of Nanjing," in Skinner, *The City in Late Imperial China,* 114–17.

The organization of the habits of everyday life similarly facilitates reflection on sources for the development of identity on the basis of economic class. Well into the Republican era, regional divisions engendered social divisions which developed together with and helped constitute class divisions. Neighborhoods often expressed regional and occupational identity more clearly than class identity. Although, as noted earlier, mention of certain native-place identities suggested class positions (Ningbo was high; Subei was low), most native-place groups encompassed a class hierarchy within their communities. Restaurants similarly were differentiated by regional cuisines rather than by the economic capacity of their clientele. Within one building many restaurants offered food at a variety of prices — inexpensive dumplings or noodles in a common room on the ground floor; medium-priced food on the second floor, and elegant banquets in private rooms on the top floor.[42] This gustatory model of all classes together (but arranged hierarchically) under one sojourning native-place roof serves as a metaphor for the nested social layers of the broader urban regional communities.

The foregoing discussion of sources for group identities contextualizes the working out of native-place identity in the city. Native-place identity was articulated in relation to (and often in combination with) other available sources of identity, territorial and economic. The boundaries of perceived or operational community at any given moment would depend on the situational context. There was nothing in native-place identity which necessarily precluded the development of other forms of community. The ways in which native-place identity intersected with people's experiences of their national or economic positions would, however, help to shape both the development of nationalism and class formation.

Native-Place Organization and Occupational Organization

Native-place organization overlapped with the organization of trade throughout the late nineteenth and early twentieth centu-

---

42. This organization may still be observed today in Shanghai restaurants. In 1985, at the venerable Xinya Cantonese restaurant on Nanjing Road, for instance, soup, noodles, porridge and crude dishes were served at large noisy garbage-strewn tables on the first floor; the second floor offered tablecloths and more expensive dishes; the third-floor private booths served dainty delicacies to a wealthier clientele.

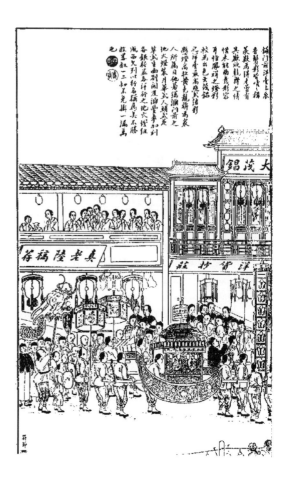

ries because sojourners from specific regions tended to specialize in one or more trades. This resulted in what William Skinner described as an "ethnic division of labor" in Chinese cities. Tea traders were from Anhui; silk merchants, from Zhejiang and Jiangsu. As Elizabeth Perry's study of Shanghai labor details, artisans and workers were similarly subdivided: "Carpenters were from Canton, machinists from Ningbo and Shaoxing, and blacksmiths from Wuxi." When competing in a trade, regional networks often carved out separate niches. The sugar trade, for example, was organized separately among groups from Chaozhou, Guangzhou, Ningbo and Fujian. Shanghai idioms expressed this identity of different regional groups with specific trades. The dominance of people from Huizhou prefecture (Anhui province) in the Shanghai pawnshop trade in the late nineteenth and early twentieth centuries, for

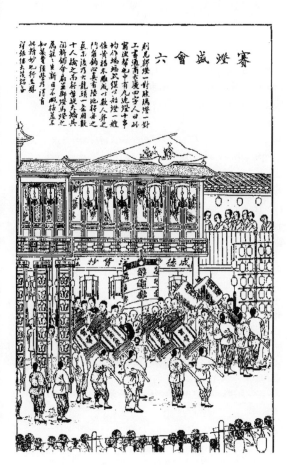

Figure 3. Ningbo partici-
pants in Parade of the
Shanghai International
Settlement. Source:
Dianshizhai huabao (Di-
anshi Studio pictorial
newspaper), 1983 Guang-
zhou reprint of late-
Qing edition (1884–
1898).

example, is evident in the expression *wu Hui bu cheng dian* ("Without a
Huizhou person, there's no mortgage).[43]

Because groups of fellow-provincials often practiced several trades
and, moreover, because trades were not always exclusively monopolized
by people from one area of China, the native-place organization of trade
is not always immediately obvious. For example, there is nothing in
the name of the Rice Trade (*Miye*) Gongsuo to suggest that it was an
organization of local Jiangsu merchants. Adding to the potential for
confusion, the names of individual associations (often the only re-

43. Skinner, "Introduction," 544; Perry, *Shanghai on Strike*, 36. Honig (*Creating Chinese Ethnicity*) provides a recent elaboration of Skinner's insight that native-place identity
could constitute ethnicity in a Chinese city.

maining evidence of their existence) frequently fail to indicate native-place or trade affiliations. When sufficient documentation is available, however, consistent overlap of native-place and trade organization is clear.[44] The various organizational possibilities under this general rule may be illustrated by several examples.

Tea, Jewelry and Silk: Native-Place Trade Associations. Examples of single trade associations whose memberships were also defined by native-place ties may be found in the Shanghai tea, jewelry and silk trades. Anhui tea merchants from Wuyuan county formed the Xingjiang Chaye Gongsuo (Star River Tea Trade Association), also called the Dunzitang (Hall for Strengthening the Native Place). A history written by the association in 1926 illustrates the intertwining of native-place and trade ties:

Our Wu is the most famous place [in China] for tea production. . . . [When] Shanghai became the major port, our Wu tea leaves were shipped to Shanghai. . . . In the Xianfeng and Tongzhi reigns of the Qing dynasty [1851–61; 1862–74] tea merchants established a warehouse in Shanghai to facilitate production, and they collected funds and established the Dunzitang Gongsuo to unite native-place sentiment and to encourage study [of tea production]. At first we purchased two buildings and called them the Xingjiang Dunzitang. In the central area we worshipped the figure of the State Duke of Hui[45] and gathered together our *tongxiang* gentlemen to make sacrifices [to him].[46]

44. The most comprehensive listing of Shanghai native-place and trade associations (*huiguan* and *gongsuo*) may be found in Xu Dingxin, "Shanghai gongshang tuanti de jindaihua" (The modernization of Shanghai industrial and commercial groups), in *Jindai Shanghai chengshi yanjiu* (Research on modern Shanghai), ed. Zhang Zhongli (Shanghai, 1990), 512–13, 518–22. Xu's attempt to list native-place and trade associations separately obscures their interrelation (as a review of the territorial names associated with many of the "trade associations" he lists demonstrates). Trade associations of native Shanghainese did not specify local origin but were commonly associations of locals, as opposed to outsiders. See Tadashi Negishi, *Shanhai no girudo* (The guilds of Shanghai) (Tokyo, 1951), 7–14; Linda Cooke Johnson, ed., *Cities of Jiangnan in Late Imperial China* (Albany, N.Y., 1993), 162–66. My argument is in accordance with Skinner ("Introduction," 542–43, 545), who suggests that historians probably underestimate economic specialization by native place and argues against reading organizational shifts as "a secular trend away from economic specialization."

45. State Duke of Hui (*Huiguo wengong zhuzi shenzhu*) is the posthumous title of the neo-Confucian scholar and theorist, Zhu Xi. Although Zhu Xi was born in Youxi county in Fujian province, his ancestral home was Wuyuan county, Anhui. For this reason he could be claimed as the illustrious patron god of the Wuyuan tea association. See Wing-tsit Chan, trans., *Reflections on Things at Hand: The Neo-Confucian Anthology* (New York: 1967), xxxviii, 2.

46. *Xingjiang dunzitang zhengxinlu* (Record-book of the Xingjiang Dunzitang), Shanghai, 1926, hand-copied manuscript, courtesy of Du Li, Shanghai Museum.

The Wuyuan tea association was not the only tea association in Shanghai, nor was it the only association of Anhui tea merchants in Shanghai in the late nineteenth and early twentieth centuries. Wuyuan tea merchants apparently participated together with other Anhui tea merchants in the Hui-Ning Huiguan, also called the Sigongtang (Hall of Thoughtful Reverence), the association of fellow-provincials from the Anhui prefectures of Huizhou and Ningguo (established in Shanghai in 1754). Because tea was a major trade among Anhui sojourners in Shanghai, tea merchants provided the financial foundation for the Anhui native-place association. This is evident from records of taxes imposed by the Hui-Ning Huiguan on all Anhui tea merchants in Shanghai, beginning as early as 1844 and continuing through at least 1897. The taxes were imposed by the *huiguan* to support social services for Anhui fellow-provincials. Tea merchants, organized in six different regional groups within Anhui (Wuyuan county among them), rotated responsibility for tax collection within the *huiguan* membership.[47]

By the end of the Qing, three separate native-place trade associations comprised the Shanghai jewelry trade. Suzhou jewelers established the Subang Zhubaoye Gongsuo in 1872. The year 1873 saw the creation of the Wuxian (Wu county) Zhubaoye Gongsuo, by a powerful contingent within the former Subang Gongsuo. Nanjing jewelers established the third association, the Nanjingbang Zhubaoye Gongsuo, in 1908, after friction with the Suzhou group (whose meeting hall they had formerly borrowed). Although all three groups were fellow Jiangsu provincials, and although their records indicate cooperation for specific purposes, they maintained separate subprovincial organizations well into the Republican era.

Separate native-place trade organizations similarly comprised the Shanghai silk trade. The names and dates of establishment of some of these associations are as follows:[48]

1853 — Shengzi and Wangjiangjing silk merchants, Jiangsu (Sheng-Jing Chouye Gongsuo)

47. *Hui-Ning sigongtang chajuan zhengxinlu* (Tea-tax record-book of the Hui-Ning Hall of Thoughtful Reverence), 1875–1934, hand-copied manuscript, courtesy of Du Li, Shanghai Museum.
48. Shanghai bowuguan (Shanghai Museum), ed., *Shanghai beike ziliao xuanji* (Compilation of materials from Shanghai stone inscriptions) (Shanghai, 1980) (hereafter referred to as SBZX), 366–68; Xu Dingxin, "Shanghai gongshang tuanti," 518–21. The Shanghai sugar and pawnshop trades offer further examples of trades divided among people from different provinces, in which native-place divisions were not bridged by an overarching trade association. By the end of the Qing, three native-place groups operated

1876 — Hangzhou silk merchants (Hang Chou Gongsuo/Qianjiang Huiguan)

1876 — Shanghai silk merchants (Shenjiang Zhouye Gongsuo)

1894 — Huzhou silk merchants, Zhejiang (Zhe-Hu Zhouye Gongsuo)

Native-Place Multiple-Trade Associations. Because merchants from one area frequently specialized in not one but several trades, they often formed multiple-trade associations. Fujian merchants from Tingzhou, Quanzhou and Zhangzhou prefectures, for example, organized the Peanuts, Sugar and Foreign Goods Association (*Huatang yanghuohang dianchuntang*). Similar native-place organization of multiple-trade associations persisted into the Republican era. For example, in 1927, when the Shanghai Municipal Government ordered the reorganization of trades from more traditional *huiguan* and *gongsuo* into more modern-style associations, Chaozhou merchants formed the Chaozhou Sugar and Miscellaneous Goods Trade Association (*Chaozhou tang zahuo gonghui*), located at the address of the Chaozhou Huiguan.[49]

Trade Associations Subdivided by Native Place. In some trades, to facilitate cooperation, several distinct regional groups joined together in one overarching trade association. For example, two major regional subgroups internally divided the Bean Trade Association (*Shanghai douye cuixiutang*). Zhejiang merchants dominated the southern group (*nanbang*); Shandong merchants controlled the northern group (*beibang*). Although the two groups cooperated in the trade asso-

---

pawnshops in Shanghai: Huizhou (Anhui), Chaozhou (Guangdong) and local Shanghai (Jiangsu) groups. Each maintained distinctive practices. In the case of sugar, Chaozhou import merchants specialized in Chaozhou sugar; Fujian merchants imported Fujian sugar. Three groups controlled Shanghai sugar shops — local (*benbang*), Zhenjiang (*Zhenbang*) and Ningbo (*Ningbang*). See Sun Xiangyun, "Jiefangqian Shanghai de diandangye" (The pawnshop trade in pre-liberation Shanghai), *Shanghai wenshi ziliao xuanji* (Selected materials in Shanghai history and culture) (Shanghai) 49 (1985):131–34; Shanghai shangye zhuxu yinghang diaochabu (Shanghai Commercial Deposit Bank, Research Section), *Shanghai zhi tang yu tangye* (Shanghai sugar and sugar trade) (Shanghai, 1933), 58–60; CHYB, April 1917.

49. CHYB, 1927. A single reference to this Chaozhou organization in the meeting notes for 1925 suggests that it existed in some fashion several years before 1927; *Shanghai shangye minglu* (Commercial directory of Shanghai) (Shanghai, 1931), sections on business groups.

ciation to facilitate business, they retained their separate organizations and did not uniformly comply with taxes and collections intended for all bean-trade members.[50]

A loose trade federation like the Bean Trade Association must have functioned in practice similarly to the separate but cooperating Jiangsu jewelry associations. Just as stone inscriptions from the separate jewelry associations provide evidence that separate organization did not preclude considerable cooperation, bean-trade records suggest that a single formal overarching trade organization did not preclude considerable native-place division.

Nonexclusive Trade Associations with Strong Native-Place Bias. The native-place organization of trade was not inflexible, and it could accommodate the strategic inclusion of certain nonnatives into what appear otherwise to have been native-place trade associations. A court case of 1879 revealed that a prominent merchant from Guangzhou prefecture, Tang Maozhi, played a leadership role in the Opium Association (formed by merchants of Chaoyang and Huilai counties of Chaozhou prefecture, Guangdong province).[51]

The Shanghai Silk Huiguan (*Siye huiguan*), organized by silk warehouse owners, offers an example of a nonexclusive trade association with strong native-place bias. Although the silk association encompassed certain non-Zhejiang merchants, documents of the association make clear the special relation of the association to Huzhou (a major silk-producing Zhejiang prefecture) and the special position of Huzhou silk merchants. The Silk Huiguan maintained a hospital for Zhejiang provincials involved in the silk trade in Shanghai, provided coffins and medicine for Zhejiang refugees from the Taiping disorders in 1861, maintained a rice-gruel "soup kitchen" in Huzhou for the indigent, arranged transportation for Huzhou sojourners returning to their native place and contributed heavily toward military expenses in Zhejiang incurred in the suppression of the Taipings. When the central government decided to bestow an honorific plaque on a benevolent association in Huzhou, it gave the plaque to the Shanghai sojourning Huzhou silk

50. "Shanghai douye gongsuo cuixiutang ji lüe" (Record of the Shanghai Bean Gongsuo, Cuixiutang), hand-copied manuscript dated 1924, courtesy of Du Li, Shanghai Museum, 13–14.

51. NCH, October 17, 1879, 385–86. In this case, all members were still Guangdong provincials.

merchants through the agency of the Silk Huiguan, which clearly served as their native-place association.[52]

Native-Place Associations Subdivided by Trade. The examples described above address the problem of overlap between native-place and trade association from the point of view of the organization of trade. The same phenomenon may be approached through a description of what were nominally native-place associations, which included under their native-place umbrella a variety of trade and occupational associations. The most elaborate of these was the Ningbo Huiguan (Siming Gongsuo), which represented sojourners from seven counties (Zhenhai, Yin, Ciqi, Fenghua, Xiangshan, Dinghai and Nantian) of Ningbo prefecture, Zhejiang province, and was the most powerful sojourners' association in Shanghai from the end of the Qing dynasty through the Republican period. In the 1930s the Siming Gongsuo encompassed numerous trade associations:[53]

Trade Associations

Fish trade (Tongshanhui)   Southern goods (Nanhuohui)

Seafood trade (Chongdehui)   Foreign goods (Yongjishe)

Wine trade (Ji'anhui)   Pork trade (Dunrentang)

Medicine trade (Yuyitang)   Butcher trade (Chengrentang)

Handicraft Associations

Stonemasons (Changshouhui)

Carpenters (Nianqinghui)

Silverworkers (Tongyihui)

52. *Siye huiguan zhengxinlu* (Record-book of the Silk Huiguan), documents dated 1860, hand-copied manuscript, courtesy of Du Li, Shanghai Museum; *Tongren fuyuantang zhengxinlu* (Record-book of the Tongren Fuyuan Benevolent Association), document excerpt dated 1861, hand-copied manuscript, courtesy of Du Li, Shanghai Museum.
53. Shanghai tongshe, ed., *Shanghai yanjiu ziliao xuji* (Compilation of Shanghai research materials, continuation) (Shanghai, 1984 reprint of 1939 ed.), 300. The Ningbo Huiguan also encompassed a variety of noneconomic organizations, including religious and charitable associations.

Trade Unions

Money trade union (Qianye Gonghui)

Five metals trade union (Wujin Gonghui)

Western food trade union (Taixi Shiwu Gonghui)

Laborers' Associations

Ningbo workers serving foreign employers (Siming Changsheng Hui)

Ningbo seamen (Shuishou Jun'anhui)

The Ningbo association represented the pinnacle of native-place organization and power. While other native-place associations did not have the wealth or population to support such extended organizational complexity they nonetheless followed a similar, if simpler, model.[54]

Although these examples suggest a variety of specific and often complex organizational arrangements, they also demonstrate the general rule of economic organization by both trade and native place. The irreducible units in each case are groups defined in terms of a single trade and a common native-place identity. Because of the dual nature of these economic and social units, they could be integrated into either overarching trade or native-place associations (or, frequently, both). Over the course of the late nineteenth and early twentieth centuries, as new associations formed and old associations faded away in the rapidly developing and constantly changing economy of Shanghai, these basic native-place trade units were involved in processes of fission or recombination with other (either same-native-place or same-trade) units. Such associational restructuring followed the rise and decline of specific trades, the diversification of sojourner economic strategies, and the influx of different immigrant populations. There was no clear trend in the direction of either overarching trade associations or overarching native-place associations

54. In the 1930s the much smaller Jiangxi Huiguan was organized around thirteen trades, each of which contributed one director. Inside the *huiguan,* each director had an office marked "Jiangxi Huiguan — — — Trade." The trades included carpentry, bamboo articles, enamel, lacquer, tailors, canvas workers, silk and pottery (interview with Shen Yinxian, Shanghai, October 1983).

until 1931, when the Nationalist government enforced laws to regularize trade associations.[55]

The Terminology of Chinese Associations

The terminology of Chinese associations in Shanghai in the period under study reveals a plethora of social, economic and religious connotations and complicates the task of describing the broad scope of phenomena related to native-place identity.[56] Distinctions among Chinese association names have been understood to reveal the underlying nature of associational practice. In contemporary usage, however, quite different terms could be interchangeable. This flexibility provides evidence of the relatedness of the forms beneath the names and of the fact that the formal and informal associations denoted were not discrete but overlapping.

Huiguan, gongsuo. Huiguan, the most studied institutional expression of native-place sentiment, were formal associations of sojourning fellow-provincials. *Huiguan* were established in Beijing as early as the late Ming by sojourning officials and scholars. Outside Beijing, particularly in centers of trade, *huiguan* were more commonly established by merchants, who patterned their meeting halls on the politically acceptable meeting halls of sojourning Confucian scholars. This was the case in Shanghai, where *huiguan* appeared as early as the seventeenth century and increased in number during the eighteenth and nineteenth centuries.[57]

---

55. After 1927 the new Nanjing government attempted to regularize commercial associations with a "commercial association law," followed by an "industrial and commercial trade association law" and "detailed regulations to enact the industrial and commercial trade association law" (1929 and 1930), requiring all trades to establish new commercial associations by 1931. Despite changes in association structure, many organizations informally retained earlier habits. Xu Dingxin, "Shanghai gongshang tuanti," 545–61.

56. In addition to *huiguan* (meeting hall) and *gongsuo* (public office), common names for native-place and trade associations included those which expressed the religious, judicial, charitable, benevolent and fraternal functions of the associations: *dian* (temple or sanctuary), *gong* (palace or temple), *ge* (pavilion), *lou* (building, also restaurant), *tang* (hall, office or court), *bang* (gang, band or clique), *hui* (association or religious society), *dang* (clique, faction, gang or party), *she* (altar, organized body or society).

57. One Shanghai association, the Guan-Shandong Gongsuo, was established as early as 1654–61 (SBZX, 509). The term *huiguan* refers both to the organization of people and the characteristic architectural form in which the association conducted its business.

The fact that nearly all Shanghai *huiguan* were established by so-journing merchants helps explain the interchangeability of *huiguan* and *gongsuo,* the latter a term many *huiguan* employed in reference to themselves, despite the fact that *gongsuo* is often considered to denote trade associations, not specifically associations of fellow-provincials. In Shanghai *huiguan* and *gongsuo* could be used interchangeably because of the overlapping of trade organization with native-place ties. It is useful, therefore, to represent most *huiguan* and *gongsuo* as organizations of fellow-provincials which also expressed trade interests.[58]

Bang. The term *bang* encompasses a broad range of meanings and occurs equally in reference to formal organizations of regional and trade identity like *huiguan* and *gongsuo,* similar but informal groups, and illegal associations like gangs, which were also frequently organized along axes of regional identity. The term *kebang,* "guest bang" (that is, outsider merchant group) occurs in reference to groups of merchants from areas outside their city of operation. Other records distinguish between *wobang,* "our bang" and *tabang* or *waibang,* "other bang" or "outside bang." *Bang* also frequently occurs in the compound *bang-pai,* or faction. In *huiguan* and *gongsuo* records, *bang* is employed in reference to subgroups within the association itself (regional and trade subgroups) and in reference to corresponding groups outside the association. In records and literature emanating from outside the associations, *bang* often means regional or trade communities, at times *huiguan* or *gongsuo* specifically.

The term *bang* and its use in regard to associations of fellow-

58. Local gazetteers (see, for example, *Shanghai xian xuzhi* [Continuation of the Shanghai county gazetteer] [Shanghai, 1918; reprint Taipei, 1970] [hereafter referred to as SXXZ], 3:1) grouped *huiguan* and *gongsuo* together for this reason. Linda Cooke Johnson (*Cities of Jiangnan,* 162–67) distinguishes between common trade and native-place organizations, arguing that sojourner associations (*huiguan*) were located outside the walled city, whereas "insider" trade associations were located within the city. She also suggests that trade associations did not provide religious services. The exceptions to these rules make the argument unpersuasive. Guangdong and Fujian *huiguan* were located within the city walls prior to the Small Sword Uprising, and a Zhejiang–Zhe-Shao *huiguan* was located there afterward. On the religious functions of trade associations, see Li Qiao, *Zhongguo hangye shen chongbai* (The worship of gods in Chinese trades) (Beijing, 1990). I would suggest that social scientists recognize the complexity of social practices like naming and accept a certain "fuzziness" here rather than force multidimensional social understandings into an inappropriate either/or categorization (economic or particularist), which reflects a way of thinking foreign to the members and contemporary observers of these associations.

provincials are significant not because it denotes a specific type of organization but because in its broadness it describes the quality of the group,
that is to say, that the group acts in the manner of a clique, faction, or
gang. This quality was recognized as both natural and potentially negative (because self-interested). Although the term is often used in a neutral sense, it is not accidental that in accounts recording unruly behavior
of regional and trade associations the associations are referred to as
bang, and not as the more respectable *huiguan* and *gongsuo,* which appear more frequently in gazetteers and in stone inscriptions left by the
associations. Unfortunately for the historian trained to find identity in
well-defined naming practices, this renaming of the association in accordance with its phase of behavior provides instead the idealized construction of what the members were doing at a given moment.[59]

New Terms in the Twentieth Century. A variety of new
terms and associational forms—*shangye lianhehui* (merchant federation), *gonghui* (public association), *youyihui* (friendly society), *xiehui*
(society, consultative committee), *tongzhihui* (comrades' association)—
appeared in the twentieth century, beginning around the time of the
Revolution of 1911. New and different forms of native-place associations
appeared under all of these new names, reflecting Shanghai residents'
striking capacity to adapt the native-place organizational principle to
new circumstances and to integrate new social and political elements
into their traditions and practices.[60]

In addition, a term employed to denote a new and self-consciously
"modern" form of general native-place association came into existence,
the *tongxianghui* (literally "association of fellow-provincials"). The full

59. The politically oriented term *dang* occurs less frequently in reference to associations of fellow-provincials, though, like *bang,* it could be used to suggest the negative
characteristics of private associations. Unlike *bang, dang* is rarely neutral. Accounts of the
Small Sword Uprising of 1853, for instance, refer to Cantonese and Fujianese *bang* and
dang. In such contexts the meaning is similar to *banghui,* or *hui;* that is, gangs and secret
societies. In these accounts of the uprising, seven participating *huiguan* appear most frequently as seven *bang* or *hui.* As a result, it can be difficult to understand the specific
connections between *huiguan* and secret societies, all organizations involved being sub-
sumed under the same rubric.

60. Examples are the Sojourning Guangdong Merchants' Federation (Yueqiao
shangye lianhehui), the Federation of Jiangsu Public Groups (Jiangsu gongtuan lianhehui),
the All-Zhejiang Association (Quan Zhe gonghui), the Subei Tongxiang Friendly Society
(Huaishu tongxiang youyihui), the Jiangxi Self-Government Comrades' Association
(Jiangxi zizhi tongzhihui) and the All-Anhui Consultative Committee (Quan Hui xiehui),
all of which were active in Shanghai during the 1920s (SB, November 1926, May 1927).

name of these associations, *lü Hu tongxianghui* (association of fellow-provincials sojourning in Shanghai), evokes again in the Republican era the permanence of (often ascribed) regional identity and the perceived transience of (often permanent) residence.

Terminology and Interpretation: Guilds and Landsmann-schaften. The dual nature of *huiguan* and *gongsuo,* which most commonly incorporated both native-place and common-trade ties, has resulted in a controversy over the basic nature of these organizations, reflecting a certain historiographical essentialism. This controversy has been expressed through variations in the western terminology which scholars have employed to characterize Chinese associations. Consideration of Chinese terminology therefore cannot alone describe the scope of the problem. We must also discuss western terminology.

In their efforts to comprehend and classify Chinese native-place and trade associations, scholars have employed two western-language terms, "guild" and "*landsmannschaften,*" to convey the nature of the groups involved. "Guild," which suggests an essentially economic organization, has been favored over "*landsmannschaften,*" which expresses the primacy of regional bonds.[61] This discrepancy in terminology results not only from the different economic arguments that have surrounded the associations but also from the fact that there appears to be no western term that incorporates both *landsmann* and trade characteristics.

It is not surprising that the Europeans frustrated in their attempts to expand trade with China adopted the term "guild" to describe the Chinese protective associations they encountered which rebuffed their attempts to penetrate Chinese markets. European interests were primarily commercial, and it was in this realm that they encountered the Chinese associations. The term "guild" offered the most obvious analogy to their historical experience. Their own economic interests, therefore, caused them to view native-place ties as an incidental and subordinate feature of Chinese guilds. They did not, in general, seek to investigate or understand the linguistic, religious and cultural basis of these associations.[62]

61. The use of the term "guild" is not restricted to western historians: Japanese scholars refer to *girudo;* Chinese scholars, to *jierte.*

62. The transcript of a trial in which British opium merchants unsuccessfully sued the Chao-Hui Huiguan (an association of opium merchants from Chaoyang and Huilai counties) for monopolizing trade reflects the Chinese merchants' exploitation of the persistent inability of the British to comprehend the nature of the Chinese association. When the British characterized their imagined "Chinese guild," the Chinese merchants used the ways in which their association did not fit the British model to "prove" that no such

The native-place characteristics as well as the noneconomic functions of these associations have accordingly been cited as evidence of irrational, particularistic or monopolistic tendencies of Chinese guilds.

Such views dovetail with historical and sociological models of the catalytic role of cities and urban associations in the development of capitalism. In particular, Weber's linkage of China's apparent failure to achieve capitalism with the failure of Chinese cities to resemble European cities—in other words, their failure to develop economically "rational" urban associations and a "commune-autonomous" form of urban settlement—has spawned numerous meditations on the nature of Chinese cities and their relation to European cities. William Rowe's study of Hankou represents the most significant recent scholarship in this vein. Because Weber stressed the particularism of Chinese business ties, arguing that urban citizenship could not develop in communities of sojourners, native-place associations have been a natural focus in studies of Chinese cities.[63]

Japanese historians like Niida Noboru and Imahori Seiji have stressed the importance of regional ties in Chinese "guilds," asserting that although common native place was not an essential condition for membership, common local-origin was nonetheless a general rule. Imahori Seiji, echoing Weber's arguments, emphasized that the closed and reactionary quality of these associations stifled China's economic development.[64]

Ho Ping-ti's major study of Chinese regional associations, developed in response to this dominant trend in Japanese historiography, empha-

---

association existed at all. See NCH, September 1879, October 1879; H. B. Morse, *The Gilds of China* (London, 1909; reprint Taipei, 1972); Herbert Giles, *Chinese Sketches* (London, 1876); D. J. MacGowan, "Chinese Guilds or Chambers of Commerce and Trades Unions," *Journal of the North China Branch of the Royal Asiatic Society* 21 (1886–87):133–92.

63. Max Weber, "Citizenship," in *General Economic History* (Glencoe, Ill., 1950), 315–51. For a detailed discussion of these arguments in the context of a critique of Weber which does not dispute Weberian logic, see Rowe, *Hankow: Commerce and Society*, 1–16. In light of recent western scholarship on the rural and regional preconditions for the development of industrial capitalism, this debate on the role of Chinese cities may appear somewhat quaint. See, for example, T. H. Ashton and C. H. E. Philipin, eds., *The Brenner Debate: Agrarian Class Structure and Economic Development in Pre-Industrial Europe* (Cambridge, Mass., 1985); Steven Hahn and J. Prude, *The Countryside in the Age of Capitalist Transformation: Essays in the Social History of Rural America* (Chapel Hill, N. C., 1985).

64. See Niida Noboru, "The Industrial and Commercial Guilds of Peking and Religion and Fellowcountrymanship as Elements of Their Coherence," *Folklore Studies* (Peking) 9 (1950):197; Rowe, *Hankow: Commerce and Society*, 267; Susan Mann, "Urbanization and Historical Change in Modern China," *MC* 10 (January 1984):90.

sized the importance of regional ties in Chinese associations. He chose the German term *landsmannschaften* to describe *huiguan* and called *gongsuo landsmann* guilds.[65] Although he emphasized the primacy of native-place ties in his choice of terminology, his assessment of the significance of these ties differed sharply with Japanese interpretations and (though not explicitly) the superimposition of Weberian typology on the Chinese historical case. The novelty of Ho's argument was his assertion that in China native-place associations played a critical positive role in economic development by facilitating interregional and social integration. Important recent work by Susan Mann on the Ningbo financial community and by Marie-Claire Bergère on the Shanghai bourgeoisie demonstrates the adaptability of traditional native-place organization to the needs of modernization.[66]

Recent scholarship by Chinese historians has addressed and restated these various arguments. The dominant trend in contemporary Chinese scholarship suggests that in the nineteenth century the nature of Chinese commercial and handicraft associations changed. Du Li and Xu Dingxin argue that feudal and particularist associations became increasingly democratic and that the significance of native-place ties gave way to more "rational" commercial alignments. This argument must be seen in the context of the abiding preoccupation with the "sprouts of capitalism" in Chinese historiography, supporting arguments that China developed or was developing an indigenous form of capitalism, in accordance with Chinese interpretations of Marxian stages of economic development.[67]

65. Ho, *Zhongguo huiguan shilun;* Ho Ping-ti, "The Geographic Distribution of Hui-Kuan (Landsmannschaften) in Central and Upper Yangtze Provinces," *Tsinghua Journal of Chinese Studies* n. s. 5 (December 1966):120–52.

66. Susan Mann Jones, "The Ningpo *Pang* and Financial Power at Shanghai," in Elvin and Skinner, *The Chinese City between Two Worlds,* 73–96. Mann's study examines how traditional locality and kinship ties within the Ningbo community not only adapted to meet the needs of modernization but also provided important resources for the developing financial power of the group. Her conclusions regarding the utility of native-place ties in the development of modern finance have been reinforced by Marie-Claire Bergère's study of regional ties and the development of modern industry in Shanghai (*L'âge d'or de la bourgeoisie chinoise* [Paris, 1986], 148–59).

67. This argument is reflected in several essays in *Zhongguo zibenzhuyi mengya wenti lunwenji* (Compilation of papers concerning the sprouts of capitalism in China), ed. Nanjing daxue lishixi Ming-Qing shi yanjiushi (Nanjing University History Department, Ming-Qing History Division) (Nanjing, 1983). See also Xu Dingxin, "Jiu zhongguo shanghui chaoyuan" (Trends in the development of old China's Chamber of Commerce), *Zhongguo shehui jingjishi yanjiu* (Research on China's social and economic history) 1 (1983):83–96. In such arguments we may observe the irony of Chinese historians recon-

Rowe's detailed study of Hankou concurs generally with this most recent judgement of mainland Chinese historians, although Rowe is more preoccupied with Weberian than with Marxist categories. Rowe employs Weber's categories regarding urban requirements for the development of capitalism but rejects Weber's conclusion that Chinese cities were irredeemably alien to the dynamic western model. He argues that (at least in cities like Hankou), China was developing an indigenous form of capitalism, which was expressed in the rationalization of economic behavior. In his choice of the word "guild," Rowe minimizes native-place organization and sentiment by insisting on fundamental economic primacy, and he suggests that by the late-nineteenth-century Chinese guilds increasingly fulfilled Weber's prescriptions for rational economic behavior.[68]

Rowe at once agrees with Ho Ping-ti's assessment of the positive economic role of *huiguan* and denies the other major element of Ho's argument, the primacy of the native-place tie. Whereas Ho suggested a separate model of "rational economic activity" based on the particularities of the Chinese case, Rowe's study concludes with the suggestion that apparent Chinese peculiarities aside, urban organization in Hankou by the late nineteenth century had come to resemble the European model.

Rowe's argument for a process of "de-parochialization" and "indigenous rationalization" in Hankou's native-place and trade associations, like the arguments of Du Li and Xu Dingxin, depends on a formalistic typing of associations. These studies deduce the presence or absence of native-place sentiment or organization largely on the basis of an organization's name, on the formal existence of new trade associations or on the basis of gazetteer accounts which provide fragmentary and uneven descriptions of association structure or constituency. Such focus on the names and formal structure of organizations can be highly distorting because native place was commonly an informal (though integral) component of new forms of trade association. This may only be evident through an examination of organizational behavior. In 1925, for instance, Chaozhou merchants had a Sugar and Miscellaneous Goods Trade Association in addition to their *huiguan*. But this did not mean a

---

structing Chinese phenomena to fit western categories. Xu has modified his position, admitting the uneven evidence for progressive evolutionary trends in his more recent work (see Xu Dingxin, "Shanghai gongshang tuanti").

68. Rowe, *Hankow: Commerce and Society,* 252, 283–85.

separation of native-place and economic functions. The apparent formal distinction between trade and native-place association (tempting for a historian eager to discover a decline in the native-place organization of trade) was in fact illusory. When the Shantou Finance Board wrote to the *trade* association in 1925, for example, the *huiguan* drafted the response. Other glimpses of how formal institutional divisions may collapse into common native-place identity are revealed by the placement of documents in archival collections. In the Shanghai Archives, for instance, the archive of the Hu She (association of sojourners from Huzhou, Zhejiang) includes the meeting records, trade rules and regulations for the Shanghai Municipal Silk Trade Association (*Shanghai tebie shi chouduan ye tongye gonghui*) and the Shanghai Huzhou Silk Gongsuo (*Shanghai Zhe-Hu zhouye gongsuo*).[69]

Because the primary focus of the present study is social rather than economic, models of economic development from feudalism to capitalism (Weberian and otherwise) are not an overriding concern. Nonetheless, the process of investigating the social behavior of *huiguan* and *gongsuo* and the availability of important new sources have led me at least peripherally into these debates. In two respects — in affirming the persistent native-place segmentation of Shanghai's urban community and the importance of native-place links which transcended Shanghai's borders — the findings of this study challenge those of Rowe which suggest the attenuation of native-place ties in the last decades of the nineteenth century and the displacement of native-place identity by an emergent urban "Hankou" identity.[70] As the story of the forms and

69. CHYB. Bean-trade documents similarly demonstrate that despite the apparent unifying structure of a bean association in the 1920s, certain regional *bang* participated in paying taxes while others did not ("Shanghai douye gongsuo cuixiutang jilüe," 13–14; SBZX, 366–68; Shanghai shi dang'anguan (Shanghai city archives), ed., *Shanghai shi dang'anguan kaifang dang'an quanzong mulu* (Catalog of the open archives of the Shanghai City Archives) (Shanghai, 1991).

70. The different conclusions of Rowe's study of Hankou and this study of Shanghai cannot be explained by differences between the two cities. Although Shanghai's commercial boom occurred later than Hankou's, Shanghai experienced commercial expansion since at least the sixteenth century (as part of the extended Yangzi delta urban network centering on Suzhou). In other respects the two cities resembled each other. Both were prominent commercial centers; both have been described as "vanguard" localities; and both attained an economic importance which outstripped their administrative importance. Shanghai was one step higher than Hankou in Skinner's hierarchy of administrative central places (a county seat rather than a market town). Nonetheless, it did not surpass Hankou in the numbers of officials assigned to the city. It may be that Rowe overestimates late-nineteenth-century weakening of native-place ties because he uses a Weberian vocabulary which presumes a contradiction between particularistic ties and economic rational-

sentiments of Shanghai urban organization told in the following pages will demonstrate, the idea of the native place remained a potent organizing principle as late as the 1930s. Moreover, native-place sentiment was not rigid but was a remarkably flexible axis for the coalition of a variety of social organizations, ranging from "feudal" to "modern" types, if these stifling labels must be used.

The fact that people retained their native-place identity did not mean they could not also develop broader (particularly national) identities. They would, and the how and why of this process is integral to the story in this book. The transformation of urban identity was a process of accretion of identities, not the displacement of native-place identity for newer, more "modern" ones. It was precisely in this process of adoption and accommodation that understandings of both tradition and modernity were forged and transformed.

The city of Shanghai did not conform to Weber's typologies of cities, European or Chinese. Perhaps more important, freedom from Weberian straight jackets permits the exploration of certain unique features of Chinese urban social and economic formations. The story of the enduring but shifting formations of native-place sentiment expressed through changing Shanghai urban institutions raises new issues of multiple and variable urban identities; connections between communities of fellow-provincials in Shanghai and their native areas (connections critical to the comprehension of both locations); connections between urban elites and non-elites through native-place ties; and the relation of native-place associations to the maintenance (or disruption) of urban order.

Finally, recognition that native-place sentiment and organization were important and enduring in Shanghai during the Republican era permits an understanding of modernization which does not presume the withering of traditional ideas and practices. Instead, we will be free to trace the ways in which "tradition" was not fixed but dynamic, not given but constructed, and the means by which elements of "traditional" Chinese culture helped facilitate and structure the process of radical social transformation we associate with modernity.

---

ity. Such an assumption need not be made in the context of a study which demonstrates the "modernization" of Chinese mentalities. Although Mary Backus Rankin (*Elite Activism,* 89) describes a transformation of consciousness which led elites to think "beyond local boundaries," she recognizes that "Zhejiang merchants in Shanghai still retained the attributes of sojourners through the last decades of the Qing dynasty."

CHAPTER TWO

Foreign Imperialism, Immigration and Disorder

Opium War Aftermath and the Small Sword Uprising of 1853

> *All the extremes of character in the empire are here brought together,*
> *so that it is difficult sometimes to tell which is, and which is not the*
> *indigenous part. . . . Among the worst, as most believe, are the*
> *Canton men. . . . These southrons are a terror . . . the officers dread*
> *coming into collision with them, since when this happens the*
> *authorities are usually resisted, and often set at naught and*
> *maltreated. . . . More numerous, and far more tractable, are the*
> *Ningbo men.*
>
> "Men and Things in Shanghai," *Chinese Repository,*
> vol. 19, February 1850

The opening of Shanghai as a treaty port in 1843 initiated one process of colonization in the city and restructured another. The first is the well-known story of the establishment of foreign settlements and the rise of foreign trade.[1] The second is the story of the rapid growth of powerful Chinese immigrant groups which aspired to assert social, political and economic control over the city while imperial forces were weak. In these interlinked processes we see the impact of western imperialism, which destabilized power relations in the city and shook the popular legitimacy of Qing rule. Native-place ties and native-place associations proved to be critical, though ambivalent, forces in the disorder which followed.

---

1. See John Fairbank's classic study, *Trade and Diplomacy on the China Coast* (Stanford, Calif., 1953); and his "The Creation of the Treaty System," in *The Cambridge History of China*, ed. John K. Fairbank, vol. 10, pt. 1, 213–63 (Cambridge, England, 1978).

The opening of Shanghai to foreign trade produced a rapidly growing and increasingly complex commercial society, with no unified structure of authority to exercise control and adjudicate disputes. In the decade following the Opium War, Shanghai suffered from an unstable and
shifting balance of power among competing interests — foreign governments and developing foreign settlement authorities; Chinese government and local officials; immigrant associations and their growing and
unruly communities. Chinese gang organizations thrived in this atmosphere of divided, weak and uncertain government, creating powerful
pockets of local, underground authority beyond the scope of foreign or
Chinese official authority.

Before a more stable system of divided rule among foreign imperialist
and Chinese imperial governments could be established, the disarray of
power in Shanghai and the admixture of immigrants and secret-society
elements combusted in a seventeen-month takeover of the city, known
as the Small Sword Uprising of 1853–55. In the event, native-place ties
and associations worked as organizational conduits and nodes, linking
state and society and channeling both social control and social disorder.
To tell this story it is necessary to begin by describing Shanghai at the
time of the Opium War.

Immigrants in Shanghai before the
Opium War

Although large-scale immigration into Shanghai did not
take place until after the Opium War, sojourners lived and traded in
Shanghai before the war, in sufficient numbers and of sufficient means
to establish *huiguan* and *gongsuo*. At the time of the opening of the port,
Shanghai's location at the mouth of the Yangzi had created a "mercantile
emporium," bustling with domestic and overseas trade: "The vessels
which arrive at this port are . . . of Fuhkien and Canton. The vessels of
the north come . . . from Kwantung, Liaotung, Tientsin, and . . . Shantung. From Fuhkien about three hundred come annually, but a greater
part of them come from Hainan or Formosa, and some from Chusan
and Ningbo, also from Manila, Bali and other ports. . . . About four
hundred come from Canton, . . . from Macao, Singapore, Penang, Jolo,
Sumatra, Siam and other parts."[2] By the mid-nineteenth century this

2. *Chinese Repository*, 1846, 467–69.

thriving coastal trade brought more than fifteen hundred vessels into Shanghai's port annually. Trade along the Yangzi River brought additionally more than five thousand vessels annually from inland ports. These boats did not go out to sea but distributed goods brought by the coastal trade from Shanghai into the interior.

The trade visible to the Europeans who arrived in the mid-nineteenth century reflected the commercial development of the Jiangnan area during the Qing dynasty. In the early Qing, the imperial government established the internal customs bureau for Jiangnan in the city of Shanghai to regulate the trade of locally produced cotton and cloth and the beans, sugar and cotton of the north–south coastal trade. The development of a commodity economy is evident from the fact that by the late seventeenth century most cultivated land around Shanghai had been transferred from rice to cotton or, secondarily, to bean cultivation. While the men in these districts farmed, the women wove, and families traded their cloth for money and rice.[3]

The development of the domestic market is evident also from the establishment of numerous native-place trade associations in Shanghai during the eighteenth and early nineteenth centuries. Stone inscriptions, or stelae, found in the old sections of the city indicate the presence of at least twenty-six such associations in Shanghai before the Opium War.[4] The earliest association recorded is the Guan-Shandong Gongsuo, established by boat owners of the neighboring northern *bang* of Guandong and Shandong.[5] They established a burial ground in Shanghai during the Shunzhi reign (1654–61). Second was the Shangchuan Huiguan, established in 1715 by boat owners of Chongming Island, at the mouth of the Yangzi. These associations of shipping merchants, distinguished

3. SBZX, 1; Du Li, "Yapian zhanzheng qian Shanghai hanghui xingzhi zhi shanbian" (Changes in the character of Shanghai trade associations before the Opium War), in *Zhongguo zibenzhuyi mengya wenti lunwenji* (Compilation of papers concerning the sprouts of capitalism in China), ed. Nanjing daxue lishixi Ming-Qing shi yanjiushi (Nanjing, 1983) 142–43; Philip Huang, *The Peasant Family and Rural Development in the Yangzi Delta, 1350–1988* (Stanford, Calif., 1990), 45; Linda Cooke Johnson, "The Decline of Soochow and the Rise of Shanghai: A Study in the Economic Morphology of Urban Change, 1756–1894" (Ph.D. diss., University of California, Santa Cruz, 1980), pp. 88–95.

4. Du, "Yapian zhanzheng qian Shanghai hanghui," 146. Because it is based on surviving stelae, Du's figure is conservative. Important *huiguan* existed for which there are no remaining stelae (of seven *huiguan* mentioned in the records of the Small Sword Uprising, for example, three are not to be found in the stela collection).

5. Guandong refers to the northeastern provinces (*Dongbei*), to which many Shandong people migrated during the Qing. The establishment of this association in Shanghai suggests an early active trade with northern ports, supplying the lower Yangzi with soy foods and fertilizer.

by native place, were followed by associations of Shanghai cloth merchants and money dealers; Beijing goods and hat merchants; Fujian
sugar and foreign-goods merchants; Fujian shipping merchants; Fujian
longan and black-date merchants; Fujian paper and rope merchants;
Shaoxing and Zhejiang bean and coal merchants; Ningbo merchants
and bankers; Anhui tea merchants; Chaozhou sugar and tobacco merchants; northern goods merchants; Jiangxi merchants and ship owners;
and Jiangxi tea merchants, among others.[6]

Many associations established buildings with meeting halls and altars
in the area of the Small East Gate, where the Chinese internal customs
office was located, or in the east and west gardens of the Shanghai City
God Temple in the north of the walled city (see Map 2). On their altars
rested images of Tianhou, local gods, or patron gods of specific trades.
The Ningbo, Guangdong and Fujian associations were especially powerful, so they are a focus of this chapter. By the early nineteenth century,
Ningbo traders were in the ascendant, consolidating control over the
Shanghai economy through two institutions, the Siming Gongsuo and
the Shanghai Money Trade Guild (*Shanghai qianye gongsuo*), outdistanc-
ing their Guangdong and Fujian rivals. This configuration of power was
disrupted in the aftermath of the Opium War.[7]

The Opening of Shanghai as a Treaty Port

Two critical shifts in the political and social structure of
Shanghai were wrought by the Opium War and the establishment of foreign settlements in the city (see Map 3). First, Shanghai's rise as a center of
commerce changed the Chinese balance of power in the city, as merchants
increasingly replaced gentry in authority and status. Merchant associa-

6. Du, "Yapian zhanzheng qian Shanghai hanghui," 146–48; SBZX, 194–258. See also
Linda Cooke Johnson, *Shanghai: From Market Town to Treaty Port, 1074–1858* (unpublished
manuscript, tentative title), on pre–Opium War associations.

7. The Fujian Quan-Zhang Huiguan (Quanzhou and Zhangzhou prefectures) was
established as early as 1757; the Guangdong Chaozhou Huiguan (Chaozhou prefecture)
was established by 1783; and the Ningbo Huiguan (Siming Gongsuo) was established by
1797 (SXXZ, vol. 3, 2–4). An early association of sojourners from Guangzhou and Zhaoqing prefectures was established in Shanghai prior to the Chaozhou Huiguan; however,
no records remain which provide a precise date. On the Ningbo group, see Shiba Yoshinobu, "Ningpo and Its Hinterland" in Skinner, *The City in Late Imperial China*, 436; and
Jones, "The Ningbo *Pang*."

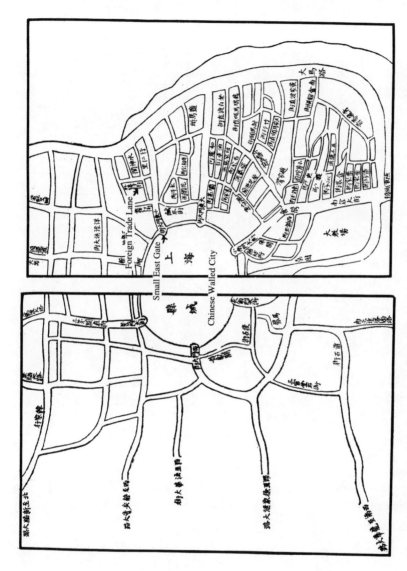

Map 2. Shanghai in the mid-nineteenth century: a Chinese view Source: *Tongzhi Shanghai xian zhi* (Tong-zhi-reign Shanghai: county gazetteer) Shanghai, 1871.

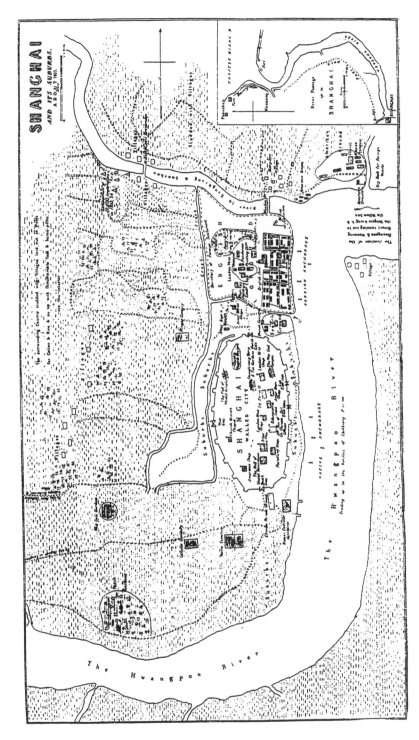

Map 3. Shanghai in the mid-nineteenth century: a Western view. Source: *All About Shanghai: A Standard Guidebook*. Shanghai, 1934.

tions grew stronger and increased their role in local governance. Second, the establishment of foreign trade initially favored Guangdong people. In the decade after the opening of Shanghai to foreign trade, Guangdong officials and merchants swiftly rose to prominence and became (briefly) the most powerful Chinese group in Shanghai.[8]

Immigration also disrupted the stability of preexisting political and economic relations, diversifying the social composition of sojourning communities and increasing the numbers of workers and semiemployed. With the new immigrants came secret-society organizations from the southeast coast, groups which thrived on the smuggling associated with foreign trade and the opium trade in particular. As smuggling spread and trade boomed, secret societies formed along native-place lines deepened their roots in the city. These developments strained the internal dynamics of individual sojourning communities. The result was an increasingly violent city.[9]

Immigrants arrived in waves. Immediately after the opening of the port in 1843, several tens of thousands of Guangdong merchants, workers and adventurers traveled north to exploit the opportunities created by foreign trade. When the Taiping Rebellion obstructed trade and threatened south and central China in the 1850s, Shanghai experienced an influx of elite immigrants, many of them merchants from Ningbo prefecture in Zhejiang province. For both groups, preexisting native-place associations provided an important institutional framework, facili-

8. See Leung Yuen-sang, *The Shanghai Taotai: Linkage Man in a Changing Society, 1843–90* (Honolulu, 1990), 122–30; Mark Elvin, "Gentry Democracy in Shanghai, 1905–1914" (D.Phil. diss., University of Cambridge, 1967), 6–8. Just as a "merchant consul system" developed within Shanghai's western community in the 1840s and 1850s, so did merchant officials come to serve in Shanghai, among them Wu Jianzhang, who served as Su-Song-Tai Circuit Intendant (the highest Chinese government official based in Shanghai) in 1852–53. Fairbank, *Trade and Diplomacy*, 213–14, 393–96.

9. Violent collective confrontations rocked Shanghai repeatedly in the second half of the nineteenth century, contrasting with Hankou in the same period, described by William Rowe as "remarkably free from open, large-scale group confrontations and protests . . . the very model of a workable social unit." Rowe argues that "urban community disaggregation occurred relatively later in China than in Europe — in China essentially awaiting rather than preceding industrialization." See Rowe, *Hankow: Conflict and Community*, 1, 8–9. Rowe suggests that subcommunity ties (including native-place ties) helped to "nurture the larger community" and keep peace. Although at times Shanghai native-place groups helped maintain order, as the Small Sword Uprising and Ningbo Cemetery Riots demonstrate, they were also critical to the mobilization of social conflict. Shanghai's experience suggests that it is problematic to generalize from Hankou's experience. Shanghai/Hankou differences might be explained by the greater western presence in Shanghai and the earlier western economic penetration. The opium trade, which boomed in Shanghai in the decade after the Opium War, was not a major factor in the Hankou economy until 1860. A more encompassing explanation must await further research on other Chinese cities.

tating the new immigrants' ability to shift businesses to Shanghai and grasp new economic opportunities in the city. As the Taipings penetrated areas close to Shanghai in the early 1860s, thousands of gentry-refugees from the Suzhou area of Jiangsu and from northern Zhejiang fled to security in the foreign settlements of Shanghai, making up another early elite immigrant wave.[10]

Guangdong *Bang* in Shanghai: A Case Study

Sojourners from the southeast province of Guangdong were the first to exploit the new frontierlike atmosphere of Shanghai, and they were key players in the upheavals which followed. Guangdong people developed expertise in foreign trade when trade with western countries was restricted to the port of Guangzhou (Canton), and this advantage facilitated their rise to wealth and power. Guangdong power in Shanghai reached both its height and its comeuppance in the Small Sword Uprising of 1853–55, when the city was occupied for seventeen months by Guangdong and Fujian rebels. When lackluster imperial forces finally crushed the internally disintegrating rebellion, the Guangdong people were defeated and disgraced. Although they made a strong comeback, the brief era of Guangdong primacy gave way before the renewed vigor of their Ningbo competitors.

Before recounting the vicissitudes of Guangdong fortunes in Shanghai, it is useful to sketch the origins and the development of the Guangdong community in Shanghai. This discussion also serves to illustrate the dynamics of native-place organization, fission, fusion and extinction, continuous processes defining and altering associational life.

What non-Guangdong natives frequently referred to as the Guangdong *bang* was not a unified group. Instead, we see a loosely connected series of subgroups, capable of combination but normally divided by native place as well as by occupational ties. Each subgroup understood itself to constitute a separate *bang*. Sojourners created at least five different Guangdong *huiguan* in Shanghai before the Opium War.

The separate organizations reflected significant ethnic and linguistic

---

10. Unlike the earlier immigrants, possibly because they lacked well-established native-place connections in the city, many of these newcomers returned to their homes after the Qing suppression of the Taipings in 1864.

differences as well as trade specializations. Three major ethnic and linguistic areas divide Guangdong province, distinguished by the Guangzhou, Chaozhou and Hakka dialects, all mutually unintelligible. The
Guang'an Huiguan represented the first linguistic group; the Jiaying
Huiguan represented the Hakka group; and the Chaozhou, Jie-Pu-Feng
and Chao-Hui *huiguan* corresponded to subdivisions within Chaozhou
prefecture.[11] Although no records from the Jiaying Huiguan survived
its demise in the aftermath of the Small Sword Uprising, it is possible
to sketch the history of the Chaozhou and Guangzhou communities.

*Chaozhou Prefecture and Chaozhou Associations in Shang-
hai.* Chaozhou prefecture is located on the eastern edge of Guangdong
province, in the lower Han River basin which extends across the provincial border into southern Fujian province. In important respects, Chaozhou people had more in common with the southern Fujianese than
with their fellow Guangdong provincials, and they therefore could only
be grouped together with them into a "Guangdong *bang*" in the context
of Shanghai, where their differences with Jiangnan and northern Chinese overshadowed their internal differences. The Chaozhou dialect is
closer to the southern Fujian (Minnan) dialect than to the dialects of
central and western Guangdong. In the nineteenth century Chaozhou
and Fujian merchants shared similar trade interests. Both regions exported sugar. Both also shipped foreign sundries from Guangzhou to
northern ports. Like the Fujianese, Chaozhou people were stereotyped
as poor, clannish and violent. Nineteenth-century Chinese records as
well as foreign records in Shanghai often failed to distinguish Chaozhou
people from Fujianese.[12]

In Shanghai, though there were separate *huiguan,* Fujian and Chao-

11. The Guang'an Huiguan, likely the precursor of the Guang-Zhao Huiguan which
emerged in 1872, represented people from Xin'an county in Guangzhou prefecture. No
records remain from the Guang'an Huiguan or the Jiaying Huiguan, both of which are
referred to in documents of the Small Sword Uprising. See Shanghai shehui kexueyuan,
Lishi yanjiusuo (Shanghai Academy of Social Sciences, Institute for Historical Research,
ed., *Shanghai xiaodaohui qiyi shiliao huibian* (Compilation of historical materials on the
Shanghai Small Sword Uprising) (Shanghai, 1980) (hereafter referred to as XDH), 39; Lu
Yaohua, "Shanghai xiaodaohui de yuanliu" (Origins of the Shanghai Small Sword Society) *Shihuo yuekan,* 3 (August 1973):14; *Tongzhi Shanghai xianzhi* (Tongzhi-reign Shanghai
county gazetteer) (Shanghai, 1871) (hereafter referred to as TSXZ), 11:32–33.
12. A British visitor to Chaozhou in 1856 described poverty-stricken villages and a local
culture that reflected a decayed social order—bloody clan feuds, kidnapping of women
and children and prominent bandit and militia groups (John Scarth, *Twelve Years in China:
The People, the Rebels and the Mandarins* [Edinburgh, 1860], 47–48, 63–70). The closeness

zhou people lived near each other in the area of the east gates of the walled city. Both groups had shops on Foreign Trade (Yanghang) Lane, also the location of the Chaozhou Huiguan (see Map 2).[13] The strong Chaozhou-Fujian presence in this area, and the foreignness of their dialects to the Shanghai people, are expressed in an old Shanghai poem:

> Hundreds of foreign goods overflowing by the market gate and wall
> Bring merchants from distant places, filling Shanghai.
> Those planning to go to Foreign Trade Lane
> All study the barbarian tongues of Quan-Zhang.[14]

The founding of Chaozhou native-place associations in Jiangsu followed the economic vicissitudes of the province. Chaozhou merchants first established a *huiguan* in Nanjing during the Ming dynasty (1368–1644). The *huiguan* moved to Suzhou along with the rice market at the beginning of the Qing dynasty, reflecting the rise of Suzhou. The later establishment of a *huiguan* in Shanghai similarly reflects the rise of Shanghai.[15] The Shanghai Chaozhou Huiguan, originally given the auspicious name Wan Shi Feng (Ten Thousand Generations of Abundance), dates from 1759. On this date, rice merchants from eight counties of Chaozhou prefecture purchased land in Shanghai to worship Tianhou.[16]

---

of Fujian and Chaozhou people, despite the provincial boundary that separated them, was institutionalized in an early *huiguan* in Shantou (Swatow — the port city of Chaozhou prefecture), the Zhang-Chao Huiguan, which jointly represented merchants of both Chaozhou and Zhangzhou (Fujian) (China, Inspectorate General of Customs, *Decennial Reports* [hereafter referred to as DR], 1882–91, 537). In an article about Chaozhou opium merchants, SB (September 3, 1879) refers to the Chao-Hui Huiguan as the Fujian Gongsuo; "The men from Canton, . . . who come from Chaochou-foo, . . . being more assimilated both in language and character to the Fokienese, they are by foreigners generally called Fokienmen" (NCH, October 5, 1850, 39).

13. In this street name, "foreign trade" refers to Chinese shops which traded in some overseas goods. After 1759, when the Qing court stopped all foreign trade outside the city of Guangzhou, goods from outside China were shipped north by Fujian and Guangdong merchants. See Wu Guifang, "Songgu mantan" (Anecdotes of the Songjiang area), *Dangan yu lishi* 1 (December 1985), 91–92.

14. Ibid., 91. "Barbarian tongues" (*jueshe*) here is a reference to Minnan dialects.

15. See Suzhou lishi bowuguan and Jiangsu shifanxueyuan lishixi (Suzhou History Museum and the History Department of Jiangsu Normal College), eds., *Ming-Qing Suzhou gongshangye beike ji* (Compilation of Ming-Qing commercial stone inscriptions from Suzhou). Nanjing, 1981 (hereafter referred to as MSGB).

16. SBZX, 249–52; Negishi Tadashi, *Chūgoku no girudo* (The guilds of China) (Tokyo, 1953), 124. In the nineteenth century, Chaozhou *huiguan* could be found as far north as Yantai (Shandong), where they purchased soybeans in exchange for sugar and soybean

After the initial purchase of land in Shanghai in 1759, the community prospered and *huiguan* property increased regularly over the next half-century. Twenty-seven deeds for *huiguan* property holdings are preserved in a stela of 1811. Chaozhou merchant prosperity depended on the community's adaptability to shifts in the Shanghai market. By the nineteenth century Chaozhou merchants had diversified their trade interests and were primarily involved in the sugar, opium and tobacco trades.[17]

Following common practice, Chaozhou merchants protected their *huiguan* through official sanction and recognition, using ties to local officials whenever possible. The rule of avoidance (which prevented officials from serving in their native areas), ensured that magistrates serving in Shanghai were all outsiders. The regular turnover of Shanghai officials increased the probability of a fellow-provincial serving in the local *yamen*. When this happened, sojourning merchants were quick to make use of native-place ties. The magistrate Chen Jianye, for example, was a major patron of the Chaozhou Huiguan at the beginning of the nineteenth century. His fellow-countrymen availed themselves of Chen's term to register their property and carve a stela bearing the magistrate's endorsement of their rules. In a similar appropriation of the mantle of Confucian legitimacy, *huiguan* merchant-directors also purchased official titles.[18]

Although the association bore the name of Chaozhou prefecture, in practice it represented only portions of the prefecture, with internal subdivisions. The original *huiguan* included merchants from eight counties: Chaoyang, Huilai, Haiyang, Chenghai, Raoping, Jieyang, Puning and Fengshun (coastal and central districts, excluding Dapu county, in the northeast, and Jiexi and Jiening counties in the west). Although the

---

"cake" fertilizer. The customs commissioner for Chefoo (Zhifou, former name of Yantai) reported that the Chaozhou association was the most powerful of the four *huiguan* in the city (DR, 1882–91, 77, 573–78; Ho, *Zhongguo huiguan shilun*, 41; James Coates Sanford, "Chinese Commercial Organization and Behavior in Shanghai of the Late Nineteenth and Early Twentieth Century" [Ph.D. diss., Harvard University, 1976], 169). Connections among Chaozhou *huiguan* in different places are suggested by the closeness of their names (which imitated family practice in the naming of brothers). The local association in Shantou was Wan Nian Feng (Ten Thousand Years of Abundance); the Suzhou association was Wan Shi Rong (Ten Thousand Generations of Prosperity) (MSGB, 340–44).

17. SBZX, 250–52.

18. Du, "Yapian zhanzheng qian Shanghai hanghui," 165; Yen-p'ing Hao, *The Comprador in Nineteenth-Century China: Bridge between East and West* (Cambridge, Mass., 1970), 184; SBZX, 250 (stela dated 1811). Of the eight directors listed on the stela, all but two had official titles (most commonly "expectant Daotai").

eight counties appear united in early records, divisions developed by the early nineteenth century, marking discrete regional groupings (*bang*): "The people of the three *bang* are very numerous. According to *huiguan* regulations, if there are misfortunes on the boats, and the goods get too wet or dry, those closest to each other must help each other. Our Chao-yang and Huilai are close and together are called the Chao-Hui *bang*. Haiyang, Chenghai and Raoping are close and make one *bang*. . . . Jie-Pu-Feng [Jieyang, Puning, Fengshun] is one *bang*. Thus they are called the three *bang*."[19]

Chaozhou population increase and prosperity permitted the different *bang* to separate. Around 1822, the Jie-Pu-Feng *bang* levied a tax on its members and formed the Jie-Pu-Feng Huiguan. In 1839, the Chao-Hui *bang* established its own *huiguan*.[20]

These divisions reflected trade specialization as well as geography. In a cryptic and defensive account of its reasons for separating from the Chaozhou Huiguan, the Chao-Hui *bang* asserted that in the period preceding the division it had derived its wealth from sugar and tobacco trading. Nonetheless, after the banning of opium by the government in 1839, tensions developed with the other *bang* over suspicions of Chao-Hui opium trading (a suggestion the Chao-Hui people deny in their stela). Because of this friction, the Chao-Hui *bang* chose independence. Despite Chao-Hui assertions that opium was not a primary business until after 1860 (when opium trade restraints were relaxed), the coincidence of the *huiguan* establishment and the date of opium prohibition suggest that Chao-Hui opium trading engendered the division.[21]

The opium connection is a likely explanation for Chao-Hui opulence. The building constructed by the Chao-Hui *bang* in 1866 (the Chao-Hui Huiguan had burned twice since 1839) was on approximately two acres (nearly ten mu) of prime city property. The land, together with the building, cost more than eighty thousand taels. Two ornate temples graced the compound, one dedicated to Tianhou, the other to Guandi (originally Guanyu, the apotheosized hero-general of the Three Kingdoms period). Other gods including Caishen (God of Wealth) were worshipped in adjoining areas. The building served the joint functions of worship and business and was, accordingly, constructed with

19. SBZX, 325 (stela dated 1866).
20. The original name was the Chao-Hui Gongsuo (ibid., 325–26, 509).
21. Ibid., 325. In an official account, the Chao-Hui *bang* would not, of course, admit to smuggling.

religious and meeting areas and with a stage for theatrical performances.[22]

*People from Guangzhou and Zhaoqing Prefectures in Shang-
hai.* In the period between the Opium War and the Taiping Rebellion,
people from the adjacent central Guangdong prefectures of Guangzhou
and Zhaoqing were at least as powerful in Shanghai as were people from
Chaozhou. Little is known about their prewar *huiguan* because records
were destroyed together with the building in 1855. Nonetheless, the Guang-Zhao community survived to rebuild a *huiguan* shortly afterward.
The wealth of this later Guang-Zhao Huiguan in Shanghai and the fame
of merchants from the two prefectures have ensured the preservation of
its history.

Guangzhou and Zhaoqing prefectures in central Guangdong (the
Pearl River delta and West River valley) were the richest and most
densely settled parts of the province. The historical prominence of the
provincial capital, Guangzhou, renders a long introduction to the Pearl
River delta unnecessary. People from these areas prided themselves on
their wealth and cultural achievements, reflected in success in the civil-
service examinations and the many officials they contributed to the
empire.

In Shanghai, natives of the two prefectures joined together in one
huiguan, which became an important node in a highly developed national network of Guang-Zhao traders. Guangdong province as a whole
had *huiguan* in forty-five cities, spread over seventeen provinces. A
number of these were Chaozhou *huiguan,* but the large proportion were
dominated by people from central Guangdong.

Prior to the Opium War, Guangzhou and Zhaoqing merchants in
Shanghai dealt in foreign goods and sundries. After the Opium War,
people from these areas continued in these trades, but also exported
their expertise in dealing with foreigners, as house-servants, clerks,
cooks, compradors and linguists. They also used their foreign connections to develop their own trade interests in tea, silk and beans.[23]

22. See Prasenjit Duara, "Superscribing Symbols: The Myth of Guandi, Chinese God
of War," *Journal of Asian Studies* (hereafter referred to as JAS) 47 (November 1988):778–95;
SBZX, 325. The ritual functions of *huiguan* are the subject of Chapter 3.

23. The two prefectures are culturally and linguistically close. Customs commissioners
of the treaty ports often noted the prominence of Guangzhou *huiguan*. The Guangzhou
association was one of the two finest buildings in the port of Jiongzhou and the wealthiest
huiguan in Fuzhou and Zhenjiang (where it shared the building with a separate Chaozhou
organization). In Suzhou, where most *huiguan* were deteriorating by the late nineteenth

The Rise of Guangdong Compradors and Officials. As foreigners moved into Shanghai, they brought with them their Cantonese
employees. During the period of restricted trading through Canton,
westerners had grown accustomed to the people, cuisine, and pidgin of
Canton. For the sake of these tastes and ties, western merchants brought
to Shanghai Cantonese compradors to organize their offices, Cantonese
cooks to staff their kitchens and Cantonese shipworkers to repair their
boats. British trade in Shanghai was initiated with the help of a Guangdong merchant referred to by foreigners as Alum. Because of his connections with the tea and silk trade he was able to persuade tea and silk
growers to consign products to Shanghai.[24]

The organization of Chinese business through native-place groups
and the system of personal financial guarantees reinforced the foreigners' initial preference for Guangzhou employees. The Hong Kong comprador for Augustine, Heard and Company naturally recommended and
guaranteed a fellow Guangzhou native for the new Shanghai office. The
Shanghai comprador for Russell and Company was chosen through
a similar process. In the case of Jardine, Matheson and Company, the
Guangzhou compradors moved north together with the company they
served. The result was a near monopoly of Guangzhou compradors in
Shanghai.[25]

Many of these individuals came from the single county of Xiangshan.
Living on a peninsula at the mouth of the Pearl River, close to
both Guangzhou and Hong Kong and harboring at its southern tip the
early international trading center of Macao (Aomen), Xiangshan residents became expert in maritime trade and trade with foreigners. The
first Xiangshan compradors recommended their relatives and fellow-
countrymen to succeed them. The wealthy and famous Shanghai
Guangdong compradors of the 1860s and 1870s, the brothers Xu Baoting and Xu Rongcun, Xu Baoting's son Xu Run and nephew Xu Yunxuan, Lin Qin (Acum), Zheng Guanying and the brothers Tang Jingxing (Tang Tingshu) and Tang Maozhi all hailed from Xiangshan.

---

century, the Guangzhou building was one of the few structures still in good condition.
See Chang Peng, "Provincial Merchant Groups"; Ho, *Zhongguo huiguan shilun,* 41–59;
DR, 1882–91, 1892–1901.

24. Like a number of those who followed him, Alum was also involved with secret
societies. In the period after his bankruptcy he found work in Ningbo operating a fence
for the disposal of booty taken by gangs of *tongxiang* pirates (Fairbank, *Trade and Diplomacy,* 220).

25. Hao, *Comprador,* 51–52, 173, 227–33. Of twenty-seven compradors in Shanghai
offices of English or American firms in the second half of the nineteenth century, twenty-
four were from Guangzhou.

While sojourning in Shanghai, these men reinvested in their native place. Xu Run and his relatives performed gentrylike functions in Xiangshan, not only remitting funds but also supervising the building and repair of dikes, canals and bridges. In times of disaster they organized relief activities from Shanghai. Zheng Guanying was mentioned for similar contributions in the local Xiangshan gazetteer.[26]

This group played a major role in constructing and leading their native-place community in Shanghai. The compradors Tang Jingxing, Tang Maozhi, Xu Run, Xu Rongcun, and Chen Geliang were all important figures in the Guang-Zhao Gongsuo, the institutional assertion of their native-place identity in Shanghai. Like the directors of other *huiguan,* they enhanced their position and the prestige of their native-place group by purchasing titles as expectant officials. Xu Baoting and Tang Jingxing both held the title of expectant Daotai. Tang Jingxing entertained in official robes and enjoyed being referred to as *guancha* (Daotai), in documents. Xu Run was not only "Daotai" but also, with a further purchase, "Honorary Deputy Director of the Board of War."[27]

While Guangdong merchants blurred former distinctions and became officials, Chinese officials serving in Shanghai played an important role in advancing the Guangzhou merchant group. Gong Mujiu, the Shandong official who served as the first Shanghai Daotai (Suzhou-Songjiang-Taicang Circuit Intendant) after the opening of the treaty port, was unprepared to face the complex foreign trade and foreign relations issues presented by his new post. He relied heavily on his functionary Wu Jianzhang, a member of the famous Samqua merchant family from Xiangshan. Wu had purchased the title of expectant Daotai and had come to Shanghai for business.[28]

Because of Guangdong merchants' facility in dealing with foreigners, Lingui, who served as Daotai from 1848 to 1851, sent a memorial to Beijing recommending that all treaty-port administrations be staffed by people from Guangzhou. Although the memorial was not adopted as policy, by the early 1850s Guangzhou predominance in Shanghai was nonetheless complete. In 1851 Wu Jianzhang rose to power as Shanghai

26. Xu Run, *Nianpu,* 14b–16b, 29b–30, 83; Hao, *Comprador,* 186.
27. Hao, *Comprador,* 188–89; Leung, *Shanghai Taotai,* 163.
28. Leung,"Regional Rivalry," 34; Leung, *Shanghai Taotai,* 150–51. Gong was of gentry background, but the incumbent magistrate Lan Weiwen, like Wu, had deep commercial connections with his own Zhejiang sojourners' community. Lan was from an area near Ningbo, in Zhejiang. In Shanghai Lan was closely connected with the Siming Gongsuo and secured a tax exemption for the association (SYZX, 295–97). After the Small Sword Uprising Lan was acting Daotai and further helped the Ningbo community.

Daotai and presided over a process Fairbank aptly described as "the Cantonization of Shanghai." Wu immediately surrounded himself with fellow-provincials at all levels to conduct his official and private business. During Wu's administration, nearly all *yamen* clerks, guards and runners were fellow Guangdong provincials. Wu also commanded a personal bodyguard of several hundred toughs, all recruited directly from Guangdong. Wu was a close friend and associate of the Guangzhou comprador group, including Xu Baoting, and the Jiaying Huiguan director, Li Shaoqing.[29]

Troublesome Arrivals: Workers, Vagabonds and Boatmen

Poor immigrants also flocked to Shanghai after the Opium War. As commercial shipping expanded, people from Guangdong and Fujian came to Shanghai as boatmen, swelling the population by tens of thousands. Accounts of the Small Sword Uprising in 1853 suggest that there were between thirty-five hundred and thirty-six hundred coastal junks operating in Shanghai by this time, bringing as many as eighty thousand people from Guangdong and fifty thousand Fujianese, in a total urban population of approximately two hundred and seventy thousand. In addition to the boatmen, Guangdong workers and adventurers involved in all aspects of the opium and foreign-goods trades (including firearms) flocked to Shanghai, hoping to capitalize on their unique familiarity with foreigners and foreign trade.[30]

Guangdong workers dominated important trades, following British enterprises as they moved north to Shanghai. This was the case with the first group of machine workers in Shanghai, who were employed in

29. Wu was also close to the Fujian merchant Li Xianyun (who, like Li Shaoqing, would be a leader of the Small Sword Uprising) as well as to the most famous Small Sword leader, Liu Lichuan, who for a time kept Wu's accounts. Leung, "Regional Rivalry," 41; Leung, *Shanghai Taotai,* 150–51; Yen-p'ing Hao, *The Commercial Revolution in Nineteenth-Century China* (Berkeley, Calif., 1986), 136; Fairbank *Trade and Diplomacy,* 393, 406.

30. "Shanghai xiaodaohui qiyi zongxu," in XDH, 10; Lu Yaohua, "Shanghai xiaodaohui de yuanliu," 16; Leung, "Regional Rivalry," 29; XDH, 519; Maureen Dillon, "The Triads in Shanghai: The Small Sword Uprising, 1853–1855," *Papers on China* 23 (July 1970):68.

foreign shipyards. Guangdong people also initially monopolized the woodworking business associated with ship repair.[31]

Native-place organization developed among sojourning workers from the moment they immigrated or were recruited to work in the city. In the case of Guangdong carpenters, for example, two *bang* divided the community — workers from Taishan county and woodworkers from other areas of Guangdong. The foreman who led the Taishan *bang* recruited new workers from his native place himself. New recruits had to first join their *bang* (paying a small fee or engaging in some form of contract) before they could work. In return these *bang* provided a degree of security, guaranteeing assistance in the event of old age, sickness and burial. The reliance of foreign (and Chinese) authorities on Chinese headmen to recruit and control labor reinforced this native-place organization of workers.[32]

As this immigrant population increased, important sectors suffered almost immediate dislocation. Chinese junks which had been attracted by the increase in coastal shipping could not compete once the use of steamboats became established. This left large numbers of Guangdong and Fujian boatmen unemployed, along with local Shanghai boatmen. The result was vagrancy.[33]

These newly swollen and dislocated populations were poorly integrated into Shanghai society and difficult to control. Unable to find employment, some boatmen became pirates. Others formed gangs, urban

31. These Guangdong shipworkers lived in a settlement around the S. C. Farnham Shipyard. In 1868 they organized the first industrial strike in Shanghai. See Marianne Bastid-Brugière, "Currents of Social Change," in Fairbank, *Cambridge History of China*, vol. 11, pt. 2, 571.

32. For accounts of early Guangdong, Ningbo and Wuxi workers, see Zhongguo shehui kexueyuan, Jingji yanjiusuo (Chinese Academy of Social Sciences, Economic Research Institute), ed., *Shanghai minzu jiqi gongye* (Shanghai's national machine industry) (Beijing, 1979), 7, 9, 13, 30, 50–68. The *bang* system could be highly exploitive. For example, in 1871 a group of laborers went to the International Settlement police to protest mistreatment. Since 1842 they had been under the control of a headman with an official Chinese license to employ the laborers as coolies for foreign labor. Arrangements were mutually satisfactory until 1862, when the headman's subassistants "squeezed" the laborers of more than one hundred thousand taels (NCH, May 12, 1871). Another example is provided by a minor riot on July 29, 1859. In this case headmen had hired their Cantonese fellow-provincials ostensibly as sailors and then sold them to British recruiters to labor in the West Indies. The British actions were protested by Cantonese merchants in Shanghai (Great Britain, Public Record Office [hereafter referred to as PRO], FO 682.1992. In 1858 Guangdong carpenters organized a temple to Lu Ban, patron deity for their trade; Ningbo carpenters formed a separate Lu Ban temple in 1866 (see Perry, *Shanghai on Strike*, 33).

33. "Zongxu," in XDH, 10; Lu Yaohua, "Shanghai xiaodaohui de yuanliu," 16.

counterparts of traditionally rural predatory bandits. In August 1850 the Chinese city authorities issued a proclamation against such gangs (preserved in the translation of the *North China Herald*): "We issue this Proclamation, addressing it to the strangers from Kwangtung and Fukien for their information. All of you who really have permanent employment must enroll yourselves in the Tee-paou's register and receive a registration ticket for your houses; each one pursuing his occupation in peace. Do not lightly . . . create disturbances."[34]

Such proclamations and attempts to register newcomers were ineffectual. The increased incidence of violence reported in the city attests to the ways in which restricted employment opportunities led to tension between native-place groups.[35] In 1850 the editors of the *North China Herald* noted that frequent fights broke out between the Fujian and Chaozhou groups who resided in the northeastern suburbs. Competing in similar professions for a diminishing number of jobs, Guangdong burglars often struck Fujian targets.[36] In such cases the relative closeness of Chaozhou and Fujian cultures which could ally the two groups against more distant outsiders was irrelevant. As tension grew on the docks and in the alleys around Foreign Trade Lane, subtle differences served as pretexts for ethnic violence.

The presence of large and underemployed populations of fellow regionals, some of whom were active in predatory gang organizations, presented new problems for native-place associations, whose activities had hitherto been confined primarily to the needs of a small merchant community. An article in the *North China Herald* of October 5, 1850, provides a graphic illustration of this new situation. A boy who belonged to a group of Fujianese boatmen was seized by a gang of vagabond Chaoyang "ruffians" and detained for ransom. The angry boatmen forcibly repossessed the boy, capturing and beating several Chaoyang

34. NCH, August 10, 1850. The "Tee-paou" (*dibao*) was a low-status constable who acted as a personal agent of the magistrate and was assigned to an area of city blocks, with responsibility for population and property registration and the maintenance of order. See John Watt, "The Yamen and Urban Administration," in Skinner, *The City in Late Imperial China*, pp. 387–8.

35. See NCH, August 17, 1850; April 5, 1851; March 29, 1851; March 13, 1852; October 23, 1853. These groups at times participated in antiforeign activity. In 1849 people from central Guangdong declared their readiness to massacre foreigners entering the walled (Chinese) city. In 1851 Guangdong and Fujian crowds protested British and French plans to build a Catholic church. In the same year, Fujianese destroyed a foreign-built bridge. France, Archives, Ministère des Relations Extérieures (hereafter referred to as AMRE), Chine 1847–51 (Correspondance Consulaire), Item dated July 10, 1849; "Zongxu," in XDH, 32; NCH, July 26, 1851, 206; NCH, March 18, 1852.

36. NCH, October 5, 1850, 39; NCH, March 29, 1851, 138.

dockworkers in the process. Rather than appealing to the Chinese authorities, local residents called on the Chaozhou Huiguan to restore order: "The heads of the Chaochou-foo Association then came forward, advising the sailors to set the men at liberty and both parties to quench their animosities. But the shore vagabonds collecting in crowds advanced to attack the junks by land and water, swords, spears, and even cannon in play." The riot continued for two full days, killing two and injuring many. In this case, neither the *huiguan* nor the local government authorities (who evinced no desire to interfere) were able to check the fighting. The Shanghai magistrate did not arrive until after the riot had ended. This incident demonstrates the popular expectation that when violence erupted the *huiguan* should keep order among its fellow-countrymen. Both the *huiguan* and the local residents considered *huiguan* intervention and mediation natural, properly prior to the appearance of Shanghai authorities. Nonetheless, as this incident makes clear, the *huiguan* was not always capable of restoring order or commanding obedience among its unruly *tongxiang*.

In this atmosphere of increasing urban disorder, *huiguan* were called on by both Chinese and foreign authorities to control their fellow-countrymen. As the preceding example suggests, the *huiguan* was conceptualized as a mediating unit, an urban institutional resource available for communicating with, controlling or disposing of sectors of the urban population. The link between immigrants and their native places, Shanghai *huiguan* became routinely responsible for shipping criminals as well as indigents back home. The county *yamen* delivered criminals to the *huiguan* gates and asked the *huiguan* directors to ensure their return passage. The Municipal Council of the International Settlement also relied on *huiguan* for keeping order in their respective communities.[37]

In many instances *huiguan* fulfilled these order-keeping functions. Nonetheless, the relation of these associations both to the formal authorities of Shanghai and to the communities with which they were identified was ambiguous. *Huiguan* could not always ensure order. Moreover, *huiguan* merchant directors were not always on the side of order. Rather than waste resources they often avoided conflicts they could not control. On occasion they even fomented riots to serve their interests. In such cases the Chinese authorities could do little on their own.

Huiguan are unmentioned in a number of instances of collective vio-

---

37. SB, October 2, 1879, 3; Skinner, "Introduction," 538; see also Chapter 5 below.

lence involving sojourners, possibly because merchants avoided antago-
nizing gangs organized along native-place lines. In August 1850 the
North China Herald reported that Guangdong and Fujian vagabonds
relied on the influence of their respective "clans" to perpetrate crime. In
one case watchmen hounded by aggrieved shopkeepers retrieved money
stolen by a Fujianese gang. The robbers, "enraged at being interfered
with by the watchmen" (who it seemed had never until then taken active
measures), returned and attacked them in the evening. The shopkeepers
complained vociferously to the magistrate, who finally sent troops to
move against fleets of Fujianese boats. Since the Fujianese escaped, the
article concluded that the Chinese authorities possessed no means of
controlling such mobs. In the next year a similar incident occurred involving a Guangdong gang, which burglarized a Fujian store. The gang
drove off a local militia mustered to pursue them and escaped from a
detachment of two hundred soldiers sent by the Shanghai garrison to
assist the civil authorities.[38]

Although in the preceding cases *huiguan* may have chosen to remain
aloof from violent elements they could not control, in the frontier atmosphere of the early treaty port *huiguan* at times clearly relied on fellow-
provincial toughs, inciting disorderly conduct. In July 1851 the Fujian
Xing'an Huiguan vigorously opposed a British purchase of land containing burial plots of fellow-provincials. Angered by the foreigners
who intended to construct a park on the site, the *huiguan* proved "a
veritable city corporation in its contumacious resistance." A large Fujianese crowd armed with staves and stones attacked the British parties
to the transaction. The crowd also seized the Chinese constable responsible for arranging the purchase.[39] This pattern of mass disturbance on
behalf of threatened *huiguan* grounds (particularly sacred burial
grounds) would be repeated several decades later by the Ningbo community.

In the meantime, poor, underemployed and marginal elements from
southeast China found security through membership in the secret societies (*banghui, huidang*) they brought to Shanghai with them. Such associations were organized along lines of regional, ethnic and linguistic
identity and were often coterminous with native-place *bang* which recruited and deployed workers. Secret-society networks from the south
were associated with Red Gang (*hong men, hong bang*) or Triad-type

38. NCH, August 17, 1850, 9; NCH, March 29, 1851, 138.
39. NCH, July 26, 1851, 206; NCH, March 13, 1852, 131.

lodges. In Shanghai they would meet with a northern Green Gang (*qing bang*) type of secret brotherhood, divided into Zhejiang and (by the end of the century) Subei branches. By 1853 sworn Red Gang brotherhoods were numerous in the Shanghai area, where they engaged in banditry, smuggling and petty crime.[40]

Although these *dang* and *hui* (unlike the government-sanctioned *huiguan*) were illegal associations, it should not be imagined that they were radically distinct in character from *huiguan*. Each organization existed for the livelihood and self-preservation of a sojourning community. Both overlapped with networks of trade. Not only was each association a meeting place for outlanders in the hostile environment of an alien city, but each also expressed a common religious community. Just as *huiguan* temples housed local gods and organized local rituals, so secret societies brought with them elements of local religion and rituals specific to their brotherhood. These religious communities merged in major public festivals organized by *huiguan* for the larger sojourning community, as for example on Tianhou's birthday, when Guangdong and Fujian boat owners and merchants worshipped for three days in their respective *huiguan*, sponsoring public opera performances and lantern displays.[41]

Respectable merchants and disreputable secret societies converged on practical as well as on ritual occasions. In the relatively lawless and unstable first decade of the treaty port, merchants as well as secret societies resorted at times to unlicensed violence. Without a commercial code or an effective legal system for the resolution of commercial disputes, secret-society "muscle" could be necessary to enforce trade agreements with outsiders. The March 11, 1852, issue of the *North China Herald* recounts one such instance, in which a "Cantonese mob" attacked the house of a Parsee opium trader to force delivery of fifty chests of previously purchased opium or the return of gold bars previously paid by a Cantonese merchant. In this example we see a link between a well-to-do merchant (one who dealt in large orders), most likely a member of his *huiguan*, and a gang employed to enforce a business contract.

40. Hu Xunmin and He Jian, *Shanghai banghui jianshi* (Short history of Shanghai gangs) (Shanghai, 1991), 26–29; Frederic Wakeman, "The Secret Societies of Kwangtung," in *Popular Movements and Secret Societies in China,* ed. Jean Chesneaux (Stanford, Calif., 1972), 29–30. Two Guangdong secret societies in Shanghai were the Double Sword Society (*Shuangdaohui*) and Small Sword Society (*Xiaodaohui*). Fujianese were organized into the Bird Society (*Niaodang*) and Blue Turban Society (*Qingjinhui*). See Lu Yaohua, "Shanghai xiaodaohui de yuanliu," 10, 14; XDH, 1158.

41. Ye Shuping and Zheng Zu'an, eds., *Bainian Shanghai tan* (One hundred years of the Shanghai bund) (Shanghai, 1988), 151.

As this case suggests, the symbiosis of *huiguan* and *banghui* was most prominent in opium trading, because of the contraband nature of the drug for most of the period under study. Opium, which was central to the nineteenth-century prosperity of Shanghai, narrowed distinctions between "respectable" merchants and secret-society smugglers. Let us consider the structural underpinnings of the opium trade.

The Opium Trade: Bridge between Respectability and Criminality

By 1845 Shanghai was the coastal center of the opium trade. No legal regulation or protection of the opium trade existed prior to 1858 because neither the Opium War nor the subsequent Treaty of Nanjing (1842) settled the opium question. Officially, the drug remained banned by the Chinese imperial government. Nonetheless, the highly lucrative and visible contraband trade flourished to the mutual profit of Chinese and western merchants and officials. The result was widespread smuggling, tolerated by local Chinese officials who were increasingly dependent on illicit opium revenues.[42]

In the booming contraband trade, Chinese merchants depended on smugglers for their goods. Waterborne smugglers moved opium along the coast; dryland smugglers carried it inland. Smugglers depended on merchants for marketing. Their contacts were necessarily regular and organized. Successful merchants were those who could effectively interact with secret-society smuggling chiefs.

Opium smugglers banded together in tightly disciplined secret societies organized along native-place lines. Many of these *banghui* were

---

42. Western receiving vessels (supplied by opium clippers) anchored at Wusong, twelve miles from Shanghai down the Huangpu River. From Wusong the drug was shipped to Shanghai and Suzhou. The Su-Song-Tai Daotai was involved in the trade, through the large sums he extracted from smugglers and their Chinese customers. In 1855, in an act of flagrant disregard for the opium prohibition, the Daotai issued permits for the passage of opium, in return for the payment of twenty-five dollars per chest (Hao, *Commercial Revolution*, 129–31; Anatol M. Kotenev, *Shanghai, Its Municipality and the Chinese* [Shanghai, 1927], 268–69). American and French consuls were often directly or indirectly involved in opium trading. The British government officially opposed smuggling, yet it also opposed any restrictions on British merchants which would not be extended equally to merchants of other nationalities. Consequently, British merchants, who carried the bulk of the trade, reaped enormous profits.

linked with the Guangdong Three Dot Society (*Sandian hui*), a branch of the Ming restorationist Triad Society. They operated through persuasion and force, bribing Chinese officials and local bandit chiefs, moving in armed convoys. These gangs protected opium shipments against the pirate and bandit gangs which were increasingly a feature of the trade routes. In these networks of interdependence, social distinctions narrowed. Petty opium dealers formed the substratum of the growing merchant class. Opportunists who made fortunes in smuggling purchased the trappings of official respectability.[43]

From the popular point of view, the opium trade was not necessarily considered disreputable. A western visitor to Chaozhou remarked on the openness with which the illicit trade was carried out in the prefectural city and on the pleasantness of the local opium men who appeared, "jolly, respectable . . . and . . . very civil."[44] In his travels, Robert Fortune was deeply impressed by the opium merchants of Shanghai: "I expected to find those merchants who were engaged in this trade little else than armed buccaneers. . . . Instead of this, the trade is conducted by men of the highest respectability, possessed of immense capital, who are known and esteemed as merchants of the first class in every part of the civilized world." Such men, as Hao Yen-p'ing has noted, were often engaged by Jardine, Matheson and Company and would form a "nucleus of the modern Chinese business class."[45]

The endemic smuggling of treaty-port trade as well as merchant participation in smuggling schemes have been recognized.[46] Unfortunately,

43. Both foreign and Chinese opium merchants resorted to gang muscle. In one case a foreign ship captain arranged to beat a Ningbo merchant who stole opium from his Fujianese client. When the case came before the British consul, the captain (an employee of Jardine's) bribed those who were beaten to stay away from the trial. In other cases, crews of foreign opium receiving ships assisted Chinese smugglers in assaults on Chinese neighborhoods (Fairbank, *Trade and Diplomacy*, 227, 246). On opium smuggling, see Lin Man-houng, "Qingmo shehui liudong xishi yapian yanjiu — gonggei mian zhi fenxi (1773–1906)" (A supply-side analysis of the prevalence of opium smoking in late Qing China, 1773–1906) (Ph.D. diss., Taiwan Normal University, 1985), 147–51.

44. Scarth, *Twelve Years*, 73.

45. Fortune, *Two Visits to the Tea Countries of China* (London, 1853), vol. 1, 172; Hao, *Commercial Revolution*, 131.

46. James Cole (*Shaohsing*, 60) notes the economic importance of salt smuggling for the survival of secret societies, technological innovations which resulted from efficient smugglers' production techniques and, most interestingly, the assumption of Chinese authorities that smugglers could be reintegrated into respectable society. Rowe (*Hankow: Commerce and Society*, 96–97) describes endemic smuggling and black-marketeering in the salt trade. The culprits were not professional smugglers nor maverick western traders but, rather, the officially licensed salt merchants themselves. Boats carrying licensed salt (on

the importance of smuggling in the development of commercial capitalism in China, the organization of domestic smuggling, the connections
between secret societies and organized smuggling, and the social composition of smuggling gangs remain largely unexplored.[47] It is clear, nonetheless, that the effect of opium smuggling on the relationship of merchants to the state provides a basis for understanding the role of
merchants and merchant institutions in the Small Sword Uprising of 1853.

When Shanghai became a treaty port, opium import and distribution
headquarters moved from Guangzhou to Shanghai. Guangdong
people, particularly those from Chaozhou, became the leading brokers
of the trade. Months prior to the formal opening of the treaty port,
foreign vessels brought Indian opium to a receiving station at Wusong,
at the mouth of the Yangzi, just north of Shanghai. Charles Hope, a
conscientious British captain, together with the Chinese acting Daotai,
responded to this apparent violation of the prohibition on trade at uno-
pened ports by reporting and rebuffing several vessels. Both he and the
Daotai were rebuked for their efforts, and the latter was removed from
office. The protection of illicit trade thus ensured, the British conducted
a brisk business in opium and foreign sundries. Goods were transferred
onto the boats of Chinese smugglers who came alongside the British vessels. These Chinese boats then either smuggled the opium ashore or made
bargains with local customs officers.[48] Thus when British Consul Balfour
established his consulate at Shanghai in the fall of 1843, the opium trade
there was already a year old, and more than six million dollars of opium
had been sold to waterborne Chinese purchasers at Wusong. Jardine's led
the trade, which penetrated the entire Yangzi basin.

To sell opium in Shanghai without obviously smuggling themselves,
foreign merchants depended on locals, including smugglers and secret-
society leaders as their brokers, to take the opium ashore and distribute
it along the Yangzi valley. Chaozhou people were so deeply identified
with these opium-marketing functions that Shanghai people deroga-
tively called them *heilao* (black guys), a reference to the dark color of
opium (opium was also called *heiyan*, black tobacco). They were also
called *jia-er-jia-da* (Calcutta; *ka-er-ka-da* in the Shanghai dialect), the
name for the intermediate grade of opium emanating from that city.

---

which duty was paid) also carried undeclared contraband salt, more than the amount
permitted by license.

47. One such study of smuggling in eighteenth-century England is Cal Winslow, "Sussex Smugglers," in *Albion's Fatal Tree*, by D. Hay et al. (London, 1975), 119–66.

48. Fairbank, *Trade and Diplomacy*, 142–43, 229–33. Fairbank does not identify the acting Daotai; most likely it was Wu Jianzhang, who served briefly in Shanghai in 1842.

The fortunes of Chaozhou magnates of the twentieth century, who were variously engaged in native banks, textiles and pawnshops, were based on the profits of this nineteenth-century opium trade.[49]

Several legendary figures dominate the lore of the early Chaozhou opium merchants. In the period following the Opium War the trade was monopolized by merchants with the surnames Zheng and Guo, who formed the first Chaozhou opium establishments in Shanghai. Both began as petty compradors. Zheng Sitai was a secret-society type who went about with a retinue of vagabonds, swindlers, armed body-guards and religious leaders. As one story goes, this following so impressed the British that they entrusted to him the task of brokering and protecting the passage of opium. Zheng became rich and founded his own Zheng Qia Ji establishment. His success inspired other Chaozhou merchants to follow his path.[50]

Guo Zibin came to Shanghai after learning some English while working as a cook for foreigners. Because English-speaking Chinese in Shanghai were "as rare as phoenix feathers and unicorn horns," foreign merchants entrusted Guo with their business. His profits financed the successful Guo Hong Tai establishment. His relatives and fellow-provincials flocked to Shanghai.

As these establishments flourished, together with others founded by Chaozhou individuals with the surnames Chen, Li and Cai, each maintained inland distribution areas. Chaozhou *huiguan* sprung up along trade routes servicing the merchants. In the important cities and market towns of Jiangsu, Zhejiang and Anhui, Chaozhou *huiguan* served as

49. Chen Dingshan, *Chunshen jiuwen* (Old tales of Shanghai's spring) (Shanghai, n.d.), 34; Negishi, *Chūgoku no girudo*, 125; Zheng Yingshi, "Chaoji yapianyan shang zai Shanghai de huodong ji qi yu Jiang Jieshi zhengquan de guanxi" (The activities of Chaozhou opium merchants in Shanghai and their relation to Chiang Kai-shek's regime), *Guangdong wenshi ziliao xuanji*, 21 (1977):1–4.

50. Zheng, "Chaoji yapianyan," 7. This memoir is by the son of a major Republican-era Chaoyang opium merchant, Zheng Zijia (also a Chaozhou Huiguan director). According to the account, Zheng Sitai was the grandfather of the famous Shanghai Ming-xing Film Studio Company owner and director, Zheng Zhengqiu. There are several possible reasons why the Chaozhou group—as opposed to the Guang-Zhao group—came to dominate the opium trade. Chaozhou merchants became involved by the early 1820s, when enterprising merchants developed a new distribution network called the "coastal system." By this means they obtained opium at a smuggling center near Guangzhou and shipped it in coastal junks to Shantou. This avoided the customary "squeeze" at Guangzhou, and they could sell at higher prices than in the south, where opium was more plentiful (Yen-p'ing Hao, *Commercial Revolution*, 119). The Chaozhou/Guang-Zhao trade divisions may also have followed social distinctions. Guang-Zhao merchants were wealthier and had connections with foreigners in the legal trades of tea and silk. The poorer and rougher Chaozhou types lacked such connections but were ideally suited for the opium trade.

hotels for opium merchants, storehouses, and branch shops, the presence of *huiguan* themselves marking the penetration of the Chaozhou opium *bang*.[51]

The connections among Guangdong opium merchants, Guangdong *huiguan* and gangs of smugglers and secret-society members are both elusive and incontestable. The uprising of the Small Sword Society which overthrew the local government in Shanghai in 1853 confirms the connections, though the records only partially clarify their nature. In the uprising, official trust in apparent distinctions between "respectable" merchants and secret society members and rebels was betrayed. In retaliation against the rebels, Qing forces razed the implicated *huiguan* in a fire that blazed for twenty-four hours and took with it the most elegant buildings of the Chinese walled city.

Losing Control and Taking the City: The Small Sword Uprising

After opening to foreign trade, the city became densely crowded, and buildings pressed against each other like barnacles on a rock. Exotic and elegant goods appeared from all over, and people who knew strange stunts and bizarre feats amazed people with their cleverness and sophistication. The people trading with this place were mainly people from Guangdong, Chaozhou, Zhejiang, and Ningbo, and their activities brought no benefit to the local people. . . . Shanghai country people are frugal and simple, but they were enticed by gambling and festivals. . . . [T]hey neglected their work, loafed and practiced martial arts. Thus they formed the Temple Gang, the Dike and Bridge Gang, the Sugar Gang, the Straw and Mud Gang. . . . In the third year of the Xianfeng reign they were seduced by the Fujian and Guangdong bandits into killing the officials and occupying the city.[52]

In the third year of Xianfeng, on the sixth day of the third month there was a tremendous earthquake, followed by days

51. Chen Dingshan, *Chunshen jiuwen,* 34; Zheng, "Chaoji yapianyan," 7–8; Chen Boxi, *Shanghai yishi daguan,* vol. 2, 60–61; Lin Man-houng, "Qingmo shehui liudong," 142–47; Zhang Jungu, *Du Yuesheng zhuan* (Biography of Du Yuesheng) (Taipei, 1967–69) vol. 1, 93, 128. According to Zhang, in the 1930s secret-society members stored opium in empty coffins in the *huiguan* coffin repository.

52. TSXZ, 1:12–13.

of successive tremors, with sounds like the howling of ghosts. In the summer, on the seventh day of the fourth month, there was an earthquake. In the fifth month, outside the north gate, blood flowed from the ground and the earth sprouted hairs. On the eighth day of the sixth month, a woman named Hong gave birth to three sons, one colored deep blue, one white, and one crimson. After this, the city was besieged.[53]

In the Small Sword Uprising of 1853[54] we see an extreme "crystallization" of trends in state–society relations during the post–Opium War, early-opium-trading years in Shanghai: the weak Chinese state, dependent on the nonstate social institutions of *huiguan* to maintain social control; the admixture of foreign elements into Chinese traditions; the powerful emergence of secret societies from the substratum of Shanghai society; the linking of secret-society elements with merchants and merchant institutions based on native-place ties; and the mediating role of *huiguan* as institutions between different levels of society and different groups in society, a role which made *huiguan* central to both the maintenance and the disruption of social order.

Huiguan *Militia.* News reverberated in Shanghai of the establishment of the Taiping Heavenly Capital at Nanjing in March 1853 and of the subsequent proliferation of smaller uprisings such as the Small Sword takeover of Xiamen in May, causing anxiety at every level of society. Shanghai's vagabond population had strengthened the ranks of secret societies, including the Guangdong Small Sword Society. "Between summer and fall, rumors buzzed in the streets."[55] Listening and spreading rumors themselves, the secret societies grew bolder.

Confronted with displays of secret-society strength and rumors of imminent rebellion (and mindful of the overextension of imperial forces), the officials governing Shanghai hastened to establish defense militia. The Guangdong merchant-Daotai, Wu Jianzhang, sought help

---

53. TSXZ, 30:19. The *North China Herald* does not record an earthquake prior to the uprising.

54. For narratives of the uprising, see "Shanghai xiaodaohui qiyi zongxu," in XDH, 7–29; Lu Yaohua, "Shanghai xiaodaohui de yuanliu"; Joseph Fass, "L'insurrection du Xiaodaohui à Shanghai," in *Mouvements populaires et sociétés secrètes en Chine aux XIXe et XXe siècles,* ed. Jean Chesneaux (Paris, 1970), 178–95; Dillon, "Triads in Shanghai"; Elizabeth J. Perry, "Tax Revolt in Late Qing China: The Small Swords of Shanghai and Liu Depei of Shandong," *Late Imperial China* 6 (1985):83–111.

55. XDH, 36.

from his friend Li Shaoqing, Jiaying Gongsuo director, and gathered together a corps of Guangdong "village braves." Li Xianyun, director of the Fujian Xinghua Huiguan similarly organized a group of Fujian "braves."[56]

The militia caused problems from the beginning. Shortly after calling the Guangdong group together, Wu found he could not support them. Disbanded, the former "braves" turned into secret-society members. In mid-August, alarmed by mushrooming secret societies, the Shanghai Magistrate, Yuan Zude, posted a proclamation denouncing banditry and accusing Li Xianyun of being a bandit leader. A week later the magistrate's runners arrested Li and fourteen others. Nonetheless, the magistrate was too frightened by threats against him to keep them in his *yamen*. He not only promptly released the group but also paid Li a large indemnity for "false arrest." According to one account, Li began to organize an uprising upon his release.[57]

The next sequence of events reflects the pivotal position of *huiguan*, providing links with and potentially influencing secret societies, as well as the unstable power relations between high and low under the native-place tie. Hearing of a plot to waylay him, Daotai Wu also feared the situation was getting out of hand. Wu negotiated with *huiguan* directors to disperse the secret societies formed by their fellow-provincials. These *huiguan* directors then discussed the situation with their "*dang,*" returning with a counterproposal that the secret-society groups be transformed instead into paid militia, as an inducement toward their keeping the peace. In the meantime, Wu bribed Li Xianyun to keep things quiet.[58]

The *huiguan* directors framed their demands in a respectful petition, which the Daotai and magistrate graced with official approval. The text is preserved in a proclamation by the Shanghai magistrate on August 31, 1853, and translated in the *North China Herald,* establishing the new forces for the defense of the city:[59]

---

56. TSXZ, 11:32; XDH, 36, 958, 985, 1018. Though the sources are not explicit, it appears that Wu imported the militia recruits from Guangdong. In the gazetteer account, the magistrate asked Li Xianyun to assemble the Fujian militia (XDH, 958).

57. NCH, September 10, 1853. It is likely the "braves" had been secret-society members all along.

58. XDH, 36; Lu Yaohua, "Shanghai xiaodaohui de yuanliu," 13; NCH, September 10, 1853. According to the gazetteer (TSXZ, 11:32), the Magistrate was also pressured to release an imprisoned ruffian named Pan to train the militia for the city, "in compensation for his crimes."

59. The petition was jointly signed by the following individuals: Li Xianyun, identified as director (*dongshi*) of both the Xing'an and the Quan-Zhang Huiguan; Tan Jing, of the Guang'an Huiguan; Guo Wenzhi, of the Chaozhou Gongsuo; Li Shaoxi, of the Jia-

We conceive that when people mutually guard a place and assist each other, a neighborhood will enjoy tranquility. . . . [If] . . . secluded villages are re-quired to maintain patroles, how much more should an emporium like Shang-hae assemble its inhabitants for military training? Moreover, just now, when the rebels are making a disturbance, and lawless banditti are availing themselves of every pretext to get up a riot—if Shang-hae which is a market of such importance, where merchants assemble, and goods are stored up in such abundance—if the place does not adopt some means of defense, then robberies will be frequent, and the hard-earned savings of the trader will be encroached upon, in which case none would venture to come hither to trade. Orders having already been communicated to the president of the Canton assembly room to collect the members of the other guilds, consult about establishing a watch and train the militia in order to aid in the defense of the place—in which are conspicuous the wish to extirpate villainy and tranquilize the people—we have in obedience thereto assem-bled the guilds belonging to Fo-kien, Canton, Ningbo and Shang-hae people to consult with the gentry of the place; all these have gladly re-sponded to the call, and have united together for the purpose above named; so that, should nothing happen, they may still be on their guard, and should anything transpire, they may resist with advantage; the watchmen on shore going backward and forward as regularly as shuttles in a loom. . . . Should this plan of calling out the militia be put into effect, the city will be as secure as the great wall, the neighborhood will be in a state of tranquility, and the merchants will feel as easy as if they were reposing on beds of down.[60]

After approving this plan, the magistrate endorsed the *huiguan* direc-tors' demand for funds from the local gentry to pay the militia. In addi-tion to this estimated annual cost of thirty thousand yuan, the magis-trate endorsed the collection of funds for salaries for the *huiguan* directors, the cost of a general office for the seven *huiguan* to use to-gether, and six smaller offices, presumably for the individual *huiguan*.[61]

The petition reflects the commanding position of the Canton associa-tion; the impecuniousness of local official government; the willingness of different regional *huiguan* to coordinate their actions for municipal defense; the demands of restive secret-society organizations to be paid off, and finally, the ability of *huiguan* to manipulate their pivotal posi-tion in the situation for their own profit and position (director salaries and official municipal offices).

---

ying Gongsuo; Zhang Gui, of the Ningbo Gongsuo; and Pan Yiguo, director of the Shanghai suburbs residents' association (*yi fu cheng dongshi*). See XDH, 39. Li Shaoxi is identified elsewhere as Li Shaoqing. Other documents refer to a Fujian Xinghua Huiguan.

60. NCH, September 10, 1853.

61. XDH, 39; NCH, September 10, 1853. Whether these funds were raised is unclear.

The Coup. On September 5, less than a week after the posting of this notice, Guangdong secret societies joined local Shanghai secret societies organized under Zhou Lichun in an attack on the district *yamen* of Jiading. On September 6 there was a run on red cloth, and Shanghai shops quickly sold out. The following day the militia formed through the *huiguan* directors' agency confederated under the banner of the Small Sword Society and festooned themselves with red headbands, red belts and other markers of rebellion. At dawn several hundred of these militiamen/rebels from Guangdong entered the Chinese walled city of Shanghai. The takeover began at the offices of the county magistrate, where there were forty guards, all Guangdong natives. The guards did not resist. According to one account they scattered "like stars" to make way for the intruders, then calmly reached into their belts and pulled out red cloths to wrap around their heads. By afternoon the rebels controlled the city.[62]

The conquest of the city claimed only two victims: one hapless guard who took it upon himself to resist and the city magistrate, who was not forgiven for his arrest of secret-society members prior to the uprising. After plundering the magistrate's *yamen* and freeing the prisoners within (leaving the corpse of the magistrate in his looted office for all to behold), the rebels proceeded to the Daotai's *yamen,* where they began to enact a similar scene, the Daotai's guard revealing matched red scarves.

Instead of killing Wu Jianzhang, the rebels reportedly shouted, "Because we are from the same native place, we will spare your life — where is the money?" Unwilling to trust his life entirely to native-place sentiment, Wu turned over his treasury, and the rebellion encountered no further resistance. In this fashion, to the wonderment of a western commentator, "a walled town of 200,000 inhabitants [was] taken by men armed mostly with spears and swords, and only one [*sic*] man killed in the struggle."[63] The city was taken, but it was more a coup than an uprising, and there was no struggle. The city's armed forces had merely taken command. Although they lacked both coherent organization and ideology, they held Shanghai for seventeen months.

An anonymous account of the rebellion written by a member of the Shanghai gentry recounts that the uprising was orchestrated by a confederation of seven major gangs (*dang*). These *dang* corresponded to seven native-place groups:[64]

62. XDH, 985, 1018–19.
63. XDH, 963, 1020; NCH, September 10, 1853, 23.
64. XDH, 36, 972.

Chaozhou (Guangdong)

Jiaying (Guangdong)

Guangzhou and Zhaoqing (Guangdong)

Quanzhou and Zhangzhou (Fujian)

Xinghua (Fujian)

Ningbo (Zhejiang)

Shanghai

The secret societies of the Shanghai area numbered more than seven. These included the following:[65]

Small Sword Society (Guangdong)

Double Sword Society (Guangdong)

Bird Society (Fujian)

Fujian Gang (Fujian)

Blue Turban/Blue Hand Society (Fujian)

Ningbo Gang (Ningbo)

Hundred Dragon/Temple/Dike and Bridge Society (Shanghai)

Luohan Society (Jiading county, Jiangsu)

Sugar Gang (Shanghai)

Straw and Mud Gang (Shanghai)

It seems fairly clear that the seven *dang* which formed the organizational foundation of the uprising overlapped with the seven regional associations which organized the city's militia. Several of the identified rebel leaders—Li Shaoqing, Li Xianyun, Pan Yiguo—were among the *huiguan* directors who signed the petition to the magistrate. At least two *huiguan* or *gongsuo* within the city served as offices for the rebels. The Guangdong rebels took Daotai Wu to their Guang'an Huiguan. The elegant Fujian merchants' Dianchuntang, with its courtyard gar-

---

65. Alternate names appear with a solidus (/). The Chinese names for these societies were *Xiaodaohui, Shuangdaohui, Niaodang, Fujian bang, Qingjin/Qingshouhui, Ningbo bang, Bailong/Miao/Tangqiao bang, Luohan dang, Tang dun, Caonidun* (XDH, 1158, TSXZ, 1:12–13; Lu Yaohua, "Shanghai xiaodaohui de yuanliu," 14).

dens and carved wood and marble furniture, was headquarters for the Fujian rebels.[66]

Connections and Tensions. It appears that the seven major regional *huiguan* were nodes for the coalescence of smaller and disparate secret societies, which conjoined on the basis of overarching regional affinities.[67] The joint militia organization provided a loose framework, connecting in turn the different *huiguan*.

The opium trade provided another critical connection. One contemporary account identified the Fujianese leaders, Chen Alin, Lin Afu, Chen Aliu, Li Xianyun, and the Guangdong leaders, Li Shaoqing and Li Shuangxuan, as opium sellers and gamblers, "accustomed to daring and lawlessness." Another noted that the Guangdong and Fujian people were engaged in transporting opium. One Guangdong leader, Liu Ayuan, was identified as the owner of an opium shop in Shanghai. Opium had clearly involved merchants in illegalities and tied them to secret societies. Opium also linked Guangdong secret societies with local Shanghai secret societies.[68]

The native-place ties which provided the axes of coalition for the rebel uprising were not linked, at this point, to an ideology which went beyond the self-interest of individual native-place groups. This is clearly reflected in the rebels' clumsy groping for symbols, causes or powers greater than themselves. Although the rebels followed secret-society rhetoric of Ming restoration and declared themselves a new Ming dynasty, they also cast about for other symbols of legitimacy, naming themselves, in foreign fashion, the Yixing Company (which may be

66. XDH, 1030. When I arrived in Shanghai in 1982 a Small Sword museum had been created in the Yu Gardens with reconstructed portions of the Dianchuntang.

67. This point is demonstrated convincingly by Lu Yaohua ("Shanghai xiaodaohui de yuanliu," 14), who charts the integration of the secret societies into the *huiguan* regional groupings.

68. XDH, 165, 985, 1022. As Perry recounts, two months before the uprising, Guangdong secret-society members transporting opium from Shanghai to Suzhou were robbed by local bandits. The opium smugglers enlisted the help of their protector, Li Shaoxi, of the Jiaying Huiguan. Li sought out a local strongman, Zhou Lichun, who had gained power among Shanghai-area secret societies because of his role in tax protests. Zhou arranged the return of the opium, which had been stolen by one of his acquaintances. Zhou's cooperation gained him friends in the Shanghai Guangdong community. Li was so pleased that he met with Zhou and introduced him to the leader of the Small Sword Society, the former sugar-broker and opium addict Liu Lichuan. The first fruit of the bond between these groups was the attack on Jiading of September 5. The second was the Shanghai uprising. See Perry "Tax Revolt," 90; XDH, 968, 1055, 1087, 1158; Lu Yaohua, "Shanghai xiaodaohui de yuanliu," 14.

taken as a reflection of their recognition of the power of foreign commerce) and hoping variously for help and sponsorship from the Taipings, from the British, French and U.S. authorities and even from the Qing official Wu Jianzhang.

From the beginning of the uprising the Small Swords were divided by the very native-place ties along which they were organized. Fujian and Guangdong groups entered the city from different directions and set up camps in different places. From their different headquarters their leaders issued independent proclamations. Each regional group wore a distinguishing badge. According to a western observer, Fujian rebels tied their heads with red bands. Although they wore red belts, Guangdong rebels wore white head cloths. There were also sartorial distinctions between sojourners and local people.[69]

On the first day of the coup the rebels argued over the fate of the Daotai, with the Fujianese pressing for execution. The Guangdong group instead protected him and took him to their *huiguan* in the western part of the city, hoping to persuade him to join them. Liu Lichuan even sent a note to the American legation proclaiming that the Small Swords intended to reestablish Wu as a high official of their new government.[70]

The rebels also argued over their conduct in the city. The Fujianese and by one report the Chaoyang group wanted to loot and plunder. They were restrained by the Guangzhou group, with ill will on both sides. A dispute arose over an estimated 200,000 taels discovered in an imperial treasury. The Fujianese wanted to divide the money; the Guangdong faction favored establishing a treasury for the defense of the city. The dispute escalated into a fight which ended only when Guangdong rebels drove the Fujianese out of the walled city.[71]

Alliances among groups were private matters, not ideological expressions of allegiance to a united Small Swords. Li Shaoxi's friendship with the local Qingpu strongman Zhou Lichun brought the Shanghai gangs into an exclusive alliance with the Guangdong group. In the treasury dispute the local Jiading and Qingpu factions sided firmly with the Guangdong group, opposing the unruly Fujianese.[72]

---

69. XDH, 40–41; Robert Fortune, *A Residence among the Chinese* (London, 1857), 123. White headcloths were reputedly a sign of mourning for the Ming dynasty.

70. XDH, 985; Fairbank, *Trade and Diplomacy,* 407–8. Wu declined the Guangdong offer and sent a message to the U.S. legation asking for protection. The Guangdong rebels permitted the Americans to rescue him.

71. NCH, September 10, 1853; XDH, 42, 141, 1025.

72. NCH, September 10, 1853.

Denouement. The fates of the Small Sword rebels similarly varied according to the native-place and personal alliances of the
different rebel subgroups. As the French-assisted Qing troops pressed
their siege, the food supply dwindled and some factions leaned toward
desertion. The Fujianese had long wanted nothing more than to return
to their native place with captured booty, but they had been prevented
from doing so by the Cantonese. As conditions and morale deteriorated, the Guangdong leader Liu Lichuan himself proposed surrender
to the reinstated Daotai (in return for an official title). His plan was
opposed by the Fujian leader Lin Afu. At times the tensions of survival
led to the emergence of savage ethnic conflict among groups previously
allied as fellow Guangdong provincials. In January 1854, in response to
a reported Hakka conspiracy (presumably referring to the Jiaying
group) to deliver the city to foreign troops, the non-Hakka Cantonese
murdered more than seventy of their Hakka fellow-provincials.[73]

In the last days of the occupation (February 1855), the Small Swords
began to flee the city in different groups. The first desertion was precipitated by Chen Alin's shooting of Liu Lichuan's secretary, an act which
aroused the anger of the Guangdong faction. Fearing revenge, Chen
and his followers escaped. Another Fujian leader, Lin Afu, and his followers also fled, joining coastal pirates. Liu Lichuan himself finally de-
serted the city for Guangdong, accompanied by more than a hundred
fellow-provincials.[74]

It was only after most rebels had vanished that the imperial forces
rushed into the city, confident of meeting no resistance. Their entrance
marked the most devastating moment of the Small Sword episode. They
beheaded, burned, tortured, drowned and raped all of the rebels, relations, sympathizers, and suspect passersby they could lay their hands
on. Amid the corpses and slaughter, the imperial troops plundered the
city and finally set it afire. Three days later, "order was restored." Nearly
half of the city lay in bloodied rubble. Houses, temples, *yamen, huiguan*
and *gongsuo* were in ruins.

As the ashes cooled, the Qing Pacification Commissioner strode into
the city to inspect the work of his troops. He issued ten regulations to
prevent the resurrection of the Small Swords. Although Ningbo and
local Shanghai people had also participated in the rebellion, Guangdong
and Fujian people (and their *huiguan*) bore the brunt of his punitive

73. Perry, "Tax Revolt," 99–100; NCH, January 7, 1854, 90.
74. NCH, February 24, 1855, 120; XDH, 961.

measures. The regulations dictated surveillance over the selection of subsequent Guangdong and Fujian *huiguan* managers; prohibition against the rebuilding of Guangdong and Fujian *huiguan* within the city walls; prohibition against the rebuilding of any "dens of rebellion"; deportation and supervised relocation of Fujian and Guangdong vagabonds; examination and registration of all Chinese in foreign employ (primarily Cantonese); prohibition of Fujian and Guangdong boats; and prohibition against vagabonds departing on these types of boats.[75]

The new acting Daotai, Lan Weiwen (from Ningbo), together with a coalition of his fellow Zhejiang merchants and officials, vigorously implemented these regulations in a full-scale campaign against people from Guangdong. In the official records, the Small Sword rebellion was increasingly attributed to "Guangdong and Fujian bandits" only. Whereas Guangdong people were forced to move outside the city and their efforts to rebuild *huiguan* repeatedly thwarted, Ningbo people were permitted to retain a temple within the city walls and use it as their *huiguan* (the Zhe-Ning Huiguan). Within a few years their former *huiguan,* the Siming Gongsuo, was restored and expanded.[76]

The outstanding feature of the Small Sword episode in Shanghai history is perhaps neither the coup nor its failure but the resemblances and overlap between the rebel and loyalist sides. Under the principle of "changing from evil ways to good" (*gai e cong shan*), secret-society members were made into defense militia for the city. The militia then turned rebel and overthrew the officials it served. This much will perhaps not seem remarkable, because attempting to coopt local strongmen was a common imperial tactic and because infiltrating city defenses was a common secret-society tactic.[77]

But the overlaps run deeper. The upstanding merchant associations, the *huiguan* which maintained urban order, were revealed in the course of the uprising to be in thrall to secret societies, as useful to the cause of rebellion as they had been in service to the government. *Huiguan*

75. Scarth, *Twelve Years,* 216; Dillon, "Triads in Shanghai," 79; TSXZ, 11:32; Leung, "Regional Rivalry," 41.

76. TSXZ, 3:4; Leung, "Regional Rivalry," 43–44. As late as September 15, 1866, there is a note in the *North China Herald* reporting the tearing down of a temporary *huiguan* erected by Guangdong natives in the Guangdong residential area of Hongkou, to the north of the walled city. The Siming Gongsuo clearly was rebuilt before 1860, when it was occupied by foreign troops for defense against a Taiping attack.

77. XDH, 191; Cole, *Shaohsing,* 60; S. Y. Teng, *The Nien Army and Their Guerilla Warfare* (Paris, 1961), 128.

directors who petitioned the authorities to maintain order, some of whom had official titles, were identified as ruffians who had been in and out of prison.

Despite their vows to overthrow the dynasty, the rebels who took the city saved the highest official in it. Not only was Daotai Wu spared, but the rebels asked him to serve in their new government. Later, when Liu Lichuan considered surrender, he planned to hand over the city in exchange for an official title.

Although Daotai Wu declined to serve in the Small Sword government, he nonetheless made few effective attempts to retake the city. Unenlightened by the lesson of his initial militia-making endeavor, Wu turned to another group of his fellow-countrymen to combat the rebels. He hired a fleet of Xiangshan pirate-boatmen to sail on Shanghai and attack the Small Swords. The pirates came as hired, but they refused to fight fellow-provincials and spent their time in Shanghai waters robbing and plundering, one more "scourge on the populace."

Meanwhile, crowning the farce at the city walls, imperial troops recruited from Guangdong (said also to be secret-society members) sallied forward daily toward the rebel forces. At the tips of their bayonets they hung ducks and other foodstuffs, for the ostensible purpose of taunting the besieged rebels. At the end of the day, taunting done, these troops returned to their camps, ducks lost among the hungry besieged.[78]

If such contradictions weakened both the rebellion and imperial attempts to suppress it, they are consistent with the limitations and corruptions of an impecunious state as well as the frontier aspects of Shanghai at the time, as a boomtown with little government. Many wealthy merchants in this period had arrived just a few years earlier as poor adventurers, rough-and-ready types who did what it took to carve out fortunes and a reputation. Such men became powerful and rose as *huiguan* leaders after the Opium War. The Jiaying Huiguan director Li Shaoqing arrived in the Shanghai area as a peddler and then became a tea-house operator with connections to opium smugglers. We see a similar type in the figure of the rebel leader Li Xianyun, whose might made him director of both the Xing'an and Quan-Zhang *huiguan:* "The Fujianese Li Xianyun was also a bandit/secret society [member]. He was nearly sixty, short and with a slight beard and moustache. Coming and going he rode a sedan chair, surrounded by a throng of his bodyguards, creating extreme dread. Whenever each brokerage or shop expected goods to

78. Fairbank, *Trade and Diplomacy,* 428; Scarth, *Twelve Years,* 211.

arrive at the docks they had to send money to Li's place in order to avoid robbery when the shipments reached shore."[79]

In an urban atmosphere in which toughs and gangs roamed the streets making their own order because little order was imposed from above, for both merchants and poor immigrants native-place ties provided one of the few means of organization and protection. The Small Sword episode reflects this centrality of *huiguan* as an organizational base for multiple purposes, as well as the significance of native-place identity as a loyalty which could cut across other ties. It was not that native-place identity determined an individual's side in the uprising (in fact, there were reports of wealthy Guangdong merchants generously donating funds to both sides). Rather, throughout the episode the usefulness of native-place ties (contrasted with the ideological weakness of both the rebel and imperial sides) diminished the participants' interest in taking other types of loyalty seriously.

In the decades that followed the uprising, while imperial forces continued to deal with the ongoing Taiping Rebellion, Shanghai *huiguan* rebuilt themselves and grew in numbers, constituency and power. Although ties to secret societies would not entirely disappear, *huiguan* leaders would become increasingly respectable, so respectable that events like involvement in a rebel uprising would become unimaginable. But even though the *huiguan* wrote the Small Sword episode out of their histories, their behavior suggests that they drew important lessons from the experience.

In the Small Sword Uprising, *huiguan* and ideas of native place appear both central and strangely powerless. Although people coalesced around native-place loyalties, at this point native-place communities did not cohere around clear leaders or clear notions. Merchant elites could not effectively direct the actions of their *tongxiang,* and their institutions and reputations suffered accordingly. After the uprising, as Shanghai merchants grew in wealth and power, they took great care to root their power more firmly within their sojourning communities. They would also deepen their connections to other sources of authority in the city—both to Chinese and to foreign institutions. Through these connections and the tensions and responsibilities they aroused they would in time embed their native-place loyalties within a more coherent politics, entirely changing the meaning of native-place sentiment.

79. XDH, 983. Li Shaoqing's description is in XDH, 1024–25. See also Perry, "Tax Revolt," 88–89.

CHAPTER THREE

Community, Hierarchy and Authority

Elites and Non-elites in the Making of
Native-Place Culture during the Late Qing

This chapter explores the dynamics of *tongxiang* community and the sources of *huiguan* authority in the late Qing. After the Small Sword Uprising, as Taiping and other refugees and immigrants swelled the population of Shanghai's sojourning communities, *huiguan* leaders extended the scope of *huiguan* activities, strengthening their connections with their communities (and their positions of power within them). Larger and more powerful *huiguan* came to rest on a broader economic base, as sojourners diversified their trade interests and carved out new occupational niches. Guangdong merchants, for example, reinvested much of their opium wealth in a multitude of new and less risky enterprises.[1] The areas of crude interdependence between wealthy *huiguan* leaders and non-elites, so visible and clumsily negotiated in the rough-and-tumble years of the early treaty port leading up to the Small Sword Uprising, change in the new social order of post-Taiping Shanghai. *Huiguan* directors of the 1860s and 1870s look considerably more respectable and sedate than did the adventurer-merchant *huiguan* leaders of the Small Sword period. They also transformed their *huiguan*, formulating new rules and procedures of association and en-

1. By 1912 Guang-Zhao Gongsuo records refer to fifteen *tongxiang* trades, including pawnshops, iron trade, steamboats, foreign goods, miscellaneous goods, wood trade and warehouses. See "Guang-Zhao gongsuo yi'an bu" (Register of Guang-Zhao Gongsuo meetings) (hereafter referred to as GZGYB), August-September 1912, manuscript, Shanghai Municipal Archives. On the diversified investments of major *huiguan* leaders in the late nineteenth century, including the Guangdong merchants Xu Run and Tang Jingxing and the leading Ningbo merchants, Takee and Yu Xiaqing, see Hao, *Comprador,* 112–52.

compassing elite/non-elite interactions within rhetorical and symbolic strategies which linked disparate elements into more stable, hierarchical communities. These strategies underlay the activities that constituted, defined and maintained the *tongxiang* community.

Huiguan leaders maintained authority by cultivating the idea of broad *tongxiang* community, regularly enacting hierarchy and continuously working out alliances with various elements of the community. Without ritually affirming community and hierarchy, they would not have been able to maintain the perception of *tongxiang* bonds.

Huiguan Business and the *Huiguan* Oligarchy

On most days in late-nineteenth-century Shanghai the large *huiguan* buildings which architecturally symbolized community were nearly empty. Periodically a small and exclusive group, calling themselves "elders" (*weng*), or "directors" (*dongshi*), met together in a central room in the *huiguan* complex to discuss matters which came before them — social, political, religious and economic.

Surviving records from the Guang-Zhao Gongsuo suggest the nature and rhythms of affairs within the *huiguan* oligarchy. In 1872, in an atmosphere of regained wealth and respectability, twenty-four directors contributed to the reconstruction of the building. All were prominent Guangdong merchants, compradors or officials in Shanghai. Records from this year show that the directors met several times each week in the early evenings after business hours, arriving casually between 6:00 and 7:00 P.M. A small group of active directors, ranging from as few as three or four to as many as ten or fifteen, normally attended. Shanghai officials, if Cantonese, often attended *huiguan* meetings.[2]

2. After the 1853 uprising, Guangdong merchants worked to restore the "face" of their community. In the late 1860s Xu Run and Tang Jingxing were leading figures in Shanghai charitable enterprises. During this period, though there was no *huiguan*, the merchants did not lack organization but met informally. It seems likely that the reconstruction of the building became convenient in 1872 because of the appointment of a Guangdong official, Ye Tingjuan, as Shanghai magistrate (Xu Run, *Nianpu*, 14–15). Records from the 1870s show attendance by several officials who are also identified as *dongshi*, including Feng Junguang (Daotai), Ye Tingjuan and Zheng Caoru (Jiangnan Arsenal Director); records for the last decade of the Qing show the attendance of Daotai Liang Ruhao. The discussion here and in the paragraphs below, unless otherwise noted, is based on GZGYB covering the years 1872 and 1891–1911. See also Lai Chi-kong, "Cantonese Business Networks

Through the last years of the Qing, a very small group controlled *huiguan* business. An 1897 discussion of protocols for use of the Guang-Zhao Gongsuo seal reveals this clearly. The seal was locked in an iron safe with two doors. Three keys fit the outer door, each kept by one director. The single fourth key, which opened the inner door, was held by a fourth director. Without the seal, of course, no documents could be signed and no financial transactions could take place.

It is sometimes assumed on the basis of collective decision making practices or fraternal rhetoric that nineteenth-century *huiguan* were sites of indigenous democratic practices.[3] Such a view should be tempered by recognition of the hierarchy embedded in *huiguan* practice. *Huiguan* rules stressed that individual sojourners did not have the right of access to the *huiguan*. Individuals who needed help were to go first to the leader of their regional subgroup. Without a letter of introduction from this intermediate authority, the *gongsuo* would not respond to an appeal. Individuals of good reputation who became implicated in lawsuits were instructed to attain a note of guarantee from a native-place shop.[4]

Even within the sojourning elite, the rhetoric of collective decision making that informed *huiguan* rules and record keeping concealed a practice of quietly coerced consensus, in which the most powerful members of the oligarchy determined the outcome of any decision. Year after year the same individuals appear in leadership roles. In the records, all decisions are unanimous. Discussion and dissent simply do not appear.[5]

In their meetings, the elders/directors discussed a wide range of busi-

---

in Late Nineteenth Century Shanghai: The Case of the Kwang-Chao Kung-So," in *Essays in Economic and Business History,* ed. Edwin J. Perkins (Los Angeles, 1994), vol. 12, 145–54.

3. Some historians have been more persuaded than have I by the quasi-democratic language of these institutions. In "The Gentry Democracy in Chinese Shanghai" (pp. 41–61), for example, Mark Elvin suggests that *huiguan* provided models of democratic management. A stela dated 1912 written by the leader of a Ningbo worker organization within the Siming Gongsuo complains of the high-handed arrogance of *huiguan* leaders and reveals oligarchic practices in the Ningbo community corresponding to those apparent from the Guang-Zhao Gongsuo records (SBZX, 429–32).

4. "Guang-Zhao huiguan guitiao" (Guang-Zhao Huiguan rules), hand-copied document, courtesy of Du Li, Shanghai Museum. Elderly Shanghai residents who remembered *huiguan* from the early twentieth century stressed that *huiguan* were not open to all, only to prominent *tongxiang* and those with letters of introduction. Others were turned away by the gatekeepers.

5. According to Guang-Zhao Gongsuo rules, individuals were to follow the decision of the group. If this was difficult and there were different opinions, then matters were to be decided by the majority. There is no mention of voting, but the rules state that "if six or seven people agree out of ten, the matter is determined." Meeting records rarely, if ever, refer to disagreements or actual votes prior to the twentieth century.

ness, including disputes over individual and business debts; family inheritance cases; price fluctuations for various goods; company shareholder arrangements; purchase and rental of *huiguan* property; insults and affronts to friends, associates and other Guangdong sojourners; injury to property (including wives and concubines); shop disputes; customs fees; disputes over purchased concubines; collections to develop factories; hiring and payment for *huiguan* employees (guards, construction workers, water carriers, janitors); bankruptcies; apprentices; charitable collections. This list is deliberately random; *huiguan* records and meeting practice did not separate diverse concerns into different categories, nor did a specialized organizational personnel deal with different problems; the "elders" addressed whatever business came before them.

Business was introduced by directors themselves; by individuals with sufficient connections to contact the elders/directors; and by businesses or trades within the Guangdong sojourning community.[6] At times representatives from particular trades or shops attended the meetings to present cases, as in 1897, when directors of two subgroups in the oil trade came to the *huiguan* to resolve a dispute. At other times the directors used the *huiguan* as a court, dispatching investigators, summoning plaintiffs and accused before them and passing judgements. Such cases were resolved when the parties involved signed an agreement "in the *gongsuo,* in the presence of all." The meeting records spell out the terms of settlement in business and inheritance cases and are marked with signatures or fingerprints and crosses, the marks of the illiterate. Those sentenced to pay penalties or turn property over to business colleagues or family members affirmed their intent to pay "before the [*huiguan*] god, with a pure heart" (*zai shen qian qing xin*), the god's authority reinforcing that of the *huiguan* directors.[7]

Although the rules of the Guang-Zhao Gongsuo refer to *huiguan*

6. Records for 1872 mention timber, miscellaneous goods, tea export, Guangdong and overseas goods, pawnshops, iron, lacquer, Hongkou iron shops and other Hongkou businesses.

7. Among those signing with fingerprints and crosses were women, in cases involving their portions of businesses or their personal property. A record from 1891 notes that meetings took place in front of the image of the god, Guandi; the terms *zai shen qian qing xin* appear in a judgment of 1895. See also MacGowan, "Chinese Guilds," 140. During my March 1984 interview Tan Xiaochuang (a native of Quanzhou, Fujian, and sometime resident of the Shanghai Quan-Zhang Huiguan) described how a *huiguan* could be more effective than a court in settling disputes, particularly in cases in which fault was difficult to determine (such as accidents at sea). In such cases, he explained, the truth could only be resolved by a process of divining before the *huiguan* goddess Tianhou. In this manner the *huiguan* temple was useful in deciding what no official could determine as convincingly.

business as *gong shi* (public or collective matters), private and public, personal and collective, were not clearly distinguished in practice during this period. Personal finances as well as business arrangements flowed through the mediating institution of the *huiguan*. Directors discussed their investments, invested together, and helped each other out in family and other business when one or another was out of Shanghai. Guangdong merchants and officials in other places contacted the Shanghai Guangdong merchants through the *huiguan* and asked them to handle various matters for them. Funds for private business transactions were often transferred through the *huiguan*. Payments for *huiguan* business, when large sums were involved, would often combine the limited "common funds" with contributions and loans from individual directors.[8]

The concerns of sojourning workers do not frequently appear in the *huiguan* ledgers, which are densely packed with the property concerns of the sojourning elite. Nonetheless, strikes or pay disputes did periodically intrude on the business of the directors. At such moments it becomes possible to glimpse in action the types of bonds, beliefs and power relations which structured class relations within the *tongxiang* community.

The day-to-day concerns of artisans and workers were handled by artisan or worker native-place associations (*bang, dian,* or *hui*). It was only when matters could not be handled at this level that the merchant *huiguan* directors stepped in as a higher adjudicating, enforcing or mediating authority. An example of such an instance may be seen in an 1879 case in which the carpenter Zeng Ajin and his brothers refused to pay the 20 percent of their earnings required by the Guangdong carpenters' Lu Ban Dian. Because the brothers worked for foreign employers, they also dodged penalties imposed by the carpenters' association. To force the unruly brothers to comply, the carpenters' association appealed to the *huiguan*. As reported in the *North China Herald,* "The carpenters' society is subordinate to the General Cantonese Guild, which ultimately took the matter in hand; and a few days ago a warrant was issued by the District Magistrate in the city . . . to compel payment." In this case we

---

8. For the flavor of *huiguan* business in this period, see also surviving correspondence of the reformist scholar-official Zheng Guanying with the Guang-Zhao Gongsuo, in Xia Dongyuan, ed., *Zheng Guanying ji* (Collected works of Zheng Guanying) (Shanghai, 1988), vol. 2, 507–8, 617–18, 917, 1139–40, 1210. Because major expenditures were frequently funded outside the "common funds," the account-books of the *gongsuo,* which indicate *gongsuo* income and regular expenses from the common fund, do not properly reflect the extent of *huiguan* activity.

see not only the Guang-Zhao Gongsuo's readiness to enforce the rule that all Guangdong carpenters had to belong to their association, but also the positioning of the *huiguan* between the carpenters and the Chinese authorities (and the willingness of the latter to enforce *huiguan* decisions).[9]

A carpenters' strike at Farnham, Boyd and Company in 1902 provided another occasion for *huiguan* intervention. Four Cantonese carpenters were arrested by foreign-settlement authorities for intimidating a Ningbo labor contractor who was responsible for employing Ningbo carpenters during the Cantonese carpenters' strike. In an effort to resolve the strike and investigate the case, the Mixed Court contacted the Guang-Zhao Gongsuo. According to the *huiguan* correspondence with the court, the directors summoned the carpenters' headmen to the *huiguan* to persuade them to return to work. The *huiguan* directors in return agreed to arrange for the release of the four arrested carpenters and provide strike-compensation funds to the workers. After investigating the situation, the directors contacted the foreign shipyard owners to secure the carpenters' release. When this initial attempt was unsuccessful, they enlisted the help of the Daotai, selected members of their community to act as guarantors to go to the court on the carpenters' behalf, and finally secured their release.[10] This example highlights the mediating role of the *huiguan,* which fashioned a compromise to both mollify fellow-provincial carpenters and return them to work. It also represented them in court as a matter of course. Although business involving foreigners was not always smooth, the action of the Mixed Court in this case nonetheless makes clear that foreign authorities, like Chinese, recognized the need to work through the *huiguan* in order to resolve the labor dispute.

9. NCH, January 10, 1879, 22–23. This case also demonstrates how foreign authorities in the city complicated *huiguan* adjudication of such matters. Because Zeng resided in the American Settlement area of Hongkou, the arrest warrant had to be signed by the U.S. Consul. Although in other cases settlement authorities often reinforced *huiguan* authority (in a 1911 case, for example, foreign-owned shipyards agreed to engage Guangdong rather than Ningbo carpenters), in this case Consul Bailey ultimately declined. See NCH, September 23, 1911, 851. See also discussions in Perry *Shanghai on Strike,* 33–34, 39.

10. GZGYB, May-June, 1902; NCH, May 28, 1902, 1069–70. *Gongsuo* records indicate that the shipyard owners prevented the payment of strike compensation. The Mixed Court was established in 1868, providing for a western "assessor" to sit with the Chinese magistrate for the purpose of examining cases involving Chinese residents in the foreign settlements and cases involving both Chinese and foreigners. See Kotenev, *Shanghai, Its Municipality and the Chinese,* 274–75.

In Chinese matters, the *huiguan* leaders not only commanded the authority to resolve routine disputes but also were capable of quickly mustering considerable resources and participation on short notice. In 1898, for instance, when rice was scarce in Guangdong and prices were rocketing, the Guang-Zhao Gongsuo responded with alacrity to appeals from hospitals in Guangzhou and Hong Kong, using native-place connections to purchase and ship more than thirteen million pounds of rice from Hankou to Guangdong. The details of this massive endeavor are precisely recorded in the *huiguan* meeting notes. Twenty sojourning Guangdong firms took on the responsibility to purchase and transport the rice, accompanying it to Guangdong to ensure that none of it would be sold along the way.[11]

In such large and smaller matters, *huiguan* authority "worked" because, in addition to serving their own interests, *huiguan* leaders understood that their long-term interest depended also on the cultivation of the larger sojourning community. For this they needed arenas which went beyond their interior meetings and courtroom dramas.

Encompassing the People

Burial and Welfare Services. Because of the importance of burial in the ancestral home, *huiguan* expended considerable amounts of managerial energy and funding on the provision of coffins, coffin storage in special repositories (*binshe* or *bingshe*) prior to shipment, and cemeteries (*shanzhuang, yimu*) in Shanghai for the "temporary" resting or burial of deceased *tongxiang* whose families could not afford the costs of shipment and burial in the native place. Such functions required not only the purchase of land and the continual building of new cemeteries and mortuaries to accommodate the growing immigrant population but, in addition, payment for geomancers, guards and sacrifices at cemetery altars.[12] Toward the end of the nineteenth century, as both western and Chinese authorities imposed limits on coffin storage, *huiguan* also

---

11. The records refer to 20 zhang of rice, each containing 5,000 dan (1 dan equals 133.3 pounds).

12. See, for example, *Guang-Zhao gongsuo zhengxinlu* (Account-book of the Guang-zhao Gongsuo), "Linian jinzhi shumu" (Record of yearly income and expenditures), 1873 and 1877, hand-copied manuscript, courtesy of Du Li, Shanghai Museum; *Shanghai Siming Gongsuo si da jianzhu zhengxinlu* (Account-book for the four major construction projects of the Shanghai Siming Gongsuo) (Shanghai, 1925); SBZX, 259–60, 266–67.

began more systematically to take on the considerable expense and management of coffin shipment to the native place.[13]

Huiguan cemeteries and coffin repositories symbolically encompassed the large community and reinforced the social hierarchy which structured it. Burial arrangements reproduced the social hierarchy of the living. Diagrams and rules for the operation of coffin repositories indicate several levels of coffin accommodations (with a corresponding scale of expenses) as well as strict separation of the sexes within each rank.[14]

Ordinary sojourners in Shanghai could depend on their *huiguan* not only for assistance when they passed away but also for help in the present. *Huiguan* often provided return passage for those who could not remain in Shanghai and intervened in court cases on behalf of those needing guarantors. An example of both forms of assistance may be found in the case of the Guangdong prostitutes Chen Yuanjin and Run Jin, who wished to redeem themselves and quit their profession. The Guang-Zhao Gongsuo petitioned the court on the women's behalf. Meanwhile, it arranged for *tongxiang* to guard the women while their case was being decided, to protect them from being abducted by their brothel keeper. The magistrate approved the petition and turned the women over to the *huiguan,* which arranged for their safe return to Guangdong.[15] Such acts, like burial provisions, reinforced the idea of a larger native-place community while establishing the *huiguan* oligarchs as the benevolent heads of a paternalistic hierarchy.

Religious Festivals and Processions. The early sojourning merchants and artisans established their associations as religious corporations. As their stone inscriptions testify, they built *huiguan* to collectively worship local or patron gods as well as to consolidate native-place

13. Stelae in SBZX (194–260) record the central role of cemetery construction and burial provisions in the establishment of *huiguan* and *gongsuo.* On coffin shipment, see Hokari Hiroyuki, "Shanghai Siming Gongsuo de 'yun guan wang' de xingcheng — Shanghai Ningbo shangren de tongxiang yishi de beijing" (Coffin-shipment network of the Shanghai Siming Gongsuo — Background for the native-place consciousness of Shanghai Ningbo merchants) (paper presented at International Conference on Urbanism and Shanghai, Shanghai, October 1991); Hiroyuki Hokari, "Kindai shanhai ni okeru itai shori mondai to shimei kōsho — dōkyō girudo to Chūgoku no toshika" (The management of human remains in modern Shanghai and the Siming Gongsuo — Native-place guilds and China's urbanization), *Shigaku Zasshi* 103 (February 1994):67–93.

14. SBZX, 360, 384–86, 416–17.

15. SB, June 25, June 28 and July 1, 1882. For records of indigent fellow-provincials returned to Guangdong, see *Guang-Zhao gongsuo zhengxinlu.*

sentiment and facilitate the enterprises of fellow sojourners. This temple function was expressed in alternate names for *huiguan* (*dian, tang, miao*), as well as in the altars that formed the ceremonial center of their buildings. The religious role of *huiguan* reinforced their symbolic centrality to the larger sojourning community.

Huiguan capacity as religious centers for sojourning communities must have been strained by immigration. The largest *huiguan* buildings could not accommodate more than several thousand people, whereas sojourning communities could number more than one hundred thousand. It was at least partly to maintain their image as community leaders that *huiguan* directors sponsored religious festivals which extended beyond their gates. Public processions displayed local strength, territorial jurisdiction, and the wealth and prestige of the merchant-sponsors, creating community among participants and enacting hierarchy.

Huiguan were major though not exclusive organizers of large festivals and processions in Shanghai in the second half of the nineteenth century.[16] They derived authority by both sponsoring and controlling large gatherings which were by their nature prone to be disorderly. *Huiguan* authority as institutions which kept order in the city was thus dependent on the periodic disruption of normal public order.

Although sojourners shared the Chinese ritual calendar with local residents, religious practices also set them apart. *Huiguan* did not participate in local earth god (*tudi*) rituals. Identification with Shanghai soil would have jarred with the fundamental identification with ancestral soil, the "projection of consanguinity into space," to use the description of Fei Xiaotong, that underlay native-place identity. The Siming Gongsuo, for example, had its own *tudi* temple, representing Ningbo soil in Shanghai. Earth god altars were also located in sojourners' coffin repositories.[17]

The two major types of popular religious rituals associated with *huiguan* were *jiao* and *yulanpenhui*. *Jiao* were Daoist rituals on behalf of

16. The funerals of prominent sojourners also occasioned processions, including such things as the distribution of spirit money, the parading of effigies and banners through the streets, horsemen, gongs, "pyramids of fruit . . . baked meats and pigs." Such extravagance attracted thousands of spectators. Because *huiguan* temporarily stored and shipped coffins, these processions often led to the *huiguan* (NCH, January 11, 1871; October 31, 1876; June 8, 1878; June 29, 1878). Other focuses of urban ritual were local temples and local government officials who performed official ritual ceremonies.

17. SB, August 26, 1879; SB, August 25, 1880; SBZX, 260; *Shanghai Siming Gongsuo si da jianzhu zhengxinlu;* Fei Xiaotong, *From the Soil: The Foundations of Chinese Society,* trans. Gary Hamilton and Wang Zheng (Berkeley, Calif., 1992), 123.

territorial cult communities, associated with the consecration and renewal of temples and temple territory. They involved ritual manipula-
tions of temple gods by Daoist priests and were often combined with a
procession by the inhabitants of a particular area associated with a temple. Smaller *jiao* with processions and theatrical performances were associated with celebrations of gods' birthdays.[18]

Yulanpenhui, Buddhist-influenced ceremonies to feed and propitiate
hungry, wandering orphan ghosts, took place in the middle of the seventh month of the Chinese calendar (see Figure 4).[19] Participants carried
grotesque representations of ghosts, set lantern boats afloat for
drowned souls, and scattered rice on the ground and in lakes, streams
and canals. They also attached lanterns to platforms or conical structures, along with sacrificial offerings.

People from Ningbo and Shaoxing prefectures in Zhejiang province,
from the Guang-Zhao and Chaozhou areas of Guangdong, and from
Fujian were known for exuberant *jiao* and *yulanpenhui* in Shanghai.
Preparations were costly and elaborate. In addition to *huiguan* resident
priests, Daoist and Buddhist priests came to Shanghai from as far away
as Guangdong to officiate. Organizers erected bamboo-and-mat platforms to enlarge the dimensions of altars for the three-day ceremony.
Open-air stages were constructed for continual opera performances.
Peddlers and food sellers flocked into Shanghai for the great marketing
opportunity presented by the throngs of participants. Such festivals
brought "enormous trade in sea slugs, glazed ducks and rice cakes,"
spirit money, incense, and ritual paraphernalia.[20]

Processions, which could extend three-quarters of a mile, consisted
of troupes of musicians, laborers dressed as bannermen and officials,
lantern carriers, ancestral tablet bearers, ornamented ponies, Buddhist
and Daoist priests, and sedan chairs carrying major contributors (see

18. *Jiao* were also used to exorcise plague gods. For descriptions of *jiao* and *yulanpenhui*, see Robert P. Weller, "The Politics of Ritual Disguise," MC 13 (January 1987):17–39;
P. Steven Sangren, "Orthodoxy, Heterodoxy, and the Structure of Value in Chinese Rituals," MC 13 (January 1987): 63–89; Stephan Feuchtwang, "City Temples in Taipei under
Three Regimes," in Elvin and Skinner, *The Chinese City between Two Worlds*, 272–73.

19. *Yulanpen* is the Chinese transliteration of the Sanskrit *ullambhana* (deliverance).
The festival was also called *zhongyuanjie*, translated both as Ghost Festival and Universal
Salvation Ritual. For the early history of this festival, see Stephen Teiser, *The Ghost Festival
in Medieval China* (Princeton, N. J., 1988).

20. NCH, August 31, 1867; August 4, 1870; August 10, 1872; August 17, 1872; September 20, 1873; August 11, 1880; September 3, 1887. References to *huiguan* employment of
resident priests may be found in DR (1882–91), 429; DR (1892–1901), 249.

Figure 4). During the period of the *yulanpenhui,* stalls bedecked with red paper invitations to the hungry ghosts filled the streets, stacked with ritual cakes to be purchased for ghostly consumption. Cakes were also distributed to the poor. At various places in the city participants set fires to transmit spirit money, paper clothes and paper houses for the suffering ghosts. Foreigners complained that these bonfires took place during periods of heavy traffic (between 5:00 and 6:00 P.M.), on major roads and bridges. They were at any rate timed and located for peak visibility.[21]

21. NCH, August 31, 1867; August 4, 1870; August 10, 1872; August 17, 1872; September 20, 1873; August 11, 1880; September 3, 1887. The *Dianshizhai* illustration (Figure 4)

Figure 4. *Yulanpenhui.*
The title and caption read, "Ghosts Making Trouble on the Street: *Yulanpen* gatherings in Shanghai are especially spectacular. In the last ten days of the last month, a crowd of Daoist priests and laymen gathered in a procession to offer incense. When they walked through the main street of the British Settlement the people who joined them burned paper ingots along the way. The [British-employed] Sikh police tried unsuccessfully to stop them, so the police dragged two participants to the police station. The people in the procession were enraged. They assembled a ghost gang, in which everyone was horse faced, cow headed, lion toothed and golden eyed. They crowded at the station and fought with their ceremonial knives. The red-turbaned police emanated black ghost power. The blue-faced devil troops exhibited barbarian rabble spirit. The two who were trapped in the devil country have not yet emerged from the door to the underworld." Source: *Dianshizhai huabao* (Dianshi Studio pictorial newspaper), 1983 Guangzhou reprint of late-Qing edition (1884–1898).

Such complex events—which incorporated religious ritual, performance and entertainment, demonstrations of wealth and prestige, charitable acts and free food, and the vigorous transaction of petty business—had multiple meanings. *Yulanpenhui,* which propitiated wandering ghosts, and *jiao,* processions associated with territorial cults, may have had particular resonance for sojourning communities. As the provision of burial services demonstrates, *huiguan* were concerned not only with live sojourners but also with sojourning souls, souls conceived as suffer-

depicts a procession on the main street of the British Settlement, presumably a reference to Nanjing Road.

ing until they could return to their ancestral home. Sojourning ghosts, far from ancestral soil and outsiders in an alien environment, bore a close resemblance to the familyless wandering ghosts invoked by *yulan-penhui*. The concerns of poor male sojourners who lived in Shanghai without wives or children appear in stone inscriptions of Ningbo worker and artisan associations: "Living, we are guests from other parts; dead, we are ghosts from foreign territory."[22]

On another level, the marginal hungry ghosts who demanded charity may have functioned as symbolic representations of the marginal and hungry in Shanghai. Despite the deportations of ruffians and vagabonds that followed the Small Sword Uprising of 1853, such people increased as the city grew, drawing their numbers from refugees and immigrants, those who lost work through the vagaries of Shanghai's shifting labor market. For the many unmarried sojourning men far away from their relatives and without families of their own in Shanghai, the festivals and processions could provide a ritual sense of public belonging. The poor among them also had the right to demand (and receive) gifts of food.[23]

It was perhaps because these ceremonies had such resonance for marginal and potentially disruptive elements that they disturbed Chinese officials. Such gatherings were condemned by the conservative reformer Ding Richang, who served as Governor of Jiangsu beginning in 1867. Ding, who had demonstrated his concern for maintaining order in Shanghai's rapidly changing and increasingly chaotic environment by ruthless beatings, imprisonment and mass deportations of vagabonds during his term as Su-Song-Tai Daotai in 1864–65, prohibited *jiao* and Buddhist festivals. He argued that these were un-Confucian and unrighteous, wasteful, and likely to encourage crime.[24]

There were many reasons why Chinese officials tried to discipline popular festivals, rituals which competed in size and grandeur with

22. SBZX, 406. See also SBZX, 384.

23. Explanation for the prominence of *jiao* — rituals associated with territorial cults — in *huiguan* religious activities may lie in another direction. The *huiguan* was not simply the institution of sojourning in the city; it also embodied a solution to the sojourning condition. Insofar as possible, *huiguan* and sojourning communities re-created or reconstituted the native place in the urban environment of Shanghai. If coffins could not be returned home, they could at least be placed with their *tongxiang* in a cemetery representing their native place, presided over by their local gods in a *yin huiguan*, or *huiguan* for the dead. Whereas *yulanpenhui* may be seen as expressing the special angst of sojourners, *jiao* rituals correspond to the creation of native-place territory in Shanghai.

24. Lu Shiqiang, *Ding Richang yu ziqiang yundong* (Ding Richang and the self-strengthening movement), Zhongyang yanjiu yuan jindai shi yanjiu suo (Academia Sinica, Modern History Institute), 30 (Taipei, 1972), 140–41. Although such concerns were far from new in this period, they were nonetheless voiced with particular urgency.

official ceremonies. The potentially violent crowds certainly worried them. Western observers noted bloody accidents and quarrels as the poor jostled and pressed to receive cakes and vied to participate in the processions.[25]

The symbolic content of these rituals also challenged the state. *Yulanpenhui* involved ritual sacrifice, not to gods (which could symbolically represent the emperor and on whom the state could inscribe values which would uphold the Confucian state hierarchy) but to orphan ghosts. Because ghosts were anomic and marginal individuals, outside the hierarchical social order, they represented illegitimate power. A ritual like the *yulanpenhui,* which recognized ghostly demands for food as legitimate, may have made the state particularly uneasy.[26]

Ding's efforts to suppress popular processions in the late 1860s were followed by yearly prohibitions by the Daotai and city magistrates for the next several decades. Official proclamations permitted merchants to construct altars and conduct ceremonies for the ghosts but forbade them to organize *yulanpenhui* processions and "incite the crowds to riot." Chinese constables, *dibao,* were instructed to intervene against processions. Anyone who dared to ignore the laws was warned of merciless punishment.[27]

Chinese officials also sought foreign assistance in suppressing the processions. The Daotai requested the Consul General of the International Settlement to issue placards to admonish and guide *huiguan* and sojourning communities. Settlement police were requested to uphold the prohibition, as they indeed appear to be doing in Figure 4.[28]

Processions continued nonetheless. Even under the strict rule of

25. NCH, January 11, 1871; September 20, 1873. A Presbyterian missionary account of *yulanpen* in Taiwan in this period suggests that this jostling may have been part of a popular ritual which followed the priestly ceremony, called "robbing the lonely ghosts:"

The most elaborate and hideous scene I ever witnessed was the "Seventh Moon Feast" . . . a very unspiritual mob—thousands and thousands of hungry beggars, tramps, blacklegs, desperadoes of all sorts . . . surged and swelled in every part of the open space. . . . At length the spirits were satisfied and the gong was sounded. . . . That was the signal for the mob; and scarcely had the first stroke fallen when that whole scene was one mass of arms and legs and tongues. . . . In one wild scramble, groaning and yelling all the while, trampling on those who had lost their footing or were smothered by the falling cones, . . . they all made for the coveted food. (Quoted in Weller, "Politics of Ritual Disguise," 23.)

26. This argument is made in Weller, "Politics of Ritual Disguise," 24. See also Duara, "Superscribing Symbols."

27. SB, August 9, 1872; August 11, 1872.

28. Letter from Daotai Liu Ruifen in Shanghai Municipal Council, *Annual Report of the Shanghai Municipal Council,* Shanghai (hereafter referred to as MCR), 1880, 57. Settlement police presumably had their own motivations for suppressing processions.

Ding Richang, the *North China Herald* observed that "[proclamations were] still hanging on the city walls when a monster procession took place." In 1872, "the autumnal religious processions . . . [were] engaged in as freely as ever." By the end of the decade, despite the Shanghai magistrate's "indefatigable" floggings of procession promoters, the "religious fervor" of Chinese residents still broke through.[29]

In the last quarter of the century, newspaper references to unruly *jiao* appear less frequently, and annual *yulanpenhui* took place within the confines of cemetery walls.[30] The Guang-Zhao cemetery was noted for the scale of its *yulanpenhui:*

The property is particularly large. There is a hall for the gods, a reception hall, an artificial hill and a small lake. In all seasons the flowers and trees can be enjoyed for the scenery. . . . Each year in the seventh moon there is a *yulanpenhui* and celebration of the *zhongyuan* festival. The *tongxiang* collect money and meet, hiring monks and Daoist masters to propitiate the roving ghosts. They not only burn mountains of incense and candles but also set up stands displaying curios and the work of famous calligraphers. Crowds persist into the night, viewing lanterns and theater. On the 14th, 15th and 16th, the people are numerous, wearing hair ornaments, scented clothing and fans, their numbers increasing into the evening. The Daotai fears ruffians, robbery and theft, thus he sends braves in addition to his attendants, arranging for each to separately patrol the area. Thus fights may be broken up.[31]

Although the Guang-Zhao festivities remained grand, a process of confinement resulted in smaller and less public festival celebrations. By the turn of the century, at least in the Ningbo community, different occupational subgroups took turns at using the *huiguan* for their individual *jiao*. The *huiguan* remained at the ceremonial center, but the community under the *huiguan* umbrella was increasingly divided by shifting ritual practices by occupation and class.[32]

This shift also reflected changes in elite public opinion. In the 1880s reformist attacks on *yulanpenhui* appeared in the *Shenbao* which echoed

29. April 29, 1871; August 17, 1872; April 27, 1878. Shanghai processions from the late 1880s are depicted in the *Dianshizhai huabao* (Dianshi Studio pictorial newspaper), 1884–1898 (Guangzhou reprint, 1983).

30. It should be stressed that, although ceremonies were confined, there is no evidence that the incidence of ceremonies decreased. See SBZX, 384–85, 403, 412.

31. *Huitu Shanghai zazhi* (Shanghai pictorial miscellany) (Shanghai, 1905), vol. 6, 8b; SBZX, 402, 404, 406.

32. Serial use of *huiguan* rooms for subgroups' *jiao* continued through the 1920s (SGY, 1922–23).

Ding Richang's conservative Confucian condemnation of superstition and waste and which intermixed traditional arguments with modern-sounding practicality: "This Seventh Moon Festival is very popular in Shanghai, and the Guang-Zhao Gongsuo's *yulanpenhui* is the most extravagant and luxurious. They make paper buildings and enormous paper constructions. Every year they spend tons of money. *Yulanpenhui* are an old custom and people believe if they contribute they will gain protection. But such things are uncertain. No one knows if helping ghosts will effect a positive result. . . . The *yulanpenhui* is to relieve the homeless ghosts. But they are already dead. . . . Why not help the living?" This writer argued, tongue in cheek, that the ceremonies did not even serve the interests of native-place sentiment. *Yulanpenhui* did not just assist Guangdong ghosts, it also helped ghosts from other places. "Now if you save the money and send it directly to Guangdong, your own place will derive all the benefit." He recommended frugality, even if tradition could not be abandoned. When floods struck Guangdong in 1880, *huiguan* directors were exhorted to restrict their festival spending and promote public righteousness by caring for their own people:[33] "Because you are from Guangdong . . . you must be concerned with the plight of your fellow-provincials. You will contribute to Guangdong because you are from Guangdong. If you don't contribute, who can they depend on? . . . You could reduce your *yulanpenhui* expenses by 70–80% and give this money to Guangdong. Sending it to the native place will improve your reputation."[34]

In the meantime, such articles did not inhibit public enjoyment of a good festival. Even elite public opinion, as expressed in the progressive *Shenbao,* was torn between reformist criticisms of "superstitious" and "wasteful" ceremonies and appreciation of festival marvels. An editorial written at the same time as the Guangdong flood (and including a few

33. SB, August 6, 1880. It should not be imagined that members of the Guangdong sojourning elite did not share these reformist sentiments. The scholar-official Zheng Guanying, whose long association with the Guang-Zhao Gongsuo culminated in his appointment as chief director in 1915, both condemned the vain waste of money for processions and—on occasion—found reason to sponsor *jiao* (Xia Dongyuan, *Zheng Guanying ji*, vol. 1, 34, vol. 2, 1226–27, 1574). Shifts in elite public opinion are analyzed in Rankin (*Elite Activism*) in the context of an emerging "public sphere" in the last decades of the Qing. On the diverging religious concerns of elite and commoner sojourners, see Peter J. Golas, "Early Ch'ing Guilds," in Skinner, *The City in Late Imperial China,* 574; R. D. Belsky, "Bones of Contention: The Siming Gongsuo Riots of 1874 and 1898," *Papers on Chinese History* 1 (Spring 1992):68–69.

34. August 6, 1880.

perfunctory comments about wastefulness) expressed clearly the popular appeal of the *jiao* for people in all walks of life:

The lights and ornaments at the Guang-Zhao Shanzhuang were even more intricate than last year. . . . In the daytime it was very crowded and lively. Most who come in the day are . . . low class people. But at night come the people with fragrant clothes, their shadows like running water. . . . The noise of carts and vehicles is like a waterfall, flowing until morning. At the east gate on a construction of about one hundred paces in length hung one hundred lights, high and low, a city of fire. Lamps hung over the gate as high as heaven, illuminating an ingenious paper Guangdong opera below. . . . Opposite were paper constellations and a marvelous crystal palace. . . . Everywhere hung calligraphy and paintings of famous people. It was very elegant. In the International Settlement some people . . . made an altar. . . . They had Ningbo fireworks . . . but it was nothing compared to the Guang-Zhao Shanzhuang.[35]

Despite increasing claims on *huiguan* money for public charity, in their confined and increasingly compartmentalized forms, festivals associated with *huiguan* remained popular into the twentieth century.[36]

If festivals incurred considerable expense and problems of control, they also represented a kind of compromise between *huiguan* leaders and groups in the sojourning community which might otherwise have threatened *huiguan* authority. Processions not only gave *huiguan* an opportunity to assert their centrality in the *tongxiang* community and their importance in the city but also provided occasions for public displays of group pride and belonging for less socially elevated but nonetheless powerful groups. The wealthy and prominent *huiguan* leaders gained popular prestige and recognition by sponsoring processions. Festivals provided poor sojourners with temporary employment, free food, and also a moment of ritual role reversal in the opportunity to dress as officials and notables. Festivals were also a likely source of profit for secret societies. Information from other cities suggests the dependence of *huiguan* leaders on professional organizers to solicit additional "contributions" for these festivals. Such organizers were often secret-society members who used this license to extort money.[37]

35. August 22, 1882.

36. Chen Boxi, *Shanghai yishi daguan*, vol. 3, 70–71.

37. SB, August 30, 1873; NCH, January 11, 1871. For a discussion of "topsy-turvy" costuming and role reversals in European festivals, see Natalie Zemon Davis, *Society and Culture in Early Modern France* (Stanford, Calif., 1965), 97–123. On secret-society involvement in festivals, see Feuchtwang, "City Temples," 287; Tanaka Issei, "The Social and Historical Context of Ming-Ch'ing Local Drama," in Johnson, Nathan and Rawski, *Popu-*

Huiguan authority depended on the leaders' ability to create a sense of community hierarchically arranged below the *huiguan*. Nonparticipation in popular festivals or serious restraint of crowd activities would have created visible lines of opposition within the community, placing *huiguan* leaders outside expressions of popular sentiment. As sponsors, they could preside over and benefit from popular enthusiasm.

Religious ceremonies also brought workers' associations (*hui*) formally into the *huiguan* institutional structure. Because rituals (including burial arrangements) were expensive, they motivated the formation of organizations to collect funds and compelled cooperation and coordination among separate organizations. In the late nineteenth century, as the merchant directors who comprised the *huiguan* elite became more focused on other forms of public activism, Ningbo workers and artisans formed mutual-aid associations which collected funds and invested in city property in order to have a stable funding base from which to assist members with burial costs and the costs of *jiao* and *yulanpenhui*. In the last decade of the nineteenth century, these associations began a process of formal incorporation into the merchant-dominated Siming Gongsuo to ensure access to *huiguan* religious halls and altars. The formation of worker mutual-aid associations and their incorporation into the *huiguan,* a process which continued into the first decades of the twentieth century, reflected necessities imposed by demographic growth. By the turn of the century Zhejiang sojourners had grown rapidly from a mid-century population of approximately sixty thousand to well over one hundred thousand. Communitywide access to *huiguan* resources even at ritual moments vastly exceeded *huiguan* capacity (and the funding capacities and inclinations of *huiguan* directors). Non-elite members of the community clearly felt the need to both organize and effectively "buy into" the powerful Siming Gongsuo in order to ensure access and protection.[38]

As early as 1863–64, Ningbo foreign-employed workers and servants

---

lar Culture in Late Imperial China, 143; Tom Shaw, "Liumang in Taipei" (paper presented at Stanford University, November 26, 1986).

38. SBZX, 360, 384–86, 403–4, 406–8, 412, 418–24; Belsky, "Bones of Contention." The concern for burial arrangements expressed in the stone inscriptions left by these worker and artisan associations makes clear the limitations of *huiguan* welfare services for members of the broad sojourning community. In contrast to rapidly expanding Zhejiang and Jiangsu populations, Guangdong sojourners declined in number from their midcentury high of eighty thousand to perhaps as few as fifty thousand. See Zou Yiren, *Jiu Shanghai renkou bianqian* (Research on population change in old Shanghai) (Shanghai, 1980); Hokari, "Kindai shanhai."

formally established the Changsheng (Long Life) Yulanpenhui, a religious association to ensure the ritual provision of *yulanpen* sacrifices at
the Siming Gongsuo for a period of three days and nights each year. In
1896–97 the Changsheng association transferred its considerable property holdings into the *huiguan*. The terms of the arrangement provided
for permanent *huiguan* management of Changsheng Hui assets in return for guaranteed provision of *yulanpen* expenses. A stone inscription
authored by Shen Honglai, leader of the Changsheng Hui, documents
the contrast between the concern of this man of the laboring classes
for protecting Ningbo coffins and the expediency of the elite *huiguan*
directors. Learning of a *huiguan* plan in 1898 to displace four hundred
coffins in order to construct a new coffin repository and road, Shen
protested to the directors, pressuring them into showing more respect
for the Ningbo dead.[39]

Ningbo carpenters similarly organized a Changxing (Lasting Prosperity) Hui and established a formal tie with the Siming Gongsuo in
1879 to guarantee access to burial services, coffin storage and shipment.
Each carpenter contributed small but steady amounts of money, which
the association kept in a fund. By 1894 the carpenters' association owned
property and capital of five thousand yuan. In 1899, following the model
of the Changsheng Hui, it asked the *huiguan* to manage its holdings,
ensuring yearly income for coffins, *yulanpen* sacrifices for hungry ghosts,
expenses for Qing Ming (the day of sweeping graves), and a *jiao* at the
end of the year. Similar arrangements, recorded in stone inscriptions,
were made by associations of Ningbo butchers, ferry workers, dockworkers and shiphands, bamboo workers, carriage varnishers and metal
workers, all of which formally placed themselves under the organizational umbrella of the Siming Gongsuo during the last two decades of
the Qing.[40]

The exuberance of religious festivals at the end of the Qing suggests

39. Additional income from the holdings went to the *gongsuo* for public works. The
gongsuo was held responsible for any necessary property repairs. See SBZX, 261–67, 428–
32. Shen's argument with *gongsuo* leaders in this incident is discussed in Belsky ("Bones of
Contention," 68), though the date of the incident is mistakenly given as 1878–79.

40. SBZX, 360, 384–86, 403–4, 406–8, 412, 416–17. Rowe discusses the process of
commendation of *hui* assets to *huiguan* control in "Ming-Qing Guilds," *Encyclopedia of
Chinese History and Culture* (Naples, Italy, forthcoming). A variety of factors influenced
this process. Rowe stresses economic motivations (inflationary pressures), the local self-
government movement and a tendency toward organizational synthesis in this period.
Hokari ("Kindai shanhai," 81–84) points out increasing restrictions on coffin storage and
workers' increased need for *huiguan* assistance with coffin shipment. The precise combina-

that although *huiguan* sponsored such events, their control over them was limited. In the immigrant, densely populated but largely unpoliced "frontier" city of Shanghai, *huiguan* interest lay in extending ritual activity to incorporate popular festivals. It is not clear that *huiguan* directors could have suppressed popular demonstrations if they had tried. The sponsorship of large-scale community events, on the other hand, established and enhanced the image of *huiguan* as patron organizations within their large *tongxiang* communities. Similarly, prominence in religious functions, including burials and propitiations of gods and ghosts, invested the *huiguan* with more sacred authority. Provision for ghosts, as well as disaster victims, the poor and the wayward all served to enhance paternalistic authority. As the *huiguan* merchant elite moved toward a more secular and national public-spiritedness, *huiguan* directors increased their distance from festivals. They nonetheless benefited from the compartmentalized incorporation of more religious sojourners into the *huiguan*. While the *huiguan* repositioned itself, shifting from organizing common religious rituals to managing group investments, the workers and craftsmen who continued to believe in *jiao* and *yulanpenhui* used *huiguan* facilities, but their rituals became private occasions.

   Opera and Native-Place Community. Huiguan performances, like the religious festivals of which they were often part, were fundamental in knitting together a community out of disparate class elements. Theatrical performances, like processions, served the twin functions of *huiguan* publicity and popular expression. The noisy open-air performance of local opera in the dialect and style of the native-place asserted sojourner presence in the city. *Huiguan* opera performances could also exacerbate preexisting tensions between regional groups.[41]

---

tion of factors motivating the property transfers remains unclear. Aside from religious concerns, stela accounts provide only formulistic motivations (references to the uncertainties of life and livelihood). Although the contexts of inflation and governmental pressure are important, the outstanding concerns expressed in the stelae are the religious beliefs of non-elite sojourners and their desire for spiritual security in a time of change. Based on SBZX records and Tōyō Bunka holdings, Hokari ("Kindai shanhai," 83) counts a total of fourteen *hui* which were incorporated in this manner into the *gongsuo*.

   41. A dramatic example of tension arising from *huiguan* performances is found outside Shanghai history in Xiangtan in 1819. Local Hunanese jeered at Jiangxi opera at the Jiangxi Huiguan, setting off a riot in which twenty people were killed (Peter Perdue, "Insiders and Outsiders," MC 12 [April 1986]:166, 176). Perdue finds in *huiguan* opera a "cultural basis for collective action" which united wealthy merchants with lower classes. As Xiangtan grew, the *huiguan* incorporated shopkeepers, porters and boatmen. This

Like the expansion of *huiguan* religious functions to incorporate the needs and interests of the broader community, dialect opera was a late development in the evolution of *huiguan* as urban institutions. In Shanghai, this change occurred in the late nineteenth century, as *huiguan* endeavored to represent the increasingly large and diverse sojourning communities which resulted from immigration.

Public theaters did not exist generally in Shanghai until the last decades of the nineteenth century. Prior to this time, as the diary of an opera connoisseur in Shanghai in the 1850s confirms, *huiguan* opera performances made native-place associations important cultural centers in the city.[42] Although most people went for the pleasure of seeing opera, *huiguan* opera was conceived ritually as the provision of entertainment for the gods (*jisi xiqu*, sacrificial theater). This ritual function was expressed in *huiguan* architecture, in which elaborate stages faced the altars of *huiguan* deities across the central courtyard. The human audience for these performances was initially small: sojourning merchants, literati and officials.

The development of popular urban theater from *huiguan* theater, a process which has been described by Tanaka Issei, reflected a prior process of popularization that took place within *huiguan* performances themselves. This popularization of *huiguan* theater followed city growth and reflected the tastes of the increasing numbers of sojourning craftsmen and workers. These performances, still funded by the *huiguan* leaders, were known as charitable, or righteous, performances (*yiyan*), conveying the idea that *huiguan*-sponsored opera was a form of community service or patronage.[43]

---

broadening of *huiguan* community worried the Jiaqing emperor, who forbade collections for opera performances, but he did not prohibit the performances themselves. This paradoxical stance reflected unwillingness to make an enemy of the *huiguan* on which the state depended for social control and other matters (Perdue, "Insiders and Outsiders," 190). Although performances at Shanghai *huiguan* had less dramatic consequences, they nonetheless incited periodic disputes over native-place turf in the city. See Chen Boxi, *Shanghai yishi daguan*, vol. 3, 181; SB, June 20, 1872; SB, July 5, 1872; NCH, June 22, 1867.

42. In an 1859 diary entry, Wang Tao recounts listening to opera at the Zhe-Shao Gongsuo: "The style was impassioned, the depiction entrancing, the scenery pleasing to both mind and eye" ("Heng hua guan riji" [Diary from the hall of fragrant splendor], in *Qingdai riji huichao* [Transcriptions of Qing diaries] [Shanghai, 1982], 256; Chen Boxi, *Shanghai yishi daguan*, vol. 3, 156). In addition to *huiguan* opera, temple festivals provided occasions for opera performances.

43. This term was used by an elderly Shanghai resident (interview with Zhu Yongfang, b. 1899, Shanghai, October 1982), who attended *huiguan* theater performances as a child. He recalled performances on the Chinese New Year, during the *Duanwu* and Mid-

Opera was not performed in local dialects until the late Qing. The earliest *huiguan* served communities of officials and scholars who favored the elite operatic styles of the court. Merchant-dominated *huiguan*, like those established in Shanghai, initially modeled themselves after the scholar-official *huiguan*. This orientation led early merchant *huiguan* to put on selections from *kunqu*, a form patronized by the court as the official national operatic style.[44]

This changed in the late Qing, when *huiguan* in expanding commercial centers began to sponsor performances by traveling opera troupes from their native places, operas performed in native-place dialect. *Huiguan* performances also began to reflect the tastes of a more popular constituency, discarding conventional and conservative tales of loyalty and filiality for the excitement of romantic love and martial heroism.[45]

As this shift suggests, by the late nineteenth century *huiguan* opera performances reflected a marriage of elite and non-elite influences. Merchant prosperity enabled *huiguan* to support increasingly lavish performances by opera troupes from the native place. The less cosmopolitan horizons of non-elite sojourners formed dialect and cultural barriers to the appreciation of any opera other than that of the native place. Because *huiguan* were the patron organizations of a large sojourning community, they could not afford to alienate that community with unfamiliar and elite cultural forms, so they catered increasingly to the parochial tastes of workers and craftsmen.[46] In this fashion, *huiguan* came increasingly to promote local native-place rather than elite culture. By cultivating a broader sojourning community, *huiguan* became less rather than more cosmopolitan cultural centers in this period.

Autumn Festivals (5th moon, 5th day; 8th moon, 15th day), and on *Zhongyuan* (date of the *yulanpenhui*, 7th moon, 15th day).

44. Tanaka Issei, "Shindai no kaikan engeki ni tsuite" (Regarding *huiguan* theater in modern times), *Tōyō bunka kenkyu kiyo* 86 (November 1981), 442–59. *Kunqu*, originally a form of Suzhou opera, was adopted and propagated by the court as the national style during the Ming (1368–1644).

45. Tanaka, "Shindai no kaikan engeki ni tsuite," 409–10, 422. See also Tanaka, "Ming-Ch'ing Local Drama," 143–60, for a typology of local opera based on the sponsorship of performances.

46. Tanaka, "Shindai no kaikan engeki ni tsuite," 408, 458–60. An account of *huiguan* opera expenditures is not possible because performances were frequently paid for by private contributions. The Guang-Zhao Gongsuo account-book (*Guang-Zhao gongsuo zhengxinlu* 1899) lists only what was paid from the general fund, to make up for spending that exceeded what was collected. A stela dated 1875–76 lists contributions of ninety-five shops belonging to the Zhe-Shao Huiguan, each of which gave ten yuan to a permanent fund for performances on the birthday of the god Guandi (SBZX, 229–30).

Tanaka identifies three phases in state attitudes toward *huiguan* opera, reflecting shifts in opera content. In the early and middle Qing, the state attempted to suppress popular opera performance but permitted the sacrificial performances of officials and merchants within *huiguan*. Such performances were considered Confucian and neither lewd nor wantonly martial. In the late Qing, as urban public theater began to develop outside *huiguan,* the government viewed *huiguan* performances as preferable to what was offered in public theaters. *Huiguan* theaters were protected because the government believed that the elite directors would exercise conservative taste and shun unorthodox plays. By the end of the Qing, as *huiguan* performances increasingly embraced the "lewd" and martial themes the state opposed, the government made weak attempts to restrict these types of performances, but it refrained from vigorous suppression of *huiguan* theater.[47]

Huiguan theater, which continued into the early twentieth century before being displaced by public theaters, may have served state interests in social control just as it served the interests of the *huiguan* leaders. Opera both brought a wide community into the *huiguan* and reinforced the hierarchy within that community. *Huiguan* leaders and their selected guests sat either on a raised platform around the stage or along the two side balconies (*kanlou* or *kantai*). The rest of the crowd, those who were not the benefactors but the recipients, pressed into the wide courtyard. From the courtyard, the audience had to look up, not only to the performance but also to the feasting and richly clothed patrons of their community (see Figure 5).

Righteousness and Reputation

A third source of *huiguan* authority and an important aspect of community identification and cohesion involved the *huiguan*

47. Tanaka, "Shindai no kaikan engeki ni tsuite," 458–60. The 1899 compilation of government institutions (*Da Qing huidian*), treats opera together with festivals, secret societies and novels, expressing the state's view of their interrelated potential for subversiveness. See Roger Thompson, "Local Society, Opera and the State in Late Imperial China" (paper presented at the 39th Annual Meeting of the Association of Asian Studies, April 10–12, 1987); Tanaka, "Ming-Ch'ing Local Drama." In 1868 Ding Richang launched a campaign against immoral theater. Lu Shiqiang, *Ding Richang,* 141–44. Ding singled out stories from *Shuihuzhuan* (Outlaws of the marsh) and *Xixiangji* (Romance of the western chamber) for encouraging violence and labeled *Hongloumeng* (Dream of red

directors' maintenance of group honor. As different regional groups interacted and competed with one another in the city, people from each native place developed reputations. An active tactic of native-place rivalry involved the creation of regional stereotypes and the defense of regional reputations. In the late Qing, as the following quotation illustrates, these reputations (and the native-place identifications they implied) were not given but contested:

> People are born lucky or unlucky. If lucky, they are born in Qufu, and the closeness of sages will enable them to get a good education. . . . People who are unlucky enough to be born in a bad place suffer from having bad people as their fellow-provincials. We were not lucky, and thus we were born in Guangdong. . . . The people we call compradors, "foreigners' dogs," "Guangdong sluts" and "saltwater sisters" all come from Xiangshan county. The people of this county are born without a sense of shame. They are too low and despicable to mention. . . . Xiangshan people use their lack of shame as a way to make money. . . . In former times people could petition to change their native place. But we cannot change our native place, and thus we are in a dilemma. Gentlemen, in the future when you write your articles . . . could you blame explicitly the compradors or the "foreigners' dogs"? Please don't say generally, "the Guangdong people."[48]

During the 1870s and 1880s economic rivalry between Guangdong and Zhejiang people, combined with a Zhejiang-dominated press, produced a lively public discourse about Guangdong identity. Frequent press attacks on Guangdong identity sensitized the Guangdong community and activated the Guangdong elite to defend Guangdong honor. The existence of a positive Guangdong identity depended on its construction and vigilant defense by a wealthy Guangdong sojourner elite. In contrast, groups without influential elites lacked the wherewithal to establish and maintain their reputation and therefore lacked a key element in the formation of a positive sense of group identity. People from northern Jiangsu, for example, lacked advocates who could contest negative stereotypes. As Honig's study illustrates, although other people

chambers) the most subversive of all. When theater disturbances occurred, officials attributed them to the immorality of the plays (SB, July 5, 1872). Magistrates also posted notices on the walls of local theaters prohibiting immoral plays (MCR for 1887).

48. SB, January 14, 1874. See Honig (*Creating Chinese Ethnicity*) on the construction of negative stereotypes of people from Subei. Honig argues (p. 4) on the basis of the Subei example that the construction of native-place identities was part of a discourse about class. Although low economic position was obviously important in the construction of Subei identity, as the discourse about Guangdong people demonstrates, relatively wealthy sojourner communities were also vulnerable to negative stereotypes.

spoke of a Subei group, Subei sojourners themselves lacked both community and well-defined native-place identity.[49]

49. Honig states (*Creating Chinese Ethnicity*, 12) that from the late nineteenth century, "conflict between Subei and Jiangnan natives, by far, was the most salient native-place cleavage." This may have been true from the perspectives of workers from northern and southern Jiangsu, but it was not obviously the case for people from Zhejiang who Honig includes in her categorization of "Jiangnan natives" or for sojourners from other areas. In the late nineteenth century, Zhejiang elites and workers were both preoccupied with Guangdong competitors. A preeminent Subei–Jiangnan cleavage is not apparent from the perspective of the *Shenbao*, which devoted considerably more column space in the late nineteenth century to the construction and discussion of Guangdong identity (a conse-

Figure 5. *Huiguan* opera.
The illustration depicts a Guangdong Huiguan opera performance
which was held to worship the
god Guandi. The moralistic caption describes the crowd as large
and disorderly, crushing and injuring a young man who was lured
inside by the sounds of gongs and
drums. Having pointed out the
dangers of attending the opera,
the author concludes by admonishing young people to avoid such
dangerous pastimes. Source: *Dianshizhai huabao* (Dianshi Studio pictorial newspaper), 1983 Guangzhou reprint of late-Qing edition
(1884–1898).

Huiguan leaders maintained their native-place reputation through a
variety of tactics. *Huiguan* prestige was bolstered by an association's
ability to appropriate for itself high claims of moral purpose. Insofar as
huiguan directors could present themselves as exemplars of Confucian
virtue, they could be regarded as deserving leaders both in the sojourner
community and in the city. As a consequence of this principle of authority and legitimation, *huiguan* were given to displays of benevolence. As

quence of the Guangdong–Ningbo economic rivalry which underlay the economic development of the city).

a correlate, *huiguan* were deeply sensitive to threats to the honor of their native place.

Righteous Charity. *Huiguan* and *huiguan* leaders demonstrated their benevolence in both ritual and substantive acts of public service and philanthropy. These included the support of hospitals and benevolent institutions (*shantang*) which cared for orphans, widows, the ill and the poor; the provision of relief to *tongxiang* in Shanghai; the maintenance of "righteous burial grounds" for paupers; the sponsorship of "righteous performances"; and the observance of the correct ritual in the worship of native-place gods.

They also served as important collection agencies, organizing and dispensing relief in periods of natural disasters. As *Shenbao* editorials criticizing festival waste made clear, maintaining "face" in Shanghai included demonstrating care for one's native place. As their Shanghai resources grew in the 1870s and 1880s, *huiguan* responded to disasters in their native areas with alacrity. When devastating floods hit Guangdong in 1885, for example, the Guang-Zhao Gongsuo launched a citywide relief-collection campaign, successfully soliciting contributions not only from *tongxiang* but also from other *huiguan* and from several foreign companies.[50]

Other demonstrations of righteousness are better understood as purely symbolic. It is difficult otherwise to explain a single roundup of three thousand beggars by the Silk Huiguan for the purpose of feeding each one a bowl of rice gruel and sending them off with fifty copper cash.[51] In a similar vein Tang Maozhi, the director of the Guang-Zhao Gongsuo, became deeply concerned with the shooting of stray dogs in the International Settlement. He arranged with a Shanghai benevolent institution that the dogs be caught and sent by boat to Suzhou, where they would be freed.[52]

Defending Native-Place Honor. Benevolent activities and the creation of a righteous image, even through the rather crude, if en-

---

50. Tang Maozhi, a Guang-Zhao Gongsuo director, also used his compradorial connections to solicit funds from western companies (NCH, April 10, 1858; NCH, July 10, 1885; NCH, July 17, 1885; NCH, September 25, 1885; NCH, October 7, 1885).

51. NCH, June 19, 1885.

52. MCR for 1894, 57.

tirely traditional, habit of labeling their works "righteous" (*yi*),[53] reveal a concern for reputation based on Confucian ideals of governance which transcended the native-place identity of the *tongxiang* group. *Huiguan* leaders demonstrated leadership qualities by joining together with directors of other *huiguan* to sponsor famine relief and contribute to local benevolent institutions. In this concern for righteous governance, *huiguan* appear as urban analogs to socially activist gentry institutions.

A contrasting area of *huiguan* concern for reputation appealed to a different source of righteousness, one which emphasized the purity and integrity of the *tongxiang* group and stressed the need for boundaries. In this regard, *huiguan* were deeply concerned with the purity and honor of *tongxiang* women. Because the *huiguan* as an institution depended on the maintenance of an idea of native-place community, it was critical for the *huiguan* leadership to act in such a way as to maintain the integrity of the community. In this type of behavior, *huiguan* acted in the manner of a lineage or kin network. A dramatic example of *huiguan* concern with community purity may be seen in the case of an ill-fated alliance between women of a wealthy sojourning Guangdong family and an actor who was not only despicable for his low profession but came from a rival native-place group.[54]

Moving Mount Tai to Squash an Egg: The Yang Yuelou Case. At noon on December 23, 1873, a young Chinese woman in bridal dress was conveyed in an open wheelbarrow through the streets of the International Settlement on the way to the Mixed Court.[55] This parody of a respectable wedding procession (in which the bride was normally hidden from public exposure, ensconced in an elaborate palanquin), attracted a crowd of people who spread notice of the impending case.

53. This labeling followed official convention—there were righteous granaries (*yicang*), righteous taxes (*yijuan*), and so forth.
54. The following narrative draws on mutually reinforcing elements in the numerous accounts in SB from December 1873 to April 1874; NCH, December 25, 1873; NCH, January 29, 1874; NCH, February 12, 1874; NCH, June 6, 1874; NCH, February 10, 1876; NCH, February 17, 1876; Chen Boxi, *Shanghai yishi daguan.*
55. In 1868 the Mixed Court moved from the British Consulate to new premises on Nanjing Road. This procession therefore took place on the main thoroughfare of the settlement. Anatol Kotenev, who completed a commissioned study of the Mixed Court in 1925, noted that in this early period the Mixed Court served as a branch of the District Magistrate's Court, commenting that, "[Mixed Court Magistrates] were marionettes in the hands of their superiors and powerful merchant guilds, who used them as a tool to regain lost positions and to get a firm footing in the Settlement" (Anatol M. Kotenev, *Shanghai: Its Mixed Court and Council* [Shanghai, 1925], 51–52, 54, 73, 75–76).

When the court convened the next day, the jostling onlookers over-flowed the courtyards, blocking traffic outside. The extraordinary inter-est aroused by the case owed to the twin attractions of a scandal staining a prominent family and rumors of illicit liaisons with the star of the Shanghai theater world.

The girl was of Guangdong origin. Her father, surnamed Wei, was a tea merchant and comprador for a foreign firm.[56] Like other wealthy sojourning merchants, Mr. Wei maintained two households, one in Shanghai and one in his native place. Mr. Wei's concubine, née Wang, was in charge of the Shanghai household. His other wives lived in Guangdong.

Madame Wei was an avid opera-goer who frequently attended the performances of the famous actor, Yang Yuelou.[57] While Mr. Wei was transacting business in Fuzhou, Madame Wei betrothed her stepdaugh-ter Abao to the actor, despite the fact that actors were considered disrep-utable.

During a trip to Shanghai, Mr. Wei's brother learned of the betrothal. Lacking the lineage solidarity he could have drawn on back home, he turned to his fellow-sojourners in the city. The *huiguan* directors dis-cussed the impending threat to the honor of their community and ruled that Yang should annul the betrothal to save the face of the Wei lineage. They notified Yang of their decision, and Yang met with his Anhui fellow-countrymen to decide what to do.

Yang's *tongxiang* reasoned that the affair was already concluded be-cause the betrothal had been properly arranged. Supported by his *tong-xiang*, Yang refused to back out and concluded the marriage through secret negotiations with Madame Wei.[58] Toward the end of December, servants delivered the bride to the Yang household. Madame Wei

56. Two merchants with the family name of Wei are mentioned in connection with the Guang-Zhao Gongsuo: Wei Wenpu and Wei Xiuchuan (Xu Run, *Nianpu,* 16; "Shang-hai Guang-Zhao huiguan yuanqi." Both names appear as founding directors ("Chongjian Guang-Zhao huiguan dongshi" [Huiguan directors at the rebuilding of the Guang-Zhao Huiguan], undated, hand-copied document, courtesy of Du Li, Shanghai Museum).

57. At the time of this case there were three or four important theaters in Shanghai, two of which—the Dan Gui Chayuan and the Jin Gui Xuan—were highly reputed. Yang performed in the latter.

58. This incident, like others related in the *Shenbao,* suggests that in a city like Shang-hai, resident wives or concubines of sojourning husbands had opportunities to take on more independent decision-making roles than did women in nonsojourner families, not only because the lineage was largely absent but also because the household itself was often fragmented. If Madame Wei stands out for her willful decision making, within the year she nonetheless conformed to a more traditional female role by committing suicide.

packed her own belongings and secretly moved in as well. When Mr. Wei's servants discovered her absence and the absence of valuable household objects they reported the matter to friends of Mr. Wei.

Mr. Wei's friends were outraged by the secret marriage and called a meeting at the Guang-Zhao Gongsuo. The *huiguan* petitioned Magistrate Chen at the Mixed Court, demanding the arrests of the women and the actor, accusing Yang of kidnapping, rape and theft. Accordingly, the magistrate dispatched his runners. The runners broke into Yang's house and arrested Yang and the Wei women, whom they found in the midst of wedding festivities.

Because of the value of Wei household objects found in the Yang compound, Magistrate Chen concluded that the magnitude of the case exceeded the jurisdiction of the Mixed Court.[59] He sent the accused for interrogation by the Shanghai District Magistrate. The District Magistrate was the Guang-Zhao Gongsuo director, Ye Tingjuan. When Yang first appeared before him, Ye ordered lictors to suspend his body and inflict one hundred and fifty blows of the bamboo rod on his ankles. Under torture, Yang confessed to abducting Abao. After a lashing on the back Madame Wei admitted that she had permitted the marriage even though the Wei family had deemed it inappropriate. The magistrate also interrogated Abao, who feebly protested that she had only followed the maxim, "If you marry a chicken then you follow a chicken." When an examination proved that she was not a virgin, Yang was accused of rape. Powder discovered at Yang's home was produced in court and declared an aphrodisiac, used by Yang to incite ill behavior on the part of the women (making Yang's crime more despicable and the women more innocent).[60] Magistrate Ye sentenced Yang to branding, exile and forced military service, a verdict the *Shenbao* described as a Guangdong victory.[61]

Although the disposal of the case reportedly pleased the guardians of

59. At this time it was common for the Mixed Court Magistrate to decline judgment on major cases and defer to the Shanghai District Magistrate, who was higher in rank (the Mixed Court Magistrate was really only a Vice-Magistrate). The move from the Mixed Court to the Shanghai District *yamen* also prevented foreign interference in the case. Ye Tingjuan is identified as a *shendong* (gentry director) of the Siming Gongsuo in GZGYB, 1872.

60. Several accounts suggest that the powder was only rouge for the actor's makeup. As an aphrodisiac, however, it partially absolved the women (and Guangdong people) from blame.

61. One account even argues that the drug so seriously altered Madame Wei's mind that she was unable to speak the truth during her interrogation. The severity of Yang's

Guangdong honor in the city, the actions of the Guang-Zhao Gongsuo also aroused criticism, as did Magistrate Ye's ruling. Editorials appeared criticizing the magistrate's regional bias. Although the first reports condemned Yang as a wanton habitué of prostitutes who had a reputation for getting into fights, they also shamed the Guangdong people by impugning the character of their women. Abao was described as being "as beautiful as a prostitute."[62] Rumors circulated that Madame Wei was lascivious and had arranged the marriage in order to live with Yang herself. Front-page editorials declared that the entire case was a false accusation by the Guangdong people, who tried to save face by pretending that a legal marriage was a matter of seduction, rape and theft.

By January the Guangdong people in Shanghai were a regular object of ridicule in the newspaper. Because they had mobilized "the power of the people of an entire province to accuse an actor and an escaped daughter," they were portrayed as "moving Mount Tai to squash an egg."[63] Not only did editorials daily debate the merits of the case, the newspaper also began to publish articles describing "saltwater sisters" and focused attention on Guangdong-organized kidnapping and trade in young women, further piquing the ire of the Guangdong community.[64]

A struggle ensued between the Guangdong people and the Shanghai Magistrate on the one hand and the Daotai, Zhejiang and Shanghai people on the other, a struggle no doubt informed by underlying economic tensions between these regional groups. On January 29, 1874, the *North China Herald* reported that the enraged Guangdong people twice

---

sentence required the approval of the Songjiang Prefect and the Provincial Judge. At the prefectural level Yang initially overturned his confession. Nonetheless, fresh torture produced a new confession. Yang was sent on to Suzhou, the seat of the Provincial officer, where he again denied his guilt and was returned to the Prefect for further investigation. In the meantime, Madame Wei committed suicide. In 1876 Yang was reported returned to his native place in Anhui province.

62. SB, December 23, 1873. Comparison with a prostitute did not always have purely negative connotations. A subsequent article defended Abao by comparing her to renowned, virtuous Tang and Ming prostitutes: "The eminent Liu Rushi committed suicide. She was a very famous courtesan but she sacrificed herself for the Ming. Gentlemen revere her martyrdom. And the famous gentleman of the Tang, Li, did not refuse to recognize [the famous Tang courtesan] Hong Fu" (SB, December 29, 1873).

63. SB, December 29, 1873.

64. These articles focus on the impurity of the Guangdong community, in particular its association with and penetration (here in terms of prostitutes serving foreigners) by the foreign community. On trade in female bondservants, see Maria Jaschok, *Concubines and Bondservants: The Social History of a Chinese Custom* (London, 1988).

stormed the Daotai's office threatening to burn down the *Shenbao* office and kill the editors if he did not take action. Daotai Shen Bingcheng, a Zhejiang native, declined. Unable to force the Daotai into action, the Guangdong people insisted the Chinese staff of the newspaper be punished, sending Magistrate Ye to make their case before the British Consul, Mr. Medhurst.[65] Failing to persuade Mr. Medhurst, the magistrate posted notices in the Chinese city and at the city gates proclaiming that the *Shenbao* had accepted the bribes of Yang's clique and printed lies.[66]

The Yang Yuelou case reveals how, in a city of immigrants like Shanghai where families were fragmented, the *tongxiang* group (through the institution of the *huiguan*) could fulfill the function of a substitute kin network. It also reveals the considerable influence of such an organization on the administration of justice. When the Guang-Zhao Gongsuo acted to prevent a marriage which would stain the reputation of the community, although the virtues of the particular response were hotly debated, the ideas that the matter concerned the *huiguan* and that the *huiguan* bore responsibility for its outcome were generally taken for granted. The central role of the *huiguan* as the organized expression of the native-place community in dealings with the courts was undisputed. Although critics attacked the *huiguan* for overreacting and exposing a matter better left out of court, they accepted as natural the role of the *huiguan* in issuing the petition and the efficacy of a petition sent to the court by the *huiguan*.[67]

Defending the public image of the native-place community was as much an integral aspect of *huiguan* activity as the public building, religious processions, ostentatious funeral rites, and charitable activities which established the native-place presence and enhanced the group's power and prestige in the Shanghai community. Newcomers to Shanghai, particularly those who had risen swiftly to wealth, like the people from Guangdong, were called on to demonstrate their moral virtue if

65. Shen was replaced in early 1874 by the Guangdong native, Feng Junguang. Unfortunately, it is difficult to trace the effect of this transition on the case. At this time the *Shenbao* was still under British ownership, although the editors were Chinese. This status protected the paper from the wrath of Chinese officials.

66. SB, February 12, 1874.

67. This was not just an illustration of the particular strength of Guangdong native-place ties. Yang Yuelou consulted his Anhui *tongxiang* as a matter of course. It might be argued that, in the case of the Shanghai District Magistrate, the influence of the *huiguan* resulted from shared native-place ties. This was not the case, however, with the Mixed Court Magistrate, who was not a Guangdong native but who ordered the arrests on the strength of the *huiguan* petition alone.

they were to exercise power in the community. If their activities back-fired, the case nonetheless suggests the lengths to which the Guangdong community would go in its attempts to save face. In this respect the case provides a notable but not unrepresentative example. In August 1873, for example, the Guang-Zhao Gongsuo repeatedly published advertise-ments correcting a report which suggested that a Guangdong woman was seen kidnapped and taken to a brothel. According to the "revised supplementary report" published by the *huiguan* (which had investi-gated the case), the woman simply went by herself to a temple near the brothel quarter to pray for her sick child.[68]

The Yang Yuelou case, in its urban approximation of the codes of honor and revenge that might be associated with rural clan feuds, in-volved a process of community definition which — like *huiguan* charity, drama and religion, bound together elite and non-elite sojourners. The case was not simply about a low-class marriage which threatened an upper-class family. The case must also be understood against the back-ground of a preexisting feud. Prior to contact between Yang and the Wei women, a street brawl had taken place between Chaozhou shop hands and Yang's acting troupe. According to one account, as a conse-quence of this fight (which engaged several hundred combatants and necessitated the intervention of local officials, soldiers and *huiguan* di-rectors before the matter was calmed) the Guangdong people had vowed everlasting enmity for Yang.[69] If a *huiguan* director's family per-mitted a marriage alliance with an individual identified as an enemy of the Guangdong people, the *huiguan* would violate community bound-aries drawn by a preexisting feud. By punishing Yang, the *huiguan* per-formed an act of revenge that endeared it to the broader *tongxiang* com-munity and maintained the purity of the group against pollution from outsiders.[70]

The Yang Yuelou case reveals, finally, how critical the maintenance of hierarchy was to community definition. The case received as much attention as it did because it involved the conduct of women and raised questions about the correct governance of women. In a Confucian con-text, in which proper management of the realm was understood to be linked to proper management of the family, the *huiguan*, as the urban

68. SB, August 25, 1873.

69. Chen Boxi, *Shanghai yishi daguan*, vol. 3, 181.

70. See Chapter 1 above for other examples involving themes of purity and pollution in native place identity.

COMMUNITY, HIERARCHY AND AUTHORITY   117

equivalent of lineage elders, was responsible not simply for defending the honor of women from its native place but also for enforcing the authority of men over women. Although female family members may have been freer in Shanghai than at home, public commentary on the case suggests that the *huiguan* (representing the absent head of the household) was expected to step in to circumvent this excessive autonomy. Using reasoning reminiscent of the Confucian classic, "The Great Learning" (*Daxue*), one critic argued that the mismanagement of the Wei household and the *huiguan*'s incorrect decision to bring a lawsuit had caused more universal disharmony. Because the *huiguan,* rather than quietly removing the women from Yang's household and covering the matter up, exposed family mismanagement, they harmed the reputation of the *tongxiang*. Moreover, because the case involved officials and the officials made an incorrect decision, it was bad for the country.[71]

This chapter has examined practices which defined and constituted the native-place community, practices without which it would be difficult to speak of community. The creation of a larger native-place community depended heavily on the wealth and status of a sojourning elite which could provide the funding for religious, recreational and charitable practices and could command the respect and influence needed for both successful adjudication of disputes within the native-place community and for maintaining community reputation in the urban area of Shanghai. Because the extent to which a given group of sojourners could constitute community depended on their wealth, native-place identity in the city ranged from the elaborate constructions of native-place culture and community found in the powerful Guangdong and Ningbo communities, to the striking absence (despite their large numbers in the city) of institutionalized community among poor sojourners from northern Jiangsu.

The practices that created native-place community reinforced an internal hierarchy which was centered on the *huiguan* oligarchs, who as directors filled a position equivalent to the heads of an extended kin network. This ensured that the *huiguan* worked to define and confirm gender hierarchy as well as economic/occupational hierarchy.

The practices of native-place community were, of course, embedded in larger networks of authority which extended beyond the sojourner group in the city. *Huiguan* oligarchs also provided a critical link to the

71. SB, December 29, 1873.

state, a link which further legitimized their local positions of authority. The next chapter describes the pivotal role of the merchant leaders in positioning the native-place community in relation to the state through the mediating institution of the *huiguan,* which served the state by assuming quasi-governmental functions. This link, which symbolically corresponded to the link between family head (as subject) and the state, meant that the practice of *huiguan* leadership could not be limited by exclusive orientation toward the native place or toward the native-place community in Shanghai. In the late nineteenth century, the directors of the major Shanghai huiguan became actors on a national stage.

CHAPTER FOUR

Expansive Practices

Charity, Modern Enterprise, the City and the State

In post-Taiping Shanghai, a number of factors converged which would expand the managerial and political horizons of native-place networks. The thinness of government administration in the face of continuing economic and population growth created a space for increased merchant power and activism in urban affairs. The merchant elite, many of whom had purchased official titles, used the organizational apparatus of native-place associations to assume order-keeping and other urban managerial functions which might have been exercised by local officials had state resources been up to the task. Such an extension of organizational activity was fed by the growing commercial fortunes of sojourning merchants, fortunes which were increasingly based not simply on Shanghai but on networks of multiport enterprises.

The developing political climate of economic nationalism also contributed to new orientations among the merchant elite. Many treaty-port merchants who daily confronted the difficulty of economic competition with foreigners in the face of extraterritoriality and unequal treaties shared the views of powerful officials like Governor General Li Hongzhang, who advocated "self-strengthening" (*ziqiang*) measures to help China compete economically with western business. Although merchant nationalism would eventually create a rift between merchants and officials in the last decade of the Qing, in the several decades of the self-strengthening movement after the Taiping Rebellion, early economic nationalism tended to both deepen reformist officials' appreciation of merchants and to involve merchants in national affairs, bringing the two groups closer together.

This strategic convergence of official and elite merchant interests resulted in a mutually profitable relationship in which each party needed the other and neither was effectively able to control the other. Limited state resources for "self-strengthening" enterprises led Li Hongzhang to recognize the need for investment and assistance from particularly wealthy merchants, especially compradors with expertise in western management and technology. Because these merchants were frequently leaders of their native-place communities, new state initiatives were quickly colonized by competing native-place networks which sought official patronage as well as profit.

The expansive managerial practices of nonbureaucratic elites in this period have been observed in the context of Zhejiang local elites and Hankou gentry-merchants in the works of William Rowe and Mary Rankin. Both Rowe and Rankin describe this elite mobilization in terms of a developing Chinese "public sphere," their choice of this term deriving from the writings of Jürgen Habermas. I have chosen not to use the term "public sphere" in this discussion of post-Taiping Shanghai society because the term is usually understood to require both nonbureaucratic initiative and autonomy and the development of independent, informed and critical public opinion through the forum of equal-access newspaper media. While sojourner associations certainly contributed to an expanding realm of nonstate public management, particularly with regard to their own sojourning populations, emphasis on merchant power and initiative must be balanced by recognition of the interpenetration of merchant and official interests, networks, institutions and enterprises in this period. The fact that *huiguan* were often established with the substantial financial and political assistance of *tongxiang* officials serving in Shanghai and that officials often attended meetings and were not infrequently *huiguan dongshi* makes attempts to distinguish "official" and "unofficial" forms of association somewhat misleading. Similarly, as the discussion of the Shanghai press in this chapter will suggest, interpretation of the significance of Shanghai newspapers needs to consider the native-place networks operating through (or excluded from) the *Shenbao*.[1]

1. Rowe, *Hankow: Commerce and Society;* Rowe, *Hankow: Conflict and Community;* Rankin, *Elite Activism.* Rankin, in particular, has carefully redefined the possible meanings of a public sphere in the context of late imperial China. The recent important debate on the existence and nature of a Chinese public sphere is summarized in articles by Wakeman, Rankin and Rowe in the April 1993 symposium volume of *Modern China.* The relevant

Managerial Practices

The Expansion of Business and Charity. As their Shanghai enterprises grew, merchant *huiguan* leaders invested their fortunes and managerial attention not simply on Shanghai and their native places but also on branch businesses in a network of cites. This was the case for the comprador-merchant leaders of the most powerful native-place groups in Shanghai in the 1860s and 1870s, Guangdong, Zhejiang and, increasingly, Jiangsu sojourners.[2] Guang-Zhao Gongsuo leader Xu Run, for example, arrived in Shanghai in 1852 as a comprador and invested in silk, tea, tobacco and opium. By 1868 he had opened his own tea firm with branches in Zhejiang, Jiangxi, Hunan and Hubei. The Zhejiang merchant-comprador Ye Chengzhong arrived in Shanghai in 1854, where he became a leading figure in the Ningbo community. Over the next several decades he transformed himself into a financier and industrialist. Although Shanghai was a base for his pioneering development of spinning mills, he established businesses in each major port, including a match factory in Hankou.[3]

As their economic concerns extended beyond the native place and beyond Shanghai, so did their charitable activities. This geographic expansion of both business and charitable activity was facilitated by improvements in transportation and communication brought about by the regularization of steam shipping among the treaty ports (including those on the Yangzi) during the 1870s. *Huiguan* increasingly organized assistance to sojourners in other cities.[4] In the process, for many *huiguan* leaders the functional native-place community became in practice a multicity, even national, network. *Huiguan* charitable activities embraced and reinforced this larger network. At the same time, *huiguan* also became contributors to charitable concerns which transcended native-place networks.

---

text by Jürgen Habermas is *The Structural Transformation of the Public Sphere* (1962; reprint Cambridge, Mass., 1989).

2. Elite Jiangsu sojourners, who fled to Shanghai to escape the Taipings in the early 1860s, became powerful in Shanghai by the late 1870s, as the Suzhou Xi family emerged as highly successful in native banks and as compradors for foreign banks. The Xis were also important leaders of the Shanghai Pingjiang Gongsuo, established 1881. See Hao, *Comprador,* 176–77; SBZX, 387–88, 511.

3. Hao, *Comprador,* 100, 142. Hao (*Comprador,* 106–53) details many of the merchant-comprador fortunes of late-nineteenth-century *huiguan* leaders.

4. The national network of Ningbo coffin shipment managed by the Siming Gongsuo in the late nineteenth and early twentieth century, for example, was very much based on the improvement of shipping and communication technology.

Although *huiguan* devoted their greatest energies when disasters hit home areas or their fellow-provincials in Shanghai or other cities, in the late Qing the major associations supported citywide charities as well. These included contributions to the Tongren Fuyuantang, the most important of the Shanghai benevolent institutions, which dispensed coffins and provided burial for unidentified corpses. *Huiguan* and *gongsuo* support for this local gentry-established institution became particularly important in the post-Taiping period, after plundering damaged the rental-income property of the charitable hall. *Huiguan* records for the late nineteenth and early twentieth centuries also reveal contributions to support Shanghai-wide disaster relief, as in the case of flooding in 1905.[5]

Shanghai sojourner associations also participated in the broad trend of charitable activism for the relief of national disasters which has been observed beginning in the late 1870s among elites in the lower Yangzi area by Mary Rankin and within Hankou merchant and gentry institutions by William Rowe. Zhejiang sojourners in Shanghai were quick to organize collection agencies which responded first to disaster in northern Jiangsu in 1876 and then on a larger scale in 1877–78, a time of severe drought and famine in the North China provinces of Henan, Zhili, Shanxi and Shaanxi. The Guangdong comprador Zheng Guanying joined the Zhejiang merchant-philanthropist Jing Yuanshan in the formation of a relief bureau for Shanxi in 1877. Stimulated by Zhejiang philanthropical ventures, encouraged by Zheng Guanying and Guang-Zhao Gongsuo director Xu Run, and not to be outdone on the pages of the *Shenbao* (which published lists of contributors), other sojourning Guangdong merchants donated heavily in 1878, as relief programs were established by Li Hongzhang.[6]

This extension of charitable activity beginning during the late 1870s is an important development, but one which — as is the case for other "expansive practices" discussed in this chapter — resists characterization in the opposing categories of "modern" or "traditional"; nonstate/extra-bureaucratic or state/official; "cosmopolitan" or "particularist." These abstracted sets of mutually exclusive opposites are as grounded in our

---

5. NCH, April 10, 1858; *Shanghai Siming Gongsuo zhengxinlu;* Johnson, *Cities of Jiangnan,* 166; GZGYB, 1905.

6. Rankin, *Elite Activism,* 142–47; Rowe, *Hankow: Conflict and Community,* 28; Leung, "Regional Rivalry," 45; Xia Dongyuan, *Zheng Guanying ji,* vol. 2, 1532. In 1878 Guangdong merchants formed a relief organization with Sheng Xuanhuai for the Henan, Zhili and Shaanxi disaster areas.

language and thinking as they are fanciful in terms of approximati
considerably more complex and ambiguous process of social chai
western-originated discourse of progress and modernity, whethe
berian or Marxist in its specific formulations, has greatly encum
both western and Chinese interpretations of development in modern
China by constructing change as a radical break and by anticipating (and
therefore finding) change in only one direction. Certainly the expansion
of charitable activism incorporated new technologies and ideas. What is
striking is the way in which "modern" tools and media facilitated the
creation of new (and expanded) notions of the native place as well as
new notions of the nation. The point here is that "modernization" in
China was multidirectional.

The larger, multiport native-place communities the new activism encompassed were in many ways constituted through new economic and
technological developments. Not only did the steamboat make communications and transport (for both business and charity) more practical,
but the Shanghai newspaper, the *Shenbao*, which both reported news
from the different treaty ports and was distributed in many of them,
helped to bring the worlds of elite sojourners in different ports together.
Although much has been made of the transformative impact of the
modern press in regard to creating in people's minds the idea of the
nation,[7] it has often been assumed that the rise of newspapers assists the
transcendence of local "particularisms." In Shanghai, the press recon-
figured people's connections to the larger polity and in certain respects
strengthened local identities, both presenting national news and creating an urban "mirror" for new reflections of native-place "face." In other
words, we are forced to recognize the paradox of national identification
being fueled by native-place loyalties.

The "mirror" of Shanghai public opinion (as articulated in the press)
motivated the broadening of both native-place charity and charity which
went beyond native-place ties. For example, in a letter to the Guang-
Zhao Gongsuo, the reform-minded intellectual/comprador Zheng
Guanying urged his fellow-provincials to coordinate multiport Guangdong collection networks to assist *tongxiang* refugees in Beijing and
Tianjin. He pointed out that Jiangsu and Zhejiang people in Shanghai
had established a relief society for northern refugees and that unless
Guang-Zhao and Chaozhou people contributed, not only would they

---

7. See, in particular, Benedict Anderson, *Imagined Communities: Reflections on the Origin and Spread of Nationalism* (New York, 1991).

lose face but foreigners would laugh at them.[8] Similarly, while conveying the new nationalism of the treaty-port elite, *Shenbao* editorials which increasingly called on *huiguan* to sponsor disaster relief in other areas of the country also stimulated native-place rivalries by publishing lists of contributors. While conveying the idea that *huiguan* were a source of funds on which the nation depended, the newspaper created a new sort of "symbolic capital" which would recur to the native-place community. Whereas *huiguan* previously vied for the grandest festival, their leaders followed shifts in public opinion and vied for reputations as public-spirited institutions. This shift is seen, for example, in a Siming Gongsuo advertisement in the *Shenbao* that it had economized and saved one hundred yuan from its *jiao,* which it donated to flood victims in Hunan.[9]

Similarly, it is difficult to disentangle *gong* in the sense of public, collective, and nonstate from *guan* (official).[10] The early stages of the charity drive to relieve the North China famine do seem to provide evidence, as Mary Rankin has detailed, of nonbureaucratic initiative and civic activism which created new models of appropriate elite behavior (as articulated in the Chinese press). But such a notion of *gong* quickly (and, for the participants, apparently unproblematically) was tied to *guan* with the involvement of Li Hongzhang. Li's sponsorship of charitable relief clearly provided further motivation for elite involvement. Shanghai merchants extended their native-place rivalries through their charitable activism into the realm of national politics. It would be naive, as Leung Yuen-sang has pointed out, to imagine that the wealthy Guangdong merchants who contributed to Li Hongzhang's relief programs did not also view their charity as a bid for the patronage of this powerful official. Li certainly became an important patron of Guangdong merchants,

8. Xia Dongyuan, *Zheng Guanying ji,* vol. 2, 1139–40.

9. SB, August 6, 1880; SB, September 7, 1880; SB, August 18, 1882 (source of the quotation). The gift of one hundred yuan, it should be noted, represented a rather small sum if festivals cost as much as several thousand yuan. This may be contrasted with considerably more substantial efforts of the Guang-Zhao Gongsuo in response to flooding in Guangdong (NCH, July 10, 1885). Western charitable activities, also reported in the press, no doubt presented an additional stimulus to a Chinese treaty-port elite which both cooperated and competed with western business.

10. The changing connotations of the term *gong* in late imperial China have been the subject of a number of important studies, in particular Mizoguchi Yūzō, "Chūgoku ni okeru kō, shi gainen no tenkai" (The Evolution of the Concepts of *gong* and *si* in China), *Shisō* 669 (1980):19–38. For discussions of *gong* with reference to the idea of a "public sphere," see Rankin, *Elite Activism,* 15–21; Rankin, "The Origins of a Chinese Public Sphere," 35–54; Rowe, *Hankow: Conflict and Community,* 61–62.

making them directors of several of his government-sponsored and -supported "self-strengthening" enterprises, even endorsing a Guangdong scheme to monopolize opium importation into all of China, memorializing the throne on the benefits of such a state-sanctioned monopoly.[11]

Finally, to present the changes in terms of cosmopolitanism versus particularism would obscure the ways in which distinctions between these apparently exclusive notions collapsed in daily practice. The management of charity reflected continuing attachment to native-place ties (even as the net of charity at times expanded beyond them). The expansion of merchant management both provided a larger stage on which to play out native-place rivalries and involved competing native-place groups in cooperative ventures in the interest of broader municipal and national goals. In fact, as charitable and other public activism grew, the elite leaders of different native-place groups increasingly cooperated in citywide joint relief agencies. During their North China famine relief management activities the leaders of the Guangdong community developed cooperative contacts with Zhejiang and Jiangsu notables sojourning in Shanghai. By the mid-1880s an ad hoc committee of sorts linked together influential merchants from different sojourning groups who repeatedly cooperated in organizing relief as disasters arose in different areas.[12]

Standing in for City Government. In post-Taiping Shanghai *huiguan* increasingly assumed urban managerial functions, including social control and taxation. Such functions developed through a combination of official and merchant initiative, reflecting officials' recognition of limited government resources as well as merchants' growing public activism. The expanded urban functions of *huiguan* broadened the range of identities associated with these institutions. At times Chinese officials even borrowed *huiguan* halls for official functions involving for-

11. Leung, "Regional Rivalry," 45; Hao, *Commercial Revolution*, 136–37. Li's memorial failed to persuade the throne.
12. Xia Dongyuan, *Zheng Guanying ji*, vol. 2, 1532; NCH, October 7, 1885. In contrast to the definite, but relatively limited, coordination among different native-place networks in late-nineteenth-century Shanghai, Rowe (*Hankow: Commerce and Society*, 10) describes more systematic coordination among different groups of urban elites in Hankou, amounting to "the rise of a guild centered, subrosa municipal government apparatus" (pp. 10, 344). For commentary on this issue, see Frederic Wakeman, "The Civil Society and Public Sphere Debate: Western Reflections on Chinese Political Culture," MC 19 (1993):125.

eigners or foreign governments, occasions which called for particularly impressive surroundings. At such moments both foreign and Chinese authorities clearly viewed *huiguan* as representing Chinese (not provincial) interests. Although the use of *huiguan* buildings at such moments does not provide evidence of *huiguan* intervention in the proceedings, it does suggest the magisterial presence of these institutions at moments of national symbolic importance.[13]

Chinese officials encouraged the use of *huiguan* as instruments of social control to defend Shanghai against bandits or uprisings, maintain order during popular festivals and settle disputes, riots and strikes in the city. *Huiguan* leaders often solicited such responsibilities, particularly when they were given license to expand their authority in the city. Major *huiguan* also contributed regularly to the coffers of local Chinese officials, paying customary fees to the Daotai's *yamen,* the Magistrate's *yamen,* and the Mixed Court.[14]

Government calls to muster *huiguan* militia did not end with the Small Sword Uprising. Five years after crushing the rebels and destroying Guangdong and Fujian *huiguan* for their complicity, Shanghai officials appealed again to *huiguan* to help defend the city. If *huiguan* militia were risky, they were perhaps no less reliable than other military bodies at the time, and there was little alternative.

Faced in 1860 with approaching Taiping rebels and the disarray of government forces, Daotai Wu Xu relied on his *tongxiang* for defense. Wu was a Zhejiang native whose extensive business interests linked him closely to the Siming Gongsuo. With *gongsuo* help, Wu created a Ningbo militia of five hundred "braves." Although this particular militia proved less than useful (reportedly fleeing the Taipings and plundering local villagers as they ran back to Shanghai) and was ultimately dis-

---

13. The grandly ornamented Shaanxi Huiguan provided the architectural setting for a treaty ratification with Japan related to Li Hongzhang's acceptance of Japanese claims for damages for the killing of Liuchiu (Ryukyu) islanders by Formosan tribes (NCH, May 10, 1873; H. B. Morse, *The International Relations of the Chinese Empire,* vol. 2 (London, 1918), 271. The Guang-Zhao Gongsuo was used as a court for the case Bennertz and Co. vs. the Jiangnan Defense and Pay Department (PRO, FO 228.1256 [1897]). In this case, the British plaintiffs claimed damages from the Chinese defendants, from whom they had chartered what they claimed were faulty steamboats. Although *huiguan* were usually cooperative in dealings with Chinese officials, they were not always willing to lend their resources for official use. In 1891 *huiguan* directors decided to "politely decline" requests by officials for use of the central meeting hall of the Guang-Zhao Gongsuo (GZGYB, 1891).

14. Guang-Zhao gongsuo zhengxinlu.

banded, other native-place associations, even the considerably smaller Shandong Huiguan, mustered and trained militia until the fall of the Taipings.[15]

Native-place ties also played a role in the organization of nontraditional forms of defense. With funding and organizational assistance from his close friend the wealthy Zhejiang comprador-merchant Yang Fang (Takee), Wu also arranged for the innovative hiring of a foreign mercenary militia, the Ever Victorious Army. This was not solely a Zhejiang project; the Guangdong merchant leader Xu Yuting also contributed heavily. The joint support of these two leaders of their respective sojourning communities for a foreign mercenary army again demonstrates the coexistence of organization by native place and innovative cooperative ventures by different sojourning elites in the service of state officials (and in their common interest of defending the city).[16]

During the Sino–French War (1883–85) social unrest in Shanghai led the Shanghai Magistrate and the Daotai to again call for merchants to raise militia.[17] Merchants in the foreign concessions also attempted to form militia, as shown by a petition received by the Shanghai Municipal Council in 1884, which also reveals their methods of militia organization:

We, the undersigned representatives of the Kwangtung [Guangdong] merchants in Hongkew [Hongkou] . . . request that the sanction of the Municipality be granted . . . to the end that merchants and other people may be assured of their safety and not remove from Shanghai in fear and trepidation. It is the purpose of the Kwangtung merchants to enlist two or three men from each shop situated in Hongkew as volunteers, thus the corps will number about 1,000 men. . . . The weapons which are to be used by the volunteers will be supplied them by . . . the Kwangtung Guild.[18]

15. Leung, *Shanghai Taotai,* 56–60; NCH, August 4, 1860; NCH, January 31, 1863. See also Hao, *Comprador,* 174–75, 191.

16. Yang Fang was the father-in-law of Frederick Townsend Ward, commander of the mercenary force (Hao, *Comprador,* 184). Yang is a good study in the compatibility of cosmopolitanism and the protection of native-place interests. His strategic cosmopolitanism in regard to his daughter's marriage to a foreigner did not impinge on his protection of the business interests of his native-place community. In addition to closely supporting the Siming Gongsuo, as Jardine's comprador Yang worked to exclude Guangdong compradors from the company. In the words of a Jardine's employee: "He is against it, saying in the first place that he and all his friends being Ningpo men would not get on well with Canton men" (quoted in Hao, *Comprador,* 175).

17. SXXZ, vol. 13, 13. The Magistrate was Li Guangdan; the Daotai was Shao Youlian.

18. Because Hongkou was located within the International Settlement, they petitioned the Shanghai Municipal Council for approval (translation in MCR for 1884, 58–59). This Hongkou Guangdong *huiguan* is also mentioned in NCH, October 4, 1884. The Municipal Council rejected this proposal. Although *huiguan* militia operated in Chinese

In the late nineteenth century local officials continued to rely on *hui-guan* to settle disputes in the city, taking for granted (and reinforcing through state practice) *huiguan* influence over sojourning communities. When cases entered the courts, courts often referred the matter back to the *huiguan* for settlement. In cases involving *tongxiang* and outsiders, *huiguan* served as legal advisors or representatives.[19]

Huiguan also averted social disorder in Shanghai by returning potentially disruptive people to their native place. A particularly volatile situation arose in 1907, when Chinese authorities closed more than five hundred opium dens in the Chinese areas of the city. Because each establishment employed a number of people, three to four thousand people stood to lose their jobs. Many of these people were connected to gangs and secret societies, and rumors spread of plots to resist the authorities. In response, the Guang-Zhao Gongsuo moved with alacrity to provide return transport to the many Guangdong provincials who had been employed in the opium dens.[20]

Local officials also relied on *huiguan* to control the popular festivals described in Chapter 3. Each year, just before the *yulanpenhui,* officials contacted the responsible *huiguan.* One such notice, written in the early 1870s, makes clear the pivotal role of *huiguan* as mediating institutions between the state and the people:

During the seventh and eighth months the people of Fujian, Guangzhou, Ningbo and Shaoxing compete in *yulanpenhui* processions. This excites and draws together unwholesome elements, who create disturbances and incidents. Thus in the past prohibitions against these processions have been recorded. Now . . . the Magistrate has notified the heads of the *huiguan* of Fujian, Guangzhou, Chaozhou, Huilai, Ningbo and Shaoxing, etc., to

---

areas of the city in times of emergency, by the late nineteenth century they were not usually tolerated in the settlements. Nonetheless, at times even foreign authorities sanctioned *huiguan* or *gongsuo* militia. For example, in 1906, because of the inadequacies of the Chinese river police, the native Shanghai Shippers' Association engaged watchmen to patrol the International Settlement wharves. The Municipal Council, unwilling to sanction the employment of private constables at municipal jetties, agreed to enroll the watchmen as Settlement employees and charge the cost to the Shippers' Association (MCR for 1906).

19. See, for example, NCH, March 14, 1878; SB, October 2, 1879; PRO, FO 228.2516 (Shanghai Mixed Court, Report of May 11, 1912); Joseph Fewsmith, "From Guild to Interest Group: The Transformation of Public and Private in Late Qing China," *Comparative Studies in Society and History* 25 (October 1985):620–22.

20. GZGYB, 1907. See also Ding Richu, "Xinhai geming qian Shanghai zibenjia de zhengzhi huodong" (The political activities of Shanghai capitalists before the Revolution of 1911), *Jindaishi yanjiu* (Modern history research) 2 (1982):230–31.

make clear . . . that such activities are uniformly forbidden. . . . The prohibitions of each former Daotai are on record. . . . All Fujian, Guangzhou, Chaozhou, Huilai, Ningbo and Shaoxing *huiguan* managers and also the people of these places are hereby forbidden from holding processions.[21]

The *huiguan*, themselves implicated in the organization of these disorderly festivities, responded to such proclamations by publicizing their commitment to maintain order in the city. The Guang-Zhao Gongsuo admonished fellow-provincials to "refrain from inciting trouble" during the seventh month, transmitted the Daotai's prohibitions and warned that processions must not enter the Chinese walled city or the foreign settlements. The *huiguan* proclaimed that it would turn in any rumormongers or troublemakers to the authorities and would absolutely refuse to assist the lawbreakers.[22]

By both sponsoring these festivals and assuming responsibility for controlling them, *huiguan* directors consolidated their leadership position as head of their respective sojourning communities. If *huiguan* did not suppress *yulanpenhui* and *jiao*, there is no reason to doubt that they exercised their joint interest with the government in keeping order. The persistence of large ritual celebrations, as detailed in the previous chapter, despite government orders to the *huiguan* to prohibit them, suggests that *huiguan* were unwilling or unable to sacrifice this source of popular authority.

Although government officials' attention was drawn repeatedly to disruptive *huiguan* activities and abuses of delegated power, *huiguan* remained generally under their protection throughout this period. Similarly, officials' delegation of authority to *huiguan* even after the experience of a *huiguan*-led uprising in the city, as the following examples illustrate, dramatizes the contingency of government power and government dependence on ambivalent, or Janus-faced, institutions which derived their power from below as well as above.

Tax Collection. Huiguan and *gongsuo* services were crucial to post-Taiping tax collection. Local officials realized that if merchant associations were not themselves involved in the collection procedures, there would be no way to control smuggling and tax evasion. *Huiguan* involvement had two effects. First, the delegation of governmental functions to specific associations increased their authority in the city. Second,

21. SB, August 9, 1872.
22. NCH, August 4, 1870.

because of native-place distinctions within trades involving more than one regional group, taxation in practice was not always applied equally to all members of a trade. Powerful native-place *bang* could manipulate tax-farming mechanisms to the disadvantage of their rivals.

After initial merchant opposition and systematic smuggling in response to the introduction of transit taxes (*lijin*) in China in the 1850s and 1860s, a system of mutual accommodation developed between merchant groups and government officials, by which important *huiguan* and *gongsuo* gradually took on tax collection. In the lower Yangzi area, this process continued through the early twentieth century.[23] This involved a significant expansion of *huiguan* functions.

The administration of tax collection involved setting up tax offices, issuing transit permits, and posting agents at roads and bridges to prevent smuggling from the tax-exempt International Settlement into Chinese territory. In 1875 the *North China Herald* described a multiplicity of such offices, some government directed, some *huiguan* or *gongsuo* directed, each of them supported by "squeeze," with the result that "every article of native produce is similarly afflicted by officers detailed in all directions for the purpose." By the 1890s the government-*huiguan*/ *gongsuo lijin*-collection symbiosis was increasingly regularized. Merchants established and ran their own highly profitable tax-collection offices, guaranteeing the government a fixed sum.[24]

The opium and foreign piece-goods trades were among the first to develop merchant-leased *lijin* tax-collection bureaus in Shanghai.[25] It seems likely that these led the process because foreign involvement in these trades facilitated smuggling (goods imported by foreigners were exempt from *lijin* transit taxation). By registering goods in a foreign name, Chinese merchants routinely avoided *lijin* payments. Local officials anxious to secure tax revenues negotiated tax-responsibility compromises with merchant associations.

---

23. See Susan Mann, *Local Merchants and the Chinese Bureaucracy, 1750–1950* (Stanford, Calif., 1987), 115–62; Luo Yudong, *Zhongguo lijin shi* (History of the Chinese *lijin* tax) (Shanghai, 1936), 111–12; Sanford, "Chinese Commercial Organization," 121–22. Mann reasons that in assuming "tax responsibility," merchants chose to trade income for secrecy and autonomy (p. 159). Attention to the organization of merchants into native-place *bang* and *huiguan* suggests an additional motive: that dominant regional *bang* sought control over taxation in order to disadvantage their competitors.

24. NCH, June 19, 1875; Sanford, "Chinese Commercial Organization," 121–24; Luo Yudong, *Zhongguo lijin shi*, III, 113–14.

25. NCH, June 19, 1875; Sanford, "Chinese Commercial Organization," 121–22; MCR for 1885, 147.

The opium trade provides an example of the workings of one tax office, illustrates the symbiosis of official and private business and shows how tax responsibility could increase the power of a native-place *bang,* helping to exclude outside (in this case western) competitors. As early as 1871 western observers remarked on the existence of a notorious "Opium Guild" (*Yangyao juanju,* or "western medicine" collection office) which leased the administration of the opium tax from the Daotai.[26]

This "Opium Guild" soon became the focus of a celebrated legal suit involving opium trade, not in Shanghai but in Zhenjiang. Before the 1870s, opium was transported up the Yangzi into Zhenjiang and the interior by Chaozhou merchants who purchased it from western companies in Shanghai, paying taxes to Shanghai officials. These merchants sold to their fellow-provincials in Zhenjiang who controlled the local opium trade. In the early 1870s David Sassoon, Sons and Company discovered that it could make a greater profit by importing opium directly into Zhenjiang. This system enabled Chinese purchasers outside the Guangdong *huiguan* in Zhenjiang to avoid taxes altogether, smuggling the purchased opium on small, armed boats under British flags. The Sassoon innovation threatened Guangdong traders in both Shanghai and Zhenjiang and also cut into opium-tax revenues collected by Shanghai officials.

The Zhenjiang Guangdong *huiguan* directors discussed the matter with the Shanghai Chao-Hui Huiguan when they went to ceremonially congratulate their *tongxiang* on the Chinese New Year.[27] Recognizing that as long as western merchants imported opium directly into Zhenjiang they could not prevent smuggling, Chao-Hui Huiguan leaders determined to end western trade in Zhenjiang. After constricting Sassoon's trade by threatening any Chinese who bought from the foreign company, they bought out the declining Sassoon enterprise, restoring the Zhenjiang opium trade to the Chao-Hui Huiguan.[28]

Surviving transcripts of a trial which undertook to expose the "Swa-

26. NCH, August 18, 1871.

27. In Zhenjiang Chaozhou merchants were organized together with other Guangdong provincials into a Yuedong (Guangdong) Gongsuo (SB, September 17, 1879; Sanford, "Chinese Commercial Organization," 130).

28. SB, October 8, 1879; SB, October 11, 1879. The *huiguan* paid a sum in excess of twenty thousand taels. This case supports the argument that despite foreign economic imperialism Chinese merchants retained considerable control over the economy and reveals how *huiguan* organizations operated to enforce this control. On the strength of Chinese merchants vis-à-vis foreign competition, see Hao, *Commercial Revolution,* 353; Rhoads Murphey, *The Outsiders: The Western Experience in India and China* (Ann Arbor, Mich., 1977).

tow Opium Guild" reveal the organization and taxation of the opium trade and the embeddedness of the trade in wider native-place interests. In September and October of 1879, the case of "Messrs. T. W. Duff and D. M. David vs. the Swatow Opium Guild" unfolded before the readers of the *North China Herald*. Duff and David were opium merchants who tried to trade in Zhenjiang after the demise of the Sassoon operation. They accused members of a Chinese "guild" of combining to exclude them from the trade. Arguing that this violated treaty stipulations, the western merchants sought compensation for losses they claimed to have incurred as a consequence. The British Vice-Consul and the Chinese Daotai presided, in addition to the British Assessor and the Chinese Magistrate, because of the importance of the case.[29]

The case was never resolved to the satisfaction of the foreign plaintiffs because they misunderstood the nature of Chinese associations, taxation arrangements, and the overlap between Chinese business and government organizations. Although the defendants were both directors of the Chao-Hui Huiguan and officers of the Shanghai Opium Tax Bureau, the prosecution failed to prove the existence of a discrete guild of opium merchants, on which its case depended.[30] Instead, there was the Chao-Hui Huiguan, which the defendants described as a club for sojourners. Whereas the defense stated that all of the several hundred opium merchants in Shanghai were from Chaozhou prefecture,[31] they argued that the *huiguan* was not a business association because merchants were but a small minority of the community it served. The large part of the community, which numbered between twenty and thirty thousand, they argued, was made up of poorer and middling classes. Moreover, there were also traders who dealt in sugar, bean-cake fertilizer and cotton. In these arguments the defense invoked the broad *tongxiang* community to mask the merchant direction of the association.

Chinese officials supported the Chaozhou merchants in this case because the *huiguan* used its tax monopoly authority to prevent smuggling associated with foreign inland trade. The *huiguan* stationed men outside British firms in Zhenjiang to monitor those who came and went. *Hui-*

---

29. NCH, September and October 1879.

30. A certain amount of confusion appears to have centered on the name *Yangyao gongsuo* (Opium Gongsuo) which appears in the Chinese account, an abbreviation of an alternative name for the Tax Bureau, the *Yangyao renjuan gongsuo.*

31. The single exception they admitted was the comprador and Guang-Zhao Gongsuo director Tang Maozhi, who was recognized as the only participating Guangzhou merchant, in return for past services to the Chaozhou association (NCH, September 23, 1879).

guan interest in protecting Chaozhou business coincided with the interests of Chinese officials who were concerned to protect their tax revenues. The Shanghai Daotai backed up all of the testimony of the Chao-Hui Huiguan, even false or misleading information.[32]

This case also demonstrates the substantial involvement of sojourning Shanghai merchants in economic matters outside both the native place and Shanghai. Although directors of the Zhenjiang *huiguan* were asked by the local Daotai to collect the *lijin* tax on opium and prevent smuggling, they acted not autonomously but in a subordinate relationship with their powerful Shanghai fellow-provincials. Joint meetings of the Shanghai Chaozhou opium merchants and the Zhenjiang Guangdong *huiguan* were held at the Shanghai Opium Tax Bureau to determine tax arrangements in Zhenjiang. The draft *lijin* tax for Zhenjiang was drawn up not in Zhenjiang but in Shanghai, by the Shanghai Chao-Hui Huiguan. The Zhenjiang magistrate even accompanied a delegation of Zhenjiang *huiguan* directors to Shanghai for discussions with the Shanghai *huiguan*.[33]

In other cases, native-place *bang* used tax-responsibility license to disadvantage Chinese competitors. In trades involving merchants from several *bang*, different groups often struck different tax bargains with local officials. The sugar trade provides an example of the maneuvering which accompanied the imposition of *lijin*. The trade was originally dominated by people from the sugar-producing region of southeastern Fujian and northeastern Guangdong (Chaozhou). By the mid-1870s Jiangsu and Zhejiang merchants (grouped together strategically as a Jiang-Zhe *bang*) had entered the trade. Relations were much closer between the Chaozhou and Fujian *bang* than between these allied southern *bang* and the Jiang-Zhe newcomers, who imported foreign sugar and shipped it to other areas. For the still powerful but declining Fujian and Chaozhou sugar *bang*, *lijin* and defense (*choufang*) tax collection offered an opportunity to regain the edge over their competitors.[34]

32. Great Britain, House of Commons, *British Parliamentary Papers*, "Commercial Reports" (Shanghai, 1879), 214–19; Sanford, "Chinese Commercial Organization," 130; SB, October 9, 1879; NCH, September 23, 1879. See also Mark Elvin, "The Mixed Court of the International Settlement of Shanghai (until 1911)" *Papers on China* 17 (1963):138; Rhoads Murphey, "The Treaty Ports and China's Modernization," in Elvin and Skinner, *The Chinese City between Two Worlds*, 54; Hamilton, "Nineteenth Century Chinese Merchant Associations," 50–71.

33. NCH, September 9, 1879; NCH, September 23, 1879; NCH, October 17, 1879.

34. SB, August 4, 1874; SB, August 25, 1874; SB, September 14, 1874; SB, November 22, 1874; NCH, September 19, 1874; NCH, October 29, 1874; NCH, July 24, 1875. Chao-

In 1874 the government-run Shanghai sugar-tax bureau lowered the taxation rate to dissuade sugar merchants from smuggling. The *lijin* tax was reduced to 61.5 percent of the former level, and the defense tax was halved. Three days later, negotiations between the Chaozhou and Fujian *bang* and the tax bureau resulted in a prejudicial enforcement of the new rules. The local Jiang-Zhe merchants complained in the *Shenbao* that only the southern *bang* received the discounts whereas they were forced to pay the full tax.[35]

Shenbao editorials, which tended to represent local interests against southerners, criticized the government for encouraging a Fujian-Chaozhou monopoly. The Jiang-Zhe *bang* complained of unequal treatment to the Daotai, who conceded their case but failed to intervene on their behalf, forcing the unhappy Jiang-Zhe merchants to accept the terms of the southern *bang:* "When we transport sugar it is confiscated by the sugar tax bureau, and we have no appeal. . . . If we want to ship it to other places, we have to ask the two *bang* [Fujian and Chaozhou] to represent us in paying the tax [to get the discount] and then they charge us for the service."[36] The Daotai in this period was Feng Jun-guang, a Guangdong native.[37]

A similar case demonstrating how native-place *bang* could manipulate tax monopolies is provided by the Shanghai Silk Cocoon Gongsuo, organized by merchants from the silk-producing prefecture of Huzhou (Zhejiang). In the 1890s this *gongsuo* used its *lijin* tax responsibility to prevent non-Huzhou merchants from shipping cocoons to Shanghai. It did this by requiring all silk boats to carry a tax-authorization certificate and then limiting the distribution of certificates to its own boats.[38]

---

zhou and Fujian merchants kept costs down by shipping Chinese sugar to Hong Kong and reimporting it as "foreign" sugar to avoid tax. Jiangsu and Zhejiang merchants competed by importing foreign sugar.

35. SB, August 4, 1874; SB, November 21, 1874.

36. SB, August 25, 1874. Within a few months the *Shenbao* reported that the Chaozhou merchants would no longer settle for a commission of 20 percent for the service of paying tax on behalf of the northern sugar merchants. The Jiang-Zhe *bang* appealed to the government for redress, to no avail (SB, November 21, 1874). On July 24, 1875, the *North China Herald* confirmed that the Fujian and Chaozhou merchants had been given a monopoly of the right of passing sugar through the tax office.

37. The tax office also pressured the Jiang-Zhe merchants to purchase sugar not from foreigners but from the Fujian and Chaozhou merchants. The Jiang-Zhe merchants criticized the Daotai for partiality and stated that they would wait for a Jiangsu official who would take up their case.

38. Peng Zeyi, "Shijiu shiji houqi Zhongguo chengshi shougongye shangye hanghui de chongjian he zuoyong" (The reestablishment and function of late-nineteenth-century

Important recent scholarship has maintained that the imposition of late-nineteenth-century taxes created a new sense of commonality among merchants which enabled them to transcend native-place ties. The examples discussed above suggest that it was equally possible (and perhaps more likely) for native-place *bang* to manipulate the new taxes and their tax-collection responsibilities in order to strengthen their position and reinforce regional distinctions.[39]

Quasi-Police Functions. To fulfill tax-collection and smuggling-prevention duties, it was not uncommon for merchant associations to hire low-paid runners. These men had to be streetwise, muscular and skilled fighters who could ferret out hidden goods and suppress smuggling. Thus *huiguan* depended on *tongxiang* toughs in order to match forces with smuggling gangs.[40] The best illustration again comes from the opium trade, which engendered the most profitable and most determined smuggling.

The employment of runners by the Opium Tax Bureau was endorsed by both Chinese and Settlement authorities to prevent smuggling. The Opium Tax Bureau initially hired seventeen runners; by 1875 the number had grown to thirty. In 1883 runners were uniformed and given identity cards stamped by both the Municipal Council and the Chinese Mixed Court Magistrate. Officially, these men were empowered to seize all smuggled opium and take it to the Tax Bureau. They could ask the police to arrest smugglers but could not make arrests themselves.[41]

---

urban handicraft and commercial associations), *Lishi yanjiu* 91 (February 1965), 91; Sanford, "Chinese Commercial Organization," 125.

39. This was also the conclusion of a western observer of the farming out of the *lijin* tax. Writing in 1905, he noted that "in this way, the guilds readily avail themselves of the opportunity to place prohibitive exactions on the goods of anyone not a member and thus debar outsiders" (T. R. Jernigan, *China in Law and Commerce* [New York, 1905], 219–20). For contrasting accounts of the effects of taxation in the late Qing, see Mann, *Local Merchants,* 25; Rowe, *Hankow: Commerce and Society,* 285–86. Mann and Rowe argue that taxation engendered bonds among merchants which transcended native-place ties.

40. *Huiguan*–gang connections persisted into the late Republican period. Lin Youren and Wang Shulin, formerly a janitor and a watchman for the Chaozhou Huiguan (interviewed in November 1983) emphasized *huiguan* need for street force in the 1930s, in particular the overlapping jurisdictions of Zheng Ziliang, a leader of a Red Gang–affiliated secret society (Sanhehui), the Chaozhou Tongxianghui and an honorary director of the Chaozhou Huiguan.

41. NCH, April 8, 1875; MCR for 1883. At first the runners worked on a commission basis, receiving rewards for each opium seizure. Because this led to abuses, in 1872 a joint proclamation by the Shanghai magistrate and the Tax Bureau provided for regular pay. By 1875 there were more than thirty paid runners, armed with bludgeons and iron bars.

In practice, agents of this Opium Tax Bureau indiscriminately seized all opium transported in the city on which no tax had been paid, including opium transported in the foreign settlements and registered under foreign names. They regularly assaulted suspects and dragged them off to the police and courts. No sooner were runners given official identification cards than police reports flowed in detailing disturbances connected with arrests of alleged smugglers. Moreover, the Opium Bureau did not hesitate to bring foreigners to court. When foreigners interfered with opium seizure, the Bureau sued for assault of its employees.[42]

Irritated by assaults on foreigners and the repeated exposure of foreigners engaged in smuggling, the Municipal Council began to limit the activities of the Tax Bureau. Police were instructed to permit certified runners to peacefully execute their duties but to suppress groups of unauthorized "rowdies" who accompanied the legitimate runners.[43]

The Opium Tax Bureau, supported by the Daotai, retaliated against Settlement police suppression by hiring foreigners to augment its forces. For Chief and Deputy-Chief runner, the wealthy Chaozhou merchants hired an Englishman and an Australian. It also engaged two foreign lawyers, Messrs. Drummond and Wainewright, to represent it in cases before the Mixed Court. Despite foreign protest, the antismuggling activities of the Opium Tax Bureau continued until smuggling was resolved by the commutation of all opium *lijin* through the addition of an increased import duty.[44]

The expansion of *huiguan* activities into the realm of urban management reflects a growing, mutually beneficial symbiosis with local officials, a relationship which in many ways resembled cycles of diminishing state initiative and local gentry activism but was also clearly generated by the new needs of a densely populated and socially and economically complex city. Given the intricacies of urban management and urban interactions, neither party to the relationship (the merchant managers or

42. MCR for 1885, 149–56, lists thirty-two official runners. In September 1885 two Filipinos carrying three balls of opium in the International Settlement were set upon by two authorized Bureau runners, accompanied by a gang of ruffians who beat the Filipinos severely. Municipal Council Chairman J. J. Keswick described such occurrences as frequent and noted that opium runners were almost always accompanied by thugs who employed violence as a matter of course. See also NCH, August 18, 1871; NCH, November 8, 1871; NCH, February 11, 1875; NCH, February 25, 1875; NCH, April 1, 1875.

43. MCR for 1885, 148–158; NCH, September 5, 1885; NCH, September 11, 1885. The Municipal Council stopped stamping the certification cards (which permitted passage through the Settlement) later in the year.

44. NCH, November 11, 1885.

the state) could be described as autonomous or controlling. In the case of opium-tax collection, Chaozhou merchants clearly exploited their bureaucratic position to increase their power in the city, making the opium-tax office an appendage to their *huiguan*. The *huiguan* merchants who operated the tax office were quick to use its influence and official status in dealings unrelated to opium. In March 1878 the opium office intervened in a case involving a Chaozhou rice-junk owner whose boat and cargo were damaged in a collision, mediating with the Shanghai Magistrate on behalf of the junk owner.[45] Such appropriations of state office for the nonofficial business of native-place groups was tolerated because such blurring of official and unofficial business was normal practice and because officials depended on the tax revenues produced by such offices.

In their quasi-governmental functions in the city, including their assumption of such bureaucratic functions as tax collection, *huiguan* directors acted in the interest of their sojourning communities. Although in the above examples sojourning merchants did not overtly take on public responsibilities out of a sense of identification with the broader municipality, such gradual identification may have been a paradoxical result. State reliance on *huiguan,* the frequent presence of *tongxiang* Shanghai officials at *huiguan* meetings and regularized assumption of bureaucratic and order-keeping functions enmeshed native-place associations increasingly in a citywide bureaucratic web.

Involvement in New Technological and Institutional Reform Projects

During the 1870s Shanghai *huiguan* leaders, the commercial elite of the city, became active exponents, investors and participants in innovative technological- and institutional-reform projects connected with the self-strengthening (*ziqiang*) and westernization (*yangwu*) movements. The Guangdong leaders Tang Jingxing, Xu Run and Zheng Guanying, because of their early compradorial experience, their exposure to western technology and the patronage of Li Hongzhang, were particularly active during the 1870s and 1880s. In the last decades of the

45. NCH, March 14, 1878.

century the Ningbo leaders Yen Xinhou, Ye Chengzhong and Yu Xia-qing joined them in influence as modernizing community leaders.

The social arrangements through which new technologies were pioneered in late-nineteenth-century Shanghai make clear the ambiguities of this important aspect of the process we refer to as "modernization." The prospects of new technological implants depended on their successful grafting onto specific native-place networks. Because of powerful competition from highly capitalized foreign firms which enjoyed the benefits of the unequal treaties and, frequently, because of a lack of support from the Chinese state, Chinese merchants could only succeed in expensive new ventures if they organized themselves into close, mutually supporting native-place networks. Important new communication and transportation technologies were spearheaded by specific native-place groups, often in competition with each other. For example, the technology of print lithography was first introduced into China through the Dianshi Studio, owned by the Englishman Frederick Major. Shortly afterward, Chinese entrepreneurs created two competing Chinese lithographic ventures, the Baishi Shanfang and the Tongwen Shuju. The Baishi enterprise belonged to the Ningbo *bang;* the Tongwen printing shop belonged to the Guangdong *bang.*[46] The stories of several outstanding Chinese experiments with new technologies bear telling because of the native-place meanings embedded in what might otherwise be imagined to be more socially neutral "modernization" processes.

The China Merchants' Steam Navigation Company. During the 1860s the steamship trade among the treaty ports was developed and dominated by the U.S. firm Russell and Company. Because traditional forms of investment provided less return, Chinese comprador-merchants with large amounts of capital were quick to invest in profitable foreign enterprises. More than one-third of the capital for Russell's joint-stock concern, the Shanghai Steam Navigation Company, was Chinese.[47]

46. Chen Boxi, *Shanghai yishi daguan,* vol. 2, 19–20. The Tongwen Shuju was established by the brothers Xu Run and Xu Hongfu. See Christopher Reed, "Steam Whistles and Fire-Wheels: Lithographic Printing and the Origins of Shanghai's Printing Factory System, 1876–1898" (paper presented at conference on Urban Progress, Business Development and Modernization in China, Shanghai, August 17–20, 1993), 16.

47. On the early history of steam shipping in China, see Kwang-ching Liu, *Anglo-American Steamship Rivalry in China* (Cambridge, Mass., 1962); Kwang-ching Liu, "British-Chinese Steamship Rivalry in China, 1873–85," in *The Economic Development of China and Japan,* ed. C. D. Cowan (London, 1964), 49–50. On compradorial investments in steam shipping, see Hao, *Comprador,* 120–21.

Viewing with dismay both foreign control over much of Shanghai's economic life in the early 1860s and Chinese investment in foreign enterprises, the reformist Shanghai Daotai Ding Richang, together with Li Hongzhang, began to consider ways to recover Chinese control over the economy by promoting Chinese ventures. In 1863 Ding attempted to make Chinese shipping more competitive by lowering taxes on Chinese junks. The next year he proposed to Li Hongzhang that the government encourage Chinese merchants to purchase and construct steamships. In 1868 Yung Wing (Rong Hong, a Yale-educated reformist entrepreneur from Guangdong), with the support of the Zongli Yamen, attempted to create a Chinese joint-stock steamship company but failed for lack of capital. Finally a joint stock company was set up under the aegis of Li Hongzhang, who viewed the enterprise as a fundamental element in a commercial war (*shangzhan*) with western companies. Li's advocacy of mercantile nationalism was shared by the vocal reformer Zheng Guanying and his Guangdong fellow-provincial compradors Tang Jingxing and Xu Run, both of whom were important investors in steam shipping. Tang, Xu and Zheng would all be participants in the China Merchants' Steam Navigation Company (CMSNC), the first attempt on the part of Chinese officials to take action to compete with western enterprise.[48]

Aware of the need for merchant investment as well as merchants' hesitancy to become involved without official patronage, financial support and security against burdensome official meddling, Li developed the idea of *guandu shangban* (merchant undertaking under official supervision) as the organizational principle of the endeavor. After an initial unproductive start, Li made Tang Jingxing commissioner in charge of the CMSNC. In 1873 Tang resigned as Jardine's comprador and brought in Xu Run to help restructure the business. The reorganized company quickly became a highly successful competitor of western shipping firms.[49]

---

48. Yen-p'ing Hao, "Changing Chinese Views of Western Relations, 1840–95," in *Cambridge History of China*, 190–92; Liu, "British-Chinese Steamship Rivalry in China," 53. The Chinese name of the company was the *lunchuan zhaoshangju* (literally, Bureau for Inviting Merchants to Operate Steamships).

49. See Liu, "British-Chinese Steamship Rivalry in China," 53, for a discussion of this principle. The CMSNC was not the only government-sponsored enterprise which involved Guangdong merchants. In 1877 Li created the Kaiping Mining Company, which would be directed by Tang Jingxing and two other Guangdong merchants, Xu Run and Wu Zhichang (Hao, "Changing Chinese Views," 423). The successful management of the CMSNC is detailed in Chi-kong Lai, "Lunchuan zhaoshangju guoyou wenti, 1878–1881"

The early success of the Chinese steamship company depended on both official patronage and subsidies and Guangdong native-place networks. Tang raised investments in the company through his close ties to Xu Run and other like-minded Guangdong merchants, who participated together in the leadership of the Guang-Zhao Gongsuo. Although Tang hired foreign experts to serve as marine superintendent, as ship captains and as engineers, he relied on sojourning Guangdong merchants as managers and to handle the freighting business. Liu Shaozong (Seating), a Hankou-based Guangdong merchant, took charge of the Hankou office. The freight-brokerage system of the Chinese company was based on the connections of the Guang-Zhao Gongsuo in other treaty ports, reinforced by generous commissions. This extended multiport native-place merchant network ensured a regular clientele for company shipping. As company business became Guangdong business, it stimulated greater coordination and communication between the Shanghai Guang-Zhao Gongsuo and the Hankou Lingnan Huiguan.[50]

Non-Guangdong merchants were not pleased by the Guangdong hold over the CMSNC. When the CMSNC published an appeal in 1875 asking all Chinese merchants to ship their cargo on CMSNC boats to support a Chinese, rather than a foreign-owned, enterprise, merchants from other areas bridled at the officially supported Guangdong monopoly:

[As a native of a central province], I have resided many years in Shanghai, as a shipper to Yangtze and northern ports. Cheap freights and attention to the convenience and interests of the shipper are important to the trader. Now the China Merchants Steam Navigation Company is entirely under

(Nationalization problems of the China Merchants' Steam Navigation Company), *Jindaishi yanjiusuo jikan* 17 (1988):15–40; Chi-kong Lai, "Lunchuan zhaoshangju jingying guanli wenti, 1872–1901" (Management problems of the China Merchants' Steam Navigation Company), *Jindaishi yanjiusuo jikan* 19 (1990):67–108; Chi-kong Lai, "The Qing State and Merchant Enterprise: Officials, Merchants and Resource Allocation in the China Merchants' Company, 1872–1902" (paper presented at the Symposium on Qing Imperial State and the Economy, University of Akron, February 22–23, 1991).

50. Xu Run had invested four hundred eighty thousand taels in the enterprise by 1882, when paid stock amounted to two million taels. His relatives and friends subscribed an additional five to six hundred thousand taels. Liu was Hankou comprador for Augustine, Heard and Company (Hao, *Comprador,* 123). Government support included generous payments for carrying government "tribute rice" as well as tax relief (Kwang-ching Liu, "Steamship Enterprise in Nineteenth-Century China," *Journal of Asian Studies* 18 [August 1959]:443–44; Liu, "British-Chinese Steamship Rivalry, 55). See Xia Dongyuan, *Zheng Guanying ji,* vol. 2, 917, for a communication between Zheng Guanying and the Guang-Zhao Gongsuo regarding Hankou business.

the charge of Cantonese — no other province man being in management. Although there are able and honorable men among them, it is to be feared they are not very experienced in the conduct of foreign steamer shipping [seeing that they employ foreign captains]. . . . When the Cantonese appeal to us to ship all of our cargo by their steamers, I reply and ask why should we, the merchants of other provinces do this? . . . Supposing that the China Merchants Steam Navigation Company, depending on their rice convey-ance profits, were really able to run off foreign vessels? We would see but one Steam Navigation Company, managed by Cantonese and controlled by the mandarins . . . , with no guarantee that the interest of the shipper would be attended to.[51]

Ningbo merchants took the opportunity offered by collisions between CMSNC steamers and other boats to criticize the company and its Guangdong management. During 1874 and 1875, along with reports of various collisions, *Shenbao* articles attacked the excessive government subsidies, the company's use of a foreign steamer to ship tribute rice and its faulty navigational skills. A legal case arising after a collision with a Ningbo junk led to conflict between the Guangdong managers of the CMSNC and the *Shenbao,* which published articles sympathetic to the Ningbo junk owners. The *North China Herald* reported that the com-pany threatened a libel suit against the newspaper for alleging that the CMSNC had extorted statements from the Ningbo crew, forcing them to take responsibility for the accident.[52]

Although the company was not uncontroversial and was clearly per-ceived as a Guangdong, as opposed to a truly national, enterprise, there is no question that it was highly successful between 1872 and 1884, while it was under merchant management. It declined in the 1885–1902 period, when, as Chi-kong Lai details, it reverted to bureaucratic management.[53]

Ningbo merchants not only complained about the CMSNC but wanted their own Ningbo shipping line. In 1882 the influential Ningbo merchant Ye Chengzhong petitioned the court requesting permission to establish a shipping company which would run steamers in competi-tion with the CMSNC.[54] Ye's petition was not granted, but Ningbo

51. NCH, April 24, 1875, 395, translation of a letter appearing in the *Shenbao.*
52. SB, April 13, 1874, regarding details of the sinking of a Ningbo boat by the CMSNC on January 13, 1874; SB, May 11, 1875; SB, August 2, 1875; NCH, July 24, 1875; NCH, August 7, 1875; NCH, August 21, 1875.
53. Lai, "Lunchuan zhaoshangju guoyou wenti"; Lai, "Lunchuan zhaoshanghu jing-ying guanli wenti"; Lai, "Qing State and Merchant Enterprise."
54. The circumstances surrounding Ye's 1882 petition are recounted in NCH, Septem-ber 10, 1887.

discontents did not rest. Several decades later, under the initiative of Yu Xiaqing, Zhejiang merchants finally realized their ambitions by establishing the Ning-Shao Steamboat Company, which successfully competed with other companies along the Shanghai–Ningbo route. The majority of passengers along this route were Ningbo and Shaoxing people who had long been irritated by the high rates of passage charged by Jardine's, Russell's China Steam Navigation Company, and the CMSNC. To assert control over their own travel and to provide less expensive passage for their community, in 1909 the Shanghai Zhejiang community raised more than one million taels in stock to purchase steamboats and construct docks for the express purpose of transporting fellow-provincials. The success of this venture owed not to state sponsorship but to the loyal patronage of a large Ningbo clientele. Once the company was established, its shipping competitors engaged in a ruthless price war to wipe out the new competition. In response, more than one hundred major Ningbo merchants formed a Ning-Shao Shipping Protection Association, which raised money to support the line.[55] Without this kind of community support, it is unlikely that the company could have survived the competitive environment.

The Birth of the Huibao. During the Yang Yuelou affair recounted in Chapter 3, the Guangdong people attempted to destroy the *Shenbao* (even reportedly threatening to burn down the office) in response to their poor treatment on its pages. Forced to abandon this approach because of the protection the *Shenbao* received through its foreign ownership, the leaders of the Guangdong community arrived at a more creative solution. As reported in the *North China Herald,* they announced that they would begin an opposition newspaper backed by the power and wealth of their *huiguan.* The result was the ambitious launching during 1874–75 of a wholly Chinese-owned and -organized daily newspaper, the *Huibao.*[56]

The most powerful Guangdong leaders — including Yong Wing

55. Similar tactics supported the founding of two Ningbo modern banks (Shangye Yinhang and Siming Yinhang) by the major Ningbo capitalists Yu Xiaqing, Zhou Jinzhen, Li Yunshu and Chen Ziqin. See SB, March 2, 1911; Chen Boxi, *Shanghai yishi daguan,* 172; Chen Laixin, *Yu Xiaqing ni tsuite* (Regarding Yu Xiaqing) (Kyoto, 1983).

56. NCH, January 29, 1874; NCH, February 12, 1874. The *Huibao* appeared a year after the brief launching of the first Chinese-owned newspaper, the *Zhaowen xinbao* in Hankou. See Ge Gongzhen, *Zhongguo baoxueshi* (History of Chinese newspapers) (Hong Kong, 1964), 120; Roswell Britton, *The Chinese Periodical Press, 1800–1912* (Shanghai, 1933), 71–2; Rowe, *Hankow: Conflict and Community,* 24.

(Rong Hong), Tang Jingxing, Rong Chunfu, and major Guangdong tea compradors—raised a fund of ten thousand taels and established the newspaper in a building adjoining the offices of the Guangdong-controlled China Merchants' Steam Navigation Company. The newspaper also received the support of Magistrate Ye Tingjuan. According to the *North China Herald*, the *Huibao* was initially distributed free of charge, in an attempt to crush the *Shenbao*.[57]

The *Huibao*, celebrated as radical and progressive in Britton's history of the Chinese periodical press (and today in Chinese press histories) and as "conservative and antiforeign" by the contemporary *North China Herald*, did not survive 1876. As the *North China Herald* response indicates, the newspaper's critical stance toward the foreign presence in China irritated foreign authorities in the city. According to Ge Gongzhen, the *Huibao* adopted a policy of "pen war" (*bizhan*) with the foreign-owned *Shenbao*, stepping in whenever *Huibao* editors felt the foreign-owned newspaper had betrayed China's interests. Through its outspoken editorial policy the newspaper also incurred the disfavor of Chinese officials, and (after experiments with greater political discretion and an attempt to create an extraterritorial shield through a nominal British proprietor) the merchant backers gradually withdrew from the venture. It stands, nonetheless, as a bold and early creation of a privately owned and instigated Chinese newspaper, stimulated by native-place tensions in the city and organized by a single native-place group.[58] The creation of the *Huibao* and the history of the Guangdong people's struggles with the *Shenbao* demonstrate that newspapers were not uncomplicated vehicles of a new urban identity. Shanghai newspapers, like enterprises in the city, bore native-place tags.

Economic Nationalism, Modern Enterprises and Cosmopolitanism

The "expansive practices" of the native-place merchant networks described in this chapter suggest the ways in which native-

57. NCH, February 12, 1874. According to Britton (*Chinese Periodical Press*, 72), *Huibao* subscriptions were paid.

58. NCH, August 4, 1874; NCH, February 10, 1876; Britton, *Chinese Periodical Press*, 72; Liang Jialu, *Zhongguo xinwenye shi* (History of Chinese journalism) (Nanning, 1984), 66–67.

place identity shaped understandings of national and urban identity in post-Taiping Shanghai and of new and "modern" things. As the charitable activities of the late 1870s and 1880s demonstrate, native-place identities and networks did not diminish as merchants broadened their "public" horizons to cooperate with non-*tongxiang* to provide assistance for people in distant areas of China. This is to say that native-place loyalties did not interfere with cooperation in citywide or (especially) national projects. Close-knit and mutually supporting sojourner networks were no obstacle; rather, they facilitated Chinese adaptations of new technologies, even as they imprinted these technologies with their native-place identities.

Continuing native-place loyalties did, nonetheless, result in a competitive tension which underlay these and other enterprises. This rivalry both resulted in the native-place colonization of particularly lucrative state-sponsored commercial enterprises and motivated groups of merchants to organize in risky private ventures in order to control powerful new technologies which (in the hands of outsiders) might be used against them.

The "expansive practices" of native-place networks, because they crossed localist and "traditional" boundaries, help us to understand the workings of "tradition" in practices of "modernity" and the uses of provincial ties within the experience of cosmopolitanism. The leaders of the major native-place communities in late-nineteenth-century Shanghai were arguably among the most cosmopolitan men in the city. The social networks and responsibilities of *huiguan* leaders were extremely broad, as reflected in Tang Maozhi's explanation to Jardine's as to why he was frequently unable to attend to all of his compradorial duties: "As chairman of the Canton Guild, I have always some cases in hand, for inquiry, arrangement or decision. Many officials and [scholars] pass up and down through this port, they pay me their formal visits and I have to return them. . . . I have to make friends all around."[59] Like Tang, many *huiguan* leaders were compradors who, as Hao Yen-p'ing has shown, were leading exponents of western legal structures and institutional arrangements to facilitate commercial development. Knowledge of western languages and compradorial and treaty-port experience gave them an expertise in foreign relations which the Chinese government relied on repeatedly in attempts to deflect and negotiate the problem of foreign expansion on Chinese soil.[60]

59. Quoted in Hao, *Comprador,* 188. The date of Tang's letter is dated September 27, 1877.
60. For example, both Yang Fang and Xu Yuting were called on by the Qing to negotiate with British and French allied forces in 1860. After China's defeat in the Sino–Japanese War (1894–95), Governor General Zhang Zhidong instructed the Shanghai mag-

These men were major actors in the highly cosmopolitan arenas of Shanghai commerce and politics, arenas which encompassed an ethnically diverse Chinese population and a foreign community of diverse nationals. But cosmopolitanism could not come to semicolonial Shanghai as a neutral or apolitical process, nor did it necessitate (among Chinese or in interactions with foreigners) either mutual tolerance or a refusal to take sides. The reform-minded merchant leaders, whose business and political activities regularly involved them in interprovincial commercial networks, close ties with reformist officials and even international relations, depended for their survival on native-place ties and clearly felt no compunction about benefiting their *tongxiang* while they pursued the broader ideals of economic nationalism in the interest of strengthening the Chinese state.

This tendency and the native-place rivalries it engendered did not impede abstract identification with the larger polity but did, in practice, limit merchants' commitment to specific state projects. As the *Shenbao* debates over the CMSNC make clear, non-Guangdong merchants did not feel that their national identity as Chinese was sufficiently compelling to make them support what they perceived to be a Guangdong shipping company acting in Guangdong interests.

In his richly researched study of late imperial Hankou, William Rowe organizes his portrait of a highly diverse, competitive urban metropolis through an interpretive framework which, while sensitively observing conflict among different native-place groups, emphasizes by the late nineteenth century "an unusually high level of cultural tolerance on the part of the urban population" and the development of *Hankou* urban identity.[61] The behavior of the most cosmopolitan Shanghai elites in this period, elites which were tied, through *tongxiang* connections, to Hankou elites and urban institutions, suggests a somewhat different framing of the issues of cosmopolitanism and urban identity. The tendency of sojourning elites to seek powerful official patrons in this period, together with their evident need to rely on native-place loyalties to support new multiport enterprises, worked against the practical usefulness of developing specific urban identity as *Shanghai* people, even though their location in Shanghai was fundamental to their transcending of provincial boundaries. The battles between the *Huibao* and the *Shenbao* and the demise of the *Huibao* in the absence of foreign pro-

istrate to seek advice from Shanghai merchants, mentioning, in particular, the Guangdong merchants (Hao, *Comprador,* 190–91).

61. Rowe, *Hankow: Conflict and Community,* 27.

tection suggest both the limitations on the development of public media at this time and the fact that exposure to urban newspapers did not necessarily result in cosmopolitanism on the municipal level. The Guangdong/Ningbo attempts to control public discourse in late-nineteenth-century Shanghai make it clear that "public media," far from acting as neutral vehicles of cultural tolerance, bore national and native-place labels and interests. The story of the *Huibao* is relevant to discussions of a "public sphere" in China which stress the role of newspapers because it shows that an independently organized Chinese newspaper with strong backers could not survive in this period, raising questions about the possibilities for public debate.

This is not to say that sojourning elites were not intimately involved with Shanghai. It is, rather, that Shanghai identity was in practice less useful, less frequently invoked and less fundamental than native-place and national identity. Sojourning elites invested heavily in Shanghai businesses and real estate and contributed to Shanghai urban management through the government of their broad sojourning communities as well as the provision of certain broader urban services. They also occasionally cooperated in specific citywide ventures. Nonetheless, in this period, prior to the existence of a Chinese municipal government which could claim the city as its own (and against which sojourning groups could position themselves), the adoption of Shanghai identity for sojourners would have been constraining. Major *huiguan* leaders of the late nineteenth century were highly cosmopolitan figures. Their cosmopolitanism, however, took place more at a national than at a municipal level; that is, they were cosmopolitan not because they lived in Shanghai but because they transcended Shanghai. Because their native-place ties extended beyond both the native place and Shanghai—and, indeed, provided multiport networks of support and an organizational basis for action on a national scale—they found it extremely useful to retain and cultivate native-place identity.

CHAPTER FIVE

Native-Place Associations, Foreign Authority and Early Popular Nationalism

Foreign authorities in Shanghai had to contend with native-place associations from the moment they established settlements in
the city, after the formal opening of Shanghai to foreign trade in November 1843. Agreements concluded between Chinese authorities and
the British and French in the 1840s regulated foreign use and purchase
of land within designated areas (see Maps 4 and 5).[1] In both the British
Settlement and the French Concession, foreigners were enjoined by
Chinese authorities to respect *huiguan* and *gongsuo* and to preserve the
integrity of the coffin repositories and burial grounds maintained by
these institutions.[2] As foreign settlements grew, *huiguan* and *gongsuo*
(which were among the largest Chinese corporate landholders in the
city) presented obstacles to foreign colonialist expansion.

Struggle over *huiguan* land soon erupted into the first violent conflicts between Chinese and foreigners in post-Taiping Shanghai. Because

1. The British settlement was formalized in 1845. The French Concession was established in 1849. These settlements were to have been reserved for foreigners (and Chinese
in their employ) only, but that arrangement lasted only until Taiping forces swept through
the Yangzi valley in 1860, bringing thousands of refugees from Zhejiang, Jiangsu and
Anhui cities and villages to the Shanghai foreign settlements. An area along the Huangpu
River, north of the Suzhou Creek, which was occupied by Americans, merged with the
British settlement in 1863, forming what would henceforth be recognized as the International Settlement. By the late nineteenth century there were approximately one-half mil-
lion Chinese living within the boundaries of the International Settlement and the separate
French Concession.

2. AMRE, Chine, Correspondance Consulaire, 1847–51, document dated November
6, 1849.

Map 4. Shanghai in 1880. Source: Section of map published by Dianshi Studio, 1880. (Courtesy of Hamashita Takeshi).

Siming Gongsuo (Ningbo Huiguan) site
and surrounding burial land.

French Concession

Chinese City

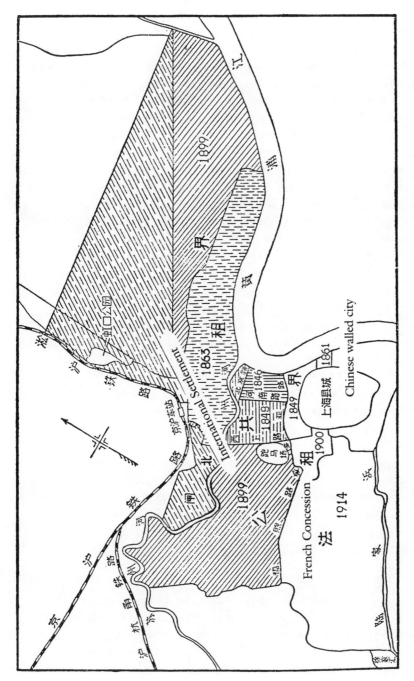

Map 5. The development of the French and International settlements. Source: Xu Gongsu and Qiu Jinzhang, eds., *Shanghai gong-gong zujie shigao* (Shanghai, 1980).

of their religious and symbolic importance to a broad sojourning community, *huiguan* could easily mobilize important sectors of the Chinese community in defense of their interests. By the turn of the century, native-place associations involved in such conflicts acquired reputations as symbols of a popular nationalist struggle against brutal imperialism.

Despite the role of native-place organization in antiforeign incidents, relations between *huiguan* and foreign authorities were not normally governed by conflict. As in their dealings with Chinese authorities, *huiguan* regularly cooperated with the administrations of the growing foreign settlements, which in turn relied upon them. This was a natural outcome of the multiplicity of administrative jurisdictions and the dispersion of public power that characterized semicolonial Shanghai. Insofar as cooperation with foreign powers reinforced *huiguan* authority, *huiguan* kept order in the settlements. When foreigners encroached on *huiguan* interests, *huiguan* did not hesitate to disturb the peace.

Foreign Reliance on *Huiguan* in the Maintenance of Settlement Order

Once the settlement governments were firmly established they began to rely on native-place associations for resources and assistance in the government of the Chinese communities within their borders. In the process the foreign authorities circumvented Chinese officials and placed the leaders of native-place associations in the position of representing the Chinese community. In this respect, the foreign presence in the city forced a certain reconceptualization of the meaning of *huiguan* as urban institutions, bringing together disparate native-place institutions into collective committees. When such committees were counterposed to and coordinated with foreign municipal authorities, they represented not the native place but the composite urban Chinese community.

Public Funding, Population Management and Judicial Functions. Throughout the 1870s and 1880s, *huiguan* and *gongsuo* provided funding for the joint Fire Commission of the international settlements. The importance of their contributions is reflected in a listing of major contributors to the commission in the Shanghai Municipal Council Report for 1875:

International Settlement   2,500 taels
French Concession   1,000 taels
Huiguan and Gongsuo   1,120 taels
Chinese Government   400 taels

Huiguan and *gongsuo* also helped fund the foreign police. Surviving account books of the Guang-Zhao Gongsuo for 1873 and 1874 list two types of payment to the settlement police (in addition to the payment of regular taxes), amounting to more than 250 taels a year from this one *huiguan*.[3]

Just as Chinese authorities relied on *huiguan* and *gongsuo* to resolve disputes within the Chinese population, foreign assessors in the Mixed Court routinely consulted with *huiguan*. As one assessor recalled:

> The guilds [*huiguan* and *gongsuo*] of China are not organized under charters from the [Chinese] Government, but the Government has always recognized their power and has usually been careful to avoid open conflict. Conflict, as we have seen, has usually resulted in defeat for the Government.
>
> The guilds . . . have their own courts, and their members, as a rule, avoid the official courts. Sometimes, however, it is impossible to do this. Outside parties bring suits against guild members. . . . In the past, however, the Government courts have usually decided such cases in harmony with the regulations of the guild concerned.
>
> While living in Shanghai it was my duty . . . to serve as American Assessor in the Mixed Court. . . . In the various civil suits that were brought before the court it was the rule to consult the regulations of the guild concerned.[4]

Foreign authorities also enlisted *huiguan* help in maintaining order among Chinese residents of the settlements during times of social and political crisis. In contrast with the periods of the Taiping threat (1860–62) and the war with Japan (1894), when Chinese took refuge in the foreign settlements, the antiforeign violence of the Boxers in North China in 1900 led to an exodus of Chinese residents who feared staying within the International Settlement. The alarmed Municipal Council posted proclamations to calm the population. Unable to allay the fleeing residents' anxieties, the Council convened representatives of "all the leading provincial guilds" to enlist their help in dissuading would-be emigrés by reinforcing security. For those determined to leave, they issued bilingual passes to control the population flow: "The measures for

3. *Guang-Zhao gongsuo zhengxinlu*, 1873, 1874.
4. E. T. Williams, *China, Yesterday and Today* (New York, 1923), 203–4.

the defense of Shanghai Settlement, arranged by the Council and the headmen of local Guilds [*ge huiguan dongshi*], have already been duly communicated to the public by notice. The Committee of the ———— Guild, having now reported that Chinese resident ———— is anxious to change his residence . . . , this pass is hereby issued to state there is no objection to his removal. Police protection provided where necessary."[5] Consultation and cooperation between major *huiguan* and the foreign authorities became general practice, as the Municipal Council recognized: "Whenever in the past any important questions have arisen affecting the Chinese community, it has been the custom for the Council to consult with the headman or committee of local guilds, so as to devise measures beneficial to those concerned. This was especially the case during the Boxer trouble of 1900, when the guilds, cooperating with the Council, did so much good in reassuring the general public."[6]

Although *huiguan* cooperated with settlement authorities, they retained considerable autonomy and remained impenetrable to foreign efforts to understand and control them. The "guilds" almost entirely eluded the settlement police who attempted an investigation in 1904. Instructed to obtain a complete list of "all guilds and similar organizations within the Settlement," the police set out to discover the rudimentary characteristics of each association, including the purpose for which they were established, the number and composition of their membership, the leaders' names and the general regulations. They were disappointed. Contrary to expectations, "information was not immediately furnished [by the guilds]. . . . The majority, beyond [some] verbal answers . . . failed to reply." The Council continued to hope that "the guilds will alter [their] policy of obstruction," but there was little it could do, and it never obtained a satisfactory accounting of these associations.[7]

Huiguan as Representative Bodies. In the period prior to 1911, the western residents of the International Settlement resisted any form of Chinese representation in settlement government. When a "Chinese Consultative Committee" was proposed by leaders of three prominent *huiguan* in December 1905, the Ratepayer's Association rejected the measure on the grounds that the plan "foreshadowed undue

5. MCR for 1900, 81–82.
6. MCR for 1904, 25.
7. Ibid., 26–28.

influence and intervention in the affairs of the Foreign Settlement," asserting moreover, that "advice regarding native interests is available
without formal organization." Nonetheless, as the Ratepayers' statement testifies, an informal system of representation existed and functioned with a certain efficacy if without legal standing.[8]

In 1910 the Municipal Council informally recognized a body of fourteen principal "guilds" in the foreign settlements:

Ningpo (Ningbo) Provincials' Guild

Cantonese (Guangdong) Provincials' Guild

Shantung (Shandong) Provincials' Guild

Nanking (Nanjing) Guild

Wusieh (Wuxi) Guild

Shanse (Shanxi) Bankers' Guild

Guild of the Chihli (Zhili) Provincials and Eight Banner Corps

Exchange Bankers' Guild

Gold Guild

Pawn Brokers' Guild

Silk Guild

(Huzhou) Silk Cocoon Merchants' Guild

Tea Traders' Guild

Foreign Piece Goods Dealers' Guild

When matters arose affecting the Chinese community, the Council addressed inquiries to some or all of these organizations to assess Chinese opinion.[9]

Close cooperation between the Municipal Council and a similarly
constituted informal committee of *huiguan* and *gongsuo* leaders helped
ameliorate an explosive situation at the end of 1910, remembered as the

8. MCR for 1906, 392–95. Such consultation was a key element in strike resolution, in
which western authorities sought *huiguan* mediation. When, for example, Guangdong
carpenters struck in the International Settlement in 1902, the Municipal Council negotiated with the Guang-Zhao Gongsuo (GZGYB, 1902).

9. For instance, when a Chinese amusement center was proposed, the Council con-
sulted the following associations: the Guangdong, Wuxi, Shanxi, Ningbo, Zhili, and
Huzhou silk *huiguan,* the foreign piece goods, exchange bankers and tea and gold *gongsuo*
(MCR for 1910, 88, 272–73).

Plague Riots of November 11–18. As was frequently the case, tension developed between Chinese residents and foreign authorities over an issue of public health. The appearance of bubonic plague in Shanghai in the fall provided the Municipal Council of the International Settlement with a pretext for enacting special public-health bylaws which enlarged the scope of foreign authority over Chinese residents.[10] Plague-infected rat corpses had appeared in the preceding year and — while counting the rat corpses brought in by Chinese laborers hired and given chopsticks for this task of collection — the Council readied itself for action. After a human plague death in the Settlement at the end of October, the Council enacted emergency plague-prevention measures. It established a plague station and surveillance system in the surrounding "plague area." Within this area (the Hongkou district), municipal health officers and sanitary investigators inspected all houses daily, forcibly removing residents suspected of harboring plague and placing those found ill and those in contact with them in an isolation hospital. Crews then evacuated the entire housing block around these designated points of disease, removed ceilings, foundations and other rat-friendly areas, surrounded the block with rat-proof barricades and fumigated with sulphur.

Not surprisingly, these measures (exacerbated by rumor and the absence of any program of public education) provoked severe unrest in the Chinese community. On November 12, 1910, hearing that the foreign authorities were seizing and killing women and children for esoteric purposes, bands of Chinese pelted foreigners with stones, beat sanitary inspectors with bamboo poles and smashed disinfecting vans and equipment. Hundreds of women and children fled the International Settlement for Chinese areas of Shanghai or the French Concession. The *North China Herald* called for "a representative committee of Chinese from the Guilds and prominent residents" to cooperate with the Municipal authorities and reach "the ignorant masses of the Chinese" in the

10. The bylaws, first proposed in 1903, made Chinese liable for notifying authorities of suspected plague cases, subject to fines and hard labor for noncompliance; Chinese were forbidden to move or bury corpses without the Health Officer's consent; the Council was empowered to evict residents and demolish houses of plague victims; finally, overcrowding was made an offense subject to penalty. Any residence inhabited "in excess of a proportion of one person for every 40 square feet of floor space and 400 cubic feet of clear and unobstructed internal air space" was considered overcrowded (this last law, proposed by the Council, was not approved by the Consular Body). See MCR for 1910, 146–49. See also Richard Feetham, *Report of the Hon. Richard Feetham to the Shanghai Municipal Council* (Shanghai, 1931), vol. 1, 59. Regarding plague in China, see Carol Benedict, "Bubonic Plague in Nineteenth Century China," MC 14 (April 1988):107–55.

urgent matter of plague prevention, admitting the Council's mistake in abruptly enforcing insufficiently explained health measures. In the meantime, the Council gave notice that the new health bylaws would be put into force on November 14.[11]

On November 13, together with the president and vice-president of the Chinese Shanghai Chamber of Commerce, prominent *huiguan* and *gongsuo* directors sent a letter to David Landale, Chairman of the Municipal Council, expressing their desire to help prevent plague but making the moderation of plague-prevention measures a precondition for their services.[12] Before acceding to this pressure, the Council made an abortive attempt to reason with Chinese residents directly in a public meeting on November 16, hoping to persuade them of the necessity of the health procedures. Prior to the meeting the Council distributed educational posters and leaflets. As a precaution, only "well-dressed, respectable Chinese" were admitted. Leaders of Shanghai *huiguan* and *gongsuo* were given front seats and were asked to speak. Nonetheless, the meeting was a disaster. The only moment of audience enthusiasm occurred when Ningbo notable Shen Dunhe (Shen Zhongli) was cheered by his *tongxiang* for promising to arrange construction of a Chinese Isolation Hospital outside the Settlement. As soon as he referred to the plague-prevention measures, the meeting was broken up by violent protests.[13]

On November 17 Council Chairman Landale notified Zhou Jinzhen (Zhou Jinbiao), Chairman of the Shanghai Chamber of Commerce, as well as directors of major Shanghai *huiguan* and *gongsuo,* that the bylaws would refer to plague outbreaks only. He forwarded a revised code (amended according to their instructions) for their approval and expressed the Council's need for help: "The Council notes with greatest satisfaction that you are in sympathy with the . . . prevention of Plague,

11. MCR for 1910, 91–97, 107, 150; PRO, FO 405.201, "China Annual Report, 1910," 36; NCH, November 11, 1910; NCH, November 18, 1910; Feetham, *Report,* 58.

12. The first signatories to the letter after the officers of the Chamber were three Siming Gongsuo directors, seven individuals identified as the "Committee of the Canton Guild," five "Canton Guild" (possibly Chaozhou Huiguan) directors and six Native Bank Guild directors. The letter protested the use of the plague outbreak as a pretext for introducing general health bylaws. The Shanghai Daotai, Liu Yanyi, separately complained that the Council had provoked the Chinese population by failing to prepare the community for the health measures. He also objected to the empowerment of foreign authorities to pull down houses, arguing that this impinged on Chinese sovereignty. See MCR for 1910, 144–45.

13. NCH, November 18, 1910; SB, November 15, 1910; SB, November 17, 1910; AMRE, Chine, Politique Étrangère, Concession Française de Changhai, vol. 277, 1911–12.

and gratefully accepts your offer of cooperation in the no less difficult task of explaining to those who are ignorant what is required and what has to be done."[14]

The next day the Municipal Council met with representatives of the Chinese community to discuss the plague measures. In attendance were Chamber of Commerce Chairman Zhou Jinzhen (also Siming Gongsuo director), vice-president Shao Qintao (of Zhangzhou, Jiangsu), Wen Zongyao (Guang-Zhao Gongsuo director), Zhong Ziyuan (director of both Guang-Zhao Gongsuo and the Shanghai–Nanjing Railway), Tian Zhimin (of Shangyu, Zhejiang, and Cotton Yarn Guild director), Shen Dunhe (Siming Gongsuo director, also representing the Imperial Bank of China), Yu Xiaqing (Siming Gongsuo director and Netherlands Bank comprador), Zhu Baosan (both Siming Gongsuo and the Foreign Piece Goods Guild director), Wang Ruizhi (Shandong Guild director), Zhu Lanfang (director of both the Huaxing Flour Company and the Xijin [Wuxi] Huiguan), Xu Gongruo (Huzhou Silk Association director), Chen Yizhai (of Shangyu, Zhejiang; Native Bankers Association director), Yang Xinzhi (of Wucheng, Zhejiang; Cocoon and Silk Guild director).[15]

The discussion lasted for six hours, during which time the Chinese representatives secured significant modifications in the proposed plague-prevention procedures.[16] The Chinese press celebrated this resolution as something of a popular nationalist victory. Praising the Chinese negotiators, the *Shenbao* stressed that citizen action had protected Chinese interests: "Despite our timid and weak officials, the strength and sincerity of the people's spirit in our country is something to be proud of."[17]

14. MCR for 1910, 146.

15. NCH mistakenly identifies Tian as a Guang-Zhao Gongsuo director (November 25, 1910). Given NCH inaccuracies, the above identifications of individuals and affiliations are based on *Shanghai shangwu zonghui tongrenlu* (Record of members of the Shanghai General Chamber of Commerce) (Shanghai, 1910); SGY, 1915; SBZX. Also in attendance was a certain "China Thompson" of the Foreign Merchandise Association.

16. NCH, November 25, 1910; MCR for 1910, 91–97, 107, 150. In addition to restricting the bylaws to plague alone, it was agreed that the search for Chinese cases should be conducted by Chinese doctors from an independently instituted Chinese plague hospital, accompanied by a female western doctor. Searches were restricted to an area within the Hongkou district (the location of the plague death). Finally, if deaths were to ensue from infection, all matters of laying out and burial were to be arranged in accordance with Chinese customs.

17. SB, November 19, 1910. The Chinese account lists the relevant actors in the negotiations as Zhou Jinzhen and Shao Qintao, the president and vice-president of the Shanghai Chamber; Ningbo *bang* directors Yu Xiaqing and Shen Zhongli; Guangdong *bang* direc-

These measures both resolved the difficulties and restricted the attempted extension of foreign municipal authority over Chinese residents. Although Chinese officials had at various points voiced protests in this matter, unofficial associations rather than the Chinese government mediated on behalf of the Chinese people in the resolution of the crisis.[18] In the meantime, Ningbo and Guangdong association leaders cooperated in the implementation of the new plague-prevention plan. In the presence of the foreign community, the Ningbo leader Shen Dunhe applauded the efforts of the Guang-Zhao Gongsuo in establishing a Chinese hospital: "I have the pleasure to inform you that through the assistance of Messrs. Lo King-sou and Chun Bing-him, members of the Committee of the Cantonese Guild, we have been able to secure a site . . . for the Paotian Hospital. This property is known as 'Verdant Villa' and formed the summer residence of Cheong Chi-pio, the well-known Cantonese merchant who parted with it to the Chinese Plague Committee for a nominal sum — an act of charity and public spirit."[19]

This case also makes clear that although the modern and inclusive-sounding Shanghai General Chamber of Commerce appeared as a new actor in the Shanghai political arena after 1902, it did not displace the older *huiguan* and *gongsuo,* particularly the more powerful ones like the Siming Gongsuo and the Guang-Zhao Gongsuo in their function of representing the Chinese community. Rather, in this period new institutional identifications were added to older ones. The interweaving of older and newer institutional forms is evident in the overlapping Chamber/*huiguan*/trade affiliations of the Chinese negotiators. Although the Municipal Council often found it convenient to direct its letters to the "guilds" through the Chamber, this practice reveals that the "guilds" continued to be important actors. The Chamber was made up, in considerable part, of *huiguan* and *gongsuo* directors and was dominated throughout its early years by the Ningbo community.[20] Although most of the individuals who met with the Municipal Council to negotiate the plague emergency were Chamber members, it is significant that

tors Tang Luyuan and Zhong Ziyuan; and the director of the foreign-goods *bang* (*yanghuobang*), Su Baosen (a Ningbo native).

18. MCR for 1910, 145–47; NCH, December 2, 1910.

19. NCH, December 2, 1910. Cheong's biography appears in Arnold Wright, *Twentieth Century Impressions of Hong Kong, Shanghai, and other Treaty Ports of China* (London, 1908), 532–34.

20. See Joseph Fewsmith, *Party, State and Local Elites in Republican China: Merchant Organizations and Politics in Shanghai, 1890–1930* (Honolulu, 1985), 34; *Shanghai shangwu zonghui tongrenlu,* 1906–15.

they were identified as leaders of their native-place *bang* in Chinese sources, this affiliation being often more significant at this time in the Chinese community. Although the Chamber provided an organizational form which appeared particularly legitimate to western authorities, it did not replace *huiguan* and *gongsuo*. What it did was redirect their focus by creating an institutional framework for the regular coordination of their activities in matters concerning Shanghai municipal affairs.[21]

The plague-related incidents of 1910 demonstrate both the advisory role of prominent *huiguan* and citywide coordination among associations in the dual interests of keeping order and defending Chinese rights.[22] This episode and, indeed, the eventual formalization of Chinese representation in Settlement government must be presented in the context of the politics of conflict — the other side of the politics of cooperation with foreign authorities. In Shanghai this history of mobilization for Chinese rights began in late-nineteenth-century *huiguan*-centered riots.

The Politics of Conflict:
The Ningbo Cemetery Riots

Two of the first violent popular conflicts between Chinese and foreigners in post-Taiping Shanghai, the Siming Gongsuo Riots of 1874 and 1898, originated in struggles over *huiguan* burial land. The riots are lauded in Chinese historiography as the first buddings of popular Chinese nationalism; recent revisionist western historiography has questioned their link to modern nationalism and has, instead, portrayed the riots as reflections of the deep concern for funerary ritual in traditional Chinese culture.[23]

For the purposes of this study, to the extent that they focus on

21. Given the Chamber's characteristics in the early period of its existence, it resembled the federations of merchant associations that appeared in various cities in the late Qing. These federations, such as the Chongqing Basheng Huiguan (which grouped together eight provincial associations), took on aspects of municipal government, formalizing previously informal meetings among *huiguan* leaders to resolve urban issues. See Skinner, *The City in Late Imperial China*, 549–51.

22. This role would later be formalized in a Chinese Advisory Board, discussed in Chapter 6, below.

23. Accounts of these riots exist in Susan Mann Jones, "Finance in Ningbo: The Ch'ien Chuang, 1750–1880," in *Economic Organization in Chinese Society*, ed. W. E. Will-

whether the label of "modern nationalism" is appropriately attached to the riots, both interpretations miss some of the significance of the events. Insofar as the riots were quickly represented in the Chinese press as models of "the people's" resistance to foreign imperialism, they provide a window onto developing popular understandings of nationalism. Moreover, although concern for coffins was certainly crucial in the riots, concern for protecting the dead could not, in itself, produce a riot. The structure of a well-organized native-place community provided the basis for mobilizing popular antiforeign protest. The presence of a managerial circle of *huiguan* leaders additionally provided a mechanism for successful negotiations with foreign authorities in defense of specific Chinese interests in the city.

The importance of the institutional presence of the Siming Gongsuo in these events is heightened by contrast with the third major violent Chinese–foreign confrontation in this period, a riot of wheelbarrow pullers in April 1897. Wheelbarrow pullers from northern Jiangsu violently protested an increase in license taxes imposed by the Shanghai Municipal Council, but they did not succeed in preventing the increase. In this incident, native-place occupational ties sustained an initial disorganized riot, but the combined lack of prestige, resources and organization among Subei immigrants made more organized and prolonged agitation (coupled with skillful negotiation) difficult.[24] What is striking in all three cases is the way in which native-place community provided a vehicle for social mobilization. Significant antiforeign protest did not take place in this period outside preexisting lines of native-place community. Sustained, focused and productive protest, however, depended on a highly organized native-place community.

The Riot of 1874. Although other major *huiguan* cemeteries within Settlement boundaries had been destroyed during the Small Sword Uprising or during French and British military operations against the Taipings, the cemetery land of the Siming Gongsuo re-

---

mott, 47–77 (Stanford, Calif., 1972), 86–88; Morse, *Gilds,* 48; Liu Huiwu, ed., *Shanghai jindaishi* (Modern Shanghai history), vol. 1 (Shanghai, 1985), 183–89, 277–81; Tang Zhengchang, ed., *Shanghai shi* (Shanghai history) (Shanghai, 1989). For a refutation of the riots' connection to Chinese nationalism, see Belsky, "Bones of Contention," 56–73. Perry (*Shanghai on Strike*) and Hokari ("Kindai shanhai") also emphasize death ritual in assessing the significance of the riots.

24. The wheelbarrow pullers achieved only a three-month delay in enforcement of the license fee (SB, April 5–8, 1897; NCH, April 9, 1897).

mained within the French Concession.[25] The considerable (and tax-free) *huiguan* holdings, protected by the presence of burial land, were an increasing irritant to the French.[26]

Unable to persuade the *huiguan* leaders to relinquish the land, the French Municipal Council resorted to the dubious tactic of using its municipal road-building authority to appropriate Siming Gongsuo holdings. At this time the area around the *huiguan* was open country. Nonetheless, toward the end of 1873 French authorities devised a plan to run two roads past the sides of the *huiguan* property, intersecting in one of the cemeteries. In January 1874 Siming Gongsuo directors protested the proposal because the roads would run through land densely packed with coffins:[27] "To make the road and have a traffic in carriages . . . over the remains of the dead is very abhorrent to our ideas, as we do not believe their spirits would rest in peace; and to disturb their remains by digging them up and carrying them away elsewhere is equally repulsive. The whole of our ground . . . is very closely filled with the graves of our people; on the east side . . . as much as . . . to the west."[28]

In place of the objectionable French proposal, the *huiguan* directors suggested alternate routes for the roads, offering not only to arrange and pay for an alternate site but to reimburse the Council for any outlays

25. In the early years of the Settlement, Fujianese clashed with the British over destruction of their graveyard (PRO, FO 228.162, 1853; PRO, FO 228.903, 1853). British and French troops occupied several *huiguan* in 1854 and in 1861–62, while defending the city from the Taipings. The pressure of French occupying armies forced the Fujian and Guangdong communities (whose *huiguan* were located in the French Settlement), to move their cemeteries in 1861 (NCH, October 5, 1861; NCH, January 3, 1890). The French were delighted at their victory: "The expropriation of the Fujian and Cantonese cemeteries, which we have so many times requested and always been refused, is finally a fait accompli. . . . This den of pestilence, which was itself a frightening expression of the politics of exclusion, has given way today to new homes (Ch. B. Maybon and Jean Fredet, *Histoire de la Concession Française de Changhai* [Paris, 1929], 238).

26. The Siming Gongsuo site, on land northwest and just outside the walled Chinese city, was incorporated into the expanding French Concession in 1849. The *gongsuo* was razed in the Small Sword Uprising but was rebuilt and expanded shortly after. In 1860 British troops razed cemetery markers and a surrounding wall; nonetheless, the *gongsuo* managed to retain title to its land and gained tax-free status in the French Concession as a charitable organization through the intervention of Daotai Ying Baoshi (a fellow-provincial) in 1868. See Leung, *Shanghai Taotai*, 151.

27. Morse, *Gilds*, 46–47; NCH, May 9, 1874; Liu Huiwu, *Shanghai jindaishi*, vol. 1, 184–86. Even NCH editorials questioned the need to build roads at this location at this time (NCH, May 16, 1874, and NCH, June 27, 1874, cited in Belsky, "Bones of Contention," 61).

28. NCH, May 9, 1874.

already expended for the current plan. Reinforcing their generosity with a caution, the directors concluded, "The Ningbo people will not allow . . . their ground to be built upon." When the French Municipal Council ignored the protest and asked the *huiguan* to clear the land, the directors refused, stating that the area was a pauper burial ground, densely packed with coffins too flimsy to move.[29]

On April 26 the leaders of each sojourning Ningbo trade (three to four hundred individuals) met to discuss the road-building emergency. The *Shenbao* reported that, "because the people from Ningbo prefecture bear great attachment to their native place," emotions at the meeting were turbulent. Two days later more than one thousand Ningbo people (including workers and shopkeepers) met at the *huiguan*, but four hours of discussion brought little agreement. Having considered the probable length of the meeting, the *dongshi* had arranged to distribute five hundred *mantou* (steamed buns). Though this could hardly feed a group more than double that number, the *Shenbao* reported that the hungry crowds stayed on to pursue the matter, reportedly calling for a strike against the French and proposing to go en masse to petition the French Consul. Having convened the crowd (and having at least symbolically provided it with sustenance), the *huiguan* directors also restrained it, sending, instead, six of their own number to negotiate with the French Consul. They also persuaded Daotai Shen Bingcheng (a fellow-provincial) to intercede with the French on behalf of the Siming Gongsuo.

In response to warnings of unrest and prodded by Consul General Godeaux (who was sympathetic to the *huiguan*), the French Council temporarily suspended roadwork and agreed to meet with the *huiguan* directors on May 4.[30] While this meeting was pending, a chance event sparked a riot. On May 3 a crowd of several hundred Ningbo people, "packed together like fish roe," stood discussing the situation outside the closed *huiguan*. A woman identified by the Ningbo crowds as a Guangdong prostitute passed by in a cart. When Ningbo rowdies hara-

29. PRO, FO 233.96, Chinese Secretary's Office, 1846–80, piece 328. The letter was signed by eleven Siming Gongsuo directors: Wang Zhenchang, Zhuang Jianren, Fang Yizhang, Zhou Dalin, Li Yuan, Hong Zhenlin, Ge Shengxiao, Zhang Sicang, Zhao Licheng, Liu Xianshen and Liu Linshu (NCH, May 9, 1874; SB, April 21, 1874).

30. SB, April 21, 1874; SB, April 27, 1874; SB, April 29, 1874; SB, May 2, 1874. French Consul Godeaux appreciated the gravity of the situation and was receptive to the skillful negotiating tactics of the *huiguan* directors; the French Municipal Council was less tractable. See AMRE, Série Chine, Correspondance Politique, Shanghai, 1871–75, vol. 7, 257–59. See also Belsky, "Bones of Contention," 59–61.

ssed her for serving French clients, she cried out for help. The policeman who came to her aid soon found himself joined by forty other policemen, fighting a Ningbo crowd of several hundred.[31]

Soon five to six hundred people had gathered at the Siming Gongsuo gate, and more filled the empty surrounding land. The French police returned in force, armed with guns, and climbed up on the *huiguan* buildings. The growing Ningbo crowd hurled stones at the police, who fired, killing one man and wounding another. The crowd, now numbering more than fifteen hundred, surged forward. Outraged by the spilling of blood, the crowd set fire to French houses, striking at French residents along the way (though apparently avoiding those who identified themselves as British). By 6:00 P.M. numerous buildings were on fire. According to the *Shenbao*, although the crowd destroyed the streetlights, the fires maintained the illumination of day. Forty foreign homes and three Chinese buildings were destroyed. Other targets were the French Municipal compound and the East Gate police station.

French troops and International Settlement volunteer forces fired into the crowd and charged with their bayonets drawn. Chinese authorities assisted in the riot suppression, sending in one hundred fifty soldiers at the request of the Consul General. After midnight, when calm was restored, seven Chinese lay dead and twenty more were badly wounded.

The next day, while western militia forces marched around the Siming Gongsuo (and while as many as a thousand Ningbo sojourners fled to their native place), the foreign consuls met to condemn the rioters and demand indemnity for their losses. To their astonishment, Consul General Godeaux independently and publicly proclaimed that upon the request of the *huiguan* directors, seconded by petitions of the Daotai and the Shanghai Magistrate, he was instructing the French Municipal Council to change its plans and preserve Siming Gongsuo buildings and graves. To the great dismay of the French Council, the riot achieved the aim of defending sacred Ningbo land against French incursions.[32]

31. SB, May 4, 1874; NCH, May 9, 1874. Sources do not indicate the policeman's nationality (or native place).

32. SB, May 4, 1874; SB, May 8, 1874; NCH, May 9, 1874. At its peak, the crowd was estimated at five thousand. The riot of 1874 was not definitively settled until 1878, when the Minister of France, the Viscount Bernier de Montmorand, accepted thirty-seven thousand taels for damages to French property and delivered in return seven thousand taels to be divided among the seven families of the Chinese killed. Accompanying this transfer of payments, he declared that Siming Gongsuo holdings would be respected in perpetuity

The Riot of 1898. More than twenty years later the French authorities precipitated a second Ningbo cemetery riot. This time they focused on the opportune issue of hygiene, which provided an excuse marked with the persuasive power of scientific imperative for the elimination of the *huiguan* coffin repositories, which were identified as unsanitary. Thus, although in nineteenth-century Europe notions of cleanliness and disease differentiated social classes and provided legitimation for a certain restructuring of the urban social landscape, in the treaty-port environment of nineteenth-century Shanghai, public health provided an important avenue for the expansion of foreign municipal authority on Chinese soil.[33]

As Shanghai population increased, so did the incidence of urban disease. Foreigners in Shanghai viewed Chinese culture in increasingly pathogenic terms, terms which justified the imposition of western institutions of cleanliness and order.[34] Cholera, normally endemic in the summer months, approached epidemic proportions in the summer of 1890. Although mortality was highest among the Chinese, foreigners also fell victim. This increased foreign repugnance for Chinese "charnel houses" in the settlements and added urgency to calls for sanitary regulations. The rise in mortality also strained the capacity of coffin repositories:

During the months of July and August . . . the deaths among the Chinese inhabiting the English, American and French concessions amounted to about five thousand. Of these the greater number have been Ningpoese. At present the Ningpo Guild-house, outside the West Gate, is filled up with coffins piled on top of each other like so many bales of cotton in a go-down. . . . Now imagine two to three thousand of these ill-made, loose-jointed, and thin-boarded coffins, each containing a corpse filled with germs of disease and in a decomposing state, all crowded into one place as is the case with the Ningpo Guild-house. When one computes the enormous

---

and that the *huiguan* would retain its tax-free status. See AMRE, Série Chine, Correspondance Politique, Shanghai, 1876–81, vol. 8, 349.

33. See, for example, Richard Evans, *Death in Hamburg: Society and Politics in the Cholera Years, 1830–1910* (Oxford, 1987); Michel Foucault, "The Politics of Health in the Eighteenth Century," in *Power/Knowledge: Selected Interviews and Other Writings, 1972–1977,* ed. and trans. Colin Gordon (New York, 1972), 166–82; Alain Corbin, *The Foul and the Fragrant* (Cambridge, Mass., 1986). See also Bryna Goodman, "The Politics of Public Health: Sanitation in Shanghai in the Late Nineteenth Century," *Modern Asian Studies* 23 (October 1989), 816–20.

34. See Kerrie L. MacPherson, *A Wilderness of Marshes: The Origins of Public Health in Shanghai* (Hong Kong, 1987), Preface, chaps. 1–2.

amount of poisonous gas that must escape from these three thousand coffins day and night, which gas is wafted all over the settlement . . . one is convinced that the present rate of mortality is very low indeed. That the Ningpo and other guild-houses are storages for coffins the Municipal Council know only too well.[35]

By this point the area around the Ningbo cemetery (the site of coffin storage) was no longer empty land but, rather, densely populated city.

Seven years later, in 1897, after much remonstrance both the International Settlement and the French Concession forbade coffin storage within their boundaries.[36] The major target of the French prohibition was the Siming Gongsuo. In January 1898 French General Consul Compte de Bezaure ordered the police to enforce the provision within six months. At this time both the French and the British were negotiating with the Chinese authorities for extension of their settlement boundaries. When the Daotai refused their request in the spring of 1898, the French responded by militantly asserting their power within settlement boundaries. At the end of May the Consul notified the Ningbo directors of French intent to expropriate Siming Gongsuo burial and coffin storage areas to build a Chinese hospital, school and slaughter-house, as well as for roads which had been postponed in 1874. The *huiguan,* backed by the Chinese authorities, refused to recognize that the French had any right to dispossess them, although the directors did arrange for shipment to Ningbo of more than twenty-five hundred coffins. As the day of dispossession neared, the Daotai hinted to the settlement authorities that civil unrest was imminent.[37]

35. NCH, September 5, 1890. The "poisonous gas" idea of disease transmission, though erroneous (the cholera vibrio is transmitted through contaminated water and food), was consistent with nineteenth-century European epidemiological theories (and fears). Nonetheless, a French municipal doctor who inspected a coffin repository in 1890 confirmed that the coffins were well sealed and, owing to the practice of packing the interior with quick-lime, posed no public-health threat (Belsky, "Bones of Contention").

36. Such regulations had to be made through the Chinese authorities under whose jurisdiction Chinese residents remained. In October 1897 the International Settlement Municipal Council asked the Chinese Mixed Court Magistrate for a proclamation forbidding the depositing of coffins in the Settlement. This document was issued November 13. See MCR for 1897, 66. Also in 1897, the French Municipal Council asked the French General Consul to insert into settlement regulations an article forbidding coffin repositories within Concession limits, following the International Settlement example. See AMRE, Chine, Politique Étrangère, Concession Française de Changhai, Compte-Rendu de la Gestion pour l'exercise, 1897, 109. Because the status of the Mixed Court Magistrate was relatively low, the effect and the legal status of these rules is unclear.

37. The notification indicated that the French would compensate the owners for the assessed value of the properties (PRO, FO 228.1293, 1898). At this time the prominent

On July 16, a day after the French served final notice, sailors landed from a French gunboat and supervised the destruction of three sections of cemetery wall by workmen (see Figure 6). Siming Gongsuo leaders responded by calling on Ningbo merchants to cease trade and meet the next morning.[38]

In the meantime, events proceeded beyond the *huiguan* leaders' control. While the French tore down the wall, crowds surrounded and harassed the intruders, although daylight and the sight of French arms temporarily prevented open conflict. When night fell, crowds armed with bricks and spiked bamboo poles filled the streets, smashing lamps, uprooting lampposts and accosting foreigners. Rioting continued through the next morning and included a contingent of Cantonese, who attacked a French police station. French troops shot and killed between twenty and twenty-five people (all Chinese), seriously wounding another forty.[39]

The next day, French and British authorities observed that the Ningbo community was on strike and that shops were closed in both settlements. Virtually all Ningbo people (who in the estimate of the British Consul comprised half of the French Concession residents) complied with the strike, which was enforced by crowds of young men. Foreign trade was seriously impaired because steamers were unable to load or discharge goods. Banks closed. Laundries closed as well, and cooks and servants left their foreign employers. Sectors of the Ningbo community also began to boycott French goods.

In the afternoon important Ningbo leaders emerged to negotiate an interim agreement with the French General Consul. Active hostilities ceased when the General Consul promised representatives of the Ningbo community a delay of three months, during which time the *huiguan* was to remove the offending graves.[40]

In the midst of this ferment the Siming Gongsuo directors distributed the following circular, urging caution and order and asserting their authority over the community:

---

gongsuo directors were Fang Mingshan, Yan Xiaofang, Ye Chengzhong and Shen Dunhe (Wei Bozhen, *Yu Xiaqing xiansheng* [Mr. Yu Xiaqing] [Shanghai, 1946], 11; Belsky, "Bones of Contention," 65).

38. This narrative is pieced together from accounts in Liu, *Shanghai jindaishi,* vol. 1, 278–80; DR, 1892–91, 469–70; NCH, July and August 1898; Chen Laixin, *Yu Xiaqing ni tsuite,* 20–21; Negishi, *Chūgoku no girudo,* 139–41; Negishi, Tadashi, *Shanhai no girudo,* 33–34; PRO, FO 228.1293, 1898; MCR for 1898; *Shenbao,* July 16–18, 1898.

39. PRO, FO 228.1293, "From Shanghai," 1898.

40. The strike lasted four days (PRO, FO 228.1293, 1898; SBZX, 430).

With reference to the affair concerning our guild-house premises, the Shanghai Daotai and the French Consul General, in company with several Foreign merchants, are trying . . . to arrange a settlement. Now, it is necessary that all who belong to our community should act peaceably at present and quietly await the results of the above conference. By no means congregate in crowds and stir up trouble on the impulse of your united indignation, for you will only be making matters worse, and perhaps suffer injuries to no avail.[41]

Despite this authoritative gesture, in the development and resolution of this incident the older directors — Yan Xiaofang, Ye Chengzhong and Shen Dunhe (who was assistant Daotai at the time of the strike) — were

41. Circular dated Sunday, July 17, translated in DR, 1892–1901, 524.

Figure 6. French destruction of the Siming Gongsuo wall, 1898. Chinese caption reads: "The Siming Gongsuo, outside the west gate of this city, was established in 1797. It has existed for one hundred years. It contains the buried remains of more than ten thousand people, the blood-pulse of the Ningbo Community, which were handled with great care. In 1874 . . . there was an incident. French General Consul Godeaux discussed this matter with the *gongsuo* and gave his guarantee of protection and asked that a surrounding wall be constructed to clarify the boundaries. This was signed by the consuls of eleven countries, recognizing the right of the Ningbo *bang* to permanently hold the property. . . . Unexpectedly the French went back on their promise. . . . They ordered soldiers to destroy three sides of the *gongsuo* wall, making three big holes, twenty feet across. When the soldiers entered the *gongsuo* they found a sea of people watching and talking. Hooligans formed a growing crowd. They were without weapons and began throwing stones like rain on the soldiers. . . . The French escaped injury only because of harsh suppression [of the crowd] by civil and military authorities. One can only say the French were very fortunate." Source: *Dianshizhai huabao* (Dianshi Studio pictorial newspaper), 1983 Guangzhou reprint of late-Qing edition (1884–1898).

forced to recognize an emergent element in the native-place community which challenged the older oligarchy. Although the *dongshi* did call the meeting of Ningbo merchants on the morning of July 17, they did not control the strike or the negotiations which followed. Intervening between them and Ningbo workers and artisans was Shen Honglai, who had come to Shanghai as a laborer several decades earlier and had worked as a cook for foreigners. Shen had attained considerable influence in the Ningbo community through his leadership of the Ningbo Changsheng Hui, which had amassed sufficient property to provide for permanent *yulanpen* ceremonies for its members and had been incorporated into the Siming Gongsuo two years prior to the riot.[42]

Shen played a major role in involving the broad community in the strike, organizing the members of his association (workers, petty artisans and people in foreign employ), along with an association of Ningbo grooms, to stop work. As Shen describes it, their decision to enter the strike took place in coordination with (but not subordination to) the *dongshi* decision to strike: "The directors Fang and Yan . . . were in charge [of the Siming Gongsuo] and wanted to strike. My *bang*, the Changsheng Hui, and the horse grooms gathered and met and we also wanted to strike." Together with the young Yu Xiaqing, who at barely thirty years of age had gone from being a "barefoot" immigrant to a respected comprador, Shen maintained effective organization among the strikers. When, four days later, Chinese and western authorities secured a resumption of trade, they achieved this through negotiation, not with the older *huiguan* leaders but with Shen.[43]

Governor General Liu Kunyi, hearing of the trouble, appointed a committee of Chinese officials (including the Shanghai Daotai and the Provincial Treasurer) to investigate the affair and negotiate with the French Consul General. Six months of tense discussion of French and Chinese rights followed, the *huiguan* side apparently handled adroitly and aggressively by Yu, whose status as a businessman and comprador and association with Shen in the strike enabled him to bridge the gap between high and low in the Ningbo community. Yu reportedly boasted to Shen during the proceedings, "If both the worker and merchant cir-

42. This practice of "funerary patronage" clearly underlay Shen's influence during the 1898 strike (see Belsky, "Bones of Contention," 67–69).

43. The quotation is from SBZX, 430. See also Chen Laixin, *Yu Xiaqing ni tsuite*, 20–21; PRO, FO 228.1293, 1898; Jones, "The Ningpo *Pang*," 87–88; Negishi, *Chūgoku no girudo*, 140.

cles back me up, no matter what atrocities the French resort to, how can they scare us?"[44]

These negotiations were rendered moot by the rediscovery of a document of 1878 which recorded the (strangely forgotten) final settlement of the 1874 troubles by the French Minister at Beijing, which provided for permanent protection of the cemetery. The French abandoned their claims to Siming Gongsuo land, and the *huiguan* agreed to cease depositing new coffins within the Concession.

Early Nationalism and Developing Class Tensions

In the differences between the riots of 1874 and 1898 it is possible to view two important developments in late-nineteenth-century Shanghai which reshaped native-place communities and popular understandings of native-place identity. The first was the merchant politicization and rising popular nationalism that followed the Sino–Japanese War of 1894–95. The second was the gradual internal restructuring of power relations between elite and non-elite elements in the *huiguan* itself.

Both riots were essentially affairs of the Ningbo community, which mobilized to defend its sacred burial ground. As such it would be problematic to assert that for the actors involved the riots involved a sense of nationalism. Although a group of Cantonese rowdies took advantage of the second riot to attack a French police station, neither riot provides evidence of common or coordinated action among different native-place groups in defense of "Chinese" rights or sovereignty.

Nonetheless, although it is important to avoid a refashioning of earlier events in accord with later sentiments, if neither riot presents a case of "modern nationalism," it is important to note the ways in which neither may be described as purely "traditional." In the 1874 incident, tension between people of different native-place groups (the Ningbo crowd versus a Guangdong woman) produced the social friction which sparked the riot. In the context of French imperialism and popular anti-French sentiment this spark produced not a Ningbo–Guangdong street brawl (with members of the Guangdong community jumping in to re-

44. Chen Laixin, *Yu Xiaqing ni tsuite*, 20.

store their native-place honor), but rather an anti-French riot. The idea that the purity or virtue of the Guangdong group was compromised by purported sexual relations between a Guangdong woman and French clients resonated with Ningbo sojourners' determination to preserve inviolate their sacred burial grounds against French incursions.

In the second incident we see a maturation of tactics, the development of a politically motivated strike and boycott, tactics which depended on the cooperation of the entire Ningbo community (across occupational and status lines) and proved most effective in impressing the foreign community. Boycotts were hardly new to *huiguan* and *gongsuo*, but they had been developed to discipline deviant members of the community or external economic competitors.[45] The French target and the context of French jurisdiction on Chinese soil resulted in the adaptation of a traditional device of collective action to new and specifically political uses.

Moreover, the experience of antiforeign riots was transformative. Such confrontations (whatever the sentiments of the rioters) were important to the gradual working out of the opposing positions of "Chinese people" versus "foreigners" in the political imaginations of Shanghai residents. Although Chinese newspaper accounts of the 1874 incident were sympathetic to the aggrieved Ningbo community, they did not immediately view the events in terms of a Chinese–foreign polarity. In contrast, *Shenbao* editorials constructed a different meaning for the 1898 incident, reflecting developing public opinion. The 1898 events were presented in more universalistic terms, as a matter of asserting and protecting Chinese rights against foreigners:

If we do not resist, the will of the [Chinese] people will appear weak and Westerners will make unlimited demands. In the future, if the people's hearts from the one county of this little *gongsuo* are as steadfast as this, this will show that even though the country might be weak and the officials might be controlled, the people can't be bullied. Foreigners will know the firmness of the Chinese people's will and they will restrain themselves in order to not offend the people. Although this act of the French demands the land of the *gongsuo*, it may also be a test of the will of the Chinese people.[46]

45. C. F. Remer, *A Study of Chinese Boycotts* (Baltimore, Md., 1933).
46. SB, July 19, 1898. See also SB, July 17, 1898; SB, July 18, 1898. As is evident here, the press played a crucial role in propagating popular nationalism. From the time of the Sino-French War (1883–1885) *Shenbao* editorials criticized Qing weakness and appealed to the Chinese people to resist foreign incursions.

This editorial clearly constructs an understanding of the incident in which Ningbo people appear as exemplary Chinese in their steadfast determination to protect one small corner of Chinese territory from foreign imperialism. Here we see a positive linking of native-place solidarity to national identity and national interests. This connection is echoed in what we know of the motivations of Shen Honglai, who, according to Negishi Tadashi's account, visited Japan prior to his activism in the Changsheng Hui. During this stay Shen contemplated China's weakness and concluded that the key to China's problems could be found in the lack of cohesive social organizations which could unite to protect China's interests. Upon his return to Shanghai he threw himself into organizing the Ningbo Changsheng Hui.[47]

Finally, the *Shenbao* editorial also expresses an appreciation of the force of popular nationalism as an antidote for China's weakness and a corresponding construction of officials as weak in contrast to the "people," presenting a critique of Qing officialdom at a time of government capitulation to foreign demands. These themes, stated cautiously here, would be voiced with considerably greater flamboyance in the early twentieth century.

It is clear that this developing articulation of popular nationalism in the press fastened on symbolic victories in the absence of substantive ability to deter the expansion of colonial control. The final settlement of the Siming Gongsuo affair was not achieved until early in the summer of 1899, when Beijing authorities finally granted the French the settlement extension they sought, in one sweep doubling the size of the French Concession. Although the Guangxu Emperor had steadfastly opposed such an extension (and had in fact proposed that the *huiguan* sacrifice its land to mollify the French), the court ultimately had no choice but to concede to French pressure.[48]

---

47. Negishi, *Chūgoku no girudo*, 200; Negishi, *Shanhai no girudo*, 34; Belsky, "Bones of Contention," 67. The roughly educated commoner Shen's diagnosis that China's weakness resulted from a lack of cohesive social groups was very similar to the contemporary diagnosis of Liang Qichao, in his 1897 article "On grouping" (*Shuo qun*), which deals with the problem of integrating Chinese people into a coherent and united political community through the formation of social groupings. See Hao Chang, *Liang Ch'i-Ch'ao and Intellectual Transition in China, 1890–1907* (Cambridge, Mass., 1971), 95–99.

48. Dong Shu, "Shanghai fazujie de fazhan shiqi" (The period of development of the Shanghai French Concession), *Shanghai tongzhiguan qikan* (Journal of the Shanghai gazetteer office), 1 (1933):701–59; Tang Zhengchang, *Shanghai shi*, 350; Belsky, "Bones of Contention," 67. By the time of the concession expansion, Empress Dowager Cixi had placed herself on the throne in a coup following the Hundred Day Reforms. Nonetheless,

The contrast offered by the simultaneous preservation of *huiguan* property and expansion of Shanghai territory under French control highlights our perception of the weakness of the Chinese central government and the local strength of Chinese associations. It also foreshadows the ways Chinese nationalism would (and would not) gain popular acceptance. Viewed from the perspective of this riot, national interests were not necessarily popular if they involved the sacrifice of local institutions (in this case the highly respected Siming Gongsuo). Although, in fact, more Chinese territory had been lost than gained by the time of the ultimate resolution of the riot, in local eyes the *huiguan* achieved a certain victory over the French, emerging ironically (if no less sincerely), as a champion of the nation.

The riot of 1898 provides another window on the process of internal restructuring that was taking place within the native-place community, visible also in the changing organizational arrangements for burial and *yulanpen* ceremonies. As noted in Chapter 3, the growing non-elite membership of the broad sojourner community provided a critical, though unstable, source of the elite *huiguan* leaders' power. As workers and artisans organized themselves and accumulated collective property, they were able to demand a somewhat greater voice in *huiguan* affairs. The hierarchy within sojourner communities would be increasingly challenged as the organizational clout of commoner sojourners grew and as popular organizations gained greater political legitimacy (as would happen in the course of popular nationalist movements).

In each Ningbo riot the *huiguan* elite attempted the delicate manipulation of the broad native-place community, the collective force of which was necessary to achieve victory in the struggle with the French. By calling a mass meeting in 1874 the *dongshi* mobilized and incited popular action. At the same time, they removed themselves from the scene of popular violence, closing the Siming Gongsuo gates until calm was restored and they could emerge as influential and respectable mediators who could negotiate on behalf of the Ningbo community while sharing the foreign authorities' goal of maintaining order.

In the riot of 1898 the paternalism symbolized by the *huiguan* directors' gift of *mantou* two decades earlier appears to have broken down. Worker and artisan sojourner groups acted on their own initiative in the later strike, organized through articulate spokesmen who could claim Ningbo victories as their own.

---

as Belsky notes, there is no reason to imagine that Cixi's court was more receptive to French demands.

The popular mobilization of 1898 hastened a process of limited de-mocratization within the association. The evident power of worker or-ganizations in the strike forced the *huiguan* elite to recognize and relin-quish a certain amount of power to non-elite leaders who could effectively mobilize workers. Not only did the maverick Yu Xiaqing break into the circle of directors, but the worker-leader Shen Honglai rose to become business manager. Within three years, Shen (still bearing the prestige of organizing the 1898 strike) forced a reformation of the system of *huiguan* governance, forming a committee of rotating repre-sentatives of each trade which met regularly with the group of *dongshi*.[49]

A stela document authored by Shen Honglai provides eloquent testi-mony of the rise of a man of the laboring classes into a position of power within the Siming Gongsuo.[50] The author expresses himself stri-dently and inelegantly, his carved words evidently an extension of his lifetime battle for acceptance by the *huiguan* elite, who frequently ex-cluded him from their company. At one point in the stone document Shen rages about an incident in which (after receiving Shen's help on various matters) the *huiguan* director Yan Xiaofang failed to answer his letter and then refused to receive him in his home, concluding resent-fully, "From this you can see the behavior of the director: When there is a problem [and he needs you], he sees you as a person. When there is no problem, you are nobody to him." In his account Shen takes evident pleasure in listing for posterity the considerable property and capital assets his Changsheng Hui brought to the Siming Gongsuo, all of the times *huiguan* leaders came to him for assistance, and all of his accom-plishments as *huiguan* manager. According to his testimony, his help was sought as early as 1875 by *huiguan* director Zhou Xiaolu in regard to an attempt by an American to seize eight feet of a Siming Gongsuo road, a large portion of which had been paved by the Changsheng Hui. He details the role of his Changsheng Hui in the 1898 strike, as well as his pivotal role in a meeting with the U.S. Consul, who threatened him, saying, "If you want to strike, we twelve nations [the international com-munity in Shanghai], together with the French, will tear down the *hui-guan*." While the U.S. Consul waited, Shen left the meeting and notified his *bang* to end the strike. According to his account, after he returned to the meeting and announced this decision the French troops retreated.

49. See Chen Laixin, *Yu Xiaqing ni tsuite,* 21; SBZX, 429–31. In the same year as the riot Shen also reprimanded the *dongshi* for inattentiveness to the protection of Ningbo coffins, causing them to lose face in the community.

50. SBZX, 429–31, document dated 1911.

As manager (while stressing his commitment to *huiguan* burial functions and providing charitable funds for impoverished members) Shen stopped wasteful practices, including the distribution of wood chips and planks from coffin construction to members as bonuses, by his estimate saving eventually forty thousand silver dollars from this alone. In addition to aggressive frugality, the talented Shen also raised funds to construct many income-producing properties (in one instance, residences with more than one hundred fifty units; in another, residences with more than three hundred units). Shen evidently gained considerable social prestige and attained a position of power by means of these accomplishments and by his consistent patronage of poorer Ningbo sojourners through provision of coffins and the construction of a clinic and hospital for the sick. Nonetheless, the stela stands as evidence of his recognition that his attainments were unusual (he repeats phrases like, "If you don't believe this, you can consult the deities" and "If this is not believed, there is a stela, you can come and see"). His account is defensive ("Ask the gentry merchants of the six counties [of Ningbo prefecture] to come and see the carelessness of the earlier managers of the *gongsuo*") and self-aggrandizing ("After this, whenever the *gongsuo* had great or small matters to resolve, I, Honglai, acted on my own with power accorded to me alone") and expresses his fears that upon his death his gains and innovations would be lost to posterity.

The dual themes of the politicization of sojourner communities and the political emergence of subordinate groups within those communities dominate the history of native-place sentiment in the twentieth century and are a focus of subsequent chapters. In the popular expressions of antiforeign resistance and growing nationalism that characterized Shanghai in the first decade of the twentieth century, the precedent of the Ningbo Cemetery Riots would be invoked repeatedly as an episode of victorious heroism. In the riots, strikes and boycotts which followed, native-place organizations, prominent among them those of the already politicized and highly organized Ningbo community, proved to be crucial actors, mobilized to defend Chinese rights against injury and affront.

As was the case in the Ningbo Cemetery Riots, in the development of popular nationalism native-place organizations would appear consistently in the familiar role of dual-edged mediator, poised between the larger, non-elite *tongxiang* community and Chinese and foreign authorities. Because of the precedent of the cemetery riots, the unspoken threat of popular violence underscored the urgency of *huiguan* demands at the negotiating table. Just as the strike success of 1898 forced the *huiguan* directors to recognize non-elite leaders who could mobilize workers, the increasingly popular nationalist politicization of the first years of the twentieth century would make links between high and low in the native-place community both imperative and tension filled. *Huiguan* leaders continued privately to encourage and publicly to restrain popular political activism in their native-place communities. Although they depended on the support of their *tongxiang* in their political battles, they also attempted to maintain order (not only to retain their respectability before Western and Chinese authorities but also in order to remain on top themselves).

Throughout this period the old elite generally did remain on top, but its control was often tenuous. Although workers frequently organized on their own, they still tried to assemble at the *huiguan,* which remained a symbolic center. Instead of abandoning the old native-place association, increasingly they would try to claim it as their own. Shen Honglai's rise and attempt to refashion the Siming Gongsuo foreshadows a broadening of association constituency which took place several years later in other native-place associations and produced an alternative, somewhat less oligarchic type of association. Although some of Shen's gains would indeed be lost after his death, his struggles and the early politicization of Ningbo sojourners during the 1898 riot were nonetheless responsible for hastening challenges to an old elite power structure which would not change without conflict.

CHAPTER SIX

The Native Place
and the Nation

Anti-Imperialist and Republican
Revolutionary Mobilization

Those desiring to take on world affairs must begin with their native
place (yu ren tianxia shi, bi zi benxiang shi).
Chinese proverb cited in Chen Laixin, *Yu Xiaqing ni tsuite*
(Regarding Yu Xiaqing) (Kyoto, 1983), 15

Informed public opinion and political organization developed rapidly in Shanghai in the years following the 1898 riot, reflecting
broad public awareness of China's humiliation in the Boxer Uprising
(1899–1900) as well as the Empress Dowager Cixi's subsequent recognition of the need to radically restructure China's commercial, educational
and political organization through a series of reforms collectively referred to as the "New Policies." This meant rapid institutional innovation at the local level: the development of Chinese Chambers of Commerce following western and Japanese models, of modern schools
featuring "western" learning and of provincial assemblies and a local
self-government movement. In the political and social movements in
Shanghai during the last decade of the Qing, native-place associations
were joined by new forms of political organizations which would increasingly take over leadership roles.

New political, economic and governmental institutions not only re-
directed Shanghai commerce and political life through new organizational frameworks but also integrated native-place groups and native-
place associations into regular, formal, overarching citywide structures.
Although reformist merchants and gentry strongly supported the new

institutions (and, indeed, agitated for them prior to their creation), the changes were usually initiated by Chinese officials in the context of reforms based on the idea that organizational restructuring along western lines (following models of western and Japanese parliaments, chambers of commerce and municipal governments) was essential to strengthen the nation. As Shanghai social organization and social thinking changed, the idea of the native place and the role of native-place associations were also redefined in the context of new political values. Native-place organizations would increasingly take on forms and practices associated with nation building and the new models of "modernity."

Although new citywide organizational structures provided a potential institutional context for the development of Shanghai identity, they did not displace native-place associations as fundamental organizational units in urban society. Moreover, people from different native-place groups did not enter into the new institutions on an equal basis. Rather, preexisting hierarchies of power and influence among regional groups provided the context for the adaptation of new forms, and native-place organizations remained important in city politics. Native-place networks inhabited and worked through the new structures, casting the new urban institutions with their imprint.

The formation and early history of the Shanghai General Chamber of Commerce provides an example of the way in which a native-place network both pioneered and maintained dominance over the major new economic institution in the city. In 1901, determined to stimulate China's economy through the creation of a more modern and unified merchant organization, Sheng Xuanhuai (Imperial Commissioner for Revision of the Commercial Treaties) asked Yan Xinhou, the wealthy merchant leader of the Siming Gongsuo (at this time the preeminent *huiguan* in the city) to oversee the formation of a Chinese Chamber of Commerce. This Yan did, in the process ensuring the selection of himself as president and of his fellow Ningbo provincial Zhou Jinzhen as vice president and an overwhelming plurality of Zhejiang merchants as founding members. The new Chamber was established in 1902 as the Shanghai Commercial Consultative Association (*Shangye huiyi gongsuo*). *Huiguan* and *gongsuo* directors, together with the officers of large, modern enterprises, comprised the membership. In 1903, after investigating commerce in the United States and Japan, the Qing court finally created a Commercial Bureau (*shangbu yamen*) and, in the next year, promulgated a law requiring the integration of all major commercial associations into Chambers of Commerce (at which point the Shanghai institution was renamed the General Chamber of Commerce). These were to be established in commercially important locations and integrated hierarchically from the locality to the national level of the Commercial Bureau.[1]

Because the Shanghai Chamber of Commerce was conceived as an integral part of a national project of commercial construction and because the organization of commerce in the city necessitated the participation of all major sojourning groups, the new organizational framework both integrated the leaders of the major regional commercial *bang* into a citywide structure and ensured that the new focus would be national as well as local. Nonetheless, the new Chamber began as a Ningbo-dominated institution, and Ningbo merchants ensured that it remained that way throughout the first decades of its existence.[2]

The new Chamber of Commerce would be important in the major Shanghai political events which took place in the years following its formation. Nonetheless, as this chapter will show, native-place networks ran through and around its meetings, motivating and shaping the direction and outcome of various movements. The major actors on the Shanghai scene (still a small handful of men) continued to be, in large part, directors of native-place associations, although these men were also the directors of the new economic and municipal institutions in the city.

1. On the origins of the Chamber, see Xu Dingxin and Qian Xiaoming, *Shanghai zongshanghui shi, 1902–1929* (History of the Shanghai General Chamber of Commerce) (Shanghai, 1991), 34–58. Yan had close ties with Li Hongzhang and had held several posts in the lucrative state salt monopoly. He traded in salt in Tianjin and owned silver shops in Shanghai, Beijing, Tianjin and various Yangzi ports. Of fifty-one founding members of the Shangye Huiyi Gongsuo for whom native place may be identified, twenty-three were from Zhejiang. Eight each came from Guangdong and Jiangsu. Other provincial groups had three or fewer. See Xu and Qian, *Shanghai zongshanghui shi,* 43–47). See also Fewsmith, *Party, State and Local Elites,* 33–34. Fewsmith mistakenly identifies Mao Zumo, the other vice-president, as a Ningbo native. Mao was from Jiangsu.

2. Xu and Qian, 88–92. In 1905, in contrast to the preceding years, Zeng Shaoqing, a Fujian *huiguan* director, was selected president of the Chamber. This resulted from Zeng's prominence in the anti–U.S. boycott of 1905. As Xu notes, Zeng's presence at the head of the Chamber did not result in a loss in power on the part of the Ningbo *bang* or in a gain in power on the part of the Fujian (or closely linked) Guangdong *bang*. During Zeng's term the Zhejiang *bang* retained absolute power in the Chamber leadership. Of twenty-one officers, thirteen were from Zhejiang (eleven of these from Ningbo)and four were from Jiangsu; no other groups (including Fujian) had more than one representative among the leadership. In 1907, once Zeng's term had expired, the Ningbo leader Zhou Jinzhen replaced him. See *Shanghai shangwu zonghui tongrenlu* for a listing of officers and membership which specifies native place. See also Marie-Claire Bergère, *The Golden Age of the Chinese Bourgeoisie* (Cambridge, England, 1989), 144–45.

Popular Anti-Imperialist Mobilization in the Last Years of the Qing

Early Chinese nationalism incorporated and built on native-place sentiments in a series of popular anti-imperialist movements which rocked Shanghai in the first years of the twentieth century. In these movements, which protested foreign insults of various dimensions (from injuries to Chinese citizens to appropriations of Chinese territory), political activists relied on native-place loyalties to stir up patriotic nationalist activity. Activists (both within and outside native-place associations) were also increasingly able to orchestrate citywide political movements which brought together merchants, students and workers of different sojourner groups.

Death on the Bund. In 1904, while the last Ningbo Cemetery Riot was still relatively fresh in popular memory, a new foreign outrage aroused and focused popular demands for Chinese rights. On December 15 two drunken Russian sailors on shore leave hired rickshaws to return to their boats. When they refused to pay, one of the rickshaw pullers persistently demanded his fare. Angered, the sailor named Ageef grabbed an adze from the hand of a nearby carpenter who happened to be repairing the jetty. As Ageef swung the adze toward the rickshaw puller, the heavy curved blade fastened on a pedestrian, threw him to the ground and crushed his skull. The Russians walked on toward their ship but were arrested by police, who turned them over to the Russian Consul. Zhou Shengyou, the man who lay dying, happened to be from Ningbo.[3]

The next day, some thirty thousand Ningbo artisans (Zhou had been a carpenter), rickshaw men and fishermen gathered to protest but were appeased at the last minute by prompt action by the Siming Gongsuo. *Huiguan* directors immediately made it known that they would aggressively demand that Ageef be turned over for trial before a Chinese official. In response to a rumor that the Russian authorities would offer an

---

3. This incident occurred at the time of the turning point in the Russo–Japanese War (1904–5). The Russian cruiser had taken refuge in Shanghai harbor. This narrative is constructed from accounts in NCH and SB for December 1904 and January 1905; Liu Huiwu, *Shanghai jindaishi,* 301–9; Xiong Yuezhi, "Shanghai ju'e yundong shulun" (A discussion of the Shanghai Resist Russia Movement), in *Shanghai shi yanjiu* (Shanghai history research), ed. Tang Zhenchang and Shen Hengchun (Shanghai, 1988), 245–46.

indemnity to the Zhou family, the directors contacted the family members, asked them to refuse any offers and promised to match any Russian indemnity.

As negotiations proceeded, the *huiguan* leaders kept the Ningbo community abreast of their efforts by means of printed handbills distributed in both the foreign settlements and in the Chinese areas of Shanghai. Such a circular, distributed on December 19 and translated later in the *North China Herald,* indicates their tactics:

With reference to the case of . . . Chou Seng-yu . . . we the undersigned now learn that the Russian Consul wishes to send the murderer and his companion back to their own vessel to be tried according to Russian naval law. This manner of conducting such a case is indeed entirely contrary to what has been the custom in the Foreign Settlements. How can we, the fellow-provincials of the murdered Chou Seng-yu, of Ningbo, then stand by and look on without making a word of protest at such a miscarriage of justice, whereby the legal prerogatives of China are taken away? It has therefore been decided to engage a foreign lawyer to draw up letters in our name addressed to the Senior Consul and also to the Municipal Council of the International Settlement. . . . We are also sending by telegraph a petition to His Excellency the Imperial High Commissioner of the Nanyang and Viceroy of the Liangkiang provinces, and a letter to the Shanghai Taotai setting forth the powers and prerogatives of a Neutral State in a case where interned prisoners are guilty of breaking the laws, and praying for the diligent and firm transaction of everything pertaining to the case under consideration.[4]

The circular reveals the political and legal sophistication of the *huiguan* leaders at this time. The case appears not simply as a Ningbo tragedy but as an offense to China's legal rights. Action in defense of the native-place group acquired new legitimacy as action in defense of the nation, with the leaders of the native-place community prompting Chinese officials in regard to national prerogatives.

On December 28 the *huiguan* leaders petitioned the Qing court, the Ministry of Foreign Affairs and Governor General Zhou Fu protesting the action of the Russian Consul in disposing of the prisoner without consulting the Shanghai Daotai. The petitioners, all of whom identified themselves with their purchased official ranks, pressed the urgency of

---

4. NCH, December 23, 1904. Circular signed by Shen Zhongli, Yu Xiaqing, Zhu Baosan, Zhou Jinzhen, Su Baosen, He Suitang and Ye Hongtao. The first four are identified as expectant Daotai; the latter three, as Prefect.

their case by stressing the threat of disorder in their communities and their efforts to keep peace:

Half a month has elapsed since the murder, and seeing nothing being done the Ningbo population of the rougher and lower orders have attempted to hold several indignation mass meetings, but they have so far been kept down with difficulty by the petitioners sending this telegram. There are, however, many murmurs circulating about amongst the petitioners' fellow-provincials, who charge the petitioners with timidity and incapability, so that there are just fears that as a first step there will be a general strike, or closing up of shops . . . thereby causing a serious stoppage of trade and setting at large crowds of disaffected men, in which case the petitioners will be perfectly at a loss what to do in the matter. Finally, had this been instead a case where a Chinese had killed a foreigner serious international complications would certainly have arisen.[5]

The petitioners insisted that the sailors be turned over for judgment by a mixed (Chinese and Russian) tribunal. In the meantime, the foreign community praised Siming Gongsuo leaders for keeping order, taking seriously the threat of a strike, remembering 1898 and imagining "an amount of inconvenience to our business and in our homes which it is appalling to contemplate."[6]

By early January the incident had become a cause célèbre in the new radical press. In a series of articles, beginning on January 5 with "A Warning to Chinese People in Killing of Chinese by Russian Sailor," the newspaper *Tocsin* (*Jingzhong ribao*) used the case to praise and amplify the anger of the Ningbo people, to identify their struggle as a nationalist struggle, and to lament China's weakness in a world ruled by force rather than justice. An article entitled "Ningbo People Can Take the Lead" urged Ningbo people to follow the precedent of their successful resistance against the French in 1874 and 1898, stressing that their struggles symbolized the struggles of the Chinese people: "If Ningbo people witnessing the killing [of their fellow-provincial] can't avenge their shame, [then] all Chinese people cannot avoid the tragic fate of being butchered by foreigners."[7] The author counseled Ningbo people to unite, to demonstrate popular indignation and to strike, disrupting for-

5. NCH, December 30, 1904.
6. NCH, January 6, 1905.
7. *Jingzhong ribao* (*Tocsin*), January 8, 1905, reprinted in *Zhonghua minguo shiliao cong-bian jieshao,* ed. Luo Jialun (Taipei, 1968), vol. 1, 163–64. The English title "Alarming Bell" appears on the masthead. Because of the awkwardness of this translation, I have used *Tocsin*.

eign business and forcing the Russians to turn Ageef over to the Chinese authorities.

On January 14, Russian military commanders found Ageef guilty of negligently killing a man, for which the minimal punishment was eight years' hard labor. But the tribunal, finding the crime "quite accidental" (in that Ageef hit someone other than the man he intended to hit!), reduced the sentence to four years.[8] On the day of the sentencing an organization of Ningbo workers distributed handbills calling for a demonstration at the Siming Gongsuo on the next day (January 15). Reacting to the workers' initiative, the *huiguan* directors called an immediate meeting on January 14, hoping to appease popular sentiment with a demonstration of leadership and resolve.[9]

At this point Ningbo leaders moved beyond their native-place community to mobilize the entire Chinese commercial elite in Shanghai, calling together leaders from all trades and native-place groups in the city. Meeting at the North Shanghai Commercial Association (*Hu bei shangye gongsuo*), they discussed ways to pressure the Russian authorities (both directly and working through Chinese authorities). First, commercial leaders from each province would send telegrams requesting support from the Ministry of Foreign Affairs, the Commercial Bureau and various national officials. Second, merchants would pressure the Daotai to meet with foreign authorities in Shanghai to make clear the extent of popular dissatisfaction with the judgement. Finally, the directors of each *bang* resolved to boycott Russian goods and Russian notes. By evening the *huiguan* leaders distributed handbills to Ningbo workers and merchants advising them of these measures and warning against reckless actions.

The *huiguan* leaders' actions did not prevent an angry gathering at the Siming Gongsuo the next day, but they did diffuse popular anger. *Huiguan* representatives persuaded the crowd of several thousand to disperse, stressing the actions which had been undertaken on their behalf. Under pressure from all sides, the Russian Consul extended Ageef's sentence to eight years.[10]

What is striking here, aside from the skillful manipulation of popular indignation by the sojourning commercial elite, is the symbolic importance of the *huiguan* for the larger Ningbo community. Rather than directly petitioning Chinese authorities or protesting before Chinese or

8. NCH, January 20, 23, 1905.
9. SB, January 15, 1905.
10. SB, January 16, 1905.

Western authorities, the Ningbo protestors called for a meeting at the Siming Gongsuo. Because the gates were closed they met in front of the *huiguan,* making their statement to their *tongxiang* leaders.

Although the non-elite Ningbo demonstrators fashioned their political statement in keeping with the boundaries and hierarchy of native-place community, the *huiguan* elite stepped beyond the Ningbo community. In a new departure (which was probably facilitated by the institutional innovation of a Shanghai Chamber of Commerce which formally brought together many *huiguan* leaders in one association), Ningbo merchant leaders were able to organize swiftly leaders of other native-place groups and trades in Shanghai and to coordinate action on the basis of Chinese nationalism.[11] A *Shenbao* editorial identified the Ningbo cause as the national cause: "Among the sojourning Ningbo people everyone is enraged . . . and among the people of all provinces sojourning in Shanghai there is not one who is not enraged. Now it is not just sojourners in Shanghai who are enraged but all Chinese, of all trades, provinces and also Chinese merchants overseas are all righteously angry. . . . This is not just a Ningbo people's tragedy, but a tragedy for all Chinese."[12]

Although the incident involved an assertion of national identity and national sovereignty, the mechanism of organization according to sub-ethnic, or native-place, identity in a nationalist struggle was not discarded but applauded. This would also be the case in a larger-scale and more famous nationalist movement which followed, the Anti-American Boycott of 1905. In this and later movements we see the formation of new political associations, often comprised of numerous distinctly organized but cooperating native-place groups. Although the new political associations (as in the case of the 1905 boycott) were responsible for producing much of the overarching political rhetoric and strategy of specific movements, their effectiveness in penetrating and mobilizing Shanghai society depended heavily on the prior organization of Shanghai residents through native-place associations.

The Anti-American Boycott of 1905. Whereas the 1898 Cemetery Riot has been viewed as China's first anti-imperialist strike and boycott, the boycott of 1905 has been viewed as the first modern anti-

---

11. Although it is striking that the leaders of the Ningbo association could call a meeting of all major commercial leaders in Shanghai on such short notice, it should be recalled that the Siming Gongsuo leaders were also the leaders of the Shanghai Chamber of Commerce.

12. SB, January 23, 1905.

imperialist boycott because it was not restricted to one native-place group but was nearly national in scope.[13] This understanding of the boycott has somewhat masked the role of native-place ties in the movement.

The immediate cause of the boycott was negotiation between the United States and China in late 1904 and early 1905 concerning the renewal of a treaty excluding Chinese labor from the United States. Lurid Chinese press accounts detailed mistreatment of Chinese workers abroad and aroused protest against U.S. immigration policies.[14]

The boycott movement began formally in Shanghai with a meeting on May 10 of prominent Shanghai merchants at the Chamber of Commerce. After speeches by activists Zeng Shaoqing and Ge Pengyun, the assembly agreed on a two-month deadline, after which no American goods were to be purchased or sold.[15] Although the Chamber declared the boycott, participation was actually determined through native-place organization and varied according to native-place group.

The Chamber was dominated by Ningbo merchants. Ningbo enthusiasm for the boycott, though not inconsiderable, did not match that of the Fujian and Guangdong *bang,* which had stronger ties to overseas Chinese communities. Dissatisfied with the Chamber meeting, Guangdong and Fujian sojourners met separately at their *huiguan* over the next two days. Both assemblies supported more radical boycott measures than those decided on at the May 10 meeting.[16]

13. For accounts of this boycott, see Zhang Cunwu, *Guangxu sanshiyi nian zhongmei gongyue fengchao* (The 1905 Chinese–U.S. labor treaty unrest) (Taipei, 1965); Liu Huiwu, *Shanghai jindaishi;* C. F. Remer, *A Study of Chinese Boycotts* (Baltimore, Md., 1933); Margaret Field, "The Chinese Boycott of 1905," *Papers on China* 11 (December 1957), 63–98.

14. The United States began to limit Chinese immigration in the Restriction Act of 1882, which excluded both skilled and unskilled laborers for ten years. Further discriminatory regulations were enacted in the next few years. They required all Chinese in the United States to register and prevented the return to the United States of laborers who temporarily visited China. The treaty under negotiation (which expired at the end of 1904) was a supplementary agreement of 1894 which provided for the absolute exclusion of Chinese workers for a ten-year period.

15. Zeng (1848–1908) was a Fujianese merchant who arrived in Shanghai in 1901, quickly made a fortune, purchased the rank of expectant Daotai and became a leader of the Fujian *huiguan.* Zeng became president of the Chamber of Commerce in 1906 as a result of his boycott leadership. Ge was an English teacher. See SB, May 11, 1905; Zhang Cunwu, *Guangxu sanshiyi nian,* 43; Tang Zhengchang, *Shanghai shi,* 411.

16. Zhang Cunwu, *Guangxu sanshiyi nian,* 44–46. Students did not really become active in the boycott until May 27, when the Shanghai Educational Association, representing twenty-four educational institutions, met to endorse the resolutions of the May 10 merchant meeting. Afterward students proved enthusiastic political activists but had little power. See Field, "Chinese Boycott of 1905," 78; Zhang Cunwu, *Guangxu sanshiyi nian,* 101.

The boycott began on July 20, the deadline set by the merchants. On July 19 the Shanghai Educational Association (*Hu xuehui*), together with representatives of Shanghai student, merchant and worker circles (*xue-shang-gong jie*) and representatives from other ports met to initiate the boycott. More than fourteen hundred people attended. Prominent among the participants were the directors of the Guangdong, Fujian, Hankou and Shandong *bang*, as well as representatives of the Chamber of Commerce, the Commercial Education Association, and leaders of the foreign-goods, silk, kerosene, native-banks, ginseng, hemp, sugar and seafood trades.[17]

On July 20, two hours before the Chamber met to announce the boycott, more than one thousand people met at the South Shanghai Educational and Commercial Association (*Hu nan xue-shang hui*). The meeting was convened by Zhou Liansheng, a Ningbo activist who advocated more radical measures than the older Chamber leadership. A representative of "Ningbo people of resolve" notified the assembly of an all-Zhejiang meeting at the Siming Gongsuo the next day.[18]

On July 21, several hundred Ningbo fellow-provincials, organized by Zhou Liansheng, rallied to protest U.S. immigration policy. Stating that Ningbo people comprised the majority of wealthy Shanghai merchants, many of whom engaged in trade with the United States, Zhou stressed the special responsibility of Ningbo people to lead the boycott, citing the precedent of the Zhou Shengyou case.[19]

As in May, the Guangdong and Fujian merchant communities met separately after the Chamber meeting. On July 25 the Guangdong and Foreign Goods Trade (*Guangbang Guangyanghuo ye*) met at the Guang-Zhao Gongsuo to set up a mechanism to end trade in U.S. goods. On the same day Fujian trade groups met at the Dianchuntang to coordi-

17. SB, July 20, 1905.
18. SB, July 21, 1905. Among those attending this meeting were representatives of the Tianjin, Chaozhou, Guangdong, Ningbo and Anhui *bang*, as well as representatives of numerous banks, including native banks, and of the metal, foreign-goods and foreign-yarn trades. Included were Zhou Jinzhen, director of the Shanghai Telegraph Bureau, and Xie Lunhui, a director of the Native Bankers' Association.
19. Zhou Shengyou was the victim of the drunken Russian sailor. The *Shenbao* article (July 22) reporting this meeting stated that it was not held at the Siming Gongsuo, as might have been expected, but that the Ningbo people borrowed the *Shang-xue hui*. This fact, and the absence of the usual *huiguan* leaders at this meeting, suggest that the *huiguan* elite demonstrated some reluctance in the proceedings or that there was some conflict within the Ningbo community over the boycott. This is also suggested by a notice calling for a Ningbo students' meeting to support the boycott, which cited uncertainty over where the meeting could be held. See SB, July 26, 1905.

nate boycott enforcement tactics.[20] Boycott pledge meetings followed at the Fujian Tingzhou Huiguan, the Zhejiang Haichang Gongsuo, the Jiangning Gongsuo, the Guang-Zhao Hospital, the Chaozhou Huiguan and the Sichuan Merchants' Gongsuo. The functions of native-place networks in the boycott are revealed in an account of a meeting of several thousand Ningbo merchants. Ningbo boycott leaders announced that they had investigated the goods Ningbo imported from the United States, had contacted leading merchants in Ningbo and had secured pledges of boycott solidarity.[21]

Through their many public meetings, circulars and published manifestos, native-place organizations mobilized, educated and regulated their communities. Although activist boycott organizers initiated the call for a boycott, sojourner institutions played organizational roles, sponsoring meetings and policing their own members, ensuring boycott participation in Shanghai and helping additionally to coordinate inland enforcement. In boycott mobilization native-place groups constituted fundamental organizational units, familiar communities for Shanghai residents, communities which made possible a high degree of mobilization, policing and compliance. In this respect native-place associations had an advantage over the Chamber of Commerce, which, as Xu Dingxin notes, could announce a boycott but lacked the institutional means to enforce compliance or discipline members.[22]

Because the boycott was organized in this fashion, different trades entered at different moments. The more resolute native-place communities persisted throughout the fall, meeting periodically to rally enthusiasm and resolve.[23]

The boycott instilled a high level of popular political awareness and participation in Shanghai residents and abetted growing alienation be-

20. SB, July 25, 1905; SB, July 27, 1905. More than eighteen hundred people attended this meeting, including the Fujian Sugar Trade and the Fujian Foreign, Guangdong, Seafood and North–South Goods Trade (*Tangye Yang-Guang haiwei nanbeihuo ye*). The Dianchuntang was established by Fujian merchants from Tingzhou, Quanzhou and Zhangzhou. The Shanghai hemp trade, bean and rice trade and a separate (not Guangdong *bang*) foreign-goods trade also met on July 23.

21. Notices of these meetings appeared in *Shenbao* from July 27 through August 1, 1905. See also Zhang Cunwu, *Guangxu sanshiyi nian*, 93. Several thousand merchants attended the Guangdong meeting (NCH, August 4, 1905). The full name of the Jiangning Gongsuo was Jiangning Qiyi Lü Hu Gongsuo.

22. Xu and Qian, *Shanghai zongshanghui shi*, 85.

23. Business losses dampened merchant enthusiasm, and the boycott waned after August 31, when the United States secured an imperial edict forbidding the boycott. Guangdong merchants persisted until at least December (SB, December 9, 1905).

tween a politically activist merchant community and the enfeebled and ineffective Qing government. Those groups which persisted after an August 31 edict banning boycott action did so in defiance of the Manchu court.

The Mixed Court Riot of December 1905. Sojourner networks played key roles in the increasingly militant nationalist protests which followed. The Mixed Court Riot, the most violent protest in the International Settlement since its establishment, occurred several months after the peak of boycott activity and involved many of the same activists. The riot developed out of disputes between Chinese and Western authorities over legal jurisdiction in the International Settlement. The case which sparked the riot joined a *huiguan* defense of fellow-provincials with the issues of national sovereignty and legal authority over Chinese citizens.[24]

The site of jurisdictional dispute was the Mixed Court. The foreign Assessor was not meant to interfere in purely Chinese cases; nonetheless, western authorities intervened increasingly in the first years of the twentieth century, sending police to supervise the court's operation. During 1905 Chinese Magistrate Guan Jiongzhi repeatedly but ineffectually protested infringements on Chinese sovereignty and interference with the principle of Chinese adjudication of Chinese cases.[25]

Smoldering resentments over western encroachment on Chinese judicial authority led to violence when a case arose which involved the interests of a prominent Shanghai native-place association. Protests began when a Guangdong widow, Li (née Huang), who was returning to her native place from Sichuan accompanied by fifteen servant-girls and her husband's coffin, was arrested by Settlement police on suspicion of

24. Secondary accounts of the Mixed Court Riot and Mixed Court history appear in Kotenev, *Shanghai: Its Mixed Court and Council*, 127–30; Xi Dichen, "Danao gongtang'an" (The Mixed Court uproar), *Shanghaishi tongzhiguan qi'kan* (Journal of the Shanghai city gazetteer office) 1 (1933):408–40; Liu Huiwu, *Shanghai jindaishi*, 318–22; F. L. Hawks Pott, *A Short History of Shanghai* (Shanghai, 1928), 166–69; Mark Elvin, "The Mixed Court of the International Settlement at Shanghai (until 1911)," *Papers on China* 17 (December 1963):131–58; Bryna Goodman, "The Native Place and the City: Immigrant Consciousness and Organization in Shanghai, 1853–1927" (Ph.D. diss., Stanford University, 1990), 226–42.

25. In addition, in April 1905 British Assessor Twyman declared the Chinese-administered Mixed Court jail unsanitary and assigned female prisoners to a new western jail. (Male prisoners for some time had been sent to an existing western jail.) See *Dongfang zazhi*, 2:11; 2:12 (1905); Liu, *Shanghai jindaishi*, 318.

kidnapping and transporting girls for sale. Tensions arose between Magistrate Guan and British Assessor Twyman over custody of Madame Li during the investigation of the case. The Magistrate ordered his runners to place her in the Mixed Court jail, whereas the Assessor (who had no jurisdiction) ordered the municipal police to escort her to a newly built western jail.[26] A fight broke out between the British police and Chinese *yamen* runners, from which the police emerged victorious. Several runners were injured, and the assisting Chinese official, Jin Shaocheng, was hit in the melee. To prevent the police from removing Madame Li, the runners locked the courtyard. Magistrate Guan withdrew, declaring that the police would have to kill him before he opened the gates. The police forced the lock and removed Madame Li.[27]

In response to this melodramatic enactment of western brutality and the pathetic weakness of Chinese officials, over the next two days (December 9 and 10) protest was organized through two institutional networks, the Guang-Zhao Gongsuo and the Chinese Chamber of Commerce. Although the voices of Chinese officials were not unheard, it was obvious to observers that merchants led officials in the matter.[28] The Guang-Zhao Gongsuo held a general meeting for Guangdong provincials and contacted the Ministry of Foreign Affairs and the Commercial Bureau, requesting help. Their telegrams vindicated Madame Li and accused the Settlement authorities of both mistreating a member of the Chinese official class and interfering with the Chinese administration of justice:

On [December 8] British police falsely accused a Madame Li née Wang of kidnapping and forcibly imprisoned her in the western jail, beating court runners and insulting the magistrate. The so-called Li née Wang is really Li née Huang, the wife of the Sichuan official Li Tingyu. Tingyu fell sick [and died] and so his father, Li Zhisheng, who is engaged in business in Chongqing and served as director of our [Sichuan] Guangdong *bang,* asked his colleagues and fellow-provincials, together with his relatives, to arrange to

26. Like the 1874 cemetery riot (which was set off by the sight of a Chinese prostitute who served foreigners), this case reveals the characteristic combustibility of crossed sexual and ethnic boundaries. Here the spark was foreign custody over a Chinese woman.

27. NCH, December 15, 1905; Liu, *Shanghai jindaishi,* 319. The International Settlement archives were not available when I worked at the Shanghai Municipal Archives in 1984 and at the date of this writing are still not generally open. On September 10, 1988, with participants in an International Symposium on Modern Shanghai, I was invited for a fifteen-minute viewing of the Settlement archives. One cabinet contained a thick file on the Mixed Court Riot. There was not time to do more than jot down a few details.

28. NCH, December 15, 1905.

send the widow, children and coffin back to Guangdong, accompanied by several household servants and slaves. All of them have "body receipts" [receipts for the sale of their person]. There were over one hundred pieces of luggage, all with transportation passes from the Sichuan Daotai. The British police . . . forced [the widow Li] into the western prison and dared to beat the court runners and insult the Magistrate. This is unreasonable. . . . Now she is still locked in the jail. . . . Popular feelings are extremely aroused and likely to erupt. . . . We pray you to assist us . . . to calm people's hearts and assert China's sovereignty. [Signed:] the sojourning gentry-merchants of all Guangdong.[29]

Xu Run, Guang-Zhao Gongsuo director and one of the few non-Zhejiang directors of the Chinese Chamber of Commerce, also led a protest meeting at the Chamber, where he was joined by boycott leader Zeng Shaoqing and Siming Gongsuo director Yu Xiaqing. This gathering of more than one thousand Shanghai notables sent telegrams to the Ministry of Foreign Affairs, the Ministry of Commerce and the Governor General at Nanjing, listing the offenses of the British Assessor and police. They requested intervention by the Beijing authorities and asserted the need for Chinese representation on the Municipal Council of the International Settlement.[30]

On December 10, after filing a protest with the Municipal Council and the British Consul in response to pressure from the Shanghai Magistrate and Shanghai merchants, Daotai Yuan called a meeting of "sojourning gentry" to discuss "the insult to Chinese officials by the Western police." Four to five hundred people attended and sent a joint official-merchant telegram to the Ministry of Foreign Affairs requesting intervention. In the meantime the Daotai asked merchant leaders to prevent disorder among their popular constituencies. On the same day the Patriotic Oratorical Society (*gongzhong yanshuohui*) organized a gathering of four to five thousand at the Xu Gardens (possibly the property of the Guangdong merchant Xu Run). This meeting featured speeches by boycott activists, notably Ge Pengyun.[31]

Over the next few days the organizational networks widened as student and student-merchant groups as well as native-place associations

29. SB, December 11, 1905. There were fifteen signatories, headed by Xu Run. The others were Huang Yiquan, Chen Weihan, Tan Guozhong, Situ Huai, Chen Qikang, Li Zhongjun, Xu Linguang, Lo Chongling, Zeng Pan, He Ying, Fang Huichang, Lu Qinghua, Yuan Qicun and Zheng Xiancheng.

30. NCH, December 15, 1905; Xi Dichen, "Danao Gongtang'an," 420–21; SB, December 10, 1905; SB, December 11, 1905.

31. SB, December 11, 1905; SB, December 12, 1905; SB, December 17, 1905.

orchestrated protests. Among the former, most of which had been mobilized during the boycott movement, were the Commercial Strive for
Progress Society (*shangye qiujinhui*), the Patriotic Oratorical Society,
the Commercial Studies Continuation Society (*shangxue buxihui*), the
Civilized Treaty Resistance Society (*wenming juyueshe*) and the Commercial Education Society (*shangxuehui*). There were also meetings of
the Siming Gongsuo, Guang-Zhao Gongsuo and Chong-Hai Fellow-
Provincials' Association.[32]

These meetings shared rhetoric which extended traditional notions
of "face" to the national body in the context of an international community. This involved "righteous indignation" at foreigners' "destruction
of China's national prestige" in beating Chinese runners and "insulting
Chinese officials." Participants assembled to discuss ways to restore China's "face." Merchant meetings appealed to Chinese officials, but they
also suggested that if Chinese officials failed to protect Chinese rights,
"we merchants will form a great assembly and decide on a means [of
action]."[33]

Responding to the spate of telegrams emanating from Shanghai merchants, the Foreign Ministry, Commercial Bureau and the Governor
General called for a meeting between the Ministry of Foreign Affairs
and the foreign ambassadors in Beijing to protest the trespass on China's
legal jurisdiction. Locally, the Daotai met with General Consul Kleime-
now, setting out the merchants' conditions for resolving tensions: 1)
release of Madame Li and her entourage; 2) dismissal of Assessor Twyman and punishment of the police; 3) exclusive use of the Mixed Court
prison for female offenders. The Consul rejected the measures.[34]

Although the Settlement authorities ignored the demands, popular
agitation continued, increasingly demanding Chinese representation on
the Municipal Council. Several thousand Ningbo fellow-provincials rallied on December 12 at the Siming Gongsuo "to preserve national integrity" (*baocun guoti*), vowing to use the power of their association to
mobilize their *tongxiang*.

Finally succumbing to pressure from the Chinese Ministry of Foreign

32. The commercial-studies society met at the Fujian Dianchuntang. The Chong-Hai
Tongxianghui represented Chongming and Haimen counties, Jiangsu (SB, December 10,
1905; SB, December 11, 1905; SB, December 12, 1905; NCH, December 15, 1905).
33. Ibid. The last quotation, from a Commercial Education Society meeting, attended
by approximately three thousand people, is typical of statements made at the other meetings, most of which advocated merchant political activism.
34. SB, December 12, 1905; SB, December 13, 1905; Liu, *Shanghai jindaishi*, 320.

Affairs, the Diplomatic Body of Beijing ordered the Consular Body in Shanghai to release the widow. The British Consul relinquished Madame Li (whose food needs in jail had been looked after by several Shanghai Guangdong restaurants) on December 15, delivering her directly to the Guang-Zhao Gongsuo.[35]

Despite Madame Li's release, agitation increased. The radical Patriotic Oratorical Society called for a strike and refusal to pay Settlement taxes. Although the collective public response of *huiguan* leaders was more moderate, *huiguan* were nonetheless the sites of large public meetings featuring radical speakers. Former boycott leaders called for a strike, for example, before an assembly at the Guang-Zhao Gongsuo on December 15. After leaving this meeting, Ge Pengyun and Yan Chengye, of the Patriotic Oratorical Society, spoke before a crowd of more than four thousand at the Chaozhou Huiguan. On December 17 the Siming Gongsuo lent its hall and grounds to the Commercial Strive for Progress Society for a large rally, at which Ge and Yan announced a strike the next day of all Chinese enterprises in the International Settlement. Radical leaders also distributed circulars announcing the strike, insisting on foreign recognition of Chinese demands in the Mixed Court case and calling for the appointment of a Chinese Municipal Councilor. As the Jiangsu Governor observed, these tactics kept the Daotai caught between the tasks of arranging Chinese–foreign negotiations and urging Shanghai merchants to control rioting.[36]

The speakers at these meetings deployed native-place sentiment to their advantage and connected the concerns of sojourner communities to the larger issue of Chinese rights and the need for Chinese representation on the Municipal Council, in recognition of the considerable Chi-

35. In this incident the British dealt directly with the Guang-Zhao Gongsuo, despite Chinese officials' demands that Madame Li be turned over to the Mixed Court Magistrate (SB, December 13, 1905; SB, December 14, 1905; Xi Dichen, "Danao gongtang'an," 430). The *North China Herald* (December 15) deplored the release order in an editorial entitled, "Mob Law": "The Diplomatic Body of Peking has decided . . . to give way to Chinese popular clamour. . . . The [protests of] the Taotai, the Canton Guild and all the noisy patriots of Shanghai under the guidance of the very men who organized and directed the boycott here . . . are enough for the Waiwupu and the Diplomatic Body."

36. SB, December 15, 1905; SB, December 16, 1905; SB, December 17, 1905; PRO, FO 228.2512. Also, on December 15 approximately one thousand people met at the Jade Gongsuo (a Jiangsu association). The Municipal Council police reported that the Ningbo *huiguan* meeting was attended by many of the "loafer and unemployed class" (MCR for 1905, 31–32).

nese property and taxes in the Settlement. While making the rounds of various *huiguan* meetings, Ge Pengyun stressed that the Mixed Court affair "affects all Chinese — whether natives of Canton, Ningbo or Swatow — everywhere in China."[37] His statement and lecture circuit during this period in which, as the *Shenbao* commented, "there was no day without meetings and no meeting without indignation," reflect the obvious organization of the Shanghai community into these prominent native-place groups and the expedience of political organization through them. Although political organization was citywide, the rationale for activism was common Chinese identity, and this did not necessitate rejection of native-place organization or identity in favor of common Shanghai identity. In meetings, telegrams and official statements, merchants were consistently described as "*sojourning* gentry-merchants in Shanghai" rather than as Shanghai merchants.[38]

On the morning of December 18 the walls of the Settlement were plastered with inflammatory placards.[39] Crowds in different parts of the Settlement simultaneously attacked the first markets and rice-gruel shops to open, exhorting owners to keep their shutters down and harassing foreigners who attempted to get to work. Shortly afterward, crowds of several thousand set fire to police stations and the town hall. Settlement authorities sent out the police, the Volunteers, sailors and marines to restore order. This was accomplished by evening, at the cost of at least fifteen Chinese lives. The strike ended the next day.[40]

Immediately after the rioting, leaders of major *huiguan* emerged with the Daotai, urged merchants to open shop, deplored the rioting, and offered their help to the municipal authorities. Although the *North China Herald* expressed bemusement at the spectacle of the "heads of

37. PRO, FO 228.2512.

38. See SB, December 15, 1905; SB, December 16, 1905.

39. Responding to the strike announcements made at the Siming Gongsuo meeting, at 10:00 P.M. on December 17, the Chamber distributed circulars denouncing the strike. Because of the late hour, these were ineffectual. See PRO, FO 228.2512; MCR for 1905, 29; NCH, December 22, 1905.

40. NCH, December 22, 1905; MCR for 1905, 29; Kotenev, *Shanghai: Its Mixed Court and Council,* 128–29; SB, December 19, 1905; Xi Dichen, "Danao gongtang'an," 431; *Shanghai xian zhi* (Shanghai county gazetteer) (Shanghai, 1935; reprint Taiwan, 1975), 14:34. Sources vary on the number killed. Many others were seriously wounded. Settlement Police identified the Patriotic Oratorical Society as responsible for printing strike announcements and hiring men to enforce the strike and singled out Ge Pengyun and Yan Chengye (identified as a coal merchant) for arrest. See NCH, December 22, 1905; PRO, FO 228.2512; MCR for 1905, 31–32.

the Ningbo guild express[ing] their regret for what has occurred,"[41] *hui-guan* leaders leapt into action in the negotiations which followed with Settlement authorities and the Daotai. Through their manipulation of events, these individuals and the associations they represented increased their influence and recognition in the order-keeping process. Yu Xiaqing, no doubt aided in this endeavor by his experience in the 1898 Ningbo cemetery affair, was the primary negotiator on the Chinese side.[42]

In the course of negotiations the municipal authorities discussed with the *huiguan* leaders the possibility of organizing a consultative committee "representative of the best native opinion," which would meet regularly with Council members and keep the Council informed of Chinese public opinion. After the experience of the riot, for the first time the Municipal Council concurred as to the necessity of this step toward Chinese representation.[43]

In early 1906 the Municipal Council approved a Chinese consultative committee of seven members (selected by representatives of forty "guilds") which reflected the power of the three most influential native-place groups in the city. Five of the merchant leaders representing the Shanghai Chinese community in this plan were from Zhejiang (three of these Siming Gongsuo directors) and one each hailed from Guangdong and Jiangsu. Although *huiguan/gongsuo* leadership was not an explicit element in the selection process, the choice of *huiguan* and *gongsuo* di-

41. SB, December 19, 1905; NCH, December 22, 1905. The *North China Herald* correspondent continued, "This . . . is in direct contradiction to the views these Uriah Heeps held . . . when they met at the Sz Ming club rooms, at which some 7,000 natives were present" (NCH, December 22, 1905).

42. NCH, December 29, 1905. Yu was flanked in the negotiations by two fellow *huiguan* directors, who portrayed themselves somewhat disingenuously as "men disassociated from the recent agitation conducted by the native Chamber of Commerce and whose sincere desire it is to restore order and maintain it." The relationship between native-place associations and the Chamber—given their intersecting memberships—deserves further examination. Certainly independent but overlapping affiliations provided merchant leaders with a convenient means of dissociating themselves from a given association in favor of an alternative identification when one institution became tainted or implicated in an unsavory affair.

43. The negotiations produced a compromise. The British declined to dismiss Assessor Twyman but agreed to investigate the conduct of the Police Inspector. Custody of female prisoners was relinquished to the Mixed Court prison. The Diplomatic Corps and the Ministry of Foreign Affairs in Beijing agreed to return to the Mixed Court regulations of 1869, disregarding intervening precedents of increased foreign influence. See Kotenev, *Shanghai: Its Mixed Court and Council*, 129–31; NCH, December 29, 1905. The principle of representation was first established in 1864, when Tang Jingxing and Xu Run were invited to attend Council meetings, but was afterward ignored by the Municipal Council until 1905. See Kotenev, *Shanghai: Its Municipality and the Chinese*, 157.

rectors to represent the Chinese community was in accordance with
Chinese public opinion as formulated in the *Shenbao,* which suggested
that *huiguan* governance provided a foundation for Chinese representative government: "All city residents should have the right to select representatives and keep order. Within the Settlement, although Chinese residents do not have this system, usually each *bang* has a meeting place
and each has merchant directors as leaders. Thus they already have the
qualities of representatives."[44] Although this committee was not ultimately approved by the Ratepayer's Association, the idea of *huiguan*
representation of Chinese interests vis-à-vis foreign authorities was re-
confirmed a decade later. In March 1915, after the French Convention of
April 8, 1914 approved the introduction of two Chinese representatives
in a consultative role into the French Municipal Council, the Senior
Consul forwarded a draft agreement to the Municipal Council for the
extension of the International Settlement which provided for a Chinese
Advisory Board, "to consist of two nominees of the Ningbo Guild, two
nominees of the Canton Guild, and one nominee of the Special Envoy
for Foreign Affairs."[45]

By both pushing for Chinese representation and placing themselves
in the position of intermediaries between the Chinese community and
foreign authorities, *huiguan* leaders advanced the cause of Chinese
rights while they also increased the power and influence of sojourner
institutions. In this manner, native-place and national interests could be
mutually complementary. The glory of Yu Xiaqing, who emerged from
the negotiations as the most influential Chinese merchant in the settlement (and was awarded an inscribed gold watch from the Municipal

44. MCR for 1906, 393; quotation is from SB, December 13, 1905. Zhejiang members
were Wu Shaoqing (Silk Huiguan director), Xie Lunhui (Native Bankers' Association
director), Zhou Jinzhen (both Siming Gongsuo and Chinese Telegraph Station director),
Yu Xiaqing (Siming Gongsuo director and Netherlands Bank comprador) and Zhu Baosan (Siming Gongsuo director and vice-chair of the Chamber). The others were You Binghan, from Shanghai county (Piece-Goods Association director), and Chen Huiting, from
Guangdong (CMSNC director). These individuals were all officers or members of the
Chamber of Commerce. See *Shanghai shangwu zonghui tongrenlu,* 1906–8.

45. This later formulation concedes one position to Chinese government authority,
though the four-to-one configuration suggests a dim evaluation of this component vis-à-
vis the native-place *bang* (AMRE, Chine, Supplément NS 613, Concession Internationale
de Changhai, 1911–16, 3–6; Kotenev, *Shanghai, Its Municipality and the Chinese,* 155–56). In
1915 the Ratepayers' Meeting unanimously accepted these conditions, but the establishment of the new Board was thwarted in a deadlock between the foreign ministers and the
Chinese government. A Chinese Advisory Committee was not finally approved by the
Ratepayers until 1920.

Council in recognition of his services in settling the affair)[46] and became somewhat of a public hero for asserting Chinese rights, magnified the "face" of the Ningbo community. Insofar as foreign authorities accepted the leaders of native-place associations as representatives of the Chinese community, they reinforced a growing tactical linkage between native-place and national identity.

Native-Place Organization and Revolutionary Mobilization

The revolutionary mobilization of society proceeded on two fronts: the early revolutionary organizations of radical students and intellectuals (often in Japan) and the more moderate, initially constitutionalist efforts of gentry and merchant activist reformers who worked through educational associations and local self-government organizations in the Shanghai area. These two wings of activism converged by late 1910 to form the fragile coalition that overthrew imperial authority in Shanghai's part in the Revolution of 1911.

Early Revolutionaries. Shanghai was a magnet for radical intellectuals, both because it was a center for the dissemination of new ideas through foreign-style schools, bookstores and newspapers and because the foreign settlements offered a degree of refuge for radicals likely to run afoul of the Chinese authorities. The most radical groups were in Japan, for similar reasons (their radicalism additionally reinforced by experience of sojourning in a militarily stronger Asian nation). These groups relied on contacts in Shanghai for disseminating their journals and as a gateway to the Chinese interior.[47]

Early radical groups were organized almost entirely through native-place ties, which provided ready networks of association among sojourning students who spoke different dialects and had different cultural

46. MCR for 1905, 93.

47. Mary Backus Rankin, *Early Chinese Revolutionaries: Radical Intellectuals in Shanghai and Chekiang, 1902–1911* (Cambridge, Mass., 1971), 5. As Rankin notes, the significance of this group diminished after 1907, as local self-government and educational associations created new (often more practical) avenues for political activism, and after mid-1909, as gentry and merchants played increasingly important roles in railway-rights disputes and agitation for constitutional government.

habits. Students in both Shanghai and Tokyo organized clubs along provincial lines. The first revolutionary associations in China were also regional networks, as has been noted by Rankin and others. Guangdong natives organized the Xing Zhong Hui (Society to Develop China's Prosperity); Hunan and Hubei activists created the Huaxing Hui (Chinese Revival Society); and Zhejiang activists established the Guangfu Hui (Restoration Society). When these groups joined together in 1905 to form the Zhongguo Tongmeng Hui (Revolutionary Alliance) they retained much of their independent existence.[48] Native-place ties also permitted activists in these groups to organize workers. For example, the early Xing Zhong Hui member Ma Chaojun, who founded the Guangdong Mechanics' Association, also traveled to Wuhan and Shanghai to organize his fellow-provincial craftsmen in shipyards and arsenals.[49]

In the first years of the twentieth century, native-place associations began to publish reformist and revolutionary journals which played a role in the developing radical press. Although journals like the *Ningbo baihua bao* (Ningbo vernacular), published by the Shanghai Ningbo sojourning community in 1903–4, featured articles about native-place industries, customs, education and literature, they also criticized national corruption. The most radical journals were published not in Shanghai (where there was more risk) but by groups of sojourning students in Tokyo, who sent them into China through Shanghai.

These journals express the combination of native-place and nationalist loyalties which provided an important context for the development of Chinese nationalism. Love for the native place and activism in the interest of local self-government were conceived as integral to national strengthening, creating local building blocks for a modern constitutionalist state. In these journals, whose titles usually bore the names of the students' home provinces, ardent nationalists explicitly considered the role of native-place ties in revolutionary nationalism.[50]

The role of native-place sentiment in the patriotic struggle to radi-

48. Rankin, *Early Chinese Revolutionaries*, 13–14, 23–25; Tang Zhengchang, *Shanghai shi*, 408–9. Jiangsu activists soon also became involved in the Guangfu Hui.

49. Ma Chaojun et al., *Zhongguo laogong yundong shi* (History of the Chinese labor movement) (Taipei, 1959), vol. 1, 52, cited in Perry, *Shanghai on Strike*, 40.

50. Among the journals published by different groups of sojourning students in Tokyo between 1902 and 1909 were *Hubei xueshengjie* (Hubei student world), *Zhejiang chao* (Zhejiang tide), *Yu bao* (Henan), *Jiangsu, Dian hua* (Words from Hunan), *Meizhou* (Mei prefecture), *Jiangxi* and *Xianglu jingzhong* (Hunan railroad tocsin). See Ding Shouhe, ed., *Xinhai geming shiqi qikan jieshao*, vol. 1 (Beijing, 1982), 239, 269–87, 329–45, 431–40, 542–43, 599–605; vol. 2 (Beijing, 1982), 622–33, 243–55, 548–53.

cally reform China was addressed in the inaugural issues of two of the most influential of these journals, *Jiangsu* and *Zhejiang chao* (Zhejiang tide). The editors of *Jiangsu* reasoned as follows: "Those who love China cry out, saying 'Our China has nothing; all it has is corruption.' And those who love Jiangsu—how much more so should they weep and say, 'Our Jiangsu has nothing; all it has is corruption.' It can be plainly said that our Jiangsu is the epitome of China, and corruption is the distinguishing characteristic of Jiangsu. Therefore, discussing corruption is the special duty of *Jiangsu* magazine."[51]

To this idea of the native place as epitome, or embodiment of the whole, is added a second rationale, that political action should properly start locally: "If you want to fight for freedom, first you must discuss self-government. You must build on the familiar local soil of human feeling, history, geography and customs. Afterwards you can take the initiative and travel beyond. First begin with Zhejiang—you can call it starting with one corner. The process doesn't end here, but [one is] limited by what one knows."[52]

This passage suggests both the notion of the native place as key to the nation (as a corner through which it may be possible to know the whole) and the idea that the native place serves as a necessary and familiar place to begin. By addressing reform in the native place, the abstract and enormous task of reforming the nation becomes concrete, manageable and familiar.[53] The passage also reflects the popularization and ac-

51. *Jiangsu* 1 (1903), reprinted in Luo Jialun, *Zhonghua minguo*, 119–20.

52. The passage contains a modified Confucian allusion, which suggests that students should infer the whole from the first corner: *ju yi yu bu yi san yu fan ze bu fu ye* (If I have presented one corner of the square and they cannot come back to me with the other three, I should not go over the points again). Analects, 7:8 (in Wing-tsit Chan, trans., *A Source Book in Chinese Philosophy* [Princeton, N. J., 1963], 31–32). See also *Zhejiang chao* 1 (1903), reprinted in Luo, *Zhonghua minguo*, 67–102.

53. These ideas recur, often in nearly identical language, throughout these journals. The native place as epitome idea is reworked repeatedly. Thus, from the foreword to the first issue of *Jiangsu:* "Our Jiangsu people [are] just like China. Our Chinese people are renowned in the world as weak and sickly; and our Jiangsu people are renowned in China as weak and sickly"; and "In the project of reforming the whole country, how is it I speak just Jiangsu dialect? I was born in Jiangsu, raised in Jiangsu, Jiangsu is the land of my ancestors. Speaking of what is most intimate, it is appropriate to begin with Jiangsu . . . beginning with one corner to win over the entire country. *Jiangsu* 1:3 (1903), reprinted in Luo, *Zhonghua minguo shiliao congbian jieshao,* vol. 1, 119. This passage, which fancifully evokes a homogeneous Jiangsu province, contrasts with the sharp north–south cultural divisions of the province. Jiangsu sojourners in Japan presumably were from the Jiangnan elite and were thus free of reminders of divisions between themselves and people from Jiangbei.

ceptance of concepts of local self-government (*zizhi*) articulated in the late Qing by reformers like Feng Guifen and Huang Zunxian, who advocated the mobilization of local elites and resources in the interest of strengthening the state. This type of localism was not seen as separatism (opposed to the state) but was viewed, instead, as necessary for the health of the polity.[54] These connections drawn between native place and nation were both sincere and pragmatic, justifying the obvious and convenient native-place networks which underlay effective social organization in this period.

Merchant and Gentry Politicization. In the course of antiforeign mobilization during the last years of the Qing, politicized merchants and gentry increasingly found Manchu incompetence and subservience to foreign demands an obstacle to their efforts to strengthen the country. As their estrangement from the government increased, merchants gradually moved from asserting Chinese rights in the face of foreign imperialism toward revolutionary nationalism directed against the Qing. The local nature of foreign political and economic encroachments on Chinese sovereignty (through the partitioning of Chinese territory in railway and mining concessions and foreign "spheres of influence") meant that native-place networks and institutions would be deeply involved in initially reformist and ultimately revolutionary nationalist mobilization. Groups of sojourning merchants in Shanghai played major roles in railway and mining-rights recovery movements in their native provinces and mobilized opposition to Qing concessions to foreign interests.[55]

Whereas in the case of the Wuchang Uprising on October 10, 1911, merchants offered support to military insurgents only after the insurrec-

54. See Philip A. Kuhn, "Local Self-Government under the Republic: Problems of Control, Autonomy and Mobilization," in *Conflict and Control in Late Imperial China,* ed. Frederic Wakeman and Carolyn Grant (Berkeley, Calif., 1975), 256–98.

55. For Jiangsu sojourners' meetings regarding foreign railroad loans and coordination with fellow-provincials in Beijing, see SB, September 20, 1905; SB, September 23, 1905. Regarding Sichuan sojourners, see Shanghai shehui kexueyuan, Lishi yanjiusuo (Shanghai Academy of Social Sciences, Institute for Historical Research), ed., *Xinhai geming zai Shanghai shiliao xuanji* (Compilation of historical materials concerning the Revolution of 1911 in Shanghai) (Shanghai, 1981) (hereafter referred to as XGZS), 607. Anhui sojourners' concerns over a mining deal with Japan are expressed in telegrams to President Yuan Shikai in Beijing and the military governor of Anhui (SB, March 18, 1912). For general background on economic-rights-recovery issues in growing merchant and gentry alienation from the court, see Michael Gasster, "The Republican Revolutionary Movement," in Fairbank, *Cambridge History of China,* vol. 11, pt. 2, 515–16.

tion, in Shanghai merchant mobilization preceded and facilitated the successful November 3 uprising led by the revolutionaries. While many of the leading merchants in Shanghai, sojourners and locals alike, participated in both the constitutionalist and the rights-recovery movements, merchant mobilization proceeded along two paths, one generally characterizing merchants in the foreign settlement areas; the other, the areas of the city under Chinese jurisdiction.

Merchants in the foreign settlements (who could not institute local self-government) agitated for Chinese representation in the western municipal-settlement governments, as we saw in the aftermath of the Mixed Court Riot. They also began to establish merchant militia. One of Yu Xiaqing's first acts after the resolution of the Mixed Court Riot in 1905 was to form a Chinese Merchants' Exercise Association.[56] Yu invited important businessmen and trade leaders to organize militia (see Figure 7), funded through collections from Chinese shops and trades. In 1906 there were between five hundred and six hundred militia members, organized into five regiments of infantry and one regiment of cavalry.[57]

While Yu used his influence to incorporate this "Chinese Volunteer Corps" into the Volunteer Corps of the Municipal Settlement, local merchant and gentry leaders in the Chinese areas of the city took steps (also in 1905) to create what foreign observers heralded as the "first attempt at purely Chinese municipal representative government."[58] Concerned by the growth of foreign authority in the city and the contrasting municipal weakness of areas of the city under Chinese jurisdiction, a group of local gentry-merchants approached Daotai Yuan Shuxun to propose a local self-government project. This was the creation of a General Works Board, a transformation of the South City Roadworks Bureau (created by officials some years earlier to oversee construction projects in the Chinese city) into what would become effectively a Chinese City Council with public works and policing authority under gentry-merchant control. According to the *Shanghai shi zizhi zhi* (Shanghai

56. Yu was association president; Yuan Hengzhi (of Jiangsu, a director of the Piece-Goods Association) was vice-president. Membership was limited to young men "of merchant circles," and the uniform caps were engraved with a Chinese merchant flag. See PRO, FO 228.1634, 1906.

57. Pan Mingxin, "Shanghai wanguo shangtuan ji qi zhonghua dui" (The Shanghai merchant volunteers and the Chinese brigade), *Shanghai wenshi ziliao xuanji* (Selected materials on Shanghai history and culture) (Shanghai) 39 (May 1982):108–9; PRO, FO 228.1634. The Shanghai Municipal Council incorporated the Chinese Brigade in 1906.

58. NCH, October 20, 1905, cited in Mark Elvin, "The Gentry Democracy in Shanghai, 1905–1914 (D.Phil. diss., University of Cambridge, 1967), 50.

Figure 7. Yu Xiaqing and his Shanghai residence. Source: Arnold Wright, *Twentieth Century Impressions of Hong Kong, Shanghai, and Other Treaty Ports of China* (London, 1908), 539.

municipality self-government gazetteer), an immediate stimulus to this development was the increasing tendency of the British and French municipal councils to build (and police) roads in Chinese areas. Yuan endorsed their plan, which in many respects consciously imitated the Municipal Council of the International Settlement.[59]

59. The Chinese Municipal Council had a succession of Chinese names prior to the revolution. It was initially known as the *Chengxiang neiwai zong gongcheng ju* (1905–9), or

Whereas sojourners dominated the struggles in the foreign settlements, local Jiangsu merchants and gentry dominated the development
of the Chinese City Council.[60] The predominance of Jiangsu leaders in
the first Chinese Shanghai municipal government project raises important issues regarding the nature and meaning of this first Shanghai
municipal structure for the actors involved. It is therefore important to
consider the background and motivations of the local gentry leader Li
Pingshu (Li Zhongjue), who initiated the project and was appointed as
the general director of the new Chinese Municipal Council.

Li was from Pudong, just across the Huangpu River from the Shanghai bund. He was therefore not a sojourner but considered himself to
be of the locality (*bendi*). He received a traditional education and
achieved the degree of senior licentiate, which led him to several posts
in Guangdong as a magistrate. His concern to defend China against
foreign encroachment led him into association with Zhang Zhidong
and other officials in the self-strengthening movement and to involvement in westernization projects. Li traveled to Singapore to write an
account of British colonial administration, and in 1903 he took up a post
as Jiangnan Arsenal inspector. Between 1903 and 1911 Li engaged in a
series of social-reform projects in Shanghai, establishing a hospital, providing running water and electrification for Chinese residents and organizing medical study societies to integrate Chinese and western medicine. He was also involved in several modern industrial enterprises. Li
was therefore a well-traveled, highly cosmopolitan individual and a pas-
sionate nationalist with a deep interest in using both western technology and administrative practices to strengthen China.[61]

General Works Board; then the Self-Government Office (*zizhi gongsuo*). On the Shanghai
local self-government movement, see Elvin, "Gentry Democracy in Chinese Shanghai,"
41–61; Tang Zhengchang, *Shanghai shi,* 427–31; *Shanghai shi zizhi zhi* (Shanghai municipality self-government gazetteer) (Shanghai, 1915). See also Li Pingshu, *Li Pingshu qishi
zixu* (Li Pingshu's autobiography at 70) (Shanghai, 1923; reprint, 1989), 52–53.

60. Yao Wennan, director of the largest Shanghai charitable hall, and leaders of local
educational projects and various Shanghai *gongsuo* worked with Li on this project. For
information on other City Council members, see Elvin, "Gentry Democracy in Shanghai,"
6; Elvin, "Gentry Democracy in Chinese Shanghai," 43–45; Tang Zhengchang, *Shanghai
shi,* 427–30. Though in a minority position, several important sojourners were included
in the Council, notably Zhu Baosan and Zeng Shaoqing, both of whom had achieved
prominence (and Li Pingshu's admiration) through anti–U.S. boycott activism.

61. For biographical accounts of Li, see Chen Zhengshu's preface to *Li Pingshu qishi
zixu,* 3–6; Yang Hao and Ye Lan, eds., *Jiu Shanghai fengyun renwu* (Leading figures of old
Shanghai) (Shanghai, 1989), 73–80. Li's ancestral home was Suzhou; in the eighteenth
century the Li family moved within Jiangsu to the Shanghai area, where they settled in
Gaoqiao (then in Baoshan county; now part of Chuansha county), in Pudong. Pudong,
literally "east of the Huangpu," is not an administrative unit but an indeterminate area

Although the Shanghai City Council is Li's most celebrated local self-government innovation in this period, it was not his only local self-government venture, nor were his self-government projects all based on western models. Also in 1905, the year he inaugurated the Shanghai City Council, Li established a Pudong native-place association, the Pudong Tongren Hui (Pudong Fellows Association, or PFA). According to Huang Yanpei, another member and an important reformist Jiangsu gentry leader, the PFA was formed out of nationalist and anti-imperialist as well as local motivations, motivations very similar to those behind the formation of the City Council. Moreover, the PFA was not concerned simply with Pudong: "At the time, we focused on resisting imperialist power. To prevent foreign merchants from building roads on [and appropriating] Pudong land; to discuss the planning of traffic and the survey of the Shanghai-Nanjing railroad; to concentrate public opinion we created the *Pudong Journal*."[62]

It is possible that Li and the others who formed the Pudong native-place association were motivated by the example of sojourner associations in the foreign settlements. Li witnessed the 1905 boycott movement and was deeply impressed by the power of merchant organization.[63] He had also witnessed the efficacity of the Ningbo and Guangdong native-place associations in mobilizing popular struggles for Chinese rights against the foreign-settlement authorities. Unfortunately, Li did not comment on his motivations in founding the PFA, of which he remained a director until at least 1911.[64] Nonetheless, the fact that a native-place association was founded at the same time and by the same activist who directed the formation of the first Chinese municipal government in Shanghai is striking. Because the PFA was created in a context in which no native-place association had previously existed, it must be seen not as a traditional defensive posture but as the innovative response of locals to the modern challenge of imperialism. Both the PFA

(including portions of Shanghai and Baoshan counties) defined by its location across the river from the commercial areas of Shanghai.

62. Gu Bingquan and Zhang Yingen, "Pudong tongxianghui ji qi dui Pudong de xianqi kaifa" (The Pudong Tongxianghui and its early development of Pudong), *Chuansha wenshi ziliao* (Materials on Chuansha culture and history), 2 (1990), 73–74; Huang Yanpei, "Pudong lü Hu Tongxianghui xuanyan" (Declaration of the Pudong Sojourner's Association in Shanghai), 1931 (courtesy of Gu Bingquan, Chuansha Gazetteer Office), 4. It was not uncommon for the Pudong Fellows Association to hold meetings across the river, in the south city of Shanghai (SB, March 30, 1911).

63. Yang Hao and Ye Lan, *Jiu Shanghai fengyun renwu*, 78.

64. SB, March 30, 1911.

and the City Council asserted local interests in a nationalist, antiforeign context. Just as Li's sanitation projects combined both Chinese and western medicine, Li appears to have simultaneously engaged in two alternative modes of organization for social and political reform, one based on a western model and one on a Chinese model, both potentially efficacious institutional forms according to his observations and experience. Both institutions accorded with Li's belief in the importance of local self-government for constructing the nation. Li used the metaphor of the body to describe the relation of the locality to the nation through the principle of local self-government: "[The locality] is the beginning point of local self-government, and when you have the point, you can lengthen it into a strand, and when you have a strand you can square it and round it into a surface, and then you can heighten and deepen the surface, creating a body."[65]

Li's activities and writings make clear that commitment to his native place was very much a part of his developing municipal consciousness. Although the City Council was not exclusively the project of Jiangsu locals, insofar as they predominated on the council it must be understood to have been primarily a locals' project. The rhetoric of local self-government also favored locals over sojourners. Because sojourners did not abandon their native-place identity, the local self-government movement was more accessible to sojourners through the home localities with which they were identified. Although Mark Elvin was certainly right to celebrate the many innovative aspects of the City Council, it is equally important to emphasize its linkages to local habits and ties. For all of its westernness the City Council should be viewed in its Chinese context, as a kind of cousin organization, in harmony with (if not the same as) the Pudong association, another type of local association created by Shanghai's local elite to prevent outsiders from encroaching on their turf. The developing municipal consciousness it expressed needs to be understood through this local emphasis. The dominance of locals on the city council was unrepresentative, given the dominance of sojourners in the general Shanghai population (one has the impression of a few powerful sojourners being asked in to provide the council with extra "clout," but in limited numbers to ensure Jiangsu dominance). In this context the municipal structure appears more like the adoption of a western form for nationalist defensive purposes than like the culmination of a new cosmopolitan urban consciousness which embraced all

65. Cited in Yang Hao and Ye Lan, *Jiu Shanghai fengyun renwu*, 77.

Chinese urban residents (or even all members of the urban elite) as citizens.

The creation of a Shanghai municipal structure nonetheless had important implications for urban consciousness and organization. It provided an institutional basis for organizing Chinese outside the settlement areas and for linking them to merchant organizations in the
Settlement. Shortly after the establishment of a Chinese militia in the
International Settlement, merchants in the Chinese areas of the city followed suit and formed exercise associations. Five physical-exercise associations were established by commercial training organizations by the end
of 1905.[66] The new City Council provided an institutional framework for
the coordination of these associations into a citywide force. In 1907, when
Daotai Rui Cheng banned opium traffic in Shanghai and ordered opium
shops in the Chinese city closed, he feared that the gang-connected opium
sellers would resist. Lacking sufficient forces of his own, he asked Li
Pingshu and Zeng Shaoqing (also a City Council member) to use the drill
associations to keep order. The five groups coalesced into an overarching
militia (*Shangtuan gonghui*) for this purpose.[67]

The merchant militia's ability to preserve peace during the opium
crisis increased its power. In the next year local authorities called on the
militia to maintain order through regular patrols. Daotai Cai Naihuang,
who took office in 1908, provided the militia with firearms and ammuni-
tion.[68] By the eve of the revolution there were approximately twenty
such militia in Shanghai, based on trade and native-place groups. As
Yang Liqiang and Shen Weibin observe, "in this manner, citizens' associations took on governmental functions and became militarized."[69]

66. Pan Mingxin, "Shanghai wanguo," 109; Shen Weibin and Yang Liqiang, "Shanghai shangtuan yu xinhai geming" (Shanghai merchant militia and the Revolution of 1911),
Lishi yanjiu (History research) 3 (1983), 67.

67. Li Zongwu, "Shanghai Daotai he shangtuan guanxi" (The connections between
the Shanghai Daotai and the merchant militia), in *Xinhai geming huiyilu* (Compilation of
memoirs of the 1911 Revolution), ed. Wenshi ziliao weiyuanhui, vol. 7 (Beijing, 1981),
526–30. See also Shen Weibin and Yang Liqiang, "Shanghai shangtuan yu xinhai geming," 68.

68. "Shanghai shangtuan xiaoshi" (Short history of the Shanghai merchant militia),
in Chai Degeng, ed., *Xinhai geming* (The Revolution of 1911) (Shanghai, 1957; reprint,
1981), vol. 7, 86–89.

69. Shen Weibin and Yang Liqiang, "Shanghai shangtuan yu xinhai geming," 67–68;
Guo Yuming, "Xinhai geming qijian de Shanghai qunzhong yundong" (Mass movements
in the Shanghai 1911 Revolution), in *Jinian xinhai geming qishi zhounian xueshu taolunhui
lunwenji* (Collected papers from the conference to commemorate the 70th anniversary of
the 1911 Revolution), ed. Zhonghua shuju (Beijing, 1982), vol. 2, 943–44.

Although initially these militia were not disloyal to the Qing and indeed reinforced government authority in the city, their formation nonetheless challenged it. By physically training urban residents in militia formations without government leadership, the merchant-gentry militia leaders (now increasingly coordinated through municipal governing structures) positioned themselves to supplant the state. In 1910–11, as conflicts over railway loan concessions led merchants previously aligned with a more moderate constitutionalist approach to a rapprochement with revolutionaries, the militia and the new City Council were poised to do precisely that.

After a wave of rice riots and tax resistance shook the Yangzi delta in 1910, in February 1911 a number of Shanghai merchants approached local self-government associations and suggested forming a Citizens' Army. On March 22, Qing officials approved, and in April 1911 a National Federation of Merchant Militia was established by local gentry-merchants, with Li Pingshu as president and Shen Manyun (a wealthy banker from Wuxi, Jiangsu) and Ye Huijun (of Pudong) as vice-presidents. Yu Xiaqing, Siming Gongsuo director and president of the Chinese Company of Settlement Volunteers, was made honorary vice-president. The militia totaled 2,490 men.[70]

On May 7 the National Federation of Merchant Militia organized a meeting of different groups in the city, bringing together sojourners and locals. The Ningbo notable Shen Dunhe was selected to chair this meeting, at which he pronounced the assembly's goals. These included the promotion of martial spirit, education for national citizenship, military training through people's militia, and the creation of "a central organ uniting each sojourning group in Shanghai."[71]

Concurrent with these developments which brought together different groups into overarching citywide frameworks, a parallel process of organizational activity deepened and reinforced native-place ties and explicitly connected native-place organization to the strengthening of the nation by stressing the importance of organizational units (*tuanti*) in building a patriotic and united China. Much of this patriotic organizational activity took place in the context of new and reformulated native-place associations, particularly among Zhejiang sojourners. On

70. Ding Richu, "Xinhai geming qian de Shanghai zibenjia jieji" (Shanghai capitalists prior to the Revolution of 1911). In *Jinian xinhai geming qishi zhounian xueshu taolunhui lunwenji*, ed. Zhonghua shuju, vol. 1, 309–10; Shen Weibin and Yang Liqiang, "Shanghai shangtuan yu xinhai geming," 68–69.
71. Ding, "Xinhai geming qian de Shanghai zibenjia jieji," 315.

March 19, 1911, a large general meeting to inaugurate a reformulated Ningbo native-place association took place at the Siming Gongsuo, with more than two thousand Ningbo sojourners attending. Shen Dunhe, who in two months would work to unite different sojourning groups into a "central organ," also chaired this meeting, which was dedicated to the special destiny of the Ningbo people, "whose footprints cover the world, and who in the future can establish branch associations everywhere, with the center in Shanghai." In his speech, Shen recalled the historic achievements of Ningbo sojourners, referring to the Ningbo people's past protection of the Siming Gongsuo and crediting the results to Ningbo organizational strength. His speech combines the recounting of Ningbo glory and destiny with a popularized version of Liang Qichao's diagnosis of China's organizational weakness: "But today, *organizations* are frequently *dispersed like yellow sand*. . . . Our Chinese people are *insulted by foreigners* because our *organizations are not solid*. . . . [Now] our Ningbo people have this great organization and this will facilitate the development of *patriotic thinking*. . . . Our association, with our protect-the-Siming Gongsuo-hearts, will go and protect the nation."[72] Later in 1911, in another act which simultaneously reinforced native-place organization and nationalist revolutionary mobilization, Yu Xiaqing (who had been active in both the railway-loan movement and the constitutionalist movement) also specially organized a Ningbo Merchants' General Assembly (*Ningshang zonghui*), located in the International Settlement. After Yu made contacts with the Revolutionary Alliance in the months prior to the Shanghai episode of the revolution, this Ningbo Merchants' Assembly provided a location for secret meetings of the Revolutionary Alliance. Given later struggles between Yu and Li Pingshu over control of Zhabei in the postrevolutionary order, it is difficult not to imagine that such activities on the eve of the revolution involved a certain positioning for power in advance.[73]

During this period Guangdong sojourner groups in Shanghai were sympathetic to Sun Yat-sen and revolutionary organization in Guangdong and appear in many respects to have focused more closely on Guangdong events and networks than on municipally focused organiz-

72. SB, March 20, 1911. Italicized words appear in large-size characters in the original. Regarding Liang Qichao's emphasis on social organization, see Chapter 5, Note 47.
73. Ding, "Xinhai geming qian de Shanghai zibenjia jieji," 317; Mark Elvin, "The Revolution of 1911 in Shanghai," *Papers on Far Eastern History* (Canberra) 29 (March 1984):157.

ing in Shanghai, which was Zhejiang and Jiangsu dominated. Indeed, there were fewer institutional links connecting them to new Shanghai municipal structures. Although Guangdong sojourners enjoyed a limited presence in the Chamber of Commerce and in the merchant militia, they did not have leadership roles and they were not a part of the City Council. Meeting records of the Guang-Zhao Gongsuo from 1906 show the Guangdong merchants in Shanghai in very close touch with the Guangzhou Chamber of Commerce, coordinating actions to be taken in regard to the Hong Kong–Guangzhou railway. In late September 1911, more than a thousand Guangdong residents in Shanghai met to hear news from two delegates of the Southern Railway Protection Association who were en route from Guangzhou to the capital. Speeches at the meeting made by Wu Tingfang and others emphasized the unity of feeling between sojourners and the people of Guangdong province. The Guangdong sojourner assembly resolved to assist their fellow-provincials "in any fight necessary to compel the government to comply with [their] wishes."[74]

Revolutionary Government and the Post-Revolutionary Order. Immediately after the Wuchang revolt on October 10, Li Pingshu met secretly with Shen Enfu and other Jiangsu leaders on the City Council, and they decided to collaborate with Chen Qimei, the regional leader of the Revolutionary Alliance.[75] Disillusioned by the Manchu response to the parliamentary movement, the Jiangsu banker and City Council member Shen Manyun (who would fund covert revolutionary organizing in this period) had already cast his lot with the revolutionaries.[76] After this, Li reportedly met daily with Chen at the offices of the

---

74. GZGYB, December 1906; NCH, September 30, 1911.

75. Mark Elvin ("Revolution of 1911") provides a valuable account of the City Council and merchant militia in the Shanghai revolutionary process. See also Elvin, "Gentry Democracy in Shanghai," 212–76. On the role of the Shanghai bourgeoisie, see Marie-Claire Bergère, *Golden Age,* 189–200; Ding Richu, "Xinhai geming qian Shanghai zibenjia de zhengzhi huodong" (The political activities of Shanghai capitalists before the Revolution of 1911), *Jindaishi yanjiu* (Modern history research) 2 (1982):219–41; Ding Richu, "Xinhai geming qian de Shanghai zibenjia jieji," 281–321. Rankin (*Early Chinese Revolutionaries,* 203–14) provides a useful overview of the Shanghai revolution. My sketch of revolutionary mobilization in this section is intended simply to supplement these accounts by outlining the role of native-place networks in the revolutionary process.

76. In 1910 Shen had traveled to the capital with other representatives of the Society to Prepare for the Establishment of a Constitution to present a petition for the rapid convocation of parliament. The petition was rejected by the imperial authorities. See Elvin, "Revolution of 1911," 145.

revolutionary newspaper *Minlibao* (funded by Shen). According to Feng Shaoshan, commander of the Paper Trade Militia, under the authority of the Militia Federation, very shortly thereafter, the united command proclaimed an uprising.[77] Li quickly took steps to render the city neutral to Chen Qimei's forces. Chen then proceeded to the Jiangnan Arsenal, which, after some mishaps and with the assistance of Li's militia, was occupied by the morning of November 3, the day Shanghai was declared republican. Within a few days Chen had organized a temporary military government which included a number of important figures in the City Council: Li Pingshu became Minister of Civil Affairs; Shen Manyun, Minister of Finance; Wang Yiting, Minister of Communications. The wealthy Ningbo capitalists Zhu Baosan and Yu Xiaqing, the Shanghai grain wholesaler Gu Xinyi and the Jiangsu piece-goods merchant You Binghan also received posts, though secondary ones.[78]

Native-place associations in a variety of ways contributed to the process of revolutionary mobilization and early "republican" government. Their frequent meetings provided arenas for the dissemination of political ideas. In addition, they printed circulars and journals and made use of the Shanghai press, publishing notices and texts of telegrams to revolutionary leaders. They collected funds for the revolutionary army and government and recruited soldiers for revolutionary armies in their home provinces.

Immediately after Chen took power in Shanghai, Shanghai youths, women and various sojourning groups formed militia. Most of the student military corps were from the two provinces of Zhejiang and Jiangsu. Other sojourners formed "northern expedition" brigades according to their native place, among these the Jiangxi Northern Expeditionary Army, the Henan Northern Expeditionary Army Branch Headquarters and the Hunan Sojourners' Northern Expedition Army. Although these names declared the participants' native-place identity, they also proclaimed their intent to contribute to the new government's project of national construction. Some, like the Sichuan Han Army, asserted their native-place and Han ethnic identity at once. This assertion of broad Han ethnic belonging did not prevent some of these militia from planning for the independence of their provinces, as was the case for the

77. Li Zongwu, "Shanghai Daotai he shangtuan guanxi," 526–30.

78. Elvin, "Gentry Democracy in Shanghai," 230–46; Bergère, *Golden Age,* 200; Marie-Claire Bergère, "The Chinese Bourgeoisie, 1911–37," in Fairbank, *Cambridge History of China,* vol. 12, pt. 1, 733. Second in command after Chen was his fellow Zhejiang provincial (and New Army officer), Huang Fu.

Sichuan Han Army, which called on Sichuanese to "unite [our collective] strength to establish an independent Sichuan."[79]

In November and December 1911 different native-place communities held meetings at their *huiguan* to gather recruits for revolutionary armies, both to serve in their home provinces and to serve the Shanghai military government. The *Shibao* observed that since the victory of the republican army in Shanghai, groups of people from each native place had volunteered to serve the revolution.[80] Notices calling for recruits published in the revolutionary newspaper, *Minlibao,* appealed to both native-place and nationalist sentiment, stressing the urgency of both national and local situations and invoking both the bravery of the revolutionaries and the special spirit or experience of the locality.[81] Such notices concretized the abstract goals of nationalism with reference to local and familiar situations.

Native-place associations also formed collection networks, raising funds for military expenses both in their native provinces and in Shanghai. A director of the Siming Gongsuo, Fang Jiaobo, later described the situation in his memoirs: "At the time in Shanghai commercial circles the Ningbo and Guangdong sojourners had the biggest groups. Their organizations were the [Siming Gongsuo] and the Guang-Zhao Gongsuo. Their members were extremely numerous and their leaders were the leaders of society. . . . [Their leaders] used utmost strength to help the revolutionary army, and called on the other sojourning commercial groups in Shanghai to help support the revolution."[82]

79. XGZS, 601–607; Wu Qiandui, "Shanghai Guangfu he Hujun dudu fu (The revolution in Shanghai and the Shanghai military government), in *Jinian xinhai geming qishi zhounian xueshu taolunhui lunwenji,* ed. Zhonghua shuju, vol. 1, 834–35; Guo Yuming, "Xinhai geming qijian," 944.

80. XGZS, 677. Among these were more than one hundred Guangdong workers who registered with the Military Government in order to enter the Dare-to-Die Corps.

81. An appeal to sojourning Sichuanese to meet to organize a righteous army (*yijun*) to aid their native place, for example, linked the national anti-Manchu struggle to the recent Sichuan railway struggle (1909–10) (XGZS, notices from *Minlibao,* November 28 and December 3, 9 and 12, 1911, 601–2, 605, 607). Such recruitment took place not only among sojourners in Shanghai but among sojourning communities in other cities as well. The advertisement of the Sichuan Army Organizational Alliance noted that Sichuanese in Yunnan, Hunan, Hubei and Japan, as well as Shanghai, were organizing armies or providing financial assistance for the army. *Huiguan* recruiting soldiers to serve in their native places arranged for transportation and coordinated the reception and accommodation of recruits with provincial authorities.

82. Wenshi ziliao yanjiu weiyuanhui (Cultural and historical materials committee), ed., *Xinhai geming huiyilu,* vol. 7, 560–61. Fang's collection team raised five hundred thousand yuan. Zhu Baosan raised two hundred thousand yuan.

Several thousand sojourning Guangdong provincials met at the Guang-Zhao Gongsuo on December 5, 1911. The assembly, led by the director Wen Zongyao, established a systematic collection program to assist (and presumably also to achieve influence in) the new military government. Wen began the meeting by stressing the Guangdong sojourners' Han ethnicity:

At this time the national situation is extremely urgent and we must rely on blood and iron. "Blood" refers to our great Han new republican citizens' blood. "Iron" refers to the firearms our great Han new republican citizens use to protect themselves. When people have blood but no iron, bleeding is useless. Moreover, it is not just our blood we shed, but the blood of our descendants. Now those citizens who are brave should mount horses and fight. Those who are wealthy should contribute to purchase the most modern weapons to prepare for military victory. In this manner it is possible not just to protect your own blood, but the blood of generations of descendants.[83]

Placing native-place networks in the service of the nation, Wen calculated that with one hundred seventy to one hundred eighty thousand people in the Shanghai Guangdong community, if everyone contributed it would be easy to raise substantial sums. All Guangdong businesses were to set aside a sum equal to 10 percent of the total paid in monthly salaries. Employees and shop clerks were to contribute one-tenth of their salaries. Collections were to continue until military affairs were settled.[84]

Other sojourning networks also invested eagerly in the new government. After a general collection, the Quan-Zhang Huiguan contributed rental income from its Shanghai properties and solicited contributions from overseas Fujianese communities in Southeast Asia. The Dianchuntang organized collections from the Fujian foreign and Guangdong goods, northern goods and seafood trades. Shandong merchant leaders personally solicited each Shandong shop for contributions, hyperbolically finding "none [who were] unenthusiastic."[85] The Shanghai Shandong community also initiated collections from fellow-provincials in Osaka, Hong Kong, Vladivostok, Qingdao and other ports.[86]

---

83. Chai Degeng, *Xinhai geming*, vol. 7, 555.

84. SB, December 5, 1911, reprinted in XGZS, 632.

85. A number of individuals visited indeed contributed more than one thousand yuan. The size of these contributions suggests that *huiguan* and *gongsuo* were important, if not exclusive, fundraisers. Large funds were similarly raised for Sun Yat-sen after the declaration of a government at Nanjing in January 1912.

86. SB, December 7, 1911; *Minlibao*, December 9 and 11, 1911, reprinted in XGZS, 634–35. Articles appeared in these papers describing collections undertaken by the Shaoxing wine trade and by the Shandong and Henan silk trade, as well as by other trade

Revolutionary leaders appealed directly to their own *tongxiang*, who responded at least initially with enthusiasm, seizing the opportunity to increase their influence while furthering the revolutionary cause. On the eve of his inauguration as president of the new republic, Sun Yat-sen attended a lengthy feast hosted by all of the Guangdong sojourning groups in Shanghai, while Guangdong groups in other provinces showered him with contributions and congratulatory telegrams. The Shanghai Guang-Zhao Gongsuo pledged four hundred thousand taels to the National Assembly, trusting at the same time that its favored candidate, Wu Tingfang, would be appointed Minister of Foreign Affairs.[87]

With similar spirit Zhejiang sojourners (especially Huzhou merchants) rallied to help Chen Qimei's Shanghai military government, while Chen shamelessly filled government posts with his Huzhou *tongxiang*. As support for his regime waned, Chen appealed to his fellow-countrymen at the Huzhou Silk Cocoon Gongsuo (*Jianye gongsuo*). When his own *tongxiang* grew reluctant, Chen imprisoned Huzhou merchants in the *gongsuo* until he had extracted substantial "voluntary" contributions.[88]

---

associations (see XGZS, 626–39). Associations of sojourning workers organized similar collections. Ningbo and Shaoxing construction workers met at the Hu Ning-Shao Shuimu Gongye Gongsuo to express their "warm-blooded" enthusiasm for the goals of the revolution and to raise money for military needs (*Minlibao*, November 24, 1911, reprinted in XGZS, 630).

87. Marie-Claire Bergère, "The Role of the Bourgeoisie," in *China in Revolution,* ed. Mary C. Wright (New Haven, Conn., 1968), 281; SB, January 1, 1912; SB, January 2, 1912; SB, January 5, 1912; SB, January 30, 1912. The only cabinet members who were not Jiangsu or Zhejiang provincials associated with the "gentry democracy" experiment in Chinese Shanghai described by Mark Elvin were Wu Tingfang and the Guang-Zhao Gongsuo leader (and revolutionary activist) Wen Zongyao. A telegram published in *Shenbao* on January 5, 1912, suggests that the Guangdong community did not feel adequately compensated for its contributions. In their message, Wu Tingfang and Wen Zongyao addressed their fellow-provincials, saying that they had just received news that the Shanghai Guangdong community was threatening to suspend its loan of four hundred thousand taels to Sun's government in protest of the minor position given Wen. Wu and Wen declared their own satisfaction with the new cabinet and chided their *tongxiang* to put aside private concerns in the interest of the public welfare. Otherwise, they warned, the new government would disintegrate from internal conflict and would become the laughing stock of foreigners. See SB, January 5, 1912.

88. Elvin, "Gentry Democracy in Shanghai," 252. For meetings of Huzhou sojourners see SB, January 7, 1912; *Shibao*, May 4, 1912, reprinted in XGZS, 970. The Zhejiang Lu Hü Tongxianghui and the Ningbo Tongxianghui supported Siming Gongsuo leaders Yu Xiaqing, Zhu Baosan and Zhou Jinzhen in cooperative efforts with Shanghai City Council members Li Pingshu, Shen Manyun and Wang Yiting (SB, January 11, 1912). The memoir of a Huzhou student who worked in the Shanghai Military Headquarters discusses collec-

Even as they invested in the new Shanghai and national governments, Shanghai native-place associations remained deeply involved with their home provinces, providing political and economic support and attempting to restore peace when undisciplined troops or friction between rival factions threw localities into disorder. In early 1912 the Shanghai Ningbo Sojourners' Association convened specially to try to preserve order in Ningbo. The fact that Ningbo Chamber of Commerce and Ningbo prefectural self-government association representatives came to Shanghai for the meetings (and under the signature of Yu Xiaqing communicated with the Zhejiang military governor) demonstrates the centrality of the Shanghai Ningbo community in managing Ningbo affairs.[89]

Not long after the establishment of the Nanjing Government, the bankers and wealthy merchants who had supported the revolution began to find the new order — which failed to establish a broad financial base and was instead supported (locally) by Chen Qimei's extortion — increasingly burdensome. As Chen's regime wore on, concern for protecting their fellow-provincials led native-place associations to deploy the rhetoric of republicanism to criticize the unscrupulous tactics of the unprincipled heirs of the revolution, just as they had criticized the Qing. Native-place associations attempted to curb the predations of the Shanghai military government by investigating specific incidents (commonly the mistreatment of wealthy fellow-provincials) and publicizing their findings in the press.[90]

tion tactics in the Huzhou Huiguan (Wenshi ziliao weiyuanhui, *Xinhai geming huiyilu*, vol. 7, 567–68).

89. SB, February 2, 1912; SB, March 24, 1912; SB, March 25, 1912. Throughout the early Revolutionary period, Chaozhou prefecture suffered disorder from military occupations. The Hong Kong Chaozhou sojourners' association sent urgent telegrams to both the Shanghai Chaozhou Huiguan and the Guang-Zhao Gongsuo describing plunder and carnage in Chaozhou and requesting help. After verifying the situation, the Shanghai associations contacted the Governor of Guangdong to protest, holding him responsible and pressuring him to rectify the situation. See SB, January 10, 1912; SB, February 9, 1912; SB, February 21, 1912; SB, March 18, 1912; SB, March 20, 1912; SB, March 21, 1912; SB, March 29, 1912. For similar actions on the part of Gansu sojourners in Shanghai, see SB, February 2, 1912. As parts of Zhejiang experienced famine in March, the Huzhou Sojourners' Association in Shanghai organized rice relief and established rice-gruel kitchens in Huzhou. See SB, March 29, 1912.

90. SB, January 11, 1912; SB, January 28, 1912; SB, March 3, 1912; SB, March 14, 1912. *Huiguan* also used the pageantry of funeral ceremonies for martyrs to make political points which could not be stated explicitly. The Shaoxing Huiguan, for example, held a dramatic funeral service for Tao Chengzhang and other "revolutionary martyrs" in January 1912, attended by approximately four thousand Shaoxing sojourners. The four flower-

When, for example, the head of Chen Qimei's secret police, Ying Guixin (a former associate of the notorious gang chieftain Van Kah-der) kidnapped and arrested Song Hanzhang, manager of the Bank of China, the Shaoxing Sojourners' Association published a formal protest addressed to Chen Qimei, accusing him of betraying the ideals of republican government and of becoming a dictator. The association also volunteered its services as Song's guarantor, citing its duty to him in recognition of his great love of his native place.[91] In March 1912 Guangdong sojourners followed the lead of their two fellow-provincials in the revolutionary government, Wu Tingfang and Wen Zongyao, and protested the actions of Chen and his associates. In telegrams to President Sun in Nanjing and Vice-President Li in Wuchang they detailed policies of extortion and asked for a restoration of law and human feeling.[92]

In his study of the revolution of 1911 in Shanghai, Elvin concludes with surprise that the fragile coalition between the revolutionaries and Chinese power networks in the city that produced the revolution in Shanghai was ever achieved. Native-place ties — which could link unlikely partners because they were not dependent on common occupation, class or outlook — were clearly a key element in the orchestration of the alliance. Linkages between Shanghai elites and the revolutionaries (indeed, the paths of revolutionary consciousness) were lubricated by native-place ties. Zhejiang ties facilitated the initial links between Chen Qimei and wealthy Shanghai capitalists. In 1909, when Chen Qimei went to Shanghai to direct revolutionary activities in the Jiangsu-Zhejiang region for the Revolutionary Alliance, he prepared the ground through native-place networks. Chen's Huzhou ties brought him support from the Huzhou capitalist Yang Xinzhi and also fellow-provincials from Ningbo. Yang had founded a school for Huzhou students in Shanghai. Chen worked briefly at the school, and through this connection also met other fellow-provincial entrepreneurs and bankers, including Wang Yi-

---

festooned coffins traveled in procession through the foreign concessions before heading to the train station for shipment to Zhejiang for burial. Tao had been vice-chair of the Guangfu Hui and became governor of Zhejiang after the Zhejiang revolution. Because Zhejiang selected him to continue as Governor, Chen Qimei perceived him as a threat and reputedly had Chiang Kai-shek kill him. See SB, January 10, 1912; SB, January 23, 1912; *Minlibao*, January 22, 1912, reprinted in XGZS, 958–59.

91. *Minlibao*, March 29, 1912, reprinted in XGZS, 431. See also Elvin, "Gentry Democracy in Shanghai," 250. Van Kah-der is a romanization of the Shanghai dialect pronunciation of Fan Gaotou.

92. SB, March 5, 1912.

ting, Li Houyu (who had repeatedly held high office in the General Chamber of Commerce), Li Weizhuang and Li Zhengwu.[93]

Linkages between the Zhejiang clique which controlled the Chamber of Commerce and the Jiangsu-dominated City Council were reinforced by the new institutional structures they inhabited (which, though they could be controlled by particular *bang*, could not legitimately — because of their new municipal and nationalist basis — be entirely exclusive) and which brought them together. Jiangsu and Zhejiang elites had also come together in the constitutionalist movement and in the course of their struggles to control the Jiangsu–Zhejiang railway.[94]

In 1906, when the Qing government promulgated "constitutional preparation," leading Zhejiang and Jiangsu capitalists (including Zhou Jinzhen, Wang Yiting, Li Pingshu and Shen Manyun) responded eagerly, and in the same year they set up a constitutional preparation society. Many of the same leading Zhejiang and Jiangsu capitalists in Shanghai had invested in the Suzhou–Hangzhou–Ningbo Railway. Li Pingshu, Gu Xinyi and Wang Yiting were all directors of the Jiangsu Railway, and the wealthy Zhejiang businessmen Zhou Jinzhen, Li Houyu, Yan Xinhou and Yu Xiaqing were heavily invested in the Zhejiang railroad company. As the Qing government began to negotiate for foreign loans, these merchants mobilized to retain control over the railroads. On November 10, 1907, a recently formed Zhejiang native-place association (*Zhejiang lü Hu tongxianghui*), led by Zhou Jinzhen (also a director of the Siming Gongsuo and the president of the Chamber of Commerce), met to organize opposition to the loans. On November 19 Jiangsu and Zhejiang merchants and gentry met to discuss the railway issue. Speakers on both occasions made clear their alienation from the Manchu government. They also reaffirmed native-place identity while they united Jiangsu and Zhejiang people in a common anti-Manchu, nationalist struggle: "If the government insists [on foreign loans], then the Jiangsu and Zhejiang people should adopt the policy of refusing to pay taxes." As Ding Richu has noted, speakers tied the rail-

93. Ding, "Xinhai geming qian de Shanghai zibenjia jieji," 312; Bergère, *Golden Age,* 195. Revolutionaries also used native-place ties to sway the loyalty of the Qing defense forces, which were organized in provincial brigades. See Rankin, *Early Chinese Revolutionaries,* 207.

94. For a summary of these railway struggles, see Rankin, *Elite Activism,* 251–81; E. T. Z. Sun, *Chinese Railways and British Interests, 1898–1911* (New York, 1954); *Jiang-Zhe tielu fengchao* (Railway agitation in Jiangsu and Zhejiang) (Taipei, 1968; reprint of 1907 ed.).

way-rights-recovery movement to the constitutionalist movement: "If we can unite, it is not just to give hope to the railroad, but [uniting] is also helpful to the future establishment of a constitution. . . . This time the people of two provinces unite resolutely. Although we unite today for the railroad matter, this is [just] a beginning."[95]

Native-place ties could link disparate individuals and provide organizational resources which reached deeper into society than the newer, more superficial municipal institutions. At the same time, precisely because they stressed native-place identity, the alliance produced was weak, and its quick disintegration and failure to produce a working government are not surprising. Despite the broad nationalist rhetoric of the new Chinese republicans, the uprisings of 1911 were notable in their failure to successfully construct a truly national order.

Instead, in a story that is well known, the ideals of revolution quickly degenerated into conflicts among local interests and battles over provincial turf. Native-place ties and organization, which had mobilized Shanghai residents for revolution and had spread nationalist and revolutionary propaganda, also provided the sentiments and associational networks of revolutionary disintegration. After the Wuchang uprising Li Yuanhong sent Li Xiehe (a Hunanese) to Shanghai as General Commander. The presence of Li and his Hunanese associates provoked the jealousy and irritation of Chen Qimei. There was also a split, as Elvin has noted, between those who felt allegiance primarily to the Guangdong-based Sun Yat-sen and those who were enmeshed in networks of loyalty to Chen Qimei. The Guangdong sojourner Wen Zongyao, for instance, appointed by Sun to govern foreign affairs in Shanghai, came into conflict with Chen's foreign affairs commissar, Xu Zhejiang.[96] Native-place differences exacerbated tensions among the different revolutionary branches which had cooperated in the uprising. There was even an intra-Zhejiang split between the northern Zhejiang supporters of Chen Qimei and Tao Chengzhang's Restoration Society, which they accused of favoring Shaoxing people over those of Huzhou, Ningbo and Hangzhou.[97]

This chapter has focused on the complex, developing relationship (and overlapping identity) of native-place and national interests and the ways

---

95. Both quotations are in Ding, "Xinhai geming qian de Shanghai zibenjia jieji," 303.
96. Elvin, "Revolution of 1911," 148–58.
97. Rankin, *Early Chinese Revolutionaries*, 211.

in which this relationship facilitated and limited developing Chinese nationalist mobilization. At the same time, the importance of native-place ties in nationalist mobilization and their reformulation in the new municipal institutions of the early twentieth century (the Chamber of Commerce and the City Council) and in the revolution of 1911 suggest the ambivalence of sojourners in regard to constructing Shanghai identities for themselves. Although we see in this period the important emergence of social organizations based on the concept of "Shanghai," examination of their practice reveals the limits of Shanghai identity. Not only did the leading commercial and political figures in the city (if they were sojourners) belong to native-place associations, but even in the context of citywide organizations they identified themselves, as we have seen, as "sojourning merchants in Shanghai" rather than as "Shanghai merchants." Indeed, identification by native place was fundamental to participation in citywide movements and institutions. The membership list of the Chamber of Commerce, for example, though providing little information other than name, age, professional affiliation and address, carefully specifies the native place of each officer and member.[98]

98. In only one obvious case does a sojourner identify himself as a Shanghai native. This exception is telling. In the 1906 membership list, Chamber president Zeng Shaoqing identifies his native place as Shanghai county. Zeng was renounced as the activist Fujian *huiguan* leader during the 1905 anti–U.S. boycott mobilization. Although we cannot know the motives behind Zeng's listing in the Chamber publication, the fact that he is remembered as Fujianese in all other accounts I have encountered suggests that his exceptional tactical assertion of Shanghai identity had little effect on how he would be known.

CHAPTER SEVEN

"Modern Spirit," Institutional Change and the Effects of Warlord Government

Associations in the Early Republic

The early Republican period presents both striking continuities and important changes in the structure of native-place associations and in their social meanings. In the radically altered social and political context of warlordism and enfeebled central government after Yuan Shikai's death in 1916, the ability of native-place associations to exert effective pressure to shape local political contexts was more constrained. As mediating institutions between state and society, native-place associations lost some of their effectiveness at higher political levels soon after 1911, as it became apparent that the revolution had failed to create a viable, stable and legitimate order to replace the imperial order which had preceded it. Although native-place associations were extremely active in the new republic, they now faced a crumbling political system in which matters were decided more often by armed force than by mediation.

At the same time, native-place associations were radically reconceived and restructured. As the polity changed, so did the form of native-place associations. Native-place sentiment acquired a new Republican vocabulary, new institutions, and took on new social, economic and political projects. Although *huiguan* continued to function throughout the Republican period and retained symbolic centrality for their communities, a more broadly based and modern form of native-place association emerged and grew in popularity — the *tongxianghui*. The 1911 Revolution, if otherwise disappointing in its accomplishments, gave birth to new forms of social organization and expression which rejected older oligarchies, closed meetings, and unwritten codes of behavior. Although wealthy *tongxiang* elites continued to find ways to assert their authority at the pinnacle of a social hierarchy, the associations of this period, like the new Republic, would have at least the forms of republicanism and representative government—constitutions, elected bodies, public meetings and public records.

Native-place associations performed manifold social functions in this period both because effective government was so minimal and because of the continuing growth of Shanghai. Between 1910 and 1927 the population of Shanghai more than doubled, growing from approximately 1.2 million to more than 2.6 million inhabitants.[1] The stream of new immigrants, including peasants seeking factory employment and refugees from natural disasters or warlord-torn areas, meant that Shanghai continued to be a predominantly immigrant city and that native-place ties continued to be called upon in the service of settling and accommodating the problems of the newcomers (see the table of Shanghai population growth in the Appendix). Prominent capitalists of this period, men such as Liu Hongsheng (Dinghai, Zhejiang), Yu Xiaqing (Zhenhai, Zhejiang) and Zheng Bozhao (Zhongshan, Guangdong) had established themselves in Shanghai through aid from fellow-provincials.[2] Like other employers, they provided assistance to destitute newcomers through the associations they sponsored.[3]

1. Zou Yiren, *Jiu Shanghai renkou bianqian*, 90, 114–15. Jiangsu and Zhejiang sojourners were numerically predominant in this wave of immigration. The proportion of Guangdong sojourners declined considerably, though the position of wealthy Guangdong merchants permitted Guangdong sojourners to retain disproportionate, if nonetheless reduced, influence. See the Appendix for a table of population growth.

2. Ding Richu and Du Xuncheng, "Yu Xiaqing jianlun" (On the subject of Yu Xiaqing), *Lishi yanjiu* 3 (1981):145–66; Chen Laixin, *Yu Xiaqing ni tsuite*, 12–15; Cheng Renjie, "Yingmei yan gongsi maiban Zheng Bozhao," *Shanghai wenshi ziliao xuanji* 1 (Shanghai, 1978):130–35. Zheng recruited Guangdong labor for his Yong Tai He (Wing Tai Wo) tobacco company in Shanghai, Hankou, Jiaxing, Huzhou and Ningbo. Because Guangdong sojourners felt he was not generous, Zheng funded a Lingnan Middle School in Hongkou to improve his image. See also Bergère, *L'âge d'or*, 158. The textile and food-products factories of the Rong brothers of Wuxi were heavily staffed with their *tongxiang*. In "Three Roads into Shanghai's Market: Japanese, Western and Chinese Companies in the Match Trade, 1895–1937," in Wakeman and Yeh, *Shanghai Sojourners*, 57–75, Sherman Cochran stresses native-place ties in Liu Hongsheng's career. Liu obtained his first job through *tongxiang* connections, became a leader of his native-place association in the 1920s and helped to establish a middle school in Dinghai, which channeled its graduates into Liu's enterprises.

3. Wealthy sojourners were so eager to build patronage networks that swindlers supported themselves by writing to Shanghai businessmen, claiming to be impoverished fellow-provincials. Two such men, who claimed "invariably to be fellow-provincials of the

Such networks of support were facilitated by what Marie-Claire Bergère has called "the golden age of the Chinese bourgeoisie." World War I produced an economic upswing in China by both temporarily protecting developing Chinese industries from European competition and by creating greater world demand for primary products from China, a demand which intensified in the immediate postwar years because of the needs of European economic reconstruction. The expansion of modern business produced an increasingly wealthy and powerful urban elite which could support an expanded scope of native-place charity.[4]

Prominent Shanghai commercial and financial leaders in this period — for instance, the Ningbo capitalists Yu Xiaqing, Zhu Baosan and Liu Hongsheng; the Jiangsu Xi family; and Wang Xiaolai, from Shaoxing — were directors of major Shanghai native-place associations. As Bergère has shown in her study of the social structures of the new bourgeoisie, native-place networks were fundamental to the constitution of the bourgeoisie and the enterprises on which it was based. Regional solidarities both substituted for and transcended family ties, enabling the development of complex and efficient networks of loyalty and patronage.[5]

Although native-place ties within the city were a boon in a competitive economic climate, the pull of the native place on these wealthy sojourners proved to be a considerable drain. In the first two decades of the Republican era, beyond the wealthy protected Chinese houses of the Shanghai foreign settlements vast rural areas experienced fighting, social dislocation and the deterioration of systems of water control, welfare and order keeping. These were the cumulative effects of the breakdown of central government, the devolution of local government and the predations of local militarists. In this period, in a way which has not been sufficiently recognized, native-place organizations gave war-torn and devastated rural areas access to the wealth of Shanghai. Weakened local elites called on their *tongxiang* in Shanghai to resolve local problems. Native-place associations responded regularly and generously to these

---

person addressed and had described themselves in the various letters as hailing from nearly all the different provinces of China," are described in *The Municipal Gazette* (June 13, 1918, 193): "That their scheme was successful was proved by the fact that they had lived well entirely on its proceeds for six months before they came under the notice of the police."

4. Bergère, *Golden Age;* Joseph Fewsmith, *Party, State and Local Elites,* 46.

5. Bergère, *Golden Age,* 141–52. See also Chen Laixin, *Yu Xiaqing,* 12–15, 26–27. The Xi family, from Dongting Dongshan (Suzhou prefecture) were leaders of the Dongting Dongshan Tongxianghui (founded in 1912); Wang Xiaolai was director of the Shaoxing Tongxianghui.

appeals. Studies of early Republican China have frequently separated urban and rural spheres and studied each in isolation, neglecting their continuous interactions through sojourner networks. Poised between urban and rural China, native-place associations mediated between the two worlds.[6]

"Modern Spirit" and the Restructuring and Proliferation of Native-Place Organizations

Although *huiguan* remained active throughout the Republican period, preexisting native-place institutions did not merely persist and adapt. In the political and social ferment surrounding the 1911 Revolution, the disclosure of China's acquiescence to Japan's Twenty-One Demands in 1915 and the May Fourth Incident of 1919, native-place sentiment experienced both rebirth and "modernization," if such a term may be applied to an old cultural tradition. It is precisely this reformulation of an old cultural institution that makes the study of "traditionalistic" social forms important for understanding Chinese modernity.

In the early Republican period new types of native-place associations (*tongxianghui*), which rejected the elitist outlook of the older *huiguan,* appeared. Spurning the religious and oligarchic rituals of *huiguan,* the new associations noisily adopted rituals of democracy, publishing voting procedures, notices of meetings, correspondence and finances and vying with the Beijing government for the numbers of times they revised their constitutions.[7] Rejecting the traditional architecture with its central altar, stage and courtyard, the new native-place organizations chose for themselves secular high-rise Western-style buildings with lec-

---

6. See Goodman, "The Native Place and the City," chap. 5 for details on *huiguan* and *tongxianghui* activities in the Republican period.

7. The meeting notes, accounts and constitutions of these new associations were published in monthly and yearly reports, and often in the newspapers as well. See, for example, *Shaoxing qixian lü Hu tongxianghui ge gong zhangcheng* (Regulations of the Association of Sojourners from Seven Counties of Shaoxing in Shanghai) (Shanghai, 1920); *Shaoxing lü Hu tongxianghui tonggao* (Report of the Association of Shaoxing Sojourners in Shanghai) (Shanghai, editions of 1911–14); SB, March 17, 1911; SB, May 14, 1919. See also Ōtani Kōtarō, "Shanhai ni okeru dōkyō dantai oyobi dōgyō dantai" (Native-place and trade groups in Shanghai), *Shina kenkyu* (China research) 19 (1929):145–56; Negishi, *Chūgoku no girudo,* 199–200; Negishi, *Shanhai no girudo,* 42–43.

ture halls, product-display rooms, newspaper-reading rooms, recreation rooms and offices built over shopping arcades.

The founding constitution of the new Shaoxing association indicates the political models which informed the organizational change.[8] The Shaoxing Lü Hu Tongxianghui was established in 1911. Following the forms and rhetoric of republicanism, it organized itself with an "assembly" (*yishihui*) and a "speaker" (*yizhang*). If the new organization and terminology were more democratic than were *huiguan*, stipulating such things as "public elections" of officers, limited terms of two years and majority rule, it is important to suggest the limitations of what these features could mean in practice. *Tongxianghui* were certainly more inclusive organizations than *huiguan*: whereas *huiguan* meeting notes generally list from ten to sixty members present at meetings (and did not have a specified membership, because it was obvious to the merchant elite who should enter and who should not), published lists for *tongxianghui* range from several hundred to as many as ten thousand members. Nonetheless, not everyone could join. The constitution stipulated that the association was limited to adult male sojourners "of good character" from Shaoxing prefecture who were introduced by members of the association and approved by the association. Such conditions obviously omitted all women and most likely the unemployed and the poor.[9]

Although these self-consciously modern associations rejected "traditionalistic" aspects of older native-place associations, in particular their

8. The Shaoxing Tongxianghui held its founding meeting in the Yongxitang (Zhe-Shao Huiguan). Its goals were to spread native-place sentiment (*lianluo xiangyi*) and to assist *tongxiang* sojourners, through: charity; education; dispute resolution; help in the case of harm to individuals, property or reputation; employment services; and improvement of customs (*gaijin fengxi*). See *Shaoxing lü Hu tongxianghui tonggao*, 1911, 2–3. Negishi (*Chūgoku no girudo*, 199–202) suggests that *tongxianghui* were a product of nationalist sentiment, the changed "spirit of the times." See also SYZX, 303. The purpose of the Ningbo Tongxianghui, founded in 1909, was "to unite the *tongxiang* group and develop the spirit of self-government." If the precise connections between association formation and political ferment remain elusive, there is no question about their coincidence, as well as the prominent nationalist and Republican rhetoric of the new associations.

9. The number of selected "assemblymen" (*yiyuan*), thirty in this case, was not much greater than the numbers of *dongshi* present at *huiguan* meetings. Although nonassemblymen could attend the meetings as auditors, they could not do so without the permission of the assemblymen. Observers could be removed for secret meetings. Members paid yearly fees which were assessed at two levels, two yuan and five yuan (*Shaoxing lü Hu tongxianghui tonggao*, 1911), 1. The exclusion of women did not go unchallenged. After petitioning unsuccessfully for membership in 1921, a certain Zhu Zhongsan organized female sojourners to protest, threatening to form a separate women's *tongxianghui* (*nüzi tongxianghui*) to mobilize public sympathy. See SB, September 29, 1922.

elitist leadership and customary procedures of governance, they did not reject the principle of organization according to native-place origin. Contrary to the presuppositions about the withering of "particularistic" and "traditionalistic" ties we have imposed on our understanding of this period, contemporaries did not view native-place ties as an obstacle to strengthening China as a modern nation. Rather, they reaffirmed the importance of native-place ties, fashioning their image of modernity out of the protean raw material of native-place community. A history of the Jiangning Tongxianghui presents a typical contemporary critique of old-style *huiguan* and explains the development of *tongxianghui:*

The functions of *huiguan* and *gongsuo* are to store coffins or ship them back to the native place, as well as to worship gods and perform *jiao* rituals. As for modern spirit . . . certainly they were insufficient as organizations. In this century, thinking about popular government increased and the spirit of organization also became more common. People with some modern knowledge all desired to associate in social organizations, solidify native-place sentiment and perform necessary acts to benefit the public. . . . Therefore the Jiangning Tongxianghui was formed in 1913.[10]

Although the rhetoric and formal institutional structure of new native-place organizations suggested a clear break with "traditional" associations, such distinctions were less clear in practice. The decade after the Revolution of 1911 witnessed growth in social organizations of all sorts, some traditional in form and function and some not. The overall number of native-place associations (*huiguan* and *tongxianghui*) increased, as did the numbers of their members. During this organizational ferment native-place sentiment became identified with the goals of nationalism and modernization that were deemed necessary to save China.

The Birth of Tongxianghui. A convenient index of social organizations in the early Republican period may be found in the successive editions of *Shanghai zhinan* (Guide to Shanghai).[11] In a section entitled "public enterprises" (*gonggong shiye*), the guidebook listed the names and addresses of Shanghai charitable, educational, and religious

---

10. *Jiangning liuxian lü Hu tongxianghui huikan* (Journal of the Association of Sojourners from Six Counties of Jiangning in Shanghai) (Shanghai, 1935), Introduction.

11. *Shanghai zhinan,* 1910, 1914, 1916, 1919, 1922, 1930. This guidebook is most reliable for commercial and professional (not worker) associations. The 1919 edition does not update the 1916 figures, so it is not included here.

associations, hospitals, museums, cemeteries, *huiguan, gongsuo* and many institutions less easily categorized. As new associations developed, they appeared in this listing. Although comparison of these listings with other sources suggests that the guidebook was not complete and listed new types of organizations only after a delay of several years, it nonetheless indicates trends in the formation of associations.

The guidebook reveals the intense organizational activity of the period and the proliferation of social organizations in general, and a comparison of the 1910, 1914, 1916, 1922 and 1930 editions shows how this general organizational "bloom" was experienced specifically in native-place organization. Growth of native-place associations is indicated by the numbers of entries in the guidebook:

	HUIGUAN	TONGXIANGHUI
1910	26	—
1914	34	—
1916	44	21
1922	53	31
1930	62	57

These numbers not only reveal growth in native-place organizations, but show, moreover, that the traditional *huiguan* increased during this period, as did the newer associations called *lü Hu tongxianghui* (literally, associations of fellow-provincials sojourning in Shanghai). *Tongxianghui*, which numbered fewer than ten in 1911, do not appear in the guidebook until 1916, when twenty-one such organizations are listed. This pattern of dual growth continued into the 1930s. Although *tongxianghui* represented greater numbers of people, the number of *huiguan* continued to exceed the number of *tongxianghui*. The *Commercial Directory of Shanghai* (*Shanghai shangye minglu*) of 1931, for example, lists sixty-eight *huiguan* and fifty-four *tongxianghui*.[12] These numbers reflect the growth of sojourning populations over most of this period, the increasing subdivision of the geographic native-place units and the persistent importance of *huiguan*. In fact, communities which did not formally organize until this period and first established *tongxianghui* went on to crown their efforts by constructing *huiguan*.[13]

---

12. Ibid., 1931.

13. For example, the Changzhou and Wenzhou *tongxianghui* raised funds to build Changzhou and Wenzhou *huiguan*, where none existed previously (SB, May 3, 1919; SB, May 8, 1919).

Let us examine the origins of these *tongxianghui,* a new and distinct organizational trend of the Republican period. The first *tongxianghui* were born in the atmosphere of the late Qing reforms and the local self-government movement surrounding the Republican revolution. They continued to increase in number throughout the Republican period, growth spurts often coinciding with periods of popular social mobilization. In May and June 1919, for example, notices in the *Shenbao* announced the formation of at least ten new native-place organizations. Many of these added the goal of resisting foreign aggression to their statements of purpose.[14]

Different native-place communities gave birth to *tongxianghui* at different times, in response to differing circumstances. Among the earliest *tongxianghui* were those of Huzhou, Haining, Ningbo and Shaoxing (all Zhejiang prefectures) and of Gansu and Anhui province. Each of these associations was established before 1912. In some communities the impetus for the formation of *tongxianghui* came from workers. In other cases it was students who demanded new, more modern and more accessible forms of association. Because of these differences, it is useful to describe the formation of two contrasting associations.

The Ningbo Tongxianghui, which would be highly influential throughout the Republican period, developed after the politicization of the Ningbo community in the 1898 cemetery riot, an event which hastened changes in the internal power structure of the sojourner community. The rise of Shen Honglai and his well-organized artisan and worker constituency challenged traditional oligarchic *huiguan* rule. When *huiguan* directors accommodated Shen by incorporating him into the *huiguan* power structure as general manager in 1901, Shen used his new position to make the leadership more accountable. As a check on the entrenched group of directors, Shen organized a second managerial group, the *gongyi lianhehui,* composed of representatives of all occupational groups within the *huiguan.* As general manager for more than a decade, Shen succeeded in modifying but not radically restructuring the traditional *huiguan.*[15]

In 1909, while still serving as *gongsuo* manager, Shen shifted tactics

---

14. These were Jiangning, Anhui (two associations), Suzhou, Hangzhou, Jiangbei, Qingpu, Jiading, Haiyan and Sichuan *tongxianghui* (SB, May 1919). Because the life of many associations was brief, these spurts of growth are not clearly indicated in the editions of *Shanghai zhinan.*

15. See Chapter 5. Although Shen instituted changes which benefited greater numbers of Ningbo people, his personal style was undemocratic and dictatorial, both as director of

and directed his energies toward the creation of a new kind of native-place institution, outside the Siming Gongsuo. The new association Shen established, called the Siming Lü Hu Tongxianghui, was a more broadly based association intended to serve the needs of ordinary Ningbo sojourners.

Although the new institution became permanent, Shen's influence ceased with his death, which came shortly after he founded the association. Without Shen the *tongxianghui* floundered. It was revived in a coopted form in 1911 by Zhu Baosan, a powerful comprador-director of the Siming Gongsuo. Zhu raised funds for a new building on Fuzhou Road and renamed the association the Ningbo Lü Hu Tongxianghui. Zhu's action suggests that the *huiguan* elite found the organization of a popular native-place association under their patronage very much to their benefit. From this moment onward, relations between the new association and the old appear harmonious. The leaders of the *tongxianghui* were *dongshi* of the Siming Gongsuo.[16]

A division of labor developed between the two Ningbo native-place associations. The *gongsuo* became, increasingly, a center for ceremonial, religious and charitable activities and was somewhat remote from day-to-day business, family, and political affairs. The *tongxianghui* devoted itself to a broad and expanding range of social, economic and quasi-juridical functions. As *tongxianghui* developed in other sojourning communities a similar institutional division of labor occurred, though some communities — Jiangxi sojourners, for instance — never developed *tongxianghui* outside their *huiguan*.[17]

---

the Long Life Association, which he considered his own, and as manager of the Siming Gongsuo. See, especially, SBZX, 429–32.

16. Negishi, *Shanhai no girudo,* 43; Negishi, *Chūgoku no girudo,* 201–2; *Ningbo lü Hu tongxianghui yuebao* (Monthly journal of the Ningbo Sojourners' Association in Shanghai) (hereafter referred to as NLTY), 1921; SGY, 1919–21.

17. *Huiguan* and *tongxianghui* leadership overlapped in other communities as well, suggesting a similar process of cooptation after the initial period of *tongxianghui* formation. This doubtless proceeded from the financial dependence of many *tongxianghui* on *huiguan*. The division of labor was not absolute. Although much Siming Gongsuo meeting time was devoted to managing a national network of coffin transportation and coffin repositories in Shanghai, as well as attending to various religious matters, the *huiguan* also built housing for the poor, supported two hospitals and a school and built a road and bridge costing more than ten thousand yuan in the south city area of Shanghai, together with other *huiguan* in the area. The *huiguan* was also closely involved with the Ning-Shao Shipping Company, which held its board meetings at the Siming Gongsuo. See SGY, 1916; SGY, March-April 1917; SGY, April-June 1918; SGY, January 1919; SGY, June 1919; SGY, August 1920.

The new Ningbo Tongxianghui proved popular and soon outgrew its headquarters. In 1916 Zhu Baosan and other Siming Gongsuo leaders sponsored the construction of a grander building on land costing fifty-six thousand yuan on Tibet Road. This *tongxianghui,* a large, western-style five-story building, was completed in 1921, for an additional construction cost of one hundred fifty thousand yuan. It became the model for later *tongxianghui.* On the first and second floors were lecture halls used for meetings and rented out for *tongxiang* marriages. The third floor housed a library and reading room and a separate periodicals room with local and Ningbo newspapers. The fourth floor served to display Ningbo products and manufactures. The fifth floor offered an exercise room and space for genteel recreations — music appreciation, arts and letters. A Chinese-style hall was maintained on the ground level for ceremonial occasions (see Figure 8).[18]

The features of the Ningbo *tongxianghui* building suggest that, like the Shaoxing Tongxianghui, the Ningbo association accommodated a restricted clientele, consisting of the literate middle and upper classes. Although we might imagine that some petty urbanites could find their way into the building if they had connections, the building was clearly not designed for the use of workers, nor could it accommodate very large crowds.[19]

The *tongxianghui* displaced the Siming Gongsuo as a social center for the community. The primary concern and constituency of the *tongxianghui* (like the *huiguan*) were Ningbo merchants and property owners in Shanghai. Nonetheless, the *tongxianghui* departed from *huiguan* social practice in significant ways. The *tongxianghui* took the service of the broader sojourning community in new directions. With the proclaimed goal of "spreading the spirit of local self-government," the *tongxianghui* sought not just to provide charity for those at the lower levels of the community hierarchy but specifically to improve and reform them. In the 1920s this involved the modern reformist and social-science-tinged practices of "investigating social conditions," "main-

18. NLTY (1921) states that more than one hundred people used the reading rooms daily (Negishi, *Shanhai no girudo,* 43).

19. Early membership figures are not available for the Ningbo Tongxianghui. Other *tongxianghui* list memberships with numbers ranging from several hundred to eight or nine thousand names. Fewer *tongxianghui* list members' occupations, but those that do reveal a middle- to upper-class group, including businessmen, scholars, journalists, clerks, teachers, shopkeepers (and in some cases by the 1920s a small number of women). The Siming Gongsuo estimated in 1920 that there were between five and six hundred thousand Ningbo people in Shanghai. See SGY, April 1920.

Figure 8. The Ningbo Tongxianghui on Tibet Road. Source: *Shanghai huabao* (Shanghai pictorial magazine) 6 (November 1985):38.

taining occupational statistics," "reforming social habits," "exchanging knowledge" and "promoting sanitation."[20]

The self-consciously modern social program of the Ningbo Tong-xianghui was not merely window dressing. In 1921 the *tongxianghui* managed five elementary and middle-level schools (with names like

20. NLTY, 1921; Negishi, *Shanhai no girudo,* 48. These reformist goals prefigure concerns of the Social Bureau of the Shanghai Municipal Government, established in 1927

"Ningbo Voluntary Republican School") for Ningbo children. This number increased to eight by 1927. The *tongxianghui* itself became an educational institution, offering a weekly adult lecture series on a range of topics concerning science, social progress and economic improvement. Among the lectures sponsored by the *tongxianghui* in 1921 (the numbers attending are noted in parentheses) were "Social Progress" (480); "Law and Morality" (352); "The Function of the Atmosphere" (220); "Epidemic Diseases" (189); "Social Darkness and Light" (450); "Product-Display Centers and Their Relation to Commerce" (285); "The Function of Coal" (293); and "The Key to Business Success" (257).[21]

In contrast to the Ningbo community, the socially more conservative Chaozhou sojourners did not establish a permanent *tongxianghui* until the late 1920s. As a result, although the Chaozhou Huiguan handled many of the new types of business thrust on native-place associations by the social problems of the Republican period, the organizational form and governing process do not appear to have undergone even superficial "modernization" or "democratization." *Huiguan* meetings were usually attended by ten to thirty directors. Although the directors deliberated as a group, the most powerful individuals among them routinely dominated discussion. Among these were the leader of the Shanghai pawnshop association, several wealthy businessmen with fortunes based originally on opium money but invested in diverse enterprises, and the director of the Mingxing Film Studio.

Although others in the Chaozhou community were not powerful enough to overturn this oligarchy, challenges developed in the early 1920s. The *huiguan* was financially strained by increased public and private demands emanating from both Shanghai and Chaozhou. In 1921, struggling over scarce resources, the three constituent regional *bang* bickered over access to *huiguan* seals, and *huiguan* managers stressed the importance of unity in order to resist outside pressures for funds.[22] In 1923–24, financial pressures worsened and the *dongshi* resolved that no matter what group or government organ pressured them to fund military expenses, they would uniformly refuse.[23]

Challenges to *huiguan* oligarchic decision making came in the con-

---

(see Christian Henriot, *Shanghai 1927–1937: Municipal Power, Locality and Modernization*, trans. Noel Castelino [Berkeley, Calif., 1993], 185–210).

21. NLTY, 1921.

22. CHYB, 1921.

23. Police accusations against *huiguan* leaders in Shanghai may indicate a pattern of extortion, though the information in the records is inconclusive. Although local pressures

text of competition for *huiguan* resources. In 1926 a group of Chaozhou students in Shanghai demanded the establishment of a more democratic native-place association. In that year the *huiguan* was considering what to do with a piece of property in the French Concession, formerly a burial ground, from which the remains had been removed to a newer cemetery. One influential *huiguan* member (whose wealth and power may be linked to opium) proposed the establishment of a hospital for indigent fellow-provincials. This traditional, conservative expression of benevolence was announced in the Shanghai newspaper as the decision of the *huiguan*.[24] Two days later a newly inaugurated Association of Chaozhou Students Sojourning in Shanghai published a counternotice calling for an immediate meeting of Chaozhou sojourners from all circles (*gejie*) to meet and discuss the most appropriate disposition of the land. The students also sent this demand to the *huiguan*.[25]

Although this was not the first time the *huiguan* had received communications from students, it was the first time student demands were presented so publicly and so forcefully. The *huiguan,* accused of representing only the merchant elite, acceded to the student demand. In the meantime, probably at the instigation of the *huiguan* leadership, a notice entitled, "Repudiate the Spurious Association of Chaozhou Students Sojourning in Shanghai," appeared in the next day's newspaper. Signed by students outside the student association, it denounced the "bogus" student association as an improperly constituted minority faction.[26]

When the student association presented its case in *huiguan* meetings on November 13 and 21, the most outspoken representative was not actually a student but Zhang Jingsheng, a notorious fringe figure of the New Culture Movement.[27] Zhang put forth two "modern" lines of ar-

---

on the Chaozhou Huiguan were greater than were those on the Siming Gongsuo (and Chaozhou resources fewer), one passage in SGY corresponds to the Chaozhou Huiguan's belt tightening. In 1916 Siming Gongsuo directors met to discuss an appeal from the Ning-Shao Philanthropic Association. They reluctantly agreed to contribute but noted that "the only reason we should contribute is that they are *tongxiang*. After this, if other provinces or prefectures raise money for disaster relief we will neither contribute nor consider this a precedent" (SGY, 1916). Such comments testify to the multiple claims on the capital of the Shanghai bourgeoisie.

24. CHYB, November 1926; SB, November 8, 1926.
25. SB, November 10, 1926. More than two hundred people reportedly attended the student meeting.
26. SB, November 11, 1926.
27. Zhang advocated sexual enlightenment, published sexual surveys in a series titled "History of Sex," ran the Esthetic Bookstore and edited *New Culture Monthly* (*Xin wenhua*

gument as to why oligarchic management of *tongxiang* property had to end. First, the *huiguan* leaders were undemocratic. Second, current practices were unprofitable: "In the past the *dongshi* have had total authority, but in these matters they need to ask people's opinions. I believe we should ask everyone to assemble for discussion and hear the decision of the majority of people from Chaozhou. The [*dongshi* plan for using the land] is secure but would only produce a limited amount of money. I think there is better way. [Building a *tongxianghui*] would not just benefit the scholarly community, but would serve the interests of all Chaozhou people." When the reluctant *dongshi* argued that indebtedness from the construction of the new cemetery precluded consideration of the students' project, Zhang criticized the lavishness of cemetery expenditures, a criticism which reflects a generational and political conflict between "enlightened" students, impatient with money wasted on old, "superstitious" rituals, and the older leaders of the *huiguan*.[28]

The student's plan for the greater social welfare of the *tongxiang* was modeled after the already well-established and powerful Ningbo Tongxianghui:

Chaozhou people in Shanghai are increasingly numerous and they don't yet have a recreational meeting place. Although there are three *huiguan* their scale is small. . . . The [new] *huiguan* will have four stories. The first two floors will have shops. On the third floor a large hall will be constructed which will be rented out for marriages, funerals and all kinds of meetings. The fourth floor will have the association offices and other clubs. The form will be like the Ningbo Tongxianghui. Although it won't be as large or magnificent, it will be as nice as we can economically afford.

The shop and meeting-hall rentals would cover the operating costs of the *tongxianghui*. Any additional profits would support educational ventures and Chaozhou students in Shanghai.[29]

The students failed in their mission, but they damaged the *dongshi* claim to represent the larger community. Compelled to confront *tongxiang* who accused them of elitism, the *dongshi* finally argued that they had the authority to make the decision because they, not the broad community, had in fact purchased the contested land. The students chal-

---

yuekan), which featured drawings of nude women and sex-counseling correspondence (Fan Jiping, "Wo suo zhidao de Zhang Jingshen" [What I know of Zhang Jingshen], *Daren* 11 [March 15, 1971]:23–27).

28. CHYB, November, 1926.

29. CHYB, November 21, 1926.

lenged the *huiguan* leaders' preemptive action in court, embroiling the *huiguan* in troublesome litigation. Other groups of Chaozhou students also published notices expressing outrage at the unwillingness of the *dongshi* to meet with the greater *tongxiang* community. Forcing a modern democratic meaning onto the paternalist rhetoric of the Chaozhou *huiguan,* they argued that although the land was *huiguan* property, the *huiguan* was the institution of the Chaozhou people. Therefore, although responsibility lay with the *huiguan,* the overall authority lay with the Chaozhou people.[30]

The students' interest in native-place organization was both natural and calculated, heightened by their desire for access to *huiguan* resources. Three demands published by the student association — the first (involving foreign encroachments on Chinese territory) expressing nationalism; the second (involving a petition to Chaozhou officials in regard to land-rent matters) expressing involvement in native-place affairs; and the third calling for democratic measures contributing to their own well-being — together illustrate the compatibility in practice of multiple loyalties (native-place, national, and student) and old and new ideas.[31]

In its struggles with contending groups of fellow-provincials, the Chaozhou Huiguan held out much longer than did other *huiguan.*[32] Nonetheless, by the early 1930s the *huiguan* coexisted peacefully with a Chaozhou Tongxianghui, a broader-based, more overtly political association which threw itself into nationalist and anti-Japanese propaganda efforts, social welfare services in Shanghai and refugee relief.[33]

Student and Worker Native-Place Associations. Although *huiguan* and *tongxianghui* were the major forms of native-place association in this period, as the stories of *tongxianghui* formation demonstrate, they were not the only kinds of organization by native place. Both *huiguan* and *tongxianghui* subscribed to the rhetoric of an all-inclusive native-place community, regardless of class or social group.

30. CHYB, November 1926; SB, December 6, 1926; SB, December 7, 1926.
31. SB, November 10, 1926.
32. CHYB, December 1926; CHYB, January–March 1927. By the time of the formation of the Chaozhou Tongxianghui at the end of the 1920s, there were already fifty other *tongxianghui* in Shanghai. The precise date of the establishment of the Chaozhou Tongxianghui is unclear (it was between 1927 and 1931).
33. *Chaozhou lü Hu tongxianghui tekan, juiguo hao* (Special issue of the Association of Chaozhou Sojourners in Shanghai, national salvation edition) (Shanghai, 1932).

They were, nonetheless, understood to have a primarily elite constituency, with the *huiguan* representing the business elite and the *tongxianghui* including a larger commercial community as well as journalists, educators and intelligentsia. The growth of these native-place institutions, associated with commercial circles (*shangjie*), was accompanied by the development and growth of associations of sojourning students (*lü Hu xueshenghui*) and coexisted with a variety of native-place trade and worker associations (*bangkou, she, gonghui*). Precise trends in the formation of these associations are difficult to outline: because their native-place composition is often not revealed by their name, many of these associations escape detection.[34]

Student associations followed a pattern of development similar to that of *tongxianghui*, finding their origins in the early-twentieth-century reforms and new educational institutions. Twenty-four student associations, associations of sojourning students among them, appear in the 1916 edition of *Shanghai zhinan*. Often student associations are listed according to school, masking the fact that many schools (particularly trade and business schools) were sponsored by native-place associations or dominated by students from one or two regions. Beneath the school-level organizations which are listed in guides and directories, students belonged to native-place student associations which are often not listed. Although there was a Fudan University Students' Association, for instance, there was also a Fudan Chaozhou Students' Association. There were also overarching native-place student associations that transcended school boundaries—for instance, the Association of Fujian Students, which met at the Fuzhou *huiguan* (San Shan Huiguan), and the Association of Zhejiang Students Sojourning in Shanghai.[35]

Although students criticized *huiguan* as superstitious and traditionalistic, the fact that "modern" students did not find native-place organization in itself objectionable is evident in the prevalence of native-place associations at the radical Shanghai University (*Shanghai daxue*, hereafter Shangda). The most radical students participated in Shangda *tong-*

---

34. Although this is also a problem in studying *huiguan* and *tongxianghui,* worker and student organizations left fewer records.

35. SB, May 5, 1919; SB, May 9, 1919; SB, May 13, 1919. On student fellow-provincial associations, see Jeffrey Wasserstrom, *Student Protests in Twentieth-Century China: The View from Shanghai* (Stanford, Calif., 1991), 127–45; Zhang Jishun, "Lun Shanghai zhengzhi yundong zhong de xuesheng qunti (1925–27)" (Regarding student formations in Shanghai political movements, 1925–27), in *Shanghai: tongwang shijie zhiqiao* (Shanghai: Gateway to the world), ed. Shanghai shi difangzhi bangongshi, *Shanghai yanjiu luncong* (Papers on Shanghai), vol. 4 (Shanghai, 1989), 104–10.

xianghui as a matter of course and as a matter of necessity.[36] A former Shangda student, Zhong Fuguang, who studied with the Communist labor organizer and party historian Deng Zhongxia, recalled the Sichuan *tongxianghui* as meeting both political and personal needs: "This was a form resulting from the party's method of organizing everyone into groups. At the time, if you didn't belong to an organization, there was no way to be politically active. Therefore there were many provincial *tongxianghui* at Shanghai University. Other schools were the same. The main activities of the *tongxianghui* were to bring together people's feelings and unite people. Everyone was studying outside his or her native place. If something came up it could be taken to the *tongxianghui*."[37] Zhong's suggestion that the *tongxianghui* form derived from party initiatives is mistaken, of course, but it confirms that there was no perceived contradiction between native-place organizations and social revolutionary goals. Zhang's statement also indicates the usefulness of native-place sentiment and organization as vehicles for effective social mobilization.

Among Shanghai workers, native-place organization developed from the moment they immigrated or were recruited to work in the city.[38] A variety of native-place *bang* — among the most prominent in Shanghai, the Guangdong *bang*, Ningbo *bang*, Shaoxing *bang*, Wuxi *bang* and local Shanghai (*ben*) *bang* — organized Shanghai labor from the opening of the port in 1843 through the Republican era.[39] Just as the contributions of *tongxiang* merchants in support of education strengthened (though by no means explains) student organization by native place, patterns of recruitment, deployment and labor control strengthened worker organization by native place. The owners of Chinese enterprises

36. Zhang Chongde (1903–37) and He Weisheng (1902–26) were student activists at Shangda. Both participated in the Shangda Zhejiang Tongxianghui, the largest native-place organization at the school. Together with their fellow-provincial comrades, they studied social and economic conditions in Zhejiang to participate in revolutionary struggles in their native place. See *Cai Xiyao and Wang Jiagui*, eds., *Shanghai daxue* (Shanghai University) (Shanghai, 1986), 67–68.

37. Cai Xiyao and Wang Jiagui, *Shanghai daxue*, 106–7. I am grateful to Jeffrey Wasserstrom for showing me this source.

38. Perry (*Shanghai on Strike*) details enduring patterns of worker native-place organization in the Republican era.

39. *Bang* was the most common term used to describe native-place organization of labor. It does not necessarily imply a formal organization. The mere presence of Ningbo workers permits the use of the term "Ningbo *bang*." That people from one native place will act as a group is assumed within the terminology. For a description of early native-place organization among Guangdong workers in Shanghai, see Chapter 2.

recruited *tongxiang* managers and foremen, who in turn recruited *tongxiang* workers. Foreign owners of Shanghai enterprises similarly relied on Chinese labor recruiters, who reproduced this pattern.[40]

Whereas regional groups monopolized specific trades in the late nineteenth century, by the early Republican period the shifting fortunes and populations of different groups led to a more complex situation of shared participation in specific trades and enterprises. That *bang* ceased to monopolize specific occupational niches did not mean that the various regional groups mixed or that the importance of *bang* diminished. Instead, labor and industry in the 1920s and 1930s were characterized by *bang* subdivision within the multi-*bang* work unit.

Shanghai textile mills were dominated by Shaoxing, Ningbo and Subei *bang*.[41] Workers at the British-owned Shanghai Tramway Company were divided between the Ningbo and Subei *bang*, which dominated separate divisions within the company. Shaoxing people, introduced by Shaoxing relatives and recruited by a Shaoxing forewoman, predominated in the leaf-packing department at the British-American Tobacco Company. Subei women worked in the more strenuous rolling department. Flour-mill workers at the Fuxin mills were divided between Hubei and Wuxi *bang*, each of which dominated different sectors of the machine room. Among those who worked on the riverfront, most of the dockworkers were from Subei; most of those who worked in warehouses, from Ningbo; and most of those who worked with cargo on the ships, from Guangdong.[42]

As with student associations, it is important to assess the social and political character of worker native-place *bang*. *Bang* divisions could

40. Chen Laixin, *Yu Xiaqing*, 12–15; Cheng Renjie, "Yingmei yan gongsi maiban Zheng Bozhao," 130–35; Shanghai shehui kexueyuan, Jingji yanjiusuo (Shanghai Academy of Social Sciences, Institute for Economic Research), ed., *Rongjia qiye shiliao* (Historical materials on the Rong family enterprises), vol. 1 (Shanghai, 1980), 118; Bergère, *L'âge d'or,* 148–59; Emily Honig, *Sisters and Strangers: Women in the Shanghai Cotton Mills, 1919–1949* (Stanford, Calif., 1986), 57–78.

41. Zhu Bangxing et al., eds., *Shanghai chanye yu Shanghai zhigong* (Shanghai industry and workers) (Shanghai, 1939; reprint, 1984), 202; Honig, *Sisters and Strangers,* 57–78.

42. Zhu et al., *Shanghai chanye,* 264–65, 625–26, 647; Elizabeth Perry, "Shanghai gongren bagong yu wuchan jieji de zhengzhi qianli" (Shanghai on strike: Work and politics in the making of a Chinese proletariat), in *Shanghai: tongwang shijie zhiqiao. Shanghai yanjiu luncong* (Papers on Shanghai), vol. 4, ed. Shanghaishi difangzhi bangongshi (Shanghai, 1989), 38–86; Shanghai shehui kexueyuan, Jingji yanjiusuo, ed., *Yingmei yan gongsi zai hua qiye ziliao huibian* (Collected materials on the British-American tobacco enterprise in China) (Beijing, 1983), 1028; Cai Xiaoqing, *Zhongguo jindai huidang shi yanjiu* (Research on secret societies and gangs in modern Chinese history) (Beijing, 1987), 333.

mean competition and rivalry, interethnic tensions, harassment and fighting.[43] In the same manner as student native-place organization, worker native-place organization occurred at levels which subdivided but could also transcend their institutions of work. In other important respects, however, the omnipresent native-place organization of workers differed from that of students. The leaders of worker *bang* tended not to be ordinary workers but foremen, labor contractors and even merchants and minor officials.[44] Moreover, membership and allegiance were more automatic than voluntary.

Communist labor organizers who surveyed Shanghai in 1921 noted that preexisting organic associations among workers — both regional *bang* and gang-type organizations — posed a major obstacle to the formation of worker unions. Nonetheless, although they viewed native-place *bang* as a kind of feudal tie which subjected workers to the manipulation of officials and compradors (not to mention retrograde gang bosses and contract brokers), in order to organize labor effectively party organizers learned that they had to work with the preexisting *bang*, making friends with their leaders and, through them, attempting to radicalize their members.[45]

Although native-place organization among Shanghai workers was enduring, this did not mean that worker organization did not change or "modernize." The continuity of the names of such organizations — *bang, bangkou* — as well as a variety of terms with religious associa-

<hr/>

43. For references to fights between workers escalating to melees between their native-place *bang*, see Zhu et al., *Shanghai chanye*, 264–65; SB, May 3, 1919; SB, May 16, 1919; SB, June 2, 1919; and Cai Xiaoqing, *Zhongguo jindai huidang*, 332. Regarding the particular prejudice of Jiangnan workers against workers from poverty-stricken Subei (who often performed the most laborious, ill-paid and demeaning tasks), see Honig, *Sisters and Strangers*, 70–78; Honig, "Politics of Prejudice," 243–74.

44. Cai Xiaoqing, *Zhongguo jindai huidang*, 331–32.

45. Deng Zhongxia, *Deng Zhongxia wenji* (Collected works of Deng Zhongxia) (Beijing, 1983), 425; "Shanghai gongzuo jihua jueyi'an" (Draft resolution on Shanghai work plans) (1926), in *Zhongguo zhongyang wenjian xuanji* (Collection of documents of the Central Committee of the Chinese Communist party), ed. Zhongyang dang'anguan (Party Central Committee Archive), vol. 2 (Beijing, 1982), 182–83; Cai Xiaoqing, *Zhongguo jindai huidang*, 331–34. See also Chen Weimin, "Zhonggong chengli chuqi Shanghai gongren yundong shuping" (The Shanghai workers' movement in the first years of the CCP), in *Shanghai: tongwang shijie zhiqiao, Shanghai yanjiu luncong* (Papers on Shanghai), vol. 4, ed. Shanghai shi difangzhi bangongshi (Shanghai, 1989), 8–37. Chen finds that "locality factions" were more numerous and more complicated in Shanghai than elsewhere. In the early 1920s native-place *bang* involved a greater number of workers than did the Shanghai gangs, though the leaders of these *bang* often tried to gain gang backing to strengthen their position.

tions — *tang, she* — suggests a certain continuity in the character of these worker associations, at least through the May Fourth period. Materials from the mid-1920s, however, reveal the growth of more secular native-place worker associations, often called *lü Hu gonghui* (sojourners' union) or *zhu Hu laogonghui* (association of laborers staying in Shanghai), reflecting both labor-organizing efforts and the increasing radicalization of the Shanghai proletariat.[46]

The Subdivision of the Native-Place Community. Some idea of the plethora of native-place associations coexisting in 1919 is provided by the partial listings of associations of Guangdong and Zhejiang fellow-provincials that appear in Tables 1 and 2.[47] These lists are not comprehensive and are meant only to suggest the range of associations within each native-place community.

This varied list of associations indicates several important developments of the early Republican period. First, it demonstrates a growing articulation of "social circles" (*jie*); that is, the separation, both in language and in organizational identity, of layers of businessmen and merchants, students, workers and sometimes journalists. Whereas several decades earlier, general appeals to the *tongxiang* community did not normally specify groups within the community, now appeals to fellow-sojourners "of all circles" (*lü Hu tongxiang gejie*) or to *tongxiang* "of commercial, student, worker and journalist circles" (*shang-xue-gong-bao jie*) expressed the differentiation of separate interest, status or economic groups. In the May Fourth period, appeals to greater *tongxiang* community were still possible, though no longer with the suggestions of brotherhood or ritual equality that characterized the nineteenth-century *tongxiang* community.

Second, although the formation of new associations certainly meant a splitting off from the old *huiguan,* this splitting was not necessarily antagonistic. New associations lacking their own buildings (as was especially the case when these associations were not commercial associa-

46. See, for example, Shanghai shehui kexueyuan, Lishi yanjiusuo (Shanghai Academy of Social Sciences, Institute for Historical Research), ed., *Wusa yundong shiliao* (Historical materials on the May Thirtieth Movement) (hereafter referred to as WYS), vol. 1 (Shanghai, 1981), 398, 401.

47. These lists are compiled on the basis of organizations mentioned in Shanghai shehui kexueyuan, Lishi yanjiusuo (Shanghai Academy of Social Sciences, Institute for Historical Research), ed., *Wusi yundong zai shanghai shiliao xuanji* (Compilation of historical materials concerning the May Fourth Movement in Shanghai) (hereafter referred to as WYZS) (Shanghai, 1980); also mentioned in SB, 1919, and in CHYB, SGY, and NLTY.

tions) commonly met at the building of the older association. For instance, the pawnshop association met at the Chao-Hui Huiguan; the Hangzhou Tongxianghui met at the Qianjiang Huiguan; the Suzhou Tongxianghui met at the Jiangning Gongsuo; the Jiading Tongxianghui met at the Cake- and Bean-Trade Gongsuo; the Fujian Student Association met at the San Shan Huiguan; and Ningbo workers' associations held important meetings at the Siming Gongsuo.

Third, the proliferation of groups reflects increasing geographical fragmentation. As the populations of fellow-provincials in Shanghai increased, there was increasing subdivision within the community according to smaller geographical units of native-place origin. Nonetheless, the interaction of these groups, viewed through the meeting notes of Ningbo and Chaozhou associations, suggests that this type of division did not mean competition or antagonism among newly subdivided units. Geographic subdivision of the native-place community resulted, rather, from growth in Shanghai's immigrant populations over the course of this period and each group's attainment of a "critical mass," a combination of numbers and wealth. In practice, on major issues groups from the same province combined forces and worked together, issuing joint telegrams and meeting together in the largest of the *tong-xiang* meeting places.[48] At moments of political urgency the increasingly diverse native-place groups coalesced into overarching federations. As Jiang Jieshi (Chiang Kai-shek) headed northward in the Northern Expedition, many Shanghai native-place associations gathered under provincial-level umbrella associations, organized to preserve peace in their native provinces and to support the formation of a Shanghai Municipal Government. Among these were the All-Zhejiang Association (*Quan Zhe gonghui*) and the All-Anhui Consultative Committee (*Quan Hui xiehui*). Multiprovince regional associations were also formed, such as the Three Provinces Federation (*Sansheng lianhehui*), created by Ningbo, Shaoxing, Wenzhou, Jiaxing, Hangzhou and other *tongxianghui*. One announcement of the formation of an all-province association explained that such an organization was needed to integrate the diverse Anhui native-place groups into a systematic and overarching organization.[49] In practice the flexibility of the native-place tie provided both the convenience of local communities for day-to-day purposes and

48. CHYB and SGY, consulted for the period 1913–37.
49. SB, November 22, 1926; SB, December 6, 1926; SB, December 9, 1926; SB, December 12, 1926.

Table 1. Guangdong Associations in Shanghai (1919)

HUIGUAN
Guang-Zhao Gongsuo
Shunde Huiguan
Nanhai Huiguan
Chaozhou Huiguan
Chao-Hui Huiguan
Jie-Pu-Feng Huiguan

TONGXIANGHUI
Zhaoqing Tongxianghui
Jiaying Wushu Lü Hu Tonxianghui
Lü Hu Dapu Tongxianghui

OTHER
Guangdong Club (Guangdong julebu)
Guangdong Sojourners' Reconstruction Association
Guangdong Sojourners' Commercial Association
Chaozhou Sugar and Miscellaneous-Goods Association
(Chao-Hui) Third-Class Pawnshop Association
Fudan Chaozhou Students' Association
Association of Guangdong Seamen

larger combinations with greater political clout when the issue was the nation.

Native-Place Burdens and Business in the Early Republican Period

Although new images of native-place community and new strategies of organization appeared in the Republican era, both *huiguan* and *tongxianghui* struggled with the considerable social and financial burdens imposed by the deterioration of local order which characterized this period. In place of effective local government and as a defense against the disorders of war, native-place associations ministered

Table 2. Zhejiang Associations in Shanghai

HUIGUAN
Siming Gongsuo
Zhe-Shao Huiguan
Zhe-Yan Huiguan
Shaoxing Huiguan
Haichang Gongsuo (Haining Huiguan)
Huzhou Huiguan
Dinghai Huiguan
Jun'an She

TONGXIANGHUI
Ningbo Lü Hu Tongxianghui
Shaoxing Lü Hu Tongxianghui
Quan Zhe Lü Hu Tongxianghui
Hangzhou Lü Lu Tongxianghui
Wenzhou Tongxianghui
Haichang Lü Hu Tongxianghui

OTHER
Shaoxing International Improvement Society
Huzhou Studen-Commercial Sojourners' Association
Ningbo Student Association
Association of Zhejiang Sojourning Students
Fudan Zhejiang Student Association
Fudan Shaoxing Student Association
Ning-Shao Cotton-Trade Welfare Association
Ning-Shao Lacquerers' Association
(Association of Ningbo Seamen)

---

to the needs of their *tongxiang* communities, maintaining social infra-structure in their native places and contributing to similar social needs in Shanghai. To some extent this activity may be seen as an extension of *huiguan* roles of the late nineteenth century, when sojourning *tongxiang* sent money and contributed to public works in their native place. None-theless, as the following discussion of the activities of the Ningbo and Chaozhou associations illustrates, the changed situation of the country-side intensified the depth and scope of involvement in the native place.

The institutional division of labor in communities which developed *tongxianghui* in the early Republican period meant that these new native-place associations displaced *huiguan* as the primary organ for so-journers' appeals and redress. This was the case for the Ningbo Tong-xianghui. In contrast, because the Chaozhou community did not produce a powerful *tongxianghui* in the early Republican period, the Chaozhou Huiguan continued to dominate the Chaozhou community until the 1930s. In respect to their management of the daily burdens of native-place business, the new Ningbo Tongxianghui in many ways functioned similarly to the early-Republican-era Chaozhou Huiguan. Although the two associations faced differing conditions in their native areas, with contrasting degrees of proximity and resources, both associations mediated among the different worlds of the native place and Shanghai, local residents, military forces and officialdom.

Involvement in the Native Place. Rich meeting records exist for the Chaozhou Huiguan, and they permit a sketch of the substantial native-place involvements of a moderately wealthy Republican-era *huiguan*. These included the management of commercial remittances and representation of Shantou shops in Shanghai, disaster relief, financing and management of local public works, support of Chaozhou charitable institutions and hospitals, tax reduction and the promotion of education.

The local Chambers of Commerce (established by law in 1904) were often ineffective or insufficiently powerful to be persuasive with provincial authorities. Although recent studies of Chinese cities have argued that a deparochialization of trade associations and commercial affairs began by the end of the nineteenth century,[50] *huiguan* records suggest that in practice this was not the case. Local business groups outside Shanghai with connections to wealthy sojourning fellow-provincials in Shanghai appealed to wealthy Shanghai *huiguan* to intervene for them in local and provincial matters, rather than limit their appeals to the local chamber. New institutions established for the more modern and rational management of business matters did not necessarily restructure

---

50. Fewsmith, *Party, State and Local Elites;* Rowe, *Hankow: Commerce and Society.* According to these accounts, such "deparochialization" involved both a weakening of native-place ties and the diminished involvement of sojourning merchants in the affairs of their native place, as well as the increasing takeover of local business matters by the newly established and more modern Chambers of Commerce. Although Bergère (*Golden Age*) emphasizes the role of native-place ties among the Shanghai bourgeoisie, by focusing on the ways in which native-place ties served the development of the bourgeoisie, she does not examine the reciprocal responsibilities of Shanghai merchants back to the native place.

common practice. Local Chaozhou merchants in Shantou — and even at times the Shantou Chamber of Commerce — brought problems to the attention of the Shanghai Chaozhou Huiguan, which then mediated with Chaozhou and Guangdong officials.

The Shantou Liuyi Huiguan (representing local merchants in Shantou) maintained regular contact with the Shanghai Chaozhou Huiguan, coordinating shipping arrangements for sugar, rice, and beans and asking for help when problems arose. For example, when the Shantou Liuyi Huiguan complained about steamboat rates in March 1921, the Chaozhou Huiguan successfully negotiated with shipping companies for lower rates. In December of the same year a boat sank off the Shandong coast carrying Shantou cargo insured for ninety thousand taels. When the insurance company delayed payment, the Chaozhou Huiguan, Guang-Zhao Gongsuo and the Guangdong Merchants' Association of Shanghai (*Yueqiao shangye lianhehui*) together pressured the company into payment. In a 1922 case the Chaozhou Huiguan, which had represented Shantou shops in reserving a large shipment of bean cakes (used as fertilizer), carefully resolved the complexities of a situation in which the northern bean-cake factory closed, bean-cake prices changed, and the Shantou clients demanded reimbursement.[51]

Native-place associations also managed financial transactions. Shanghai merchants kept accounts at the *huiguan* which also regularly managed remittances for shops in Shantou. When remittance tickets were lost, as happened in 1914, the *huiguan* sorted out the situation, registering each shop's remittance tickets, printing notices in the newspapers, annulling lost remittances in the court of the French Concession (where the *huiguan* was located) and spreading losses among the entire Chaozhou *bang*. When warfare obstructed the flow of remittances in 1916, the *huiguan* managed the affair jointly with the Shantou Chamber of Commerce.[52]

A byzantine incident demonstrating the role of a Shanghai native-place association in local finance (and the importance of sojourner financial networks for an area with many overseas Chinese) occurred in 1925. When the local Shantou currency, the longyin, suffered devaluation, the Chaozhou Huiguan rallied to bolster the currency and prevent market panic. The devaluation was rooted in the pattern of remittances to Shantou from overseas sojourners. Chaozhou merchants in South-

51. CHYB, April 1917; CHYB, March 1921; CHYB, December 1921; CHYB, 1922.
52. CHYB, November 1914; CHYB, Spring 1916.

east Asia remitted money to their native place through fellow-countrymen in Hong Kong. Fluctuations in the Hong Kong currency caused a decline in the dependent local currency. The Shanghai Chaozhou Huiguan coordinated a broad effort to support the longyin which involved the Shantou banks, the Shantou Chamber, the Shantou Remittance Association, the Hong Kong Chaozhou Merchants' Association, and (through the latter) *tongxiang* at each Southeast Asian port.[53]

Although these valiant measures did not revive the failing Shantou currency, this episode demonstrates the wide coordinating role of the *huiguan*. When local and sojourner institutions finally recognized the necessity of canceling the old currency and adopting dollars (yuan), the *huiguan* notified all old-style banks and shops, printed notices in the newspapers, sent word to the Shanghai Fruit Gongsuo and the Pawnshop Gongsuo (both Chaozhou interests) and canceled old remittance tickets. When the Shantou Finance Board contacted the Shanghai Sugar and Miscellaneous-Goods Association (also a Chaozhou concern), it was the *huiguan* that drafted the response. The *huiguan* also imposed a five-thousand-yuan fine against anyone not using dollars.

The *huiguan* sent representatives to Shantou to help regulate finance according to the yuan. These representatives came into conflict with Shantou old-style banks, which stood to suffer from the changes. When the banks threatened to take them to court, the *huiguan* paid their expenses. This incident demonstrates not only the wide regulatory power of the Shanghai *huiguan* in Shantou finance but, in addition, *huiguan* regulation of financial affairs among different Chaozhou concerns in Shanghai — sugar, pawnshops, and fruit — each of which was organized into a separate business association.[54]

The Ningbo Tongxianghui, which represented a wealthier and more powerful sojourner community than did the Chaozhou Huiguan, was similarly involved — and was highly influential — in local Ningbo affairs. Robbery victims routinely asked influential friends to appeal to the *tongxianghui* on their behalf. The *tongxianghui* then urged local officials to

---

53. CHYB, February 1925; CHYB, March 1925.

54. Involvement in Shantou business and finance in this period meant also longer-term and new-style investments. In June 1920 the Shanghai Chaozhou Huiguan pledged to raise five hundred thousand taels for a handicraft factory in Shantou. It also sponsored a professional school in Shantou (the *Chaozhou bayi zhiye xuexiao*), which it funded and provided with management personnel until at least 1925. See CHYB, November 1919; CHYB, February 1920; CHYB, June 1920; CHYB, September 1922; CHYB, June-September 1925.

deal with the case. The repetitions of this process leave the firm impression that without influential letters of introduction the *tongxianghui* would not have intervened and that without the intervention of the *tongxianghui* the cases would have been ignored. Once the *tongxianghui* took up a case, local authorities acted promptly to hasten its resolution.[55] At times the Ningbo Tongxianghui initiated local administrative reforms and even selected local administrators. For example, in October 1921, after deciding that Zhenhai county needed a Dike Works Bureau, the *tongxianghui* asked the Ningbo Daoyin to order the Zhenhai Magistrate to direct local self-government committee members to organize this bureau. The Daoyin endorsed the plan and asked the Shanghai association to select the Bureau head.[56]

The Ningbo Tongxianghui also helped moderate local taxes and bureaucratic obstruction. In October 1921 sugar merchants in Shipu county complained to the Shanghai association of an oppressive sugar tax levied by the Shipu Chamber of Commerce. Pressured by the *tongxianghui,* the Shipu Chamber rescinded the tax. In the same year, Sijiao Island (Dinghai county) residents appealed to the *tongxianghui* because the Jiangsu Financial Bureau was interfering with rice transport to the island, delaying a required rice-transport license. The *tongxianghui* mediated with the Jiangsu office on behalf of the islanders.[57]

The substantial involvement of native-place associations in native-place affairs meant that when the native place suffered, association directors and sojourners reached deeply into their pockets. Guangdong province was beset by both natural and militarily induced disasters throughout the early Republican period.[58] When disasters occurred, Guangdong gentry and also officials appealed for help from their *tong-*

55. NLTY, correspondence of November 4, 5, 28, 29, 30, 1921; October 3, 7, 10, 13, 1921. In a number of instances, the association clearly became involved in criminal cases, though *tongxianghui* regulations generally stipulated that *tongxiang* could only appeal in civil cases.

56. NLTY, correspondence of October 15 and 19, 1921. "Daoyin" was the title used in the Republican period for the former office of Daotai.

57. The resolution of the rice case is unclear. See NLTY, correspondence of October 1, 2, 3, 9, 10, 11, 12, 20, 1921.

58. The death of Yuan Shikai in June 1916 is conventionally understood as the beginning of the warlord period in China, when national unity was destroyed by the rise of competing regional military governments with a pattern of shifting alliances and intermittent civil war which persisted until at least 1928. Warlord fighting and the rapacity of various warlord regimes tended to exacerbate the effects of natural disasters by depleting local resources and permitting local institutions of water control and welfare to deteriorate.

xiang in Shanghai. In the event of small and localized disasters, each Guangdong *huiguan* assisted its home area. In the case of large-scale disasters, as in 1915 when the three major Guangdong rivers flooded, the Guang-Zhao Gongsuo and the Chaozhou Huiguan coordinated their efforts, at times in conjunction with the Hong Kong Chaozhou Commercial Association (*Xianggang bayi shanghui*). When an earthquake hit Chaozhou prefecture and Mei county in January 1918, the Chaozhou Huiguan provided primary relief, with help from the Guang-Zhao Gongsuo. Two Chaozhou Huiguan directors traveled from Shanghai to investigate the situation with the Shantou Chamber of Commerce, and the *huiguan* collected funds for dike repair to prevent spring flooding. As was common in the case of major disasters, relief organization on this occasion involved a multicity sojourner network. The Shanghai *huiguan* coordinated efforts with *tongxiang* in Guangzhou, Hankou and Beijing.[59] If *huiguan* meetings called to determine relief measures were occasions for hyperbolic expressions of native-place sentiment ("In philanthropy, there are no limits. Now we think of our native place — how could we not be moved to action . . . all good men dearly love our native place with fervent hearts"),[60] they do nonetheless demonstrate abiding commitments to the native place and a means of apportioning responsibility among the different groups of sojourning Shanghai *tongxiang*.

In times of extraordinary disaster the Chaozhou Huiguan acted as a local administration in exile, funding and managing relief and also directing local Chaozhou authorities and institutions. Catastrophic flooding in August 1922 destroyed Chaozhou dikes and homes. Huiguan investigators reported at least a hundred thousand deaths in Chenghai, Raoping and Chaoyang counties. When the scope of the disaster exceeded available funds, *huiguan* directors campaigned and swiftly raised seventy-five thousand yuan. Citing the losses due to flooding, the directors interceded with Guangzhou military authorities to reduce taxation in the area. They also directed a local Shantou benevolent institution (Cunxintang) to investigate the needs of orphans, ar-

59. CHYB, March 1918; CHYB, February 1920. After the relief work was over and the dikes were all repaired, the Shanghai Chaozhou Huiguan distributed a report detailing the Shantou earthquake disaster contributions.

60. CHYB, June–August 1913; CHYB, July 1915; CHYB, January-May 1918. *Huiguan* contributions to the maintenance of Chaozhou water control were common. Dike repair was the subject of meetings in May 1924; a major dredging project, involving substantial *huiguan* investment, is noted in CHYB, January 1919.

range for adoptions, and charge the expenses to the *huiguan*. Ten thousand sets of clothing for disaster victims were made in Shanghai and shipped to Shantou.[61]

These interventions took place outside official channels. If anything, local government acted as a hindrance to disaster relief. Noting the influx of *huiguan*-raised capital, Chaozhou officials attempted to deflect some money for their own uses, nominally to rebuild a local *yamen*. They were rebuked by the Chaozhou Huiguan, which embarked on the repair of local dikes, contributing another fifty-one thousand yuan. The *huiguan* also sent an inspector to traverse local dike networks for more than a year, to complete a comprehensive investigation of damage and reconstruction.[62] Clearly, at such times the Shanghai association was capable of stepping in and serving in the capacity of caretaker government for local Chaozhou affairs.

Zhejiang was not as disaster stricken in this period as was Guangdong, nor were Ningbo officials as unreliable; nonetheless, when calamity struck, the Ningbo Tongxianghui responded. In August 1921, for example, in response to flooding in Yin and Fenghua counties, the *tongxianghui* established a Ningbo Flood Disaster Collection Committee (*Ningbo shuizai jizhenhui*), headed by Zhu Baosan, to care for refugees and bury corpses. The committee raised almost seventy-four thousand yuan, most of which was remitted to the Ningbo Daoyin, who organized local relief.[63]

In such cases the *tongxianghui* worked closely with Ningbo officials. Though Ningbo officials appear to have been more scrupulous than those in Chaozhou, when they were negligent the *tongxianghui* chided them. Residents of western Yin county, exasperated by frequent robberies, complained to the Shanghai *tongxianghui*, which prodded the

61. CHYB, August-December 1922. Although sources do not permit measurement of these expenditures in comparison with total available Chaozhou sojourner funds, these were nonetheless major expenses. Such claims by the native place on sojourning merchants' resources diverted Shanghai capital away from the city and from more economically productive investments. For a discussion of the implications of this phenomenon in comparative perspective, see Joseph Esherick and Mary Rankin, eds., *Chinese Local Elites and Patterns of Dominance* (Berkeley, Calif., 1990), 333.

62. CHYB, August 1922–December 1924. At the conclusion of these relief efforts, the *huiguan* paid for the purchase of a local cemetery for disaster victims, storing the Shantou cemetery deed in Shanghai.

63. Siming Gongsuo records for 1921 do not mention the Yin-Feng disaster. Apparently *huiguan* directors decided that the Ningbo Tongxianghui would deal with the tragedy. See SGY, 1921; NLTY, 1921.

Ningbo Director of Police into action.[64] Residents of eastern Yin county complained of both robberies and harassment by a local "peace-keeping militia" (*baoweidui*), producing a successful appeal by the *tongxianghui* to the Yin county magistrate to disband the militia.[65]

The urgency of warfare in the Republican era reinforced the mediating role of Shanghai *huiguan* in the networks of power that infused the native place and the nation.[66] When possible, *huiguan* mobilized to protect local property from military conflict. Threats of fighting between the northern Anfu clique which controlled Duan Qirui's Beijing government and the southern allied forces in December 1917 led local Shantou institutions to seek help from the Chaozhou Huiguan, which — together with the Guang-Zhao Gongsuo, Jiaying Tongxianghui and Dapu Tongxianghui — joined in telegraphing both sides to avoid war.[67] There were limits to the resources of *huiguan* in such matters, however. Ineffectual in preventing war in this and other incidents, the Chaozhou Huiguan took steps to manage its effects. In 1918 Yunnan soldiers posted in Chaozhou extorted money, took hostages and imposed levies on shops and charitable institutions. Together with the Guang-Zhao Gongsuo, the Shanghai *huiguan* contacted the Chaozhou authorities, Guangzhou military commanders, the Provincial Military Governor and the Provincial Assembly. The results reveal the limits of governance in warlord times. The Military Governor of

64. The *tongxianghui* wrote on October 13; the Ningbo police responded by October 15.

65. NLTY, correspondence of October 8, 10, 16, 1921.

66. The examples in this section are from entries in the CHYB for the dates specified. Because Guangdong was particularly beset by military problems during this period, the Shanghai Guangdong *huiguan* were more preoccupied with military affairs than were *huiguan* representing areas with less warfare.

67. In 1917 two governments claiming constitutional legitimacy came into existence, one in Beijing and one in Guangzhou (established by Sun Yat-sen). Each claimed to be carrying out the Provisional Constitution of the Republic of China. To suppress the dissident movement in the south, Duan Qirui decided in July to attack Guangzhou via Hunan. Hunan militarists declared independence from Beijing in August, and fighting broke out. This began the first major war of the warlord period. In late December, southern allied forces responded to the northern military intrusion by entering Hunan in order to help the Hunanese expel the northerners. Within Guangdong there was tension between the forces of Long Jiguang, Guangdong Military Governor (and former supporter of Yuan Shikai), and Yunnan forces allied with Lu Rongting, Guangxi Military Governor (Guangxi was allied with Yunnan and Guizhou in tenuous support of the Guangzhou Military Government). See Ch'i Hsi-sheng, *Warlord Politics in China, 1916–1928* (Stanford, Calif., 1976), 18–27; Li Chien-nung, *The Political History of China, 1840–1928* (Stanford, Calif., 1956), 343–88.

Guangdong responded with alacrity to the *huiguan* appeal, but the representative he sent to rectify the situation in turn used his position to extort.

In August 1920 conflicts between Guangxi and Guangdong forces led to appeals to the Shanghai *huiguan* from Chen Jiongming, Commander of the Guangdong Army and newly appointed governor of the province. The *huiguan* complied, affirming its determination to aid Guangdong and keep out outside troops.[68] But even *tongxiang* troops proved to be a burden for the native place. In November soldiers from the Military Expense Bureau of the Chaoyang County Magistrate occupied the house of Guo Weiyi, a member of the local Chaozhou gentry, demanding twenty thousand yuan. Because Guo had already contributed to the Guangdong forces, he begged his Shanghai *tongxiang* for help. The *huiguan* telegraphed the Chaoyang Magistrate and Governor Chen, asking them to discipline the Shantou Military Expenditure Bureau. *Huiguan* directors Huang Shaoyan and Jiang Shaofeng went the next day to plead their case with Sun Yat-sen, Wu Tingfang and Tang Shaoyi, leaders of the southern government.[69]

As the strains of local militarization produced increasingly demoralized behavior, not only did *huiguan* influence with civilian officials reach its limits but the *huiguan* itself became an object of extortion. Having exhausted local resources by the beginning of 1924, the Chaozhou government targeted sojourning merchants (*lüwai shangmin*) for taxation. Although *huiguan* protests persuaded the Shantou Military Provision Board to cancel the tax, one county magistrate, Xie, refused to give up this source of funding and sent troops to extort funds from the families of sojourners.[70]

Such experiences both depleted *huiguan* resources and dampened en-

---

68. The *huiguan* meeting notes do not specify the sum contributed. There is no doubt, however, that the Shanghai merchants were sympathetic to Chen's espoused program of consolidating self-government in Guangdong province, which the merchants saw as a means of protecting the province from outside troops.

69. The effectiveness of this intervention is not clear. On December 4 the Chaozhou Huiguan received a response from Governor Chen, promising to rectify the matter, though Guo's complaints continued.

70. The Chaozhou Huiguan records neither provide the magistrate's full name nor identify the county in which he served. In this case, the *huiguan* could do little other than try to shame provincial officials into action by publicizing the situation in the newspapers, demanding the magistrate's dismissal and asserting that a Republican government should respect the people. Whereas the Chaozhou Huiguan dealt with the military exactions of Chen Jiongming's forces, the Guang-Zhao Gongsuo was more concerned with Sun Yat-sen's military government in Guangzhou. The Guang-Zhao Gongsuo supported the

thusiasm for Chen's government. In February 1925, when Chen sent representatives with bond subscriptions to Guangdong sojourners' associations in Shanghai, they were politely but unenthusiastically received.[71] Perhaps in response (or simply desperate from lack of pay and provisions), in May troops entered a Chaoyang village and tied up the village elders. This time *huiguan* intervention coincided with the arrival of a more humane military commander,[72] who removed the offending soldiers. In recognition of his care for the Chaozhou people, the Shanghai Chaozhou Huiguan sent him an inscribed honorary plaque.

Such incidents and unremitting pressure on its funds caused the Chaozhou Huiguan to organize a Shanghai Chaozhou People's Livelihood Consultative Committee (*Shanghai Chaozhou minsheng xiehui*) in 1926 to deal with military collections in the native place and with associated pressures on sojourning merchants. The committee went into immediate action to ward off the military requisitioning of merchant property in Chaozhou.

Minding Tongxiang *Business in Shanghai and Beyond.* While attempting to ameliorate the effects of war and ineffective government in the native place, sojourner associations continued to function as primary sources for the protection of sojourners' business, family and property interests. Both the Chaozhou Huiguan and the Ningbo Tongxianghui devoted considerable energy to managing the problems of their sojourning communities. The relative strength and centrality of Shanghai native-place institutions made Shanghai associations a resource for sojourners in areas beyond Shanghai, extending the management concerns of *huiguan* into distant areas where local *tong-*

Guangzhou Merchant's Association militia in defense against excessive taxation by the Military Government. In July 1924 the Guang-Zhao Gongsuo called all Shanghai Guangdong sojourners' associations together to discuss the militia organization and, in August, Sun's confiscation of the merchant militia's arms. See CHYB, July-August 1924. Unfortunately, the Chaozhou Huiguan meeting notes are brief, reporting little beyond the resolution to provide assistance to those involved in the militia and to their families, should they come to harm.

71. This reception may be compared with Sun Yat-sen's fund-raising activities among his Shanghai *tongxiang* in February 1923, when his Guangdong Military Collection Board, "noting the love of *tongxiang* for their native place," asked for loans from one hundred shops. The Chaozhou meeting notes comment that only twenty stores out of the group sent representatives to the meeting. CHYB, February 1923.

72. Probably Xu Zhongzhi. The meeting notes mention only family names, when names are given at all. CHYB, May 1923.

xiang resources were much weaker.[73] The associations intervened in four general areas: family matters, disputes affecting property and reputation, charitable activities and problems with taxation or troublesome bureaucracy.

The Ningbo Tongxianghui, less preoccupied than the Chaozhou Huiguan with crises in the native place, spent proportionally more time resolving the personal problems of its Shanghai community. The family matters dealt with by the *tongxianghui* often concerned runaway or kidnapped wives and daughters, cases which appear in the records as affronts to (male) property and reputation. The *tongxianghui* investigated each such case and contacted local officials, with striking success in securing the return of the woman or girl in question.[74]

The Chaozhou Huiguan also played a mediating role in family matters, often supplying a distinctly traditional form of justice. In a case from 1922, the daughter of a Chaozhou person named Guo Guangshan married Cai Zaiqian (also from Chaozhou) as his third wife. Within a year she hung herself, unable to bear her mother-in-law's cruelty. At Guo's appeal, the *huiguan* convened a meeting to publicize the daugh-

73. This is most obvious in the national Siming Gongsuo coffin-shipment network and in the work of the Chinese Society for Assistance to Women and Children discussed below, but it is evident also in the appeals even modest *huiguan* received from other places. The Chaozhou Huiguan aided fellow-provincials in nearby Nantong when their cemetery was threatened by construction plans of the Nantong gentry. It assisted the Suzhou Chaozhou Huiguan so regularly (funding or supervising building repairs, land rental, tenant relations, legal problems, debt collection, accounting procedures and housing construction) that the Suzhou association appears as an appendage. More distant Chaozhou sojourners received varied treatment. When a Chaozhou sojourner in Sichuan was arrested, the Chaozhou association combined forces with the Guang-Zhao Gongsuo to help. When the Hankou Chao-Jia Huiguan requested funds for renovations, it received only a lukewarm response. See CHYB, August 1914; CHYB, February-April, June, October 1917; CHYB, March, December 1918; CHYB, October-November 1921; CHYB, March, November 1923; CHYB, January, June 1924; CHYB, July 1925; CHYB, October 1926.

74. NLTY, correspondence of October 1, 5, 9, 12, 13, 22, 1921; November 1, 3, 12, 23, 24, 25, 26, 1921. In one case which suggests both the extent and the limits of Ningbo Tongxianghui abilities, a woman named Zhang Asu was abducted and taken to Changchun in the northeastern province of Jilin. The Ningbo Tongxianghui worked with the *Zhongguo furu jiujihui*, which had no Changchun branch and was finally unable to help. The Ningbo Tongxianghui, lacking institutional connections in Changchun, worked through a *tongxiang* banker there. It is striking that in this case the *tongxianghui* did not contact local officials. This was perhaps because with a limited sojourning community it had little influence with such distant local governments. In a similar case in Wuxi, the *tongxianghui* dealt with the Wuxi Magistrate as efficiently as it dealt with local Ningbo magistrates.

ter's ill treatment and to demand punishment of the Cai family. The *huiguan* also registered the case with the Mixed Court. Threatened by this action, the Cai family requested a *huiguan* settlement. Two *huiguan* directors investigated and pronounced that the Cai family should pay a penalty of five hundred yuan to build a tomb for the girl in Chaoyang. The *huiguan* also contacted the local Chaoyang county court, which ordered the head of the Cai family to bring his son before the Guo family formally to apologize.[75]

The Chaozhou Huiguan regularly intervened to help *tongxiang* collect debts, as well as to investigate and clarify shop-accounting procedures and disputes. In such instances, the *huiguan* freely demanded (and received for review) account books of *tongxiang* businesses. One such case fell into *huiguan* hands in 1917, when the Mixed Court of the French Concession asked the Chaozhou Huiguan to examine forty-seven account-books dating back to 1893 in order to unravel the profit-sharing records of the Lin family's enterprises. Shareholders in the largely family concern were not all family members and were divided among Shanghai and Shantou residents, which complicated the research. Four *huiguan* members met daily for two hours a day to review the accounts. After several weeks they determined that Lin Yunqiu owed the other shareholders seven thousand yuan each. This did not settle the problem: "The Lin brothers, uncle and nephew, each maintain their prickly temperaments. They have repeatedly been urged to resolve things, but their relations are not harmonious." When attempts at reconciliation failed, the *huiguan* threatened the Lins with court action. This worked, and the *huiguan* supervised the transfer of the funds and signing of documents, notifying the court that the matter was concluded.[76]

Although specialized Chaozhou trade associations existed in Shanghai in the early Republican era, the Chaozhou Huiguan frequently mediated business disputes and commercial negotiations for sojourners in Shanghai and in other cities. The consistent activity of native-place associations in such matters makes it clear that trade associations did not displace the customary conduct of business by native-place associations. For example, the Chaozhou Huiguan played a decisive role in the general conduct of the north–south sugar trade, which was divided among

75. CHYB, September-December 1922.
76. CHYB, February-March 1917; CHYB, May-June 1917. In this case the *huiguan* had persuasive power because several of the Lins had accounts at the *huiguan*. Toward the end of the case, the *huiguan* withdrew one family member's funds in order to pay legal fees. See also CHYB, October 1919; CHYB, May 1924.

Chaozhou and Fujian *bang*.[77] The records of the Ningbo Tongxianghui provide similar evidence of involvement in trade issues. In some commercial disputes the *tongxianghui* resolved matters; in others, the *tongxianghui* referred the matter to the *tongxiang* trade association. The records leave the impression of an overlapping network of organizations, any of which disputants might approach, depending on where their connections were stronger (as opposed to hard-and-fast functional differences between organizations).[78]

Coffins, Hospitals, Schools and New Public-Welfare Projects. Both *huiguan* and *tongxianghui* invested in a range of public welfare and charitable services, though in this area a division of labor between their areas of focus is more apparent. Coffin storage remained the preoccupation of *huiguan; tongxianghui,* in contrast, focused energy on services for the living, at times through innovative institutional arrangements.

As in the nineteenth century, coffin storage and shipment drew *huiguan* administrative energy and resources. When sojourning populations grew, so did the numbers of the sojourning dead (or "sojourning coffins," *lüchen*) and so did the complexity of the arrangements for storing and transporting coffins. Because warfare often obstructed transportation, unburied coffins accumulated in Shanghai, and burial grounds expanded.[79] A western guide to Shanghai of 1920 noted that the principal sights to be seen in the Xinzha (Sinza) district, north of Nanjing

77. In 1917 the *huiguan* dealt with an appeal of the Jiyitang, an association of sugar merchants in Beijing (likely a Chaozhou concern). A group of merchants in Shanghai had stopped following customary trade regulations established by agreement with Fujian sugar merchants in Shanghai. The Beijing association apparently hoped to use this pretext in order to break with the former trade arrangement. The Chaozhou Huiguan reprimanded the Beijing association, reasserting Chaozhou commitment to the customary rules (CHYB, April 1917).

78. NLTY, correspondence of October 4, 6, 13, 14, 17, 1921; November 6, 7, 9, 17, 18, 19, 20, 22, 29, 1921. Often these cases involved the distribution of dividends or profits among several partners or shareholders. Reading the accounts of family and business disputes in this period, one is struck by the frequency of cases involving women's property and of appeals to the association initiated by women who were independent property holders or shareholders. Widows often appealed to *huiguan* to defend holdings which were threatened by male relatives. This use of *huiguan* is striking and seems new in this period, though the paucity of records for the nineteenth century makes comparison difficult.

79. This expansion took place largely outside the foreign settlements; nonetheless, CHYB and SGY both record incidents of friction with municipal authorities over cemetery boundaries. See CHYB, May 1917; CHYB, December 1918; SGY, August 1915; SGY, February–March 1916; SGY, January-May 1919.

Road, were the monumental coffin repositories and graveyards established by different native-place associations. Indeed, the guidebook remarks, "as Shanghai has more Chinese from other parts of the empire than any other place, its mortuaries are the largest and most numerous."[80] Such facilities (referred to as *binshe, bingshe, binfang, chang* or *shanzhuang*) numbered at a minimum seventeen in 1910, twenty in 1914, thirty-three in 1919 and forty-one in 1931.[81]

These sojourner coffin repositories, which took up increasing amounts of space in the Chinese areas of the city, contained arbors, courts, trellises, kiosks, zigzag pathways, ornamental rocks and shrubs, elaborately carved wood and furniture, and calligraphic scrolls. Coffins were stored in locked rooms — with silk covers and plenty of space for the wealthy, and dormitory-bunk-type arrangements for the less fortunate.[82] By 1931 the sojourning Zhejiang community would have at least eleven cemeteries and coffin repositories, divided by Zhejiang locality. The Guangdong community in Shanghai would have eight.[83]

The Ningbo Siming Gongsuo built and managed an increasing number of coffin repositories over the course of the early Republican period. The 1920 guidebook describes the scale of one of these, located in Zhabei. "Of great vastness," its side walls extended for a quarter-mile. An immense hall on one end contained fourteen hundred coffins. More coffins filled rooms on either side of a long, arched passageway.[84] *Huiguan* officers coordinated a national system of shipment, storage and

80. C. E. Darwent, *Shanghai: A Handbook for Travellers and Residents* (Shanghai, 1920), 68–70.

81. These figures are from the 1910, 1914, and 1919 editions of *Shanghai zhinan* and from the *Shanghai shangye minglu*, section labeled *gongmu bingshe*. These figures are probably lower than the actual numbers, because smaller concerns went unlisted. The SXXZ (1918) list is very incomplete. Mortuary building in this period extended the borders of the city, because new mortuaries were generally built at the periphery for reasons of space and sanitation. *Huiguan* coffin repositories were thus a cause for the extension of roads and canals, to facilitate the transport of coffins. The meeting notes of both the Chaozhou and Ningbo *huiguan* are full of reports concerning the engineering and bureaucratic problems associated with road and canal extensions.

82. An unpublished Shanghai Museum survey of extant *huiguan* buildings (Shanghai bowuguan, 1984) provides an ironic commentary on these coffin accommodations. One entry, marked "Chong-Hai Tongxianghui Huiguan," mentions a room from a former repository which had been built to house four coffins. At the time of the museum survey the room was occupied by eight living Shanghai residents.

83. *Shanghai shangye minglu*, section labeled *gongmu bingshe*. In the case of Chaozhou burial grounds, burials were divided by county, with long ditches serving to divide coffins from different *xian*. Males and females were also separated. See CHYB, Fall–Winter 1920.

84. Darwent, *Shanghai*, 106.

burial of the coffins of Ningbo fellow-provincials.[85] As part of this complex enterprise, between 1918 and 1922 the Siming Gongsuo embarked on four major construction projects, including the building of north, south and Pudong mortuaries and a Siming Hospital, as well as the renovation of older east and west mortuaries. The scale and expense of Ningbo mortuary construction provide eloquent testimony to Ningbo wealth in Shanghai. For each project the *huiguan* established collection teams (*mujuan tuan*), which raised considerable sums from a large number of *tongxiang* in a short period of time. A 1918 funding drive produced five hundred twenty thousand yuan in all; for the north mortuary alone, two hundred three thousand yuan were collected in a single month.[86]

Smaller *huiguan* could not match the Ningbo coffin network but were nonetheless concerned with arrangements for the deceased, securing reasonable coffin-shipping rates from steamboat companies and printing obituaries. In 1922 the storm sewers in the overcrowded Chaozhou cemetery clogged, creating concern that the bones of the deceased were suffering from moisture. The three Chaozhou *bang* purchased a new site and embarked on complex arrangements to ship large numbers of old coffins back to Chaozhou, moving the rest to the new Chaozhou Shanzhuang in Zhabei (this entailed construction of a canal). The new coffin repository and *yin huiguan* were consecrated after geomantic consultation and three days of Daoist ritual, for which *tongxiang* enterprises contributed funds and sacrificial offerings. A representative from the Shantou Cunxin Benevolent Association assisted in these ceremonies.[87]

Although burial functions remained a primary and exclusive *huiguan* concern in the early Republican period, charity for the living (on the part of both *huiguan* and *tongxianghui*) expanded and became more modern. Native-place associations established new, functionally differentiated charitable institutions. The Siming Gongsuo operated a sepa-

85. SGY, May–June, 1915; SGY, December 1916; SGY, January 1919; SB, March 14, 1912; Hokari, "Shanghai Siming Gongsuo"; Hokari, "Kindai shanhai".

86. SGY, 1918–19; *Shanghai Siming Gongsuo si da jianzhu zhengxinlu* lists the contributors and contributions. See also SYZX, 298–99; Negishi, *Shanhai no girudo*, 32–34. Ōtani Kōtarō, who stressed the scale of these collections and their efficiency, calculated that the expense required for collecting this money was less than 6 percent of the total raised ("Shanhai ni okeru," 282, 285).

87. CHYB, 1922; CHYB, July 1923; CHYB, January 1924; CHYB, 1925; CHYB, April 1926. Chaozhou sojourners also supported a Lingnan Shanzhuang, together with the Guang-Zhao and Dapu sojourning communities.

rate clinic and hospital for needy *tongxiang*. It also provided housing for the poor. In 1920 the *gongsuo* established the Siming Number One Charitable School (*Siming diyi yiwu xuexiao*) and paid for student fees and supplies. The fact that the school was set up in the great hall of the *gongsuo* suggests increasing disuse of the former religious and ceremonial center.[88] The Chaozhou sojourning community supported a number of schools beginning in 1913 with a Chao-Hui Elementary School, which provided free education for *tongxiang* children. In 1917 the Chao-Hui Huiguan established the Chao-Hui Industrial School for poor boys in the International Settlement, on land purchased for more than two hundred thousand taels.[89] In 1926 the community initiated a Chaozhou hospital project.

These new charitable projects followed trends in social reorganization involving increasing functional specialization together with the appearance of "modern," frequently western-influenced institutional forms. At the same time, organization by native place was preserved. This was true even for institutions which did not formally limit their services to people of their native-place group. A glimpse into the functioning of a new, apparently "modern" and public-minded institution reinforces this impression. In the first year of the new republic, the Shaoxing, Ningbo and Huzhou *tongxianghui* (all Zhejiang institutions) joined forces and established the Chinese Society for Assistance to

88. SGY, March–April 1917; SGY, April 1918; SGY, November 1919. *Huiguan* still contributed to traditional Shanghai *shantang* in the Republican period, though they spent more on their own charitable enterprises. *Shanghai cishan tuanti baogaoce* (Statistical report of Shanghai charitable groups) (Shanghai, 1915) lists *huiguan* and trade groups among contributors to Shanghai benevolent associations. Although the Siming Gongsuo established the charitable school, the Ningbo Tongxianghui bore the larger share of educational work, operating eight schools by the 1920s (*Shanghai xian zhi* [Shanghai county gazetteer] [Shanghai, 1935; reprint Taiwan, 1975] [hereafter referred to as SXZ], juan 9); Kōtarō, "Shanhai ni okeru," 156; SGY, November 1919.

89. CHYB, November 1926; SXZ, juan 9; MCR for 1917, 211a–213a. The sum expended on the Chao-Hui School suggests the continued opium-based wealth of the Chao-Hui Huiguan. The Guang-Zhao Gongsuo established a Guang-Zhao middle school in 1913. There was also a Guangdong public school (*Guangdong gongxue*), established in 1912, with 509 students in 1926 (*Shanghai Guangdong gongxue shiwunianzhou jiniankan* [Fifteenth anniversary publication of the Shanghai Guangdong Public School] [Shanghai, 1926]); and also, by 1920, a Guangdong elementary school (*Guangdong xiaoxuexiao*) (see *Guangdong xiaoxuexiao jiniance* [Guangdong Elementary School yearbook] [Shanghai, 1920]). Systematic government development of a public-school system awaited the establishment of a municipal bureaucracy in Shanghai in 1927, after which various Chinese and foreign private schools came under the formal control of the Bureau of Education, which exercised some curricular control and supervision. See Henriot, *Shanghai*, 193–95.

Women and Children (*Zhongguo furu jiuji zonghui,* or CSAWC) to deal with the rise of kidnapping.[90] This was a public-spirited response to the growing social problems of the new republic. The association name also reflects the paradoxical embrace by native-place associations of institutions which announced themselves as Chinese, as opposed to representing local interests. But it is important to look beyond the name. Shaoxing Tongxianghui archives provide ample evidence of the efforts of this association on behalf of Shaoxing kidnapping victims, efforts which involved the CSAWC in activity over a wide geographic area; however, the CSAWC was not only less active on behalf of non-Zhejiang victims, it also harassed rival native-place groups under the guise of seizing potential kidnappers. In a revealing perversion of their "all-China" charitable function, Ningbo zealots associated with the CSAWC at times descended on Guangdong provincials en route home. Guangdong travelers with wives and children were questioned, dragged off boats, and separated from their belongings (which tended to disappear in the process).[91]

Other welfare activities included relief for the poor and return passage to the native place.[92] As in the nineteenth century, such benevolence reinforced structures of patronage and dependence that maintained community hierarchy. Despite the rhetoric of community, ordinary people could not gain admission into association buildings; without a letter of introduction they were stopped by guards at the gate. *Huiguan* opened to them only two or three times a year, on holidays when there were free opera performances and sometimes free noodles. Nor was charity automatic. For this, too, many associations required letters of introduction. Although some of my interviewees suggested that many people could not have requested assistance because they lacked necessary connections, others stressed that they would not have imagined asking because charity carried with it the brand of social disgrace. Some associations physically "branded" recipients to prevent cheats, marking the hands of those who received money or boat tickets.[93]

90. Chen Boxi, *Shanghai yishi daguan,* vol. 3, 9–10; Zhongguo furu jiuji zonghui, Archives, Shanghai Archives.

91. Shaoxing Tongxianghui, Archives, Shanghai Archives; CHYB, August 1914; CHYB, March 1917. The problem was resolved after the Chaozhou Huiguan and the Guang-Zhao Gongsuo negotiated with the CSAWC.

92. CHYB, October 1926.

93. Interviews with: Zhu Yongfang (Jiangsu native), Shanghai, October 1982; Yan Xianggu (Shaoxing native), Shanghai, February 25, 1983; Er Dingqi (Ningbo native), Shanghai, March 1983; Shen Yinxian (former Jiangxi Huiguan doorkeeper), Shanghai, October 1983; Tan Xiaochuang (Quanzhou [Fujian] native), Quanzhou, March 19, 1984;

Defending Tongxiang. In the early Republican period, as before, native-place associations mediated disputes among *tongxiang* and between *tongxiang* and outsiders and influenced the course of justice in both Chinese and foreign courts. Associations intervened in and out of court and routinely responded to court inquiries. Although both the Chaozhou Huiguan and Ningbo Tongxianghui preferred to settle cases outside the courts, they also used the threat of legal action to enforce compliance within their community and rarely hesitated before interfering in formal lawsuits. Courts continued to call on native-place associations to vouch for individuals under suspicion, as well as to check shop accounts.[94]

As might be expected, the recipients of this aid tended to be among the more influential members of the native-place community, or at least those with connections to association directors. In cases involving individuals' reputations the associations investigated charges and worked with authorities to clear the besmirched individual's name. When a Ningbo Tongxianghui leader was himself accused of a crime, the association both protested to the local Chinese authorities and printed letters declaring his innocence in the Shanghai newspapers.[95]

The refutation of criminal accusations could also become a matter of saving native-place face. As in the nineteenth century, Guangdong people in Shanghai continued to struggle to overcome affronts to their reputation, though the gestures of face-saving in the twentieth century were restrained compared with the Yang Yuelou case decades earlier. In 1914 a newspaper article contended that Chaozhou people operated *huahui* (a form of gambling considered to be particularly corrupting), to the detriment of honest Shanghai residents.[96] The matter was raised with some fanfare at a meeting of *huiguan* directors, who hyperbolically recorded their astonishment at the accusation. Incensed by the insult to the reputation of Chaozhou sojourners and determined to clear itself of all association with vice, the *huiguan* announced that it would conduct a public investigation and punish any wrongdoers. In this case the rhetoric of the meeting notes appears as part of the community public-

---

Lin Youren (former Chaozhou Huiguan janitor), Shanghai, November 13, 1983; Wang Shulin (former Chaozhou Huiguan watchman), Shanghai, November 13, 1983.

94. CHYB, January 1915; CHYB, June 1921; NLTY, 1921.

95. NLTY, correspondence of October 30, 1921; November 4, 14, 16, 20, 1921.

96. This accusation was probably well grounded, though *huahui* were clearly not the exclusive preserve of Chaozhou people. Contemporary guides to Shanghai also associate *huahui* with Ningbo people.

relations work taken on by the *huiguan*.[97] A decade later *huiguan* director and Chao-Hui Industrial School sponsor Guo Zibin was arrested and accused of opium trafficking. *Huiguan* records for this matter insist on Guo's respectability and reputation, though they do not entirely remove him from suspicion ("For a long time he has not been involved in the opium business"). Declaring the police action an affront to their native-place group, the *huiguan* protested to the Mixed Court.[98]

This description of native-place associations in the early Republican period has necessarily focused on three contexts affecting the direction of change: 1) ideological developments of the period, in particular the ways in which Shanghai residents conceived of "modern" organizations and criticized what was "traditional"; 2) the institutional apparatus of early Republican society and the interactions of "old" and new-style institutions; and 3) the political and economic effects of the disorders of the warlord period and the social imperatives these posed for the native-place associations which coped with such difficult times. The combination of ideological, institutional and material contexts illuminates the concurrent possibilities and processes of change which affected native-place organization and the particular paths of "modernization" (ideal and practical) charted by Shanghai society. In the early republican period, concepts of ideal organizational structure, the imperatives and proliferation of social organization and the burdens managed by native-place associations all reflect the perceived and experienced limitations of government and the efforts of urban residents to bridge evident gaps (between tradition and modernity, between state and society and between the city and the countryside). These struggles all represented issues for Chinese nationalism, as Chinese nationalism focused increasingly on the construction of a strong state. In the process, as the following chapter will show, the nationalist preoccupations of native-place associations were increasingly engaged with the envisionment and rectification of the Chinese state.

97. Although the meeting notes were not published for public consumption, they recorded resolutions which reflected wordings agreed upon for use in the *huiguan*'s public response to various issues. Most of the actual discussion, particularly in regard to sensitive issues, was not recorded.

98. The charge against Guo cannot be verified but is not unlikely. Chaozhou opium business was lively in this period (see Zheng Yingshi, "Chaoji yapianyan," 1–31; CHYB, February 1925). In this account the Chaozhou community refers to itself with the phrase *bang tuanti*, joining the more modern and public-sounding "*tuanti*" to the older (and more self-interested-sounding) "*bang*."

CHAPTER EIGHT

The Native Place and the State
Nationalism, State Building and
Public Maneuvering

Viewing the disarray of the polity in the warlord period, two great architects of the modern Chinese state, Sun Yat-sen and the young Mao Zedong, contemplated the task of nation building. As activists, not merely visionaries, they each sought building blocks in the social realities which surrounded them, through which to begin the construction of the new national unity they imagined. In a 1919 essay written a few months after the May Fourth Movement, Mao expressed great optimism in regard to the Chinese people's capacity for organizing and argued for the creation of a "great union of the popular masses" (*minzhong de da lianhe*), an overarching national union of the Chinese people.[1] The great union was to be built from what Mao referred to as "small popular unions" (*minzhong de xiao lianhe*). In response to his rhetorical question as to whether Chinese people had the motivation to build a "great union," Mao celebrated the political associations which had developed since the last years of the Qing and the formation of provincial assemblies, educational associations and chambers of commerce. Mao then noted three types of voluntary associations which could provide a basis for popular mobilization, worker unions, student

1. Mao Zedong, "Minzhong de da lianhe" (Great union of the popular masses), in *Mao Zedong ji* (Collected works of Mao) (Tokyo, 1974), 57–69 (originally published in serial format in *Xiangjiang pinglun* [Xiang River Review], July 21, July 28 and August 4, 1919). Stuart Schram translated this essay into English; my own translations are not always identical to his. See Schram, trans., Mao Zedong, "Minzhong de da lianhe" (Great alliance of the masses), *China Quarterly* 49 (January-March 1972):76–87. I am grateful to David Strand for calling my attention to Mao's early essay.

and educational associations of various sorts, in China and abroad, and *tongxianghui,* all of these associations made possible by "the recent opening up of government and of thinking" in the Republican period. Based on his observations in the May Fourth movement, Mao argued that political disorder and foreign oppression had begun to motivate such "small unions" to combine into "large unions." Among the several examples Mao provides of "large unions" were two sojourner associations in Shanghai, the Hunan Reconstruction Association (*Hunan shanhou xiehui*) and the Shandong Association (*Shandong xiehui*). He also noted a commercial federation of fifty-three groups in Shanghai, formed in that year. Mao based the "how-to" portion of his essay not on the western theorists he mentions in passing as possible sources of inspiration (whose works would not have led him to include native-place associations in his own theorizing) but on his personal observations of Chinese realities. As a result, student associations and (among native-place associations) Hunanese figure prominently in his essay.[2]

When Sun Yat-sen conceived the task of uniting China as a national community in his "Three People's Principles" lectures of 1924, he constructed a similar model for building what he referred to as "a large united body" (*da tuanti*). While lamenting that foreigners laughed at Chinese for being "no more than a sheet of loose sand" in regard to national consciousness, Sun stressed that Chinese society did provide other kinds of useful loyalties, family and native-place loyalties, which might be extended to the nation: "If we are to recover our lost nationalism, we need to have unified groups, a very large united body. An easy and effective way to create a large united body is to build on the foundation of small united groups, and the small units we can build upon in China are lineage groups and native-place groups. The native-place sentiment of the Chinese is very deep-rooted; it is especially easy to unite people from the same province, prefecture or village."[3]

That Mao and Sun recognized the strengths of native-place communities and imagined their integration into a larger national unity is not surprising—their writing was based on their observations of Chinese society and their pragmatism. Although their visions were compelling, their rhetoric was not particularly original—as we have seen from the

2. Mao, 62–68. Other "large unions" provided as examples by Mao were the national federations of education associations, chambers of commerce, the seventy-two Guangzhou guilds, the fifty-three Shanghai associations and student federations in large cities.

3. Sun Yat-sen, *Sanmin zhuyi* (The three principles of the people) (Shanghai, 1927), p. 77.

language of native-place associations involved in nationalist mobilization in the first years of the century. Their words were persuasive precisely because they embraced familiar Chinese social realities and because they repeated ideas of nation building based on popular notions, which constructed the idea of the nation by conceiving local social units as building blocks for broader coalitions.

This chapter begins by examining the role of native-place associations in the May Fourth Movement, as a means of demonstrating that Mao's and Sun's visions of broader nationalist coalitions based — in significant part — on native-place associations were not fanciful. Nonetheless, as the history of the May Fourth moment and its passing make clear, native-place associations united only in a piecemeal and ephemeral fashion and did not (given the loyalties that separated them and the tensions within the communities they encompassed) unite in an enduring fashion to create a new national "popular union." The last part of this chapter contrasts the political possibilities of native-place associations in the May Fourth moment — a period of feeble central government — with their situation during the Nanjing decade, under a reconstituted and considerably more powerful state.

New Culture, Old Habits: Native-Place Organization and the May Fourth Movement

Studies of the May Fourth Movement in Shanghai have not stressed native-place organization. It would be surprising if they did, because the period is celebrated for its themes of iconoclasm, enlightenment, nationalism and modernity, themes that are understood to constitute a rupture with old, "particularistic" social ties. The nationalism of the May Fourth Movement and the self-proclaimed cultural radicalism of the associated New Culture Movement have led sympathetic historians to seek out expressions of new cultural and political forms and to relegate cultural continuities to the status of remnants. In the process we have lost track of some of the social networks and organizations which underlay and facilitated the movement.[4]

4. This section appeared originally in slightly different form in Bryna Goodman, "New Culture, Old Habits: Native-Place Organization and the May Fourth Movement," in Wakeman and Yeh, *Shanghai Sojourners,* 76–107. For a critique of May Fourth historiography along these lines, see Arif Dirlik, "Ideology and Organization in the May Fourth

Although May Fourth historiography has not stressed the role played by native-place associations in providing organizational forms for the patriotic activities of students, businessmen and workers, some notice of several of the most influential of such organizations—the Ningbo, Shandong, and Guang-Zhao *huiguan,* associations of Zhejiang and Shandong students and seamen's associations of Ningbo and Guang-dong, for instance—has been unavoidable.[5] Moreover, the persistence and adaptability of native-place ties throughout this period and ex-tending into the 1920s have been a focus in other contexts—in studies of the Shanghai bourgeoisie by Marie-Claire Bergère and Susan Mann and, more recently, in Elizabeth Perry's study of Shanghai workers.[6] Nonetheless, neither the full role of native-place organizations nor the way in which these "traditionalistic" organizations changed over this period has been recognized.

Native-place organization underlay many of the social coalitions that staged the Shanghai student, commercial and worker strikes following the news of the May Fourth arrests of students in Beijing. Moreover, they formed the component elements of the more celebrated, more "modern" organizations of the period—those overarching organiza-tions formed along occupational lines, such as the Shanghai Student Union (*Shanghai xuesheng lianhehui*), the Shanghai General Chamber of Commerce and the more politically activist Shanghai Federation of Commercial Groups (*Shanghai shangye gongtuan lianhehui*).

Merchant mobilization preceded the surge of student activism in Shanghai and sustained the political mobilization that followed the news of the arrests of students in Beijing. Merchant-led native-place as-sociations organized for patriotic political activity early in 1919.[7] On February 6, 1919, seven associations jointly signed a telegram asking the Beijing government to resist Japanese demands and preserve China's sovereignty in the Paris conference. Four of the seven were the Guang-Zhao Gongsuo and the Zhejiang, Ningbo and Shaoxing *tongxianghui*.[8] Concern over the disruption of the North–South peace negotiations in

Movement: Some Problems in the Intellectual Historiography of the May Fourth Pe-riod," *Republican China* 12 (November 1986):5.

   5. See, for instance, Joseph Chen, *The May Fourth Movement in Shanghai* (Leiden, 1971).

   6. Bergère, *Golden Age,* 148–59; Jones, "The Ningbo *Pang*"; Perry, *Shanghai on Strike.*

   7. Chen, *May Fourth Movement,* 194–95.

   8. The other three associations were the Foreign-Goods Trade Association, the Export Trade Association, and the World Peace Federation (WYZS, 144–45).

Shanghai prompted the formation of the Shanghai Federation of Commercial Groups (*Shanghai shangye gongtuan lianhehui*) on March 3, 1919, in the Ningbo Tongxianghui building.[9] The federation of fifty-three organizations which Mao would soon point to as an example of a "large union" was composed primarily of native-place associations and trade associations. The native-place associations involved were:

Ningbo Lü Hu Tongxianghui

Guang-Zhao Gongsuo

Chao-Hui Huiguan

Zhaoqing Lü Hu Tongxianghui

Danyang Lü Hu Tongxianghui

Jianghuai Lü Hu Tongxianghui

Wenzhou Lü Hu Tongxianghui

Jiaying Lü Hu Tongxianghui

Guangdong Sojourners' Commercial Association

Dapu Lü Hu Tongxianghui

Sichuan Lü Hu Tongxianghui

Jiangning Lü Hu Tongxianghui

Jiangsu Pottery Trade Association

Shaoxing Lü Hu Tongxianghui

Zhejiang Lü Hu Tongxianghui

Pinghu Lü Hu Tongxianghui

Jie-Pu-Feng Huiguan

Hubei Lü Hu Tongxianghui

Jiangxi Lü Hu Tongxianghui

9. At the time, two separate governments, the Beijing government and the Guangzhou Military Government, both claimed legitimacy in China and were engaged in a north–south civil war. The purpose of the federation (comprising fifty-three groups) was to exert pressure to end the civil war, resume peace talks and bring a return of political stability needed to foster business.

This group was active throughout April, agitating both for peace within China and for a favorable resolution of the Qingdao question internationally.[10]

On May 6, the first day of activity after news of the May 4 events reached Shanghai, the Shandong *tongxianghui* sent a telegram to the Beijing government protesting the failure to protect Qingdao. The Federation of Commercial Groups urged businesses to participate in an urgent upcoming "Citizens' Meeting" (*Guomin dahui*) called to discuss the situation. On May 7 and 8 the Federation sent telegrams to the president, the cabinet, and the Ministry of Education in Beijing pressing for release of the students to calm the angered public. The Federation also urged the Chinese delegates at the Versailles conference to refuse to sign the treaty. Finally, the Federation served as a watchdog organization for the more reluctant Shanghai General Chamber of Commerce, admonishing it for its less radical stance.[11]

After meetings held by educators at Fudan University on May 6, and a preparatory meeting at the Jiangsu Provincial Education Association, a "Citizens' Meeting" was held on May 7 to protest the loss of Qingdao, the arrests of the students in Beijing, and the actions of the "traitorous" officials. This gathering brought together fifty-seven associations, including representatives of twenty-four schools (several of which, like the Shaoxing Sojourners' School, were sponsored by native-place associations) and eleven native-place associations. These included a number of associations not included in the Shanghai Federation of Commercial Groups, among them:

Henan Tongxianghui

Jiangbei Sojourners' Preservation Society

Anhui Consultative Committee

Sichuan Lü Hu Tongxianghui

Shandong Lü Hu Tongxianghui

Fujian Reconstruction Committee

Hunan Affairs Preservation Society

10. WYZS, 648–54. At the Paris Peace Conference the powers decided on April 30 to accept Japan's demands for the transfer of all previously German interests in Shandong and to reject China's position. Knowledge of this decision touched off the Beijing University student protests on May 4.

11. WYZS, 158, 171–73, 233.

Quan Zhe (All-Zhejiang) Lü Hu Tongxianghui

Hubei Reconstruction Committee

Shaoxing International Improvement Society

On May 9 merchants began to boycott Japanese goods. Newspapers announced the closings of numerous schools and businesses, to observe the fourth anniversary of China's acquiescence to Japan's Twenty-One Demands. Prominent among the private schools which closed were those of Guangdong, Ningbo and Huzhou sojourners in Shanghai. All of this activity occurred prior to the formal establishment of the Shanghai Student Union on May 11.[12]

In the next week, workers and artisans, organized by trade and native place, joined in the protest. One such group, the association of local Shanghai and sojourning Shaoxing construction workers (*Hu-Shao shuimuye gongsuo*) printed several notices in the *Shenbao*. In language both traditionally deferential and also borrowing terms from a more modern political vocabulary, the workers expressed their concern, outrage and determination to act: "All those with blood and breath are profoundly affected. We who belong to worker circles [*jie*] are also a sector of the citizenry. Witnessing the tragedies of national subjugation, past and present, is like being flayed. Accordingly, in conscience we advocate following the manner of the gentlemen of each *jie* who prepare meetings, and ourselves suggest a means of resistance. All of those in our trade belong to worker circles, but we should not, because of that, speak only of labor."[13] The workers announced that they would no longer use Japanese wood, metal, glass and cement. Declaring that, "for the purpose of saving the nation from extinction," all of the workers must obey the boycott and "exhibit the determination of citizens," the workers also enjoined their foremen and the owners of the enterprises which employed them to obey. In a notice printed in the *Shenbao* on May 17, the workers addressed the directors of their trade as follows:

In the importing of Japanese goods you could say our trade is at the top of the list . . . all of our people are united . . . and from this day on will not use Japanese goods. If you meet with foreign-organized engineering projects which have already arranged the purchase of Japanese goods, you must find a way not to use them. . . . If it is a Chinese project which has arranged to use Japanese materials, the materials should be immediately replaced

12. WYZS, 181–83, 186–88, 192, 195–96.
13. WYZS, 212.

with Chinese materials . . . and the proprietor of the enterprise should compensate [the relevant parties]. If the proprietor does not consent, there is only one suitable approach—we will stop work. Although there are many fools and dimwits among our workers, our blood is warm and honest. We will do our utmost hoping to protect our nation's territory.[14]

During these weeks of agitation, *tongxianghui* throughout the city called meetings to discuss the political situation and to send telegrams to the authorities in Beijing and in their native provinces. Networks of fellow-provincials served as conduits for the transmission of information. The telegrams of these groups to their fellow-provincials in Beijing and to the authorities of their native provinces fill the pages of the *Shenbao,* both as paid advertisements and as news items. Jiangsu fellow-provincials sojourning in other provinces similarly sent telegrams to the Shanghai General Chamber of Commerce to exert pressure and exhort the Chamber to defend China's national sovereignty. Native-place associations repeatedly printed declarations of their unity and resolve to boycott Japanese goods, urging all Chinese (in their own respective groups) to do the same.[15]

Shanghai students declared a strike on May 26 and began to encourage merchants and industrialists to maintain their boycott. When news arrived of the June 2 arrests of students in Beijing, the students began to exert pressure for a general strike. The strike was already under way when merchants announced their solidarity with the movement in a meeting on June 5 which included students, educational leaders, leaders of native-place and trade associations and journalists. In this meeting the merchant leaders of native-place associations spoke out in support of and to coordinate actions already taken by their constituencies. Among the impassioned speakers identified as belonging to "merchant circles" was Cao Muguan, school principal and also a delegate of the Shaoxing Tongxianghui. Cao announced that Shaoxing merchants had met and resolved to strike in unity, demanding the punishment of the traitorous officials, the recovery of citizens' rights, and the release of the students. Cao was followed by Guang-Zhao Gongsuo delegate Zhou Xisan, who expressed similar resolutions. These were echoed by the Jiangning Huiguan representative as well as by Chen Liangyu, who represented both the Ningbo Tongxianghui and the Tobacco and Wine

14. WYZS, 226–27.
15. SB, May 1919.

Federation.[16] At a second meeting, of "student, commercial, industrial, and newspaper circles" held at the General Chamber on June 7, participants resolved to maintain the strike until the "national traitors" Cao Rulin, Lu Zongyu and Zhang Zongxiang had been punished and dismissed. Among the merchants, the three *bang* of Shandong, Ningbo and Guangdong were reportedly the most determined.[17]

Native-place networks were vital links in the extraordinary merging of student, business and worker concerns and in the formation of the "united front" that characterized this period of the movement. In the organization of strike activity, native-place associations performed a number of critical tasks, disseminating information, organizing political activity and maintaining order. On the day of the strike announcement, the Ningbo Tongxianghui met and published a manifesto attesting to the fervent patriotism of Ningbo fellow-provincials and urging unified Ningbo action.[18] The manifesto also stressed the need to maintain order, resolve disputes, and to refrain from incidents involving foreigners. The Siming Gongsuo sent the following telegram to the Beijing government, expressing concern for public order: "Shanghai's commercial, student and worker circles indignantly rise in fervor and strike. People's hearts beat wildly; danger extreme. If situation not immediately resolved, fear social structure will collapse. Humbly ask release students in prison. Dismiss three officials to ease people's indignation and stabilize situation. Presented on behalf of Shanghai Siming Gongsuo's full body of 400,000 people."[19]

The *huiguan* also disseminated public notices calling for order in its sojourner community: "Urgent Announcement of the Shanghai Siming Gongsuo: Compatriots, you have patriotically stopped work. In your actions be civilized. Shanghai's population is great and order is critical. If we can be organized and unified we can show our spirit more strongly. On no account assemble in the streets. On no account take part in demonstrations. If you encounter foreigners be calm. Maintain mutual respect and they will respect us. We pray everyone will pay attention and be careful."[20] The Guang-Zhao Gongsuo similarly sent telegrams to the Beijing government exhorting the officials to listen to public opinion. On June 7 the Guang-Zhao Gongsuo published an appeal

16. WYZS, 300–5. Chen was also a director of the Siming Gongsuo.
17. WYZS, 324–25.
18. SB, June 6, 1919.
19. SGY, June 1919.
20. SGY, June 1919.

to fellow-provincials to maintain public order and avoid fights with foreigners.[21]

As in the boycott of 1905, native-place organizations — more than the new Chambers of Commerce — spread the merchant strike to other areas and enforced the boycott in Shanghai. The Ningbo Chamber of Commerce joined the strike after it received a telegram from the Shanghai Ningbo Tongxianghui. Once the Ningbo strike went into effect, the Ningbo Chamber and the Ningbo labor union, in addition to a variety of other Ningbo associations, kept in close contact with the Shanghai Ningbo Tongxianghui, requesting news and direction. *Huiguan* and *tongxianghui* investigated individuals suspected of business with Japanese and held public meetings to proclaim individuals guilty of traitorous behavior and barred from the native-place community. One such offender, Lu Zongyu, was denounced by the Lü Hu Haichang (Haining) Gongsuo, which published announcements that Lu would no longer be recognized as a Haining *tongxiang*.[22]

Communication between the Shanghai Chamber of Commerce and Shanghai businesses went through the intermediary of native-place associations.[23] Although the Chamber did appeal to these organizations, it was unable to exert its will upon them. When, after a secret meeting with the Chinese authorities, the Chamber urged *tongxianghui* on June 10 to counsel their communities to stop the strike, it was rebuffed. Guangdong, Ningbo and Shandong shopkeepers met with their native-place groups and repudiated the Chamber's action. Ningbo Tongxianghui directors printed a notice in the *Shenbao* stating that they had rejected the Chamber's appeal, stressing that Ningbo merchants would not resume business. Shandong merchants published a similar notice.[24]

When the Beijing government finally responded to the strike demands and dismissed the "national traitors," powerful native-place asso-

21. SB, June 7, 1919.
22. For example, see SB, June 9, 1919; SB, June 10, 1919; SB, June 12, 1919; SB, June 14, 1919; WYZS, 391.
23. Many Chamber of Commerce leaders were also directors of their native-place associations. Yu Xiaqing at the time was a director of the Chamber, a Siming Gongsuo director, and a leader of the Shanghai Federation of Commercial Groups. When tension developed between the conservative Chamber and the radical Federation, Yu responded by ceremonially resigning from all three roles. He did not resign, however, as director of the Ningbo Tongxianghui. See SB, June 15, 1919.
24. A heated meeting of the Commercial Federation was called in response to the action of the Chamber and held at the Shaoxing Tongxianghui. See WYZS, 389–91; SB, June 10, 1919; SB, June 11, 1919.

ciations announced the decision to end the strike. The Ningbo Tong-xianghui exhorted Ningbo people to return to work but to use only Chinese products. It also sent a telegram to Ningbo residents in Han-kou advising them to return to work, saying, "the Ningbo market in Shanghai has reopened" (*Hu Yongshi kai*).[25] These instances suggest that native-place *bang,* rather than the Chamber or the Commercial Federation or any other overarching organization were crucial in determining the opening and closing of businesses. This was particularly evident in cities in which the general strike was partial. In Hankou, for instance, the businesses of sojourning Guangdong and Ningbo merchants closed, initiating the strike, but many other shops remained open.[26]

Native-place associations exerted themselves on behalf of arrested *tongxiang.* The Shanghai Sojourning Anhui Consultative Committee expressed concern over the arrest of Chen Duxiu and contacted the Beijing Anhui *huiguan* to help secure his release. The Shanghai Fujian Reconstruction Committee worked for the release of arrested Fuji-anese students.[27]

In the activities of native-place associations in the May Fourth period, we see the articulation of "modern" values and practices that have been attributed, in their origins, to May Fourth student activism. These included the organization of workers for educational and patriotic purposes. For example, at the end of April or during the first days of May, the Jiangbei Sojourners' Preservation Society (*Jiangbei lü Hu weichihui*) established a lecture hall in Zhabei, "to organize Jiangbei manual and commercial workers to attend educational classes in their leisure time." Lectures were designed to enlighten and improve the morality of the many "unlearned country bumpkins" in the Jiangbei (Subei) community, as well as to encourage patriotism, lawfulness and sanitation.[28] If such activities expressed an old-fashioned paternalism, both the mechanism (organized classes for workers) and the content (patriotism and sanitation) were new.

It is also critical to note the strategic uses of traditional practices in the organization of modern political activity. Though less important in this period than in the late nineteenth century, *huiguan* still staged pop-

25. The Chinese phrase is striking. The *tongxianghui* could have simply said that Shanghai business had resumed. Clearly, Ningbo people saw it as *their* market, simply located in Shanghai. See SB, June 13, 1919.
26. SB, June 15, 1919.
27. SB, June 16, 1919; SB, June 20, 1919; SB, June 21, 1919; SB, June 24, 1919.
28. SB, May 5, 1919.

ular ritual events for the larger native-place community. Such events provided propaganda opportunities. Although most native-place associations held meetings to discuss the political situation and write telegrams, some, like the Jiangyin Huiguan, met political crises with religious ceremonies. Gathered together for a feast Jiangyin *tongxiang* prayed before the altar of Guandi to ask for his assistance and protection and for strength and unity to "wipe away China's shame" in a time of national danger. Other traditional practices could be put to similar uses. On the occasion of a *yulanpen* gathering in the summer of 1919 the Siming Gongsuo printed and distributed special notices urging the use of national products.[29]

The events of 1919, which reveal not only the appearance of new groups but also their combination into larger federations, verify that — at least on a temporary basis — native-place associations could be integrated as constituent elements in overarching nationalist bodies. The rhetoric of native-place sentiment vigorously asserted the contribution of native-place associations to nationalism and bears examination.

The rhetoric of native-place associations throughout the Republican period spoke to the urgent need for existing social organizations (and native-place associations specifically) to form a foundation for nationalist mobilization. The Ningbo Tongxianghui (which organized lectures on the benefits of native-place organization and the promotion of national products) and other associations, like the Suzhou Tongxianghui, used slogans such as "In unity against the outside, love the native place, love the country" (*yizhi duiwai aixiang aiguo*) and "Business and enterprises must unite in groups. The nation is but one big group [*da tuanti*] encompassing and uniting many small groups [*xiao tuanti*]. For the wealth and strength of the country, it is imperative to unite in groups."[30] *Tongxianghui* throughout the Republican era presented themselves as instruments of nationalist mobilization:

There is not a day we do not suffer the incursions of economic imperialism. If we do not intensively organize and strengthen our spirit of unity, we will not avoid defeat and elimination. [We must] assemble many people with similar language and customs who can conform to and communicate with

29. SB, June 11, 1919. This article, entitled, "Jiangyin Tongxiang Do Things in an Unusual Way," concludes with a combination of May Fourth secularism and pragmatism: "Although this type of activity borders on the superstitious, it may also be seen as a sincere expression of will." SGY, July 1919.

30. SB, May 25, 1919; SB, May 26, 1919. The Suzhou Tongxianghui was formed in the midst of May Fourth agitation.

each other and together organize in a group to plan for public welfare. This provides a basis for struggles against the outside and also gives the struggle for internal reform something to rely on. It also helps to prevent oppression and insults. This is the essential idea behind *tongxianghui*.[31]

and:

[In order to establish] nationalism it is necessary to have organizations. But seeking strong groups, we must first mutually and effectively unite. Our people's ability to organize is weak. But "love one's home, love one's native place" sentiment is very strong. For instance [this is expressed in] *huiguan* and *tongxianghui*. Using this as a base, it is possible for our people to go from the small to the great and from weakness to strength. Nationalism becomes gradually possible. Our Henan Tongxianghui serves people of all *jie*, represents a large population and moreover has a long history.[32]

Such statements illuminate a paradox: universal identity (nationalism) depended on the further articulation of specific identity. Public spirit was to be developed by grouping people by native place, and the mobilization of the native-place group was to serve the nation. In this fashion native-place strength contributed to national strength.[33] By means of synecdoche, in a fashion similar to that apparent in *Jiangsu* magazine much earlier, the native-place group stood for the national community. In the process, abstract ties were personalized and concretized through local relationships and community.

In any event, throughout the May Fourth period in Shanghai, division of the Shanghai populace into native-place groups proved no obstacle to jointly organized expressions of nationalism. Despite the increasing geographic subdivision of provincial native-place communities, different associations routinely combined and worked cooperatively. Many small groups (*xiao tuanti*) were perceived as the organic constituents of the large group (*da tuanti*), the nation.[34] In the May Fourth

31. *Chaozhou lü Hu tongxianghui niankan* (Annual of the Association of Chaozhou Sojourners in Shanghai) (Shanghai, 1934), Introduction.
32. *Henan lü Hu tongxianghui gongzuo baogao* (Report on the work of the Association of Henan Sojourners in Shanghai) (Shanghai, 1936), 1–3.
33. The practice of native-place organizations makes clear that native-place sentiment by itself was not sufficient for nationalism but that organization was critical, that people needed to be organized through membership in native place-associations which could mobilize and coordinate patriotic action.
34. See SB, May 25, 1919; SB, May 26, 1919. Such slogans from the May Fourth period reechoed throughout the 1920s, 1930s and even into the 1940s. A special commemorative issue of a Jiangsu sojourners' publication explained *tongxianghui* as follows: "All these

Movement in Shanghai, native-place groups clearly acted as units for the organization, expression and dissemination of nationalist ideology. Without these groups, it is difficult to imagine how such effective social mobilization could have occurred.[35]

At the same time, the social mobilization of the May Fourth movement reveals a changing institutional context. In regard to native-place associations, *tongxianghui* — constructed as "modern" Republican institutions — had emerged as important political actors, with agendas different from those of the older *huiguan*. The external institutional context was changing as well, in a manner which would affect the political role of these new native-place associations in Chinese society. Although in May 1919 native-place associations were vital political actors, their actions took place in the context of (and in interaction with) a plethora of new occupationally and functionally differentiated organizations — student, worker, commercial and political associations.

One such new organization was the Shanghai Federation of Street Unions (*Shanghai ge malu shangjie lianhehui,* or SFSU), formed in the immediate post–May Fourth period by a broader spectrum of shopkeepers and merchants than the elite Chamber of Commerce. The radical SFSU developed to protest an increased tax levy in the International Settlement. Using the slogan "no taxation without representation," activists used a tax strike to press (this time with ultimate success) for a Chinese Advisory Board to the Municipal Council. The formidable organizational apparatus of the Federation of Street Unions represented merchants from forty streets in the International Settlement (from as many as ten thousand shops), bringing together a newly politically mobilized middle bourgeoisie more forcefully and with better coordination

various *bangpai* divisions are organizational units for individuals, and each group forms a circle of life. The different circles knit together to form an extremely long interlocking mechanism" (*Dongting dongshan lü Hu tongxianghui sanshizhou jinian tekan* [Thirty-year commemorative issue of the Dongting Dongshan Tongxianghui] [Shanghai, 1944], Introduction).

35. In "The Historian's Use of Nationalism and Vice Versa" (in *The South and Sectional Conflict* [Baton Rouge, 1968], 34–84), David Potter offers an important critique of the historiographical tendency to objectify nationalism as generically different from "traditional" forms of group loyalties. He argues, instead, that the emotional attachment or group loyalty of nationalism may be better understood as continuous with, strengthened by, even deriving from other loyalties (pp. 37–40, 55, 57). The history of native-place sentiment in Shanghai illustrates this, suggesting a continuum of concentric circles of native-place identities which permitted individuals to identify first with their counties, prefectures, provinces and so on, up to the unit of the nation. I am grateful to Lyman Van Slyke for calling my attention to Potter's work.

than was possible through either the more elite Chamber of Commerce or the disparate native-place associations.

One May Fourth activist who was involved in the tax strike and struggle for Chinese representation and who would become SFSU president in 1921 was an outspoken member of the sojourning Guangdong community. This was Tang Jiezhi, a U.S.-educated physician with interests in two Shanghai trading companies, who also edited the *Shanghai Journal of Commerce* (*Shanghai shangbao*). In 1918, together with Wen Zongyao, Tang had engaged in a power struggle with more conservative elements of the Guang-Zhao Gongsuo and had succeeded in reorienting the *huiguan* in a more politically radical direction. After this, Tang effectively combined use of his power base in the Guangdong community with his leadership of the SFSU in struggles with both the Municipal Council and the more politically conservative Chamber of Commerce. Tang's tactics suggest the continuing utility of native-place organization in this period, together with a characteristic tendency of activists to work through multiple organizational forms to achieve multiple points of leverage.[36]

Nonetheless, in a very short period, the new associational forms— broadly based merchant associations like the Federation of Street Unions, labor organizations and political parties, would develop a dynamism and centrality in political life and social mobilization that would displace, though not eliminate, native-place associations. This had clearly begun by the May Thirtieth Movement of 1925. Although historical materials from the May Thirtieth Movement do feature *huiguan* and *tongxianghui* performing functions similar to those they performed in 1919, they appear less prominent and the traces of their activity are overshadowed by the activities of workers' unions and the Communist

36. When the Municipal Council approved the Advisory Board, the SFSU was unable to promptly resolve the issue of how Chinese advisors would be selected. The Municipal Council turned to the Chamber of Commerce, which solicited major native-place and trade associations for nominees. When solicited, Guang-Zhao Gongsuo activists used the opportunity to rebuke Chamber involvement in the matter, arguing that the *gongsuo* represented only one sector of the urban population, whereas the Advisory Board should be selected by the full body of residents. (The Ningbo Tongxianghui responded in similar fashion.) Tang then used the *gongsuo* as a pressure group and, together with activists in the Ningbo Tongxianghui, pushed for the establishment of a Chinese Ratepayers' Association to counterbalance the power of the foreign Ratepayers' Association in the city. The new Chinese Ratepayers' Association then selected the Advisory Board, inaugurated in 1921. See GZGYB, June 6, 1920; GZGYB, September 19, 1920; PRO, FO 228.3291, 1921; *Shanghai gonggong zujie shigao* (Draft history of the International Settlement of Shanghai) (Shanghai, 1980), 539. See also Fewsmith, *Party, State and Local Elites,* 57–59.

party. The impression is that history has edged native-place associations at last onto the margins of the political stage.[37]

This ultimately did not happen, at least not for long, because the conditions which fueled labor and party organization were cut short in 1927. Nonetheless, crucial in the nascent organizational trend toward occupationally and functionally differentiated civic associations—a trend which might have resulted in the fading of native-place associations if it had not been stunted by the formation of the Nanjing government in 1927—was the increasing political radicalization and mobilization of Shanghai workers. It is therefore important to conclude this discussion of May Fourth mobilization in Shanghai by considering class articulation within the native-place community.

Chapter 7 considered divisions within the native-place community according to *jie,* or circles of interest, occupation, age or class. The birth of *tongxianghui,* at least initially, involved the formation of new, more broadly based groups with more open structures of governance. Divisions by *jie* within the native-place community reflect a certain consciousness of the need to organize according to one's interests rather than to submit to being organized by native-place elites. It is therefore critical to consider the extent to which overarching native-place community existed in this period and whether class tensions precluded identity with and cooperation within the larger group.

It is possible to speak of the larger native-place community as an idea which could be evoked effectively for specific purposes throughout the early Republican period. Underlying this idea, as shown in Chapter 7, in their charitable and educational functions *huiguan* and *tongxianghui*

---

37. The May 30 protests followed the shooting of the Chinese worker, Gu Zheng-hong, by Japanese foremen at one of the Naigai Wata Japanese factories on May 15. Richard Rigby (*The May 30th Movement: Events and Themes* [Canberra, 1980]) provides an excellent account. See also Nicholas Clifford, *Shanghai, 1925: Urban Nationalism and the Defense of Foreign Privilege,* Michigan Papers in Chinese Studies, no. 37 (Ann Arbor, Mich., 1980); Ren Jianshu and Zhang Quan, *Wusa yundong jianshi* (Short history of the May Thirtieth Movement) (Shanghai, 1985); Li Jianmin, *Wusa can'an hou de fanying yundong* (The anti-British movement after the May Thirtieth tragedy) (Taipei, 1986). On the role of native-place associations in the May Thirtieth Movement, see Goodman, "The Native Place and the City," chap. 5. The distinguishing feature of the May Thirtieth Movement of 1925, compared with the May Fourth Movement of 1919, was the appearance of a militant labor movement, organized through both the Guomindang and the Communist party. While party involvement did not preclude grass-roots organization of Shanghai workers, students and merchants through their native-place associations, native-place associations may no longer be described as occupying a portion of the center stage. The major document collection on the May Fourth movement is WYS.

served larger communities beyond their predominantly merchant memberships. *Huiguan* also continued ritually to serve a large religious community, though the numbers of sojourners now rendered the sorts of community gatherings that took place in the nineteenth century impossible. The presence of *huiguan* resources to some extent ensured that their *tongxiang* would have an interest in maintaining some degree of community and identity, in order to partake of *huiguan* services and support.

The egalitarian language of native-place sentiment, by which both wealthy and poor could share equally in the *tongxiang* bond as fellow-provincials, could be exploited by both high and low. When dissenting groups came to demand a piece of *huiguan* property, they could argue that it was, in effect, already their own, because it was *tongxiang* property. *Huiguan* leaders were then forced to maintain the rhetoric of brotherhood and community or breach it by pointing out — as did Chaozhou Huiguan directors in 1926 when confronted by demanding students — that it was in fact their property, not the property of the *tongxiang*.[38] In general, *huiguan* leaders chose to preserve the rhetoric of community in order to gain the allegiance of the community. For this reason *huiguan* came to modify their practices as the new organizational form of the *tongxianghui* gained legitimacy. *Huiguan*, as well as *tongxianghui*, adopted public constitutions, formal voting procedures, more representative assembly, and at least the appearance of openness and more democratic rule.

Evidence that the larger community could in fact be mobilized by the old institutions may be found in *huiguan* ability to tap the larger community for funds. In the course of mortuary and hospital construction in 1918, for example, the Siming Gongsuo engraved the names of contributors on stone and wood (more durable carvings for more generous contributors). It counted 320 contributors of more than 50 yuan; 17,320 contributors of 1–50 yuan; and 2,770 contributors of "a few coins." A total of 20,470 people "fervently contributed out of love for their native place." Although far shy of the community of four hundred thousand claimed by the *huiguan* in the May Fourth agitation of the next year, it is nonetheless an impressive number.[39]

38. CHYB, 1926.

39. SGY, 1918–19. This pool was increased in January 1919, when the *huiguan* brought together leaders of "each Ningbo trade and *bang*" (more than one hundred representatives in all) to the *gongsuo* to increase the effectiveness of money-raising efforts. In this meeting it was decided that all those "in commercial circles" would deduct pay from all of their *tongxiang* workers, five fen from each yuan of salary for one month.

At the end of May 1919, when the French Consul asked the *huiguan* to move a Ningbo children's burial ground, the *huiguan* called a public meeting and vowed to use the full strength of the Ningbo community to oppose the French. Through this manifestation of mass unity (or at least the persuasiveness of the threat), the Siming Gongsuo secured from the French a promise to preserve the integrity of their graveyard in perpetuity.[40] Despite such demonstrations of the existence of effective community in certain contexts, it is evident that by the May Fourth period there was also considerable tension within native-place communities, particularly between workers and their *tongxiang* employers.[41] Although native-place associations still occasionally resolved strikes and labor disputes, by this time this was more the exception than the rule. French authorities lamented in 1921 that whereas worker-employer negotiations through the intermediary of "guilds" had been possible in the past, those days had given way to a preference for intimidation and direct action.[42]

One example of this new preference for intimidation and even violence may be found in the strike of Ningbo and Guangdong seamen and stokers which followed the May Fourth commercial strike announced on June 5, 1919. In a reminiscence of the strike, a worker who was the leader of the Association of Ningbo Seamen (Jun'an She) describes how workers heard the slogans of the May Fourth period and "could not stifle [their] patriotic sentiment." Feeling the seamen should support the movement, this man and other organizers propagandized their coworkers, with the result that more than five thousand workers struck and stopped seagoing traffic.[43]

Concerned by the crippling economic effects of the work stoppage, Ningbo *huiguan* directors negotiated with the strikers. The striking Ningbo seamen, in a group of more than one thousand, agreed to meet at the Siming Gongsuo to discuss their actions. This much was possible. But when *huiguan* director Fang Jiaobo (also a leader of the Chamber of Commerce) began to lecture the seamen on their duty to return to work, his *tongxiang* refused to listen. A large worker jumped behind Fang, grabbed his collar from behind and ripped his shirt. The other

40. SGY, 1919.

41. This tension might be compared to that which developed earlier (in the nineteenth century) between rich and poor branches of south China lineages. See Frederic Wakeman, *Strangers at the Gate* (Berkeley, Calif., 1966), 112–15.

42. AMRE, Série Asie, Chine 31, Shanghai, 1918–22, Report of June 13, 1921.

43. WYZS, 343–44, 358.

seamen applauded (according to several accounts) and yelled, "Beat him, beat him." Fang fled and the workers declared a victory. Here we have an obvious case of the failure of greater *tongxiang* community and evidence of independent class organization and solidarity among the *tongxiang* worker *jie*.

Nationalism played an important role in the workers' radicalism in this instance. Armed with the righteousness of nationalism, workers felt justified in their rebellion against those at the pinnacle of the *tongxiang* occupational hierarchy. Nationalism also lubricated the coordination of the separate native-place organizations of Ningbo and Guangdong seamen.[44] This incident parallels actions taken by the Shanghai and Shaoxing construction workers' association as they expressed their determination to enforce the anti-Japanese boycott. Worker subdivision into Shanghai and Shaoxing *bang* did not prevent joint organization. Like the Ningbo seamen, the construction workers were radicalized by their organized assertion of nationalism, threatening to strike if their foremen and the chiefs of the enterprises which employed them did not adhere to the boycott.

Other evidence suggests a weakening of the vertical native-place ties which might bind together a greater *tongxiang* community. In this period, for the first time, *huiguan* and *tongxianghui* contemplated and in some cases instituted badges of membership.[45] This practice would have been unnecessary in the nineteenth century, when the relevant communities were not only smaller but also better ordered by structures of deference. At that earlier time, unlike the May Fourth period, artificial means were not necessary to decide which *tongxiang* could enter the building and which would do best to remain outside.

While suggesting these important tensions in the larger native-place community, research on native-place associations in the May Fourth period makes two points clear. We cannot understand social organization and social movements in the early Republican period without recognizing the crucial role of native-place associations, old and new. Nonetheless, we cannot understand native-place communities without recognizing the emergence of class ties and consciousness. Although native-place organizations persisted and indeed grew in numbers in this period, their "particularism" did not preclude integration into larger wholes. Just as native-place organization did not subvert nationalism, native-place ties

44. WYZS, 358–61; SGY, June, 1919; SGY, July, 1919.
45. SGY, April 1920.

complicated but did not preclude class consciousness. A study of the growth of native-place associations in the May Fourth period suggests the possible ironies of an unexpected fit: how apparent anachronisms — *huiguan* and *tongxianghui* — accommodated themselves to (and even promoted) the community-transcending imperatives of national mobilization and class formation.

Native-Place Associations in the Nanjing Decade

The contrast between the "associational bloom" of the May Fourth period and the constricted associational possibilities of the Nanjing decade (1927–1937) provides an opportunity to view native-place associations in a political context which differed radically from prior periods, periods in which native-place associations had championed the cause of the "nation" in the absence of a strong state. Chiang Kai-shek's 1927 purge, which crushed both the Shanghai labor movement and, for the moment, the Communist party, severely constrained the development of the mass-based political associations which had begun, by the time of the May Thirtieth movement, to displace native-place associations as information conduits and organizational networks for social mobilization. Other important public associations — like the Chamber of Commerce — would be quickly brought under the control of the new state.[46]

In this altered context, which irrevocably transformed associational life, native-place associations experienced somewhat of a public reemergence. The "public reemergence" of native-place associations in the Nanjing decade was modest and limited by constraints imposed by the new state apparatus. Within these constraints, native-place associations emerged in the 1930s as popular public associations, important both for the expression of public opinion and for social mobilization. They also appeared as prominent actors in the narrowing zone of public criticism of a government viewed as failing in its duty to the people, preserving,

46. See Kōhama Masuko, "Nankin kokumin seifu ka ni okeru Shanhai burujoa dantai no saihen ni tsuite" (The reorganization of bourgeois groups in Shanghai under the Nanjing Nationalist government), *Chikai ni arite* 13 (May 1988):33–51.

in transformed fashion, their past role as institutions which mediated between state and society.

An additional critical development further transformed the nature of native-place associations in the Nanjing period. This was the rise of the Shanghai gangs. Whereas underground organizations were not unrelated to native-place associations in the past, they had not since the Small Sword Uprising been so important in Shanghai society, nor had they altered the basic power hierarchy within sojourner associations. The historical possibilities of the 1930s were, of course, very different from those of the mid-nineteenth century. Just as the *tongxianghui* of the 1930s were new and highly "modern" native-place associations, the secret societies with which they would interact had been transformed into highly "modern" gangs.[47] A sense of the vastly altered context — prerequisite to an outline of the activities of native-place associations in the Nanjing decade and their relations to the new state — may be conveyed by a sketch of a new native-place association founded in the 1930s and characteristic of — indeed defining — the new era.

The Pudong Tongxianghui: Product of a New Era. On November 21, 1936, at 10:00 A.M., celebrants inaugurated the new building of the Shanghai Pudong Tongxianghui on Avenue Edward VII (now Yenan Road) in the International Settlement. It was a grand eight-story edifice, designed to overshadow all of the buildings in the neighborhood (see Figure 9). After the formal ceremony, during which the city notables Yu Xiaqing and Wang Xiaolai — neither of them from Pudong — gave speeches before an overflowing crowd, entertainment continued until 3:00 A.M. the next day. In all, more than twenty thousand guests paid their respects to the new building. The list of those who sent ceremonial calligraphic scrolls reads like a who's who of the political and economic elite — among them H. H. Kung, Zhang Qun, Zhang Jia'ao, Pan Gongzhan, Lin Sen and Sun Fo. Photographs of the event show visitors packed into the capacious auditorium, called the Du Hall

---

47. The modernization of Shanghai gangs is a topic beyond the scope of this study. The political transformation of the Green Gang (Qing bang) is discussed in Brian Martin, "Warlords and Gangsters: The Opium Traffic in Shanghai and the Creation of the Three Prosperities Company to 1926," in *The Nationalists and Chinese Society, 1927–1937,* ed. John Fitzgerald (Melbourne, 1989), 44–71; Brian Martin, "The Green Gang and the Guomindang Government: The Role of Du Yuesheng in the Politics of Shanghai" (paper presented at the International Conference on Urban and Shanghai Studies, Shanghai, October 20–24, 1991); Brian Martin, "The Green Gang in Shanghai, 1920–1937: The Rise of Du Yuesheng" (Ph.D. diss., Australian National University, 1991).

Figure 9. The Pudong Tongxianghui. Source: *Pudong tongxianghui huisuo luo-cheng jinian tekan* (Special commemorative publication for the inauguration of the Pudong Tongxianghui building) (Shanghai, 1937).

(named after Du Yuesheng). Above the rows of seats hung hundreds of commemorative scrolls. More guests lined the balcony. All eyes were on the stage, which framed the figures of the two leaders of Shanghai. The Mayor, Wu Tiecheng, stood on the right. By his side stood the man of many roles—Green Gang boss, entrepreneur, anti-Japanese patriot— Du Yuesheng, the founder of the Pudong Tongxianghui.[48]

The scene captured in these photographs conveys characteristic features of politics and public associations in 1930s Shanghai. The grandeur of the Pudong Tongxianghui ceremony suggests a new kind of flourishing of *tongxianghui*. In the Nanjing decade, a period commonly described in terms of the themes of unprecedented state building, state penetration and the reorganization of society, native-place associations remained major formations in the mental and social landscape.[49] They were important to Shanghai residents in this period because they performed critical quasi-governmental functions—as juridical, investigative and order-keeping institutions; as organs of social mobilization; and as organs of grievance, mediation and redress. In many cases they provided channels of access to limited government services. In these roles native-place associations continued economic and social services which they had performed in the past, functions in which they had not, ultimately, been displaced by more occupationally and functionally specialized economic and political associations. In addition, in the Nanjing decade, because the Guomindang suppressed any form of representative government and, especially after 1932, restricted the independence of the General Chamber of Commerce and other potentially oppositional urban institutions, native-place associations provided an important avenue for civic organization. To accomplish these things in this period, native-place associations needed both to respond to new social needs and to come to terms with new sources of power in the city.

The Pudong association was new among Shanghai *tongxianghui*, because the backwater suburb of Pudong had relatively little means and less "face" in Shanghai prior to the rise of Du Yuesheng. Du's prominence was critical to the establishment of a new association in 1932, long

48. *Pudong tongxianghui huisuo luocheng jinian tekan* (Special commemorative publication for the inauguration of the Pudong Tongxianghui building) (Shanghai, 1936); *Pudong tongxianghui nianbao* (Yearly report of the Pudong Tongxianghui) (hereafter referred to as PTN) (Shanghai, 1936).

49. Henriot, *Shanghai 1927–1937;* Parks Coble, *The Shanghai Capitalists and the Nationalist Government, 1927–1937* (Cambridge, Mass., 1980); Duara, *Culture, Power and the State;* Fewsmith, *Party, State and Local Elites.*

after the fading of the earlier Pudong Tongren Hui. In certain respects, Du's existence re-created Pudong as a native place. In other words, Du's wealth and power provided impetus for the institutionalization and re-spectability of Pudong native-place sentiment. As one of Du's followers described it in his memoir-biography: "It was because a Du Yuesheng emerged from Pudong that for a long period the Pudong dialect became fashionable in Shanghai. At the very least, loafers and their friends could all say a few sentences of Pudong dialect in order to show off, implying that they had connections to Du's group and that they were not alone in the world."[50]

This quote makes clear that native-place sentiment was not necessarily traditional or automatic. It could arise where there was little tradition, and it flourished especially where it was useful. It could also exist outside real connections to the supposed native place — in the case of the Pudong association, members did not necessarily have to be from Pudong. The Pudong Tongxianghui was a historical creation of 1930s Shanghai and marked the apogee of a new trend in native-place associations, associa-tions which were very large and organized with powerful backers. As the stream of respectful visitors indicates, such native-place associations were taken very seriously. If the Pudong Tongxianghui was unique in its con-nections to Du Yuesheng, it was neither the largest nor necessarily the most powerful of the 1930s Shanghai native-place associations.

Characteristics of Tongxianghui *in the 1930s.* The nature and day-to-day business of native-place associations in the Nanjing de-cade reflect the possibilities of urban civic association and expression in this period. The first thing that is striking about these associations in the 1930s is their number and their size. As many as sixty solidly estab-lished native-place associations existed in Shanghai in this period, with offices, regular meeting places, and memberships sufficiently large to support the organization (minimally several hundred, often many thou-sand). The larger and more powerful organizations, like those of Ning-bo and Pudong, developed impressive memberships for voluntary as-sociations in this period. More than twenty-two thousand Ningbo sojourners paid to belong to their *tongxianghui;* for the Pudong Tong-xianghui the figure was just under twenty thousand, a remarkable num-ber for a brand-new organization. These membership figures were also considerably higher than those of the previous decade had been.

50. Zhang Jungu, *Du Yuesheng zhuan,* vol. 2, 312.

As in the early Republican period, *tongxianghui* in the Nanjing decade were socially inclusive but hierarchical organizations. They had a graded hierarchy of membership types. Honorary or special members might contribute as much as several hundred or a thousand yuan in a year. Lower-ranking members joined for as little as one yuan — sometimes just fifty cents. The most common occupation for members was merchant (*shang*) — usually more than 60 percent — followed by smaller percentages of office workers, government clerks, policemen and occasionally workers and students. (In the case of the Pudong association, nearly 20 percent of the membership was made up of workers.) Membership requirements for introductions from two current members, together with the mandatory annual fee, even if minimal, ensured that associations drew the large portion of their members from the upper, middle and lower-middle class and excluded the very poor. They were, nonetheless, organizations accessible to a large sector of the working public. Although the constitutions of most *tongxianghui* in this period now stipulated that men and women were equally free to become members, in practice women were only a minimal presence at meetings — generally they comprised no more than 2 percent of *tongxianghui* membership throughout the decade. However minimal, their presence was an innovation. Women appear in the ledgers of *tongxianghui* activity with surprising frequency, initiating correspondence and casework of the associations.[51]

Although membership was accessible to many people, decision making within the organizations was concentrated within the ranks of a small but powerful minority. The most important decisions took place outside the largely ritualistic general meetings and were the exclusive domain of a handful of directors, usually a combination of the most influential businessmen, intellectuals, politicians and/or gang leaders within the community. These were the people on whom native-place associations depended for their finances and their influence. The relationship was mutually beneficial; native-place associations provided these individuals with considerable social followings and public "face," intangible but critical factors in the calculus of power in the Chinese city.

51. PTN, 1935; *Ningbo lü Hu tongxianghui dibajie zhengqiu jiniankan* (Commemorative publication of the eighth membership drive of the Ningbo Tongxianghui) (Shanghai, 1933); *Jiangning liuxian; Guangdong lü Hu tongxianghui disijie huiyuanlu* (Fourth anniversary membership record of the Guangdong Tongxianghui) (Shanghai, 1939); *Hu She dishisanjie; Henan lü Hu tongxianghui gongzuo baogao; Ningbo lü Hu tongxianghui dishiyijie zhengqiu huiyuan dahui jiniankan* (Shanghai, 1939).

One might well ask, noting the growth and size of these associations in this period, what exactly they did and what prompted so many people to join. By this time the rituals of appearing "public" and "democratic" had caused the major *tongxianghui* to produce regular detailed yearly (sometimes monthly) reports through which many of their day to day public activities may be observed. It is not surprising to find that they performed many traditional functions — supporting schools and orphanages, providing disaster relief and sending the indigent back to their native place. But native-place associations were also deeply involved in functions one might have assumed were taken over and developed by either the bureaucracy of the newly established and much heralded Shanghai Municipal Government,[52] by recently reorganized commercial and economic associations — the Chamber of Commerce and the *tongye gonghui* (trade associations mandated by the new government) or by new civic and political associations. The range of their activity may be indicated through a brief sketch.

The Range of Tongxianghui *Functions.* The order-keeping functions of *tongxianghui* are apparent from voluminous records of casework involving kidnappings, runaway women, beatings, thefts and fights. Tongxianghui ledgers for the 1930s abound in cases of kidnapping, a crime which flourished especially under the Nanjing regime. When their wives and children were kidnapped, family members did not routinely go to either the police or the Chinese Society for Assistance to Women and Children (*Zhongguo funu jiuji zonghui,* or CSAWC).[53] The aggrieved appealed instead to their native-place associations. In such cases (and in cases of fights or thefts), as before, native-place associations investigated, mediated, or brought the case to the relevant authorities. Both civic organizations like the CSAWC and government offices (courts and public security bureaus) relied on *tongxianghui* for evidence and cooperation and turned lost or indigent individuals over to *tongxianghui* custody.[54]

---

52. See Henriot, *Shanghai 1927–1937.*

53. An impressionistic comparison of *tongxianghui* and Public Security Bureau kidnapping cases suggests a division of labor along gender lines. *Tongxianghui* cases involved women and children; police focused their efforts on the kidnappings of male residents. See Frederic Wakeman, "Social Control and Civic Culture in Republican Shanghai" (paper presented at the Shanghai Seminar, University of California, Berkeley, November 2, 1991).

54. *Hu She dishisanjie; Ningbo lü Hu tongxianghui dibajie;* CHYB, 1934; PTN, 1933–36; *Jiangning liuxian.* The procedures outlined in the reports of these associations are corroborated by CSAWC and Shaoxing *Tongxianghui* archives at the Shanghai Municipal Archives.

Throughout this period *tongxianghui* continued to investigate commercial disputes. By the mid-1930s many *tongxianghui* (even smaller associations like the Jiangning Tongxianghui) maintained teams of lawyers to deal with the many types of business they handled. For example, the Sojourning Indigo Dye Trade Association appealed to the Jiangning Tongxianghui for help in dealing with merchants who illegally misappropriated trade-association property. The *tongxianghui* investigated and presented the case in court.[55] Shipwrecks frequently occasioned the intervention of native-place associations. When a foreign boat hit and sank a barge belonging to a Madame Shen, a Pudong native, she contacted her *tongxianghui*, which represented her in the negotiations. When a boat belonging to Huzhou sojourners capsized and fifty people drowned, the parties concerned notified the Huzhou association in Shanghai. The Hu She registered each family's losses, contacted the authorities of the counties bordering the river where the boat had sunk, and initiated an investigation. The Hu She reported its findings to the government authorities concerned and mediated a settlement with the boat company.[56]

Workers' associations at times appealed to *tongxianghui* (if they had influential *tongxianghui*) when their livelihood was threatened. In the case of a strike of electrical workers in the International Settlement in 1933, the Ningbo Tongxianghui organized a Federated Committee of Sojourning Tongxianghui to jointly lobby the Settlement Municipal Council on behalf of the workers. In the next year, a ferryworkers' union contacted the Pudong Tongxianghui complaining that the Shanghai city government had awarded the ferry business at their dock to an outside company, resulting in the loss of their livelihood. The Tongxianghui set up a special investigative committee and petitioned the Shanghai Municipal Government on the workers' behalf. The city authorities responded with alacrity, asking the *tongxianghui* to send negotiators to party headquarters to arrange the matter. No doubt the settlement of this case was facilitated by the fact that Du Yuesheng himself took up the matter with the Shanghai mayor, Wu Tiecheng.[57]

55. *Jiangning liuxian*, 17.

56. *Jiangning liuxian* PTN, 1934, entry of January 19; *Hu She dishisanjie*, section 1, 72–74.

57. *Ningbo lü Hu tongxianghui dibajie*, entries for October 1933, 7–8; PTN, 1933, 9; PTN, 1934, entries of March, April and June. The disposal of this case follows a typical pattern, in which difficult or important cases were referred to the most powerful member of the organization. In the case of the Ningbo Tongxianghui, difficult cases were referred to Yu Xiaqing; for the Chaozhou Tongxianghui, difficult cases were referred to Zheng Ziliang.

In this period native-place associations continued to defend Chinese interests against foreign trespasses. At times *tongxianghui* coordinated activities to create a united citywide front. When a Vietnamese policeman in the French Settlement shot and wounded several Chinese civilians, the Chaozhou Tongxianghui enlisted other associations in a collective effort to exact reparations and punish the transgressor. Within a day, the Ningbo and Chaozhou *tongxianghui* called a "City-Wide Meeting of Representatives of All Associations" (*quanshi getuanti daibiao dahui*) to orchestrate a united response.[58]

An incident involving the dumping of Japanese rice on the Chinese market reveals the persisting native-place organization of commerce in the 1930s. Both the Shanghai Sojourning Anhui Rice Merchants' Trade Association (*Lü Hu Wanshang miye gonghui*) and the Shanghai Sojourning Guangdong Merchants' Miscellaneous Grain Association (*Lü Hu Yueshang zaliang bang*) notified the Ningbo Tongxianghui of an attempt in 1933 to dump more than twenty-five thousand piculs of Japanese rice on the Shanghai market. The Guangdong association asked the Ningbo Tongxianghui to notify Ningbo rice merchants and warn them against purchasing Japanese rice. The Anhui association asked the Ningbo Tongxianghui to take up the matter with the city government in order to restrict the import of Japanese rice and to increase the taxation rate on imported Japanese rice. The Ningbo association printed notices in the newspapers and contacted both the city government and the Chamber of Commerce in order to safeguard the Shanghai market. What is striking here is not just that the Anhui and Guangdong trade groups initiated a concerted response to a threat to trade through native-place organizations but also that the Anhui association did not itself go directly to the relevant commercial and governmental authorities. Instead, it appealed to the more influential Ningbo Tongxianghui, asking this association to take up the matter up with the city government and the Chamber of Commerce. This path of action becomes explicable if the influence of Ningbo sojourners on both the city government and the Chamber of Commerce are taken into account.[59]

<hr />

58. PTN, 1933, "Dashiji," 2, 6. The Pudong association joined these efforts. When it then discovered that a Pudong person had been wounded in the incident, it investigated separately and demanded (and received) additional compensation.

59. *Ningbo lü Hu tongxianghui dibajie,* entries for October 1933. See also Marie-Claire Bergère et al., "Essai de prosopographie des élites Shanghaïennes a l'époque republicaine, 1911–1949," *Annales: Economies, Sociétés, Civilisations* 4 (July-August 1985):901–30; Bergère, *Golden Age;* Henriot, *Shanghai 1927–1937.*

Another type of case prominent in *tongxianghui* ledgers and particular to the Nanjing decade suggests the way in which *tongxianghui* served as defensive mechanisms against an oppressive state. In the face of arrests or false accusations of merchants by local Guomindang headquarters or by Guomindang-supported anti-Japanese resistance associations, the relatives of abducted or arrested persons notified their *tongxianghui*, which then provided evidence that the individuals in question were legitimate merchants and not traitors, and negotiated, often successfully, for their release.[60] In similar fashion, people in the native place complained to Shanghai *tongxianghui* to curb the excesses of local officials. In one case of this sort, thirty-seven shops in a Nanhui market town struck because the local tax-collection agent beat up a merchant. The Pudong Tongxianghui took the matter up with the local authorities.[61]

Tongxianghui also served to moderate, if not entirely reduce, tax burdens imposed in their native place, in response to appeals from native-place trade associations. In one case of this type, the Silk and Tea Trade Association appealed to the Shanghai Hui-Ning Tongxianghui, asking for help in their struggle with the Anhui government. The provincial government overcharged the tea merchants in the course of collecting a tea tax. The Shanghai association pressured the provincial government, asking for the return of the merchants' money and publicizing the affair in the *Shenbao*. Success in such negotiations depended, naturally, on the strength of the single *tongxianghui*. The Pudong and Ningbo associations were often successful in such matters. Weaker *tongxianghui* attempted similar interventions, with mixed results.[62]

In these instances, native-place associations used newspapers and the force of public opinion to shame and reform rapacious officials or agencies. For instance, in 1932 the Shanghai Anhui Tongxianghui became

60. See for example, PTN, 1934, entries for February 23, 1934; *Ningbo lü Hu tong xianghui dibajie,* entries for October 16, 1933: *Hu She dishisanjie; Chaozhou lü Hu tongxianghui niankan.* It should not be imagined that all of the arrested or detained were innocent. One category of appeals to the Chaozhou Tongxianghui came from merchants whose goods or cash had been detained by the Shanghai customs. Given Chaozhou involvement in the smuggling of contraband, *tongxianghui* actions here appear to have protected illicit trade as handily as legitimate business. See *Chaozhou lü Hu tongxianghui niankan.*

61. PTN, 1935.

62. SB, August 27, 1932, p. 16. Some solutions were creative. When the Guangdong Merchants' Miscellaneous Grain and Oilcake Association complained of overtaxation, the Chaozhou Huiguan mobilized representatives of the Shanghai Chamber of Commerce and arranged a deal with Guomindang officials. In return for the rescinding of the tax, the native-place association would make a contribution to the Nanjing Zhongyang University. See CHYB, May 21, 1934.

concerned about official corruption and embezzlement in Anhui. In a joint effort with the Beijing Anhui Tongxianghui and local people in Anhui they secured proof of fraud and printed the details of the case in the *Shenbao*.[63] In the process, *tongxianghui* acted as watchdogs on municipal and local officials and moderated tax burdens in their native place.

Tongxianghui also lobbied for their native place, procuring government assistance in local construction, transportation, policing and welfare projects. The Hu She, in collaboration with the Crepe Trade Association, lobbied for increased security on the waterways connecting Huzhou and Shanghai. The Pudong and Ningbo *tongxianghui* solicited and secured government assistance with public-works projects in home areas (docks, bridges, roads, telephone lines). While they lobbied for government funds, these associations continued to pour capital, time and labor back into their native places.

Managing Wartime Shanghai. In wartime Shanghai, native-place associations proved to be powerful and efficient organizations, able immediately to provide capital and personnel resource networks to deal with a crisis of great magnitude — the social consequences of war with Japan. In the face of the catastrophic bombing of the densely populated districts of Hongkou and Zhabei in August 1937, coordinating committees established by the Shanghai Municipal Government had neither the funds nor the human resources to do more than attempt to straddle a massive movement initiated from below the level of the government. Native-place organizations provided institutional networks critical to the popular mobilization which developed to meet the crisis.[64]

The impact of the bombings on the Shanghai Guangdong community was especially great because many Guangdong people worked in the areas which were bombed. The Guangdong Tongxianghui, in coor-

63. SB, August 16, 1932.

64. The discussion below concerns the events of 1937. For evidence of immediate *tongxianghui* response to the January 1932 bombing, see Lian Kang, "Ji aiguo shiyejia Lan Meixian" (Remembrance of the patriotic entrepreneur Lan Meixian), in *Kangri fengyun lu* (Record of the War of Resistance Against Japan) (Shanghai, 1985), 309–12; *Chaozhou lü Hu tongxianghui tekan, jiuguo hao* (Special issue of the Association of Chaozhou Sojourners in Shanghai, National Salvation Edition) (1932); and notices of the Ningbo, Taizhou, Guangdong, Chaozhou, Suzhou, Huzhou, Henan, Sichuan, Jianghuai, Shandong, Fujian, Jiangxi, Shaoxing, Wuxi, Pudong and Anhui associations printed in SB between January 28, 1932, and February 10, 1932.

dination with the older Guang-Zhao Gongsuo immediately established five refugee centers, borrowing for this purpose property of Guangdong merchants in Shanghai. *Tongxianghui* members managed the centers, enlisting refugees as additional in-camp personnel. In his memoir, a refugee-camp employee, a former office manager for the China Merchants' Steam Navigation Company (CMSNC), reveals that his *tongxiang* employer at the CMSNC directed him and seven fellow office workers to shift jobs and work in the refugee center. Their new office was a floor of a Guangdong restaurant. Guangdong students volunteered to register, distribute food and otherwise care for the refugees. In this manner, the Guangdong community sheltered approximately fifty thousand people, all of them from Guangdong. They also arranged and subsidized transportation costs to send their fellow-provincials safely back to Guangdong.[65] Those sheltered represented nearly half of the total Guangdong population in Shanghai at the time.

The records of the Ningbo Tongxianghui tell a similar story on an even greater scale. Immediately after the Marco Polo Bridge Incident, the Ningbo Tongxianghui organized a battalion of crisis committees, divided by functions — money raising, defense, supplies acquisition, records and documentation. On August 13, when Hongkou and Zhabei became war areas, refugees immediately poured into the Ningbo Tongxianghui building in the International Settlement, which became a temporary shelter. The *tongxianghui* arranged convoys to take them to other Ningbo shelters. Before long it maintained fourteen refugee centers housing nearly twenty-five thousand refugees. As the pressure of refugees in Shanghai increased, the *tongxianghui* arranged boats to provide passage to Ningbo. Between August 15 and September 17 they returned eighty thousand people. By the time the operation was finished they had returned two hundred thousand people, or one-third to two-fifths of the total Shanghai Ningbo population. Those without money for the trip were funded by the association (which provided money to more than eighty-two thousand such people). Ningbo refugees without homes to return to in Ningbo were nonetheless sent to a refugee center in Ningbo, also managed by the *tongxianghui,* which provided food and housing for these refugees until March 1938. In addition, it provided

65. Fang Yinchao, "Guangdong lü Hu tongxianghui gongzuo zhuiji" (Remembrance of the work of the Association of Guangdong Sojourners in Shanghai), *Dacheng* 45 (August 1977):26–27; *Guangdong lü Hu tongxianghui jiuji nanmin weiyuanhui baogaoshu* (Report of the Refugee Relief Committee of the Guangdong Tongxianghui) (Shanghai, 1938).

medical care to twenty-five hundred fellow-provincials. The Siming Gongsuo provided coffins for those who died in the attacks.[66]

Guangdong and Ningbo refugee relief efforts were notable for their scale but not unusual in terms of their design. Smaller associations, like the Quan-Zhang Huiguan and the Dongting Dongshan Tongxianghui, raised funds, organized relief committees, mobilized rescue militias, hired cars to enter occupied areas and transport the wounded to shelter, established refugee centers and shipped refugees to their native place.[67]

In other ways as well, native-place associations protected their *tong-xiang* from the disasters of war. The war disrupted the market and disastrously affected the livelihood of the cotton-growing people in Pudong. In response, the Pudong Tongxianghui established a Cotton Transportation and Sales Society in October 1937 which raised one million yuan to purchase Pudong cotton and transport it by convoy across the Huangpu River and through the French Concession to the Pudong Association, where it could be safely stored.[68] The *tongxianghui* raised these funds in just a few weeks, while supporting twelve refugee centers for Pudong people.[69]

These examples demonstrate commonly accepted lines of native-place identity, organization and mobilization in the city, on a large scale, and associations which could, when necessary, muster capital, property and personnel on short notice and function with remarkable efficiency. If both refugee relief work and the efforts of the Pudong Tongxianghui to maintain the livelihood of Pudong people were (despite their unprecedented scale) "traditional" types of activity for native-place associations, *tongxianghui* were also very active in the primary area of emerging popular dissent in the Nanjing decade, the voicing of anti-Japanese nationalism and criticism of Guomindang accommodation to Japanese occupation of

66. *Ningbo lü Hu tongxianghui jiuji beinan tongxiang zhengxinlu* (Record-book of assistance provided to fellow-provincial refugees by the Association of Ningbo Sojourners in Shanghai) (Shanghai, 1939), 1–36.

67. See for example, Huang Zepan, "Shanghai Quan-Zhang huiguan yange ji kang-zhan shiqi de huodong" (The evolution of the Shanghai Quan-Zhang Huiguan and its activities during the War of Resistance), *Quanzhou wenshi ziliao* (Quanzhou cultural and historical materials) 13 (1965?):63–67; *Dongting Dongshan*, 86–87. Feng Yi, "Le problème des réfugiés à Shanghai, 1937–40" (Memoire de DEA, Université Lumière-Lyon 2, September 1993, 38), counts twenty-one native-place associations active in relief efforts.

68. Shanghai Municipal Police Report, National Archives, Washington, D. C., D–8133, October 20, 1937.

69. PTN, 1938.

Chinese territory. Responding to the explosive events in Manchuria and Shanghai in the fall and winter of 1931–32, Shanghai native-place associations published strident criticisms of Zhang Xueliang and rallied considerable financial support for Ma Zhanshan, one of the few Chinese military commanders to seriously engage Japanese forces.[70]

Tongxianghui also provided shelter and resources for anti-Japanese activists. Especially notable in this regard was the Pudong Tongxianghui, which in 1937 housed at least eight anti-Japanese associations, including the All-Shanghai Association for the Support of Armed Resistance, the Shanghai Citizens' Committee for Severance of Economic Relations with Japan, the Shanghai Wartime Literature and Art Society, and student and worker groups.[71] Even smaller associations, like the Shangyu Tongxianghui, played an active role in organizing anti-Japanese activity.[72]

The scope of *tongxianghui* activity at this point in time is striking. In 1937, a decade after the establishment of an activist government committed to the reorganization, modernization, taxation and control of Shanghai urban associations through the considerable bureaucratic machinery of the Shanghai Municipal Government,[73] it is intriguing to find native-place ties and native-place associations so prominent in urban civic activity. Indeed, in a time of crisis, it appears that for a large number, probably the majority, of refugees, native-place identity remained their primary identity. Even those Ningbo people who no longer had homes or family in Ningbo to go back to appealed to the Ningbo Tongxianghui and were returned to Ningbo. Given the uncertainties of life under Japanese aggression, native-place identity developed a new utility. Even if the native place was entirely unfamiliar to Shanghai-born "sojourners," maintaining sojourner consciousness meant that they had another home if life in Shanghai proved to be untenable.

Shanghai businessmen commonly put their greatest efforts into helping their *tongxiang* first, contributing secondarily, if at all, to govern-

70. See, especially, *Chaozhou lü Hu tongxianghui tekan*, 1932; *Quan Zhe gonghui huiwu baogao* (Report of the work of the All-Zhejiang Association) (Shanghai, 1931–32).

71. The other anti-Japanese associations housed at the *tongxianghui* were the Shanghai Municipality Students' Wartime Service Group, the Shanghai Municipality Educationalists' Race Salvation Association, the Shanghai Young Writers' National Salvation Propaganda Group, the Shanghai Municipality Cooperative Social Circles National Salvation Association and the National Salvation Workers' Training Institute. See Shanghai Municipal Police Report, D–8141, November 15, 1937.

72. Ibid., D–7758, April 12, 1937.

73. See Henriot, *Shanghai 1927–1937*.

ment-sponsored or international relief efforts.[74] A good but not unusual example is Lan Meixian, a wealthy entrepreneur and major shareholder of the Shanghai Dalai Bank, the Jiaxing Minfeng Paper Factory, the Hangzhou Huafeng Paper Factory and the Ning-Shao Steamboat Company. After the bombings of August 13, 1937, Lan decided to help the Chinese forces by contributing the sum needed to purchase an airplane. He did this through the Ningbo Tongxianghui.[75] Local-level governments outside Shanghai similarly made their famine-relief contributions to their native-place associations in Shanghai rather than to the Shanghai government-sponsored committee.[76]

Public Maneuverings: Native-Place Associations between State and Society

Throughout the Nanjing decade native-place associations were understood as belonging to "society" as opposed to the "state." *Tongxianghui* represented themselves as people's organizations and pub-

74. Before the war broke out, Wu Tiecheng, Shanghai mayor, established a disaster-relief committee. Six months after the war began, this committee published a report claiming to have played a commanding role in the relief efforts (*Shanghai cishan tuanti lianhe jiuzai hui jiuji zhanqu nanmin weiyuanhui bannian gongzuo baogao* [Report of the Disaster Relief and War Refugee Assistance Committee of Federated Shanghai Charitable Organizations] [Shanghai, 1938]). This "command center" image cannot be reconciled with accounts of the Guangdong community's relief efforts (which do not mention the semi-official disaster relief committee) or with the detailed account-book of the Ningbo Tongxianghui disaster-relief effort. (The committee is not mentioned in correspondence or among monetary donors, only at the bottom of a list of individuals and groups which provided goods like clothing and biscuits.) In six months the government-sponsored committee raised approximately one million yuan, the amount raised by the Pudong Tongxianghui for cotton transport alone. The memoir of a refugee-relief director who worked with the committee suggests that Guomindang officials formed the organization as a propaganda ploy: "When the war broke out, the leaders of society inevitably shouldered the task of helping wounded soldiers and aiding refugees, and in this manner the officials received credit for assuming (in name) positions of leadership" (Zhao Puchu, "Kangzhan chuqi Shanghai de nanmin gongzuo" [Shanghai refugee work during the early part of the War of Resistance], *Wenshi ziliao xuanji* [Shanghai] 4 [1980]:31–50). An international relief committee cared for 23,727 refugees in the first six months of war, a figure slightly lower than the 24,858 refugees cared for by the Ningbo Tongxianghui. See K. Y. Lee, *Annual Report of the International Relief Committee* (Shanghai, 1938). See also Feng, "Le problème des réfugiés."

75. Lian Kang, "Ji aiguo shiyejia," 309–12. Later, when the refugee situation was critical, Lan delivered his household silver and his silver steamboat models (a considerable collection) to the Ningbo Tongxianghui to help Ningbo refugees.

76. The Ningbo Tongxianghui, for example, received contributions from county and prefectural governments and from local benevolent associations. Such contributors are

lic organizations (*minjian tuanti, minzhong tuanti, shehui gongtuan*). The government classed them similarly as in the realm of society, as social organizations, or as people's organizations (*shehui tuanti, renmin tuanti*). Although such understandings were strategically useful (on both sides), they masked a complexly overlapping relationship with the state.

State Penetration. Like other social organizations in the Nanjing decade, *tongxianghui* registered with the government, filled out government surveys and received state instructions, particularly with regard to their ritual and educational activities and accepted "the leadership and guidance" of representatives of the Social Bureau and the Party Branch Office in Shanghai in their general meetings. Their published records suggest cooperation in all of these activities, even as they also organized at strategic local points in opposition to the state. It is important, therefore, to consider the extent to which they were "penetrated" by the state and to ask what strategies and features of their makeup enabled them to carry on the multitude of civic activities they engaged in which were not mandated by the state.

The extensive efforts of the Nanjing government to neutralize or control public associations and political activity have persuaded some historians that little civic activity was possible at this time outside the realm of the state. Records of native-place associations provide a useful index of state penetration of society. Because native-place associations performed a broad range of social services and because they were not explicitly political in this period, they were not a major target of control; nonetheless, beginning in 1928, they became increasingly subject to the regulations and interventions of the Social Bureau of the Shanghai Municipal Government and the Shanghai party branch office.

A survey of the publications and archives of native-place associations, as well as publications of the Shanghai city government and the Nanjing government, permits an impressionistic account of state attempts to identify, register, investigate and reform native-place associations, as well as of the ability of these associations to delay, resist, and deflect these state intrusions.

---

largely absent from the list of donors to the government-sponsored committee, which received contributions from provincial governments. It is striking that even some provincial governments sent their contributions through their *tongxianghui* (this was the case, for instance, with the Sichuan government). See *Shanghai cishan tuanti lianhe; Ningbo lü Hu tongxianghui jiuji beinan tongxiang.*

In 1928, shortly after the establishment of the Shanghai Municipal Government, native-place associations were notified that they had to register with the Social Bureau and with the Shanghai branch party headquarters. It was not until the spring of the next year that native-place associations began to take seriously the registration regulations. Nonetheless, finding these regulations "obstructive" and "trouble-some," most associations developed delaying tactics. As late as 1931 the Chaozhou and Ningbo associations were still delaying. When the Chaozhou association finally did register, they did not list their property holdings, as noted in their meeting records, "to avoid conflict."[77]

By 1932 the Social Bureau had made some headway. Shaoxing Tongxianghui archives record the process of state investigation of the association. After a period of delay, the Shaoxing Tongxianghui finally petitioned the Social Bureau to register in 1932. The license petition provided the bureau with a one-sentence statement of purpose ("We establish the Shaoxing Tongxianghui to promote the public good, provide charity, unite native-place sentiment and work for the benefit of our native place and our sojourning *tongxiang*"), a list of officers and employees, and a copy of the association constitution and rules. A survey of 1934 provided the Social Bureau with somewhat more information: the total number of members (not a name list), the names of the officers, a one-sentence description of internal organiza-tion, and a statement of sources of income (property rentals and membership fees), though the exact property holdings were not listed.

In a section devoted to "special types of associations" in a *Report of the Conference on the Guomindang Central All-China Mass-Movement Leadership Committee* (1934), party activists argued for the need to funda-mentally reorganize native-place associations to make them more sys-tematic and to facilitate party guidance and direction. *Huiguan* were to be turned over to *tongxianghui* management; county- and city-level *tongxianghui* were to be subordinated to provincial-level *tongxianghui*. Party investigators complained of the unsystematic names of native-place associations and stressed the need to clarify these names to facili-tate precise classification. These suggestions reflect a bare state of ac-quaintance with the associations under consideration and ignorance of

77. CHYB, May 1929; CHYB, February 1932; CHYB, March 4, 1932; SGY, April 1929; SGY, March 22, 1931.

the realities of native-place association. There is no evidence that these reforms were implemented.[78]

One instance in which native-place associations did follow a government directive to "modernize" their practices reveals the tendency of these associations to make surface compromises with state regulations. In 1930 associations received notice that they were not to celebrate the Chinese New Year with their traditional practice of ritual *tuanbai* greetings. They were instructed to change to the Republican calendar and more modern modes of comportment. The Chaozhou native-place association responded by replacing the name *tuanbai* with the more modern-sounding *kenqinhui,* a term used to denote all sorts of purposeful modern gatherings. From 1930 on, the Chaozhou association set aside a Sunday in February to hold a *kenqinhui,* a time for greetings among all Guangdong sojourner groups.[79]

Despite repeated efforts to register and restructure these associations, as late as 1936 the Shanghai Municipal Government could only claim that twenty-seven of the sixty-five *tongxianghui* of which it was aware were fully registered according to all of the procedures of the law.[80] Although at times the power of the city government and public security forces was clearly more efficient, particularly in the area of extracting funds and even temporarily requisitioning buildings of native-place associations,[81] there was nonetheless an evident gap between state aspira-

78. *Zhongguo guomindang quanguo minzhong yundong gongzuo taolunhui baogaoshu* (Report of the Conference on the Guomindang Central All-China Mass-Movement Leadership Committee) (Nanjing, 1934). Guang-Zhao Gongsuo records note an earlier reorganization effort by the Shanghai Municipal Merchant Association Reorganization Committee (*Shanghai tebieshi shangren tuanti zhengli weiyuanhui*) of the Social Bureau, which attempted to reform association election procedures through the creation of a Federation of Sojourning Huiguan and Gongsuo (*Lü Hu huiguan gongsuo lianhehui*). The *gongsuo* rejected the election rules of the new federation and notified the Social Bureau that it would await the development and publication of more satisfactory guidelines before they would respond. See GZGYB, January 1930.

79. CHYB, 1930. See also *Hu She dishisanjie* regarding yearly *tuanbai.*

80. Shanghai shi nianjian weiyuanhui (Shanghai municipal yearbook committee), comps., *Shanghai shi nianjian* (Shanghai municipal yearbook) (Shanghai, 1936), E–13. The remaining *tongxianghui,* with one exception, are listed as being in the process of registration.

81. In 1929 the Siming Gongsuo was notified that Shanghai branch party headquarters wanted to requisition huiguan buildings. The *huiguan* rebuffed this attempt, though records of the following year note a second request, this time from the public-security-bureau police. In 1930 the *huiguan* rented rooms for the police, subsidizing the rent until the police moved out in the fall of 1931 (SGY, November 13, 1930). Records of July 1932 note that one hundred police had quartered in a temple of a Siming Gongsuo coffin repository (SGY, July 1932).

tions for control and state limitations. In this gap, and in a relationship which encompassed mutual accommodation and at times strategic co-operation in a broad scope of activities, native-place associations provided spaces for certain degrees of political activism that would not be curtailed by the state.

The Interpenetration of State and Society. Although much is to be gained from a consideration of state penetration — namely, an index of state initiatives as well as a record of successes and limitations — this type of discussion obscures the considerable overlap of state and society characteristic in the makeup of these associations, historically and in this period. This overlap is evident in association personnel, proclaimed affiliation with state organs, performance of services to the state, and state recognition of native-place associations.

Membership lists and collection records point to striking areas of overlap between state and society. The 1936 membership list of the Henan Tongxianghui includes two Public Security Bureau branch chiefs, two police chiefs, and 97 police and Public Security Bureau employees among the members (in some cases as many as 30 police from one station, or something approximating the full-scale incorporation of work units into the *tongxianghui*).[82] Similarly, 179 Hu She members were employed in "party and government," and another 69 were employed in military, police or social-control institutions (totaling 248 of approximately 1,300 members).[83]

Substantial government-employee membership is also revealed in a *Shenbao* report on the 1930 collection drive of the Pudong Tongxianghui, which established seventy-two collection teams among members in a campaign to fund the new building. Among these teams, organized according to residence locality and occupational group, one covered collections in the Shanghai party headquarters, one covered collections among the military, two focused on national-government employees and one focused on city-government employees.[84] Obviously, these

82. *Henan lü Hu tongxianghui gongzuo baogao.* Additionally, members included a number of police employed by the International Settlement and employees of the Social and Sanitation bureaus of the Shanghai Municipal Government.

83. *Hu She dishisanjie.* Government employees are also prominent among the nearly eight thousand members of the Guangdong association (*Guangdong lü Hu tongxianghui disijie huiyuanlu* [Fourth anniversary membership record of the Guangdong Tong-xianghui] [Shanghai, 1937]).

84. SB, September 2, 1931. An article of October 10 cites the total collected as 53,445 yuan (SB, October 10, 1931).

kinds of membership links served the associations well in their day-to-day interactions with branches of the Public Security Bureau and bureaucrats of the Shanghai Municipal Government.

Published association records (as opposed to their unpublished archives) make a point of their affiliation with the Social Bureau and the party, their acceptance of party "guidance and supervision" and their enthusiasm in regard to government campaigns. Their published reports begin with photographs of their state licenses; their constitutions vow adherence to the Three People's Principles, the guidance of the Guomindang, and their determination to eliminate counterrevolutionaries. Their general meeting summaries highlight the presence at these meetings of government officials. These items all appear in their published meeting notes like protective badges.[85]

State organs and state officials recognized native-place associations in a multitude of ways, licensing them, bestowing symbolic recognition, attending *tongxianghui* meetings, relying on *tongxianghui* as quasi-governmental organizations to carry out government programs. Government recognition was on display at the inaugural ceremony for the new Pudong Tongxianghui building described above, in which the calligraphy of government luminaries graced the walls of the auditorium, while the mayor shared the stage with the founder of the *tongxianghui*. Sun Fo did calligraphy for Chaozhou Tongxianghui publications; Wu Tiecheng provided his calligraphy for the Guangdong Tongxianghui.[86]

Representatives from provincial governments, as well as from Shanghai party headquarters and the Social Bureau, attended the yearly general meetings of *tongxianghui*. Although they did this "to supervise and guide" the work of the associations, their presence also helped to legitimate the associations. A Guomindang party representative attending a Pudong Tongxianghui meeting praised the association and its contribution to the nation: "Shanghai is a model for China, and your association is a model for all *tongxianghui* nationally. You contribute to the well-being of the native place and contribute to the glory of the country."[87]

85. For example, see *Henan lü Hu tongxianghui gongzuo baogao*.

86. *Shanghai Guangdong zhongxue xinxiao luocheng jinian ce* (Publication commemorating the completion of the new Guangdong Middle School) (Shanghai, 1935). For a discussion of the political uses of calligraphy, see Richard Kraus, *Brushes with Power* (Berkeley, Calif., 1992).

87. SB, March 1, 1937. Although party and Social Bureau representatives did attend these general meetings, it is important to point out that general meetings were largely ceremonial occasions; they did not affect the real work of the *tongxianghui*.

Creating "Civic Ground." Overlap with the state, state affiliation and state recognition all contributed to the legitimacy of native-place associations in this period. Nonetheless, *tongxianghui* were not entirely dependent on the state for their legitimacy. Association records and activities suggest a variety of other strategies which helped them to create a kind of "civic ground," an independent basis of legitimacy for their public activities. This involved the manipulation of "governmentality," of connections and of higher claims to nationalism.

Whereas in earlier periods native-place associations took on the trappings of republicanism to proclaim their modernity and dedication to the project of building a strong nation, during the Nanjing decade the "governmentality" of native-place associations helped them to create a civic space for their activities. As in the early Republican era, the 1930s associations incorporated into their modes of conduct influential and recognized ideals of governance (constitutions, elections, provisions for the welfare and governance of their member populations, the rhetoric of local self-government). They now also incorporated into their reports and procedures all of the trappings of modern social science, forming "statistics committees" and "social-survey committees" and prominently featuring pie charts and bar graphs with inventive graphic motifs (airplanes and steam engines, alongside Olympic-style torches) in their publications.[88] Because these were ideals with broad public legitimacy, ideals to which the state was also subject, native-place associations could in a sense displace the state, or in any event compete with it for legitimacy by outshining it.[89]

The tactic of governmentality is evident in the way native-place associations inserted the language of local self-government and the rhetoric of Sun Yat-sen into their constitutions and public statements, making it the foundation of their existence. By rhetorically marking themselves as Sun's descendants, *tongxianghui* were seen (and could act) not as merely self-serving "particularistic associations" but rather as constituent building blocks of a strengthened constitutional state. This is clear in a publi-

88. On modernist discourse, see Duara, "Knowledge and Power in the Discourse of Modernity: Campaigns against Popular Religion in Early Twentieth-Century China," JAS 50 (February 1991):67–83.

89. Although the tactics of governmentality usually meant simulating ideal government rather than imitating the actual government, it involved degrees of imitation as well. At approximately the same time as Mayor Wu Tiecheng began to conduct group marriage ceremonies (*jituan jiehun*) at the Shanghai Civic Center, *tongxianghui* also began to conduct group marriage ceremonies for fellow-provincial couples. See *Hu She dishisanjie*, section 1, pp. 66–67; SB, June 18, 1938; SB, June 30, 1938.

cation of the Ningbo Tongxianghui: "Fellow-provincials unite and form the Ningbo Tongxianghui. People from other places also unite and form other *tongxianghui*. Then each native-place group joins together and forms an extremely large national organization. In this manner, domestically, it will be possible to consolidate the strength of local self-government, and internationally, it will be possible to resist the insults of foreign powers."[90] A second example is from a manifesto printed by the associations of Fujianese sojourners in Shanghai and Beijing: "The locality is the foundation of the state and self-government is the stepping-stone for constitutional government. Thus those who wish to do good for their country must realize local self-government, causing the people to devote themselves to the public service of their locality in order to develop their ability to deal with public affairs. After this they may participate in national affairs, supervise government and bring the nation to constitutional government, achieving the freedom of full citizens."[91] Such statements both legitimated the public activities of *tongxianghui* and rebuked the government at higher levels for its lack of dedication to the long-sought-after goals of Republican government.

Another "tactic" which bolstered the social force of native-place associations in the Nanjing decade involved the use of powerful connections. In the 1930s native-place associations coalesced and grew around specific individuals with auras of power. In the case of the Ningbo Tongxianghui the figure was Yu Xiaqing. Wang Xiaolai and Shi Liangcai served the same function as leaders of the Shaoxing and Jiangning associations, respectively. The usefulness of *tongxianghui* and the rise of several new associations in this period were also linked to the ascendant power of Shanghai gangs. The prominence and efficacy of the Pudong Tongxianghui clearly reflected the power of the Green Gang leader Du Yuesheng. Other *tongxianghui* followed suit. The Subei gangster Gu Zhuxuan was the director of the Jianghuai Tongxianghui and the vice-chairman of the Subei Sojourners' Federation.[92] The Red Gang leader Zheng Ziliang was prominent in the Chaozhou Tongxianghui. Given the limitations of government services and the realities of government taxation, corruption and inefficiency, compounded by protection rack-

90. *Ningbo lü Hu tongxianghui dibajie.*

91. SB, January 29, 1932, 12.

92. See PTN; Gu Shuping, "Wo liyong Gu Zhuxuan de yanhu jinxing geming huodong (I used the cover of Gu Zhuxuan to carry out revolutionary activities), in *Jiu Shanghai de banghui* (The gangs of old Shanghai), ed. Zhu Xuefan (Shanghai, 1986), 360. Gu Zhuxuan was also vice-chairman of the Subei Refugee Assistance Committee.

ets and gang organization in the city, it is not surprising that Shanghai residents in this period reinvested their energies in native-place communities, particularly when affiliation provided linkages to icons of power and influence.

The need of public associations for powerful patrons meant that although membership was accessible to many people, despite their constitutions and democratic rhetoric, decision making on important issues was probably less democratic in this period than it had been in earlier periods. Although the gang "muscle" behind certain native-place associations is obvious, it would be mistaken to view native-place associations in the Nanjing decade as essentially gang-type organizations. Their archives offer voluminous evidence of substantial charitable, civic and nationalist commitments. These commitments were maintained at considerable cost, even danger, and they consumed the energies of individuals who may have needed the protection of people like Du Yuesheng but who were often themselves intellectuals, influential reformers, deeply committed nationalists and anti-Japanese activists.

A Higher Kind of Loyalty. The most potent tactic for creating civic "ground" on which to stand was through the articulation of a more steadfast nationalism than that upheld by the state. The process by which *tongxianghui* could become a location for urban reformist — and at times oppositional — sentiments in the 1930s may be illustrated through the career of the influential educational reformer Huang Yanpei. In the early Republican period, in accordance with his faith in rational education, Huang worked to reform Chinese society through two influential institutions, the Jiangsu Provincial Education Association and the Chinese Vocational Education Association. These efforts, begun in the early Republican period, represented a growing institutional collaboration between Shanghai capitalists and Jiangnan intellectuals who believed in the necessity of economic modernization and educational reform to strengthen the nation. Education, perhaps the only realm which might possibly have enjoyed the type of free and uncoerced public discussion which Habermas associates with a "public sphere," was an early victim of the Guomindang "partification" (*danghua*) process. Both the Jiangsu Provincial Education and the Chinese Vocational Education Associations came under attack in 1927, and Huang temporarily fled to Dalian to escape assassination. Increasingly constricted in the political influence he could exercise on the basis of these organizations and persuaded that educational initiatives were bound to fail because they promoted individualism and that individuals were doomed to inefficacy outside membership in large groups, Huang Yanpei rechanneled much of his patriotic and reformist energy into his leadership (together with Du Yuesheng) of the Pudong Tongxianghui.[93]

In a manifesto written in 1933, Huang linked the existence of *tongxianghui*, along the model of the Ningbo Tongxianghui, to the imperative of anti-imperialist resistance:

Our Chinese population is over 470,000,000 and we are repeatedly affronted by Japan, which has a population of less than 70 million. Our land is occupied; our people have been butchered, and we are forced to accept foreign control . . . while we are unable to help ourselves. . . . A critical reason is that we don't unite. How should we save China? Many people have ideas, all of which require one thing: People must abandon their selfish individualism and begin to form small groups. Then they should knit together small groups into large groups and unite the large groups into one great national group. When the entire country becomes one group, the mass foundation for the nation will be established, the nation will be strong and long-lived. . . .

And what will be the starting point for the small groups? Human feelings really develop only when people leave their native place and manifest their sincere mutual love. For this reason, the uniting of locals is often not as powerful as the uniting of sojourner groups who are motivated by the common experience of sojourning in a foreign place. The connections which result from the sojourning condition create large and solid groups. In the entire [Shanghai] population . . . what group manifests the greatest strength? It is a sojourner group. Those responding say in unison, Ningbo people! Ningbo people! . . . And why is [the Ningbo people's] ability to unite especially strong and solid? . . . At the beginning, when [Ningbo] people came to Shanghai [the Ningbo native-place association] arranged work for them, helped them through sickness. . . . Those seeking work could receive introductions. . . . [I]f they encountered hardship they could help each other and provide relief. . . . From the time Shanghai opened as a treaty port, Ningbo people have occupied the dominant position. . . . In 1874 and 1898 because of a threat [by the French] to their cemetery, they gathered a crowd to resist, and a long-weak country forced the westerners to submit. . . . Any group, if only they could have the strength to organize the masses by helping its members, may be similarly strong and great. [Without their *tongxianghui*] I fear the Ningbo people's accomplishments would not be as great or their unity as solid. . . . Our Pudong fellow-

93. My account of Huang's pre-1927 career relies on Ernst Schwintzer, "Education to Save the Nation: Huang Yanpei and the Educational Reform Movement in Early Twentieth Century China" (Ph.D. diss., University of Washington, 1992).

provincials deeply believe in this theory, and in the force of precedent. Therefore we gather together people from all circles to meet, intellectuals and laborers, and ... together build the awesome building of the future. .... [W]ith the Pudong Tongxianghui the ... business of the Pudong people increases and their contribution to society and the country is daily greater. The mass foundation of the state is established, national power will be strengthened, the life of the nation will be long, and from this there will be no more national disasters.[94]

By combining nationalist rhetoric and Confucian reasoning, the *tongxianghui* becomes the center for the ordering of the nation. This lessens the "particularism" of the native-place tie. Huang's manifesto also suggests a number of observations about civic activity and rhetorical rationales for civic activity in this period. First, Huang makes clear that civic activity is to be based not on individual autonomy or citizenship, but on tightly organized mutual-protection associations based on native place, not on urban residence. Second, public action, or action in the public realm, is grounded not in individual rights but in the imperative to save the nation. Third, the tie to the nation is the foremost factor in motivating and legitimating public activity. It is through their anti-Japanese activity that we may understand the basis for native-place associations' expressions of dissent. Dissent in itself was not valued. Public associations viewed themselves as being forced into the public realm when the government failed to serve the interests of the nation. Because the anti-Japanese movement was under attack by Chiang Kai-shek, particularly after the assassination of Shi Liangcai, under whose editorial supervision the *Shenbao* had become increasingly anti-Japanese, anti-Japanese activists and propagandists needed shelter. Shelter and institutional resources were available to individuals like Huang, and others, in the form of native-place organization.

Whereas in the period prior to 1925, it seems that native-place associations remained vital actors on the Shanghai scene because of a continuing absence of strong government and the limited development and impact of newer and more functionally differentiated social organizations, it would appear that in the Nanjing decade they reemerged in importance because of the imperfect, uneven and at times oppressive nature of the new state.

94. Huang Yanpei, "Shanghai Pudong tongxianghui mujin goudi jianzhu xuanyan" (Manifesto for Shanghai Pudong Tongxianghui land purchase and building-construction fundraising) (pamphlet, Pudong Tongxianghui, Archives, Shanghai Archives).

Recent discussion of civic activity in the Republican era has been dominated by the concepts of "civil society" or a "public sphere," terms which, employed in a Chinese context, have aroused considerable debate.[95] Civil society/public sphere discussions as they have been articulated in the China field have often focused on efforts to document practices of "urban citizenship" and the existence of social arenas which were entirely independent from the state. This emphasis on autonomy or its inverse, state control, has inhibited consideration of the modes of public maneuvering described above, which were neither fully autonomous nor state controlled. As the activities of native-place associations in the Nanjing decade reveal, a rich associational life coexisted with the ever-present (if often ineffectual) threat of state coercion. The history of these associations in the Nanjing decade raises questions about the extent to which city residents wished to develop a common urban identity or to operate on the basis of urban citizenship. It is not clear that such things were imaginable. Shanghai citizenship (whatever it could mean) was clearly less useful, in practice, than membership in a powerful native-place association. Even the most powerful businessmen (not to mention people like Du Yuesheng) found it desirable to establish, direct or at least contribute heavily to their native-place associations. Among the leaders of Shanghai native-place associations we find many of Shanghai's most prominent and outspoken capitalists, journalists and politicians, among them Liu Hongsheng, Wang Yiting, Wang Xiaolai, Shi Liangcai and Yu Xiaqing.[96] Sponsoring native-place organizations not only gave them considerable "face" and large networks of followers but also permitted them to acquire the legitimacy of speaking as selected leaders of large "people's" associations.

It is important to note the civic activity of native-place associations

95. David Strand, *Rickshaw Beijing: City People and Politics in the 1920s* (Berkeley, Calif., 1989); David Strand, "An Early Republican Perspective on the Traditional Bases of Civil Society and the Public Sphere in China" (paper presented to the American-European Symposium on State vs. Society in East Asian Traditions, Paris, May 29–31, 1991); Frederic Wakeman, "The Civil Society and Public Sphere Debate: Western Reflections on Chinese Political Culture," *MC* 19 (April 1993):108–38; William Rowe, "The Problem of 'Civil Society' in Late Imperial China," *MC* 19 (April 1993):139–57; Mary Backus Rankin, "Some Observations on a Chinese Public Sphere," *MC* 19 (April 1993):158–82; Judith Farquhar and James Hevia, "Culture and Postwar American Historiography of China," *positions* 1 (April 1993):486–525.

96. Liu was a director of the Dinghai Tongxianghui; Wang Yiting was a Pudong Tongxianghui director; Wang Xiaolai was a Shaoxing Tongxianghui director; Shi Liangcai was Jiangning Tongxianghui director.

in the 1930s and their impressive ability to mobilize their resources for "public" or "civic" goals—their use of public meetings, newspaper advertisements and media events, and the frequency with which they united in citywide federations of associations for more effective economic or political action. At the same time, given the features of public opinion and the urban environment outlined above, it is equally important not to confuse such developments with a European model of a "public sphere" as described by Habermas. We should, instead, attempt to find a model more suited to the Chinese context. What the persistence of native-place organization and the scope of *tongxianghui* activity suggests is that even the notion of civic activity could only be sustained in the 1930s if Chinese city residents were organized in large and influential protective groups. As the activities of *tongxianghui* throughout the Republican era suggest, it was these groups, not individual citizens, which formed the constituent elements of the newer, more celebrated, more "rational" forms of political and commercial organization, including the Chamber of Commerce and trade and occupational associations. Because government services were minimal, it was necessary to contend for them through powerful groups. It was also necessary to create alternative subgovernments in the city which functioned to mediate disputes and dispense justice. The corruptions of government in this period also necessitated such groups as a means of recourse and protection.

Native-place associations did not provide the only access to this kind of broad public identity, of course, but because of their size, constituency, legitimacy and public acceptability they were extremely useful and popular. The large constituency of *tongxianghui* both provided considerable resources and gave legitimacy to the claim of being "people's" organizations (*minzhong tuanti*). By embracing both native-place sentiment and modern civic and nationalist values, they eased the anomie of modern political and economic organization. They were, moreover, viewed as legitimate civic organizations and were not generally vulnerable to repression because they were not explicitly political.[97] *Tongxianghui* could also continue to function because they were at times quite useful to the Guomindang government. They not only provided welfare

97. It was for this reason that in 1940 underground Communist organizers followed a party directive for work in Guomindang-controlled areas which counseled working through *tongxianghui*, among other popular legal organizations. See Zhang Chengzong, "Kongzhan banian de Shanghai dixia douzheng" (Shanghai underground struggle in eight years of the War of Resistance Against Japan), in *Kangri fengyun lu* (Record of the War of Resistance Against Japan), vol. 1, 16.

and social services beyond the capacity of the Shanghai Municipal Government but also, at times, actively promoted state programs, particularly as propaganda organs in the New Life Movement.[98] Finally, as an organizational form *tongxianghui* could defend their presence in terms of the popular and well-accepted rhetoric of local self-government and preparation for national constitutional government, the eternally repeated goals of politics throughout the Republican period. The relationship between *tongxianghui* and the state is best understood as expressing not autonomy but shifting areas of partial autonomy, interpenetration and negotiation. This combination suggests a conception of power different from Habermas's "public sphere" idea. Such reconceptualization is crucial to understanding both the possibilities and the limitations of civic action in the Nanjing decade.

98. *Hu She dishisanjie.*

CHAPTER NINE

Conclusion

Culture, Modernity and the
Sources of National Identity

The exigencies of wartime relief efforts depleted the resources of native-place associations, which were also constrained by the
Japanese occupation of Shanghai and the outflow of population from
the city, reversing earlier immigration trends. The economic crises of
the civil war period further limited the possible activities of native-place
organizations. Although these associations survived past 1949 to be investigated by the new Communist government in 1951, the investigators
faced greatly diminished associations.[1] Maoist policies of fixing rural
and urban populations prevented the influx of new immigrants to the
city. Nonetheless, the old *huiguan* — shells of their former selves — lived
on (while their properties were nationalized and transformed into
schools and housing units) as social clubs and as neighborhood religious
temples. Their twilight ended with the Cultural Revolution, when *huiguan* gods were smashed and the habits of everyday life — at least temporarily — were radically restructured.[2]

In the post–Cultural Revolution era native-place associations have
experienced a gradual and mild comeback, again in altered form and
context. Although the *tongxianghui* were illegal within the People's Republic, the state encouraged them in overseas communities as a means

---

1. "Shanghai shi gongsuo huiguan shanzhuang lianhehui diaocha biao" (Survey of the
Shanghai Municipal Federation of *Huiguan, Gongsuo* and *Shanzhuang*), 1951, Shanghai
Municipal Archives, 118-1-8.

2. Shen Yinxian, interviewed in October 1983, cared for the Jiangxi Huiguan gods
until they were destroyed in the Cultural Revolution.

of promoting investment in the mainland.[3] Students were known to have informal *tongxianghui* when I studied in Shanghai from 1982 to 1985. As Deng Xiaoping's economic reforms loosened restrictions on travel from the countryside to the cities and as rural populations again began to swell urban areas, sojourner institutions of various sorts have reemerged. Informal regional *bang*-type associations and recruiting mechanisms organize the new immigrant "floating population" currently swelling Shanghai and other Chinese cities. At the other end of the social spectrum, with the opening of trade opportunities new native-place formations have developed in the shape of trade and study associations. In major commercial cities like Shanghai these function to protect and promote trade and technological development in specific areas. The new associations use new names, like the "Develop Wenzhou Friendly Association" (*Zhenxing Wenzhou lianyihui*), because the name *tongxianghui* bears a "feudal," old-society connotation.[4]

Studying an idea over a long period of time through the institutional and social practices to which it gives rise (and which construct it) permits a reappraisal of our habits of viewing Chinese history. This study suggests that we need to interrogate two of the primary interpretive frameworks through which we look at China in the modern period. The first is "culture," which we should see as historically constructed — as a loose assembly of terms, habits, notions, and institutions which seem

3. There is a striking contrast between articles criticizing *tongxianghui* in the domestic edition of *Renmin ribao* (see, for example, "Hexu chengli tonxianghui" [Why establish *tongxianghui*?], September 5, 1985, 1) and the overseas edition, which promoted *tongxianghui* (see "Huashengdun Fujian tongxianghui zhuxi Ren Lizeng" [Ren Lizeng, Chairman of the Washington Fujian Tongxianghui], December 9, 1985, 8; "Ningbo he Ningbo bang" [Ningbo and the Ningbo *bang*], November 15, 1985).

4. Dorothy Solinger, "The Floating Population in Chinese Cities: Chances for Assimilation?" in *Urban Spaces: Autonomy and Community in Contemporary China*, ed. Deborah Davis et al. (Cambridge, England, 1995). Fujianese students at six top Shanghai universities in 1985 formed a Zhenxing Fuzhou Lianyihui, which used the slogan, "To Develop China, First Develop Fujian; To Develop Fujian, First Develop Fuzhou" (*Tuan de qingkuang* [News of the Shanghai CCP Youth League], March 26, 1985). On contemporary student and worker groups, see Elizabeth Perry, "Labor's Battle for Political Space, The Role of Worker Associations in Contemporary China," in *Urban Spaces*; Jeff Wasserstrom, "Student Associations and Student Protest in Contemporary China," in *Urban Spaces*. Preliminary observation of contemporary native-place formations suggests an important contrast with pre-1949 native-place associations. The new organizations appear to be strictly divided along functional and occupational lines. They do not incorporate rhetoric of overarching native-place community which transcends class; similarly, they do not appear to engage in charitable activities which service a larger community.

fixed or familiar or "traditional" but which turn out in practice to be continually adaptable, changing and subject to new meanings and new ideologies. Recent controversies over the classical anthropological view of "culture" as a coherent and self-contained unity of ideas and practices have led to the gradual elaboration of a considerably more fluid and open notion of culture, as "a porous array of intersections where distinct processes crisscross from within and beyond its borders."[5] Although this idea of culture is considerably more difficult to envision abstractly than is the more fixed classical notion, it serves much better in approximating the "story" told in these pages.

The idea of the native place and the practice of sojourner organization in the city were two powerful, familiar and easily recognizable "cultural elements" in the urban landscape of nineteenth- and twentieth-century China. Although such ties and organizations have been increasingly recognized as a fundamental element in modern Chinese history, they have nonetheless borne "cultural" tags bearing an ahistorical meaning. Evidence of native-place ties has been taken as a sign of cultural continuity, as a marker of "particularism" and of a failure to evolve new conceptions of individual and social identity. That which bears the label of Chinese "culture" is commonly understood as "tradition," the static foil to "modernity." By considering changes in the meaning of native place over time, innovation and invention in the institutional context of native-place networks and differences between elite and non-elite perceptions of native-place community, it becomes possible to bridge the gulfs between "history" and "culture," and between "culture" and "modernity."[6]

As this study has shown, the idea of the native place was imbued with different meanings at different times and by different historical actors and therefore (though undeniably an element of Chinese culture) cannot be divorced from changing political and ideological contexts or be understood merely as a cultural "remnant." The dynamism of the native-place tie should be taken, instead, as a testament to the protean character

5. Renato Rosaldo, *Culture and Truth: The Remaking of Social Analysis* (Boston, 1989), 20. For a critique of the notion of culture in Chinese historiography and the equation of culture with nonmodernity, see Farquhar and Hevia, "Culture and Postwar American Historiography," 486–525.

6. Several recent studies of urban China have made important contributions along these lines. Honig's study of northern Jiangsu immigrants in Shanghai (*Creating Chinese Ethnicity*) notes the invention of Subei identity. Strand (*Rickshaw Beijing*) provides an important, nuanced discussion of the interpenetration of tradition and modernity.

of "culture." Native-place ties could be materialized in male religious fraternities or in secular political associations which came to admit women by the 1920s;[7] they could be inhabited by secret-society members and adventurers or reformers and industrialists. Native-place institutions (and their social meanings) changed radically as well, permitting young student radicals to reject "feudal and superstitious" *huiguan* while championing the cause of reformist, constitution-bearing *tongxianghui*.

Native-place associations and native-place identities were created at specific times, not simply as a reflexive "traditional" cultural response to demographic shifts but because the creation of such organizations and identities served specific and changing economic and political purposes. As a cultural form, native-place associations cannot be divorced from their material basis, as is evident in the contrast between the strength of Ningbo and Guangdong ties and institutions and the weakness of native-place institutions and identities among people from Hubei and northern Jiangsu. The emergence of native-place associations must also be seen as having a political basis. Li Pingshu's establishment of the Pudong Tongren Hui in 1905 needs to be understood not as the contradictory and anachronistic act of a cosmopolitan, westernizing social reformer but as of a piece with his larger municipal reform and nationalist projects. The meaning of the activist U.S.-returned physician Tang Jiezhi's effort to reformulate and lead the Guang-Zhao Gongsuo needs to be integrated with his leadership of the radical Shanghai Federation of Street Unions, his battles for Chinese representation in the International Settlement in Shanghai and his efforts to create a National Constitutional Assembly. The result is a more complex view of the meanings of the cultural iconoclasm which underlay the May Fourth era. Simi-

7. Although most *tongxianghui* in the 1920s and 1930s admitted women, there were few women members. For example, the Jiangning Tongxianghui membership list for 1935 reported a total of 608 men and 7 women, just over 1 percent of the membership. See *Jiangning liuxian lü Hu*, 100. *Huiguan* also began to admit women. In the spring of 1920, Siming Gongsuo directors ruled that any *tongxiang* woman who gave a sufficient (unspecified) sum to the *huiguan* and otherwise qualified (qualities unspecified) could also receive a membership badge. Gender equality had been extended to the spiritual realm two years earlier, when *dongshi* created a "female director spirit-niche" (*nüdong shenkan*) in the *huiguan* temple, in return for a generous donation. Henceforth all wealthy widows who contributed as generously were to be honored by a niche and worshiped in the *huiguan*. See SGY, June-July 1918; SGY, April-May 1920. No (live) female directors appear in any Siming Gongsuo sources throughout the Republican era, nor do they appear in the records of the Chaozhou Huiguan. The same was true of *tongxianghui*.

larly, despite some continuity in personnel, the newly established Pudong Tongxianghui of the 1930s evoked new social projects and pro-
jected entirely different social meanings. In the course of Nanjing-era
transformations, native-place associations acquired new social connotations, becoming imprinted by the gang connections which often sustained them during this difficult period. It was not coincidental that
when I arrived in Shanghai in 1982 and asked elderly residents what they
remembered about *huiguan* and *tongxianghui,* most of them initially
thought that I was asking about *huidang* and *banghui* (gangs), from
which they seemed indistinguishable.

A final problem with the utility of Chinese culture as an interpretive
framework has to do with assumptions about the "pure Chineseness"
of Chinese culture. In the modern period it should not be possible to
ignore the permeability of cultural boundaries. This kind of cultural labeling, and antithetical notions of cultural difference, are rendered
highly problematic by the easy ability of native-place associations to take
on aspects of "western" ideologies and institutions which might have
seemed antithetical to their cultural basis, by the role of western authorities in the city in shaping the meaning of native-place associations when
they treated *huiguan* as organs representing the Chinese community, by
the way native-place networks flowed through new "western" institutions like the Chamber of Commerce and by the fluency with which the
same individuals worked through both "Chinese" and "western" institutions.

The second interpretive framework, "modernity," is also highly contested but has nonetheless enduringly tended — through our standards
for "modernity" and the signs by which we recognize it — too often to
look like something western.[8] Although we have long been trying to
understand Chinese modernity, it has been difficult to see the ways in
which "China" and "modern" fit together. Insofar as we model modernity after ourselves, "modern China" will remain an oxymoron with
which we interact but to which we refuse admission into our modern
pantheon. The notion of modernity as something with fixed standards,
as a recognizable threshold, is troublesome, moreover, because it has

8. Recent contributions toward developing definitions of modernization that encompass more than westernization are Pierre-Étienne Will, "Modernization Less Science?
Some Reflections on China and Japan before Westernization" (paper presented at the
Seventh International Conference on the History of Science in East Asia, Kyoto, August
5, 1993); Rowe, "The Problem of 'Civil Society,'" and Strand, "An Early Republican Perspective."

displaced efforts to understand the process of change with measurements and markers of change, which cannot provide historical explanations.

"Modernity" should not be a remote abstraction, an elusive goal derived from western experience, against which we measure China and (seeing Chinese difference) find it continually wanting. This study provides, I hope, some paths toward a clearer understanding of several specific processes of change we associate with "modernity," even as it warns against overemphasizing understandings of modernity that presume a radical break with "tradition." The shifting forms of native-place association, changing institutional structures over time and the changing ideological justifications for these forms should make us realize that the elements of "culture" are not inherently "traditional" or "modern" but the necessary, often useful and always constraining paths of change. To express this notion more dynamically, the "cultural elements" that make up the practices of everyday life are the conduits through which change is interpreted and made real and through which it may penetrate society.

Among the processes associated with "modernization" which have been themes in this study are technological and institutional innovation, democratization, "westernization," the growth of nationalism and the broadening political mobilization of society. Rather than focus on abstract or presumed meanings for these processes, the ideas themselves (or the understandings we have about them) have been contested in order that we may reshape our understandings in accordance with the Chinese context. Rather than simply celebrating the introduction of new (western) technologies, we need to look carefully at the Chinese social arrangements through which new technologies were pioneered (as in the case of print lithography, steam shipping, and newspapers) and the ways in which technology was not autonomously socially transformative but susceptible to colonization by native-place networks. Rather than focusing exclusively on the emergence of new institutions like the Chamber of Commerce or the 1905 Shanghai City Council (presuming that we understand the meaning of these changes for society), we need to consider the ways in which apparently new organizational forms interacted with "older" organizations or were invested with similar social purposes. The point is not to deny the importance of these changes or to relabel them as "traditional" or incomplete. The result in each case should be a shift from a preoccupation with a signpost of a "resemblance" to our modernity toward a concretization of actual processes of change in Chinese society and a redefinition and reconceptualization of our terms and presuppositions. This shift should also permit us to rediscover the dynamism of Chinese culture even as we note cultural continuity.

During the Cultural Revolution native-place associations died out not because they were useless in modern times but, rather, because they were drained of resources and suppressed by the mechanisms of a new political culture. Similarly, they have reemerged today not because Deng's reforms have returned China to its traditions or because native-place ties have themselves become modern. In altered form, native-place associations are back because immigration has resumed, because they provide useful services and because the demographic, economic and political restraints which obstructed their formation have loosened. It is not that China is now returning to its past but rather that native-place ties have once again been reinvented.

Although this study does not attempt to comprehensively redefine "Chinese modernity," through a more open notion of culture, through a deemphasis on boundaries or thresholds of "modernity" and through a concretization of processes of social and ideological change (observed through the functioning of social institutions), it has made a preliminary foray in this direction. It has also suggested ways in which our understandings of two key, if highly contested, concepts associated with "modernity" drawn from western experiences need to be rethought in the Chinese context: the idea of a "public sphere," and the idea of Chinese nationalism. Recent debates over the emergence of a "public sphere" in late traditional and early Republican China, though excessively preoccupied with whether Chinese culture is capable of producing a "public sphere" along even loosely interpreted Habermasian lines, have been highly productive in delineating state-society relations and possibilities for action in a public realm. By stressing both the consistent overlap between state and society and the possibility (nonetheless) for public activity which is not under state control, this study has suggested ways in which we may refine our notions of a developing public realm, one which may be specific to China, rather than an imperfect Chinese reflection of a superior European "public sphere." This involves a shift from a search for absolute social autonomy toward an understanding of the kinds of social maneuvering which may take place in a situation of limited social autonomy and even overlap with the state. It also involves a shift from an analytic insistence on individual rights toward an understanding of other grounds (like nationalism or dedication to local self-government) which may legitimize certain forms of resistance to the state. Although the use of concepts from western historical experience has enabled us to fruitfully interrogate China's experience, we need to relinquish both our insistence on strict western markers for historical development and our search for comparable Chinese "equivalents." The idea is to abandon the historically dubious idea of "equivalence" and to understand more precisely the nature of Chinese difference, not as a foil to us, but as its own entity.

This study of native-place associations and their role in social mobilization and developing Chinese nationalism contributes, finally, to our understanding of the broad phenomenon of nationalism. Benedict Anderson's recent study of "the origin and spread of nationalism" has been influential in part because, through his apt term "imagined communities," Anderson expressed and explored the socially constructed nature of national communities and highlighted processes by which national entities and national identities become imaginable.[9] Although Anderson's study and other recent theoretical literature on nationalism has suggested that nationalist movements could mobilize "certain variants of feelings of collective belonging which already existed" in society, consideration of the conscious integration of preexisting ties (preexisting imagined communities) into a larger national imagined community has been minimal.[10] Prasenjit Duara's study of modern Chinese nationalism calls into question the utility of Anderson's and other modernist frameworks for understanding developing ideas of the Chinese polity. By tracing the role of older cultural elements in the imagining of the nation, this study of native-place sentiment and organization in the era of developing nationalism contributes to this developing discussion by providing a counterweight to excessive emphasis on the contribution of new historical elements.[11]

Subethnic native-place networks institutionalized in sojourner associations played a formative role in the anti-imperialist and state-building nationalisms and in popular social mobilization in these causes in late Qing and Republican Shanghai. It is important, therefore, to recognize

---

9. Benedict Anderson, *Imagined Communities: Reflections on the Origin and Spread of Nationalism*, rev. ed. (New York, 1992).

10. E. J. Hobsbawm, *Nations and Nationalism since 1780: Programme, Myth, Reality* (Cambridge, England, 1990), p. 46.

11. Anderson (*Imagined Communities*), for example, stresses the role of print vernacular languages, newspapers and colonial administrations. Cf. Prasenjit Duara, *Rescuing History from the Nation: Questioning Narratives of Modern China* (Chicago, 1995).

the ways in which national sentiment was fueled by native-place loyalties and to understand the position of local identities in the developing idea of the Chinese nation.

The distinctiveness of native-place identity, as an intermediate group identity which might be integrated into a construction of a broader national identity, is twofold. First, in contrast to family, clan or village communities, in which feelings of common identity could be based on a familiar and known community of people, sojourners' native-place communities (which could involve hundreds of thousands of people in a large city like Shanghai) exceeded the boundaries of finite, familiar and knowable groups of people and were based on imaginary as well as institutionalized reconstructions of the native place in the city of sojourning residence. Second, in contrast to newer types of urban associations (merchant, student and worker associations), native-place identity incorporated feelings for territory, ancestors and cultural and linguistic ties, all of which have tended to play important roles in the formation of modern nationalisms.

As the evidence in the preceding chapters indicates, I am not suggesting that native-place networks were not motivated by self-interest or that they entirely transcended "particularistic" sentiments. Native-place associations, as this study has shown, encompassed a range of loyalties and political stances. The point here is that the label of "particularism," applied simplistically to such associations, fails to provide an explanation of their evident historical role in the construction of urban nationalism. If the presence of native-place sentiments and networks in the development of Chinese nationalism is not recognized, we will fail to understand component contradictions and tensions which make up the character of what we refer to as "nationalism."

As we have seen, native-place ties and institutions were involved in nationalist social mobilization not simply because "they were there" and could be useful, though certainly their utility was important. Also important was the process by which the sojourning condition and sojourning networks enabled the transcendence of "localisms" and the manner in which the imagined link to the native place and native-place community, through the operation of synecdoche, permitted the imagining of national community. In this exploration of the "place" of native-place identity in national identity, in this probing of the complex relationship of national interests and native-place interests, we may both modify our general understanding of nationalism and more precisely describe the ways in which nationalism developed and worked in a Chinese context. We can also see the importance of the state for structuring institutions at the local level. The institutional forms of native-place associations changed in accordance with changing conceptions of the broader political polity, with *tongxianghui* adopting constitutions and assemblies while politicians remodeled the state along similar lines. This process of mirroring, of aligned social and political transformation at the state and local levels, in "traditional" as well as more "modern" local institutions, is surely a critical element in the creation of national citizens.

Appendix

Population Growth in the International Settlement, 1910–30, by Provincial Group

	1910	1915	1920	1925	1930	1935
Jiangsu	180,331	230,402	292,599	308,096	500,000	591,192
Zhejiang	168,791	201,206	235,779	229,059	304,544	388,865
Guangdong	39,336	44,881	54,016	51,365	44,502	53,338
Anhui	5,263	15,471	29,077	26,500	20,537	30,956
Shandong	2,197	5,158	10,228	12,169	8,759	14,765
Hubei	3,352	7,997	11,253	14,894	8,267	9,674
Hunan	680	2,798	2,944	7,049	4,406	4,315
Jiangxi	1,488	5,353	7,221	10,506	4,406	5,540
Fujian	2,134	5,165	9,970	12,464	3,057	3,787
Total	413,314	539,215	682,476	723,086	910,876	1,120,860

Note: Jiangsu figures do not differentiate northern and southern Jiangsu, sojourner or Shanghai native. The first figures available for areas of Shanghai under Chinese jurisdiction are as follows:

1929

Jiangsu	1,046,622
Zhejiang	283,995
Anhui	51,099
Guangdong	36,947
Shandong	20,395
Hubei	19,681
Hebei	14,462
Fujian	9,654
Hunan	5,282
Jiangxi	5,926
Total	1,500,500

SOURCE: Zou Yiren, *Jiu Shanghai renkou bianqian de yanjiu* (Research on population change in old Shanghai) (Shanghai, 1980), 114–15. The total includes provinces with smaller sojourning populations.

Glossary

Anhui gongjie xiejinhui
安徽工界協進會
Anhui lü Hu xueshenghui
安徽旅滬學生會
Anhui tongxianghui 安徽同鄉會
Anhui zhu Hu laogonghui
安徽駐滬勞工會
Bailong bang 百龍幫
Baishi shanfang 拜石山方
bang 幫
banghui 幫會
bangkou 幫扣
bangpai 幫派
baocun guoti 保存國體
baotu 暴徒
baoweidui 保衛隊
Bayi 八邑
beibang 北幫
beiwen 碑文
benbang 本幫
bendi 本地
binfang 殯房
bingshe 丙舍
binshe 殯舍
bizhan 筆戰
Cai Naihuang 蔡乃煌
Caishen 財神
Cao Muguan 曹慕管
Cao Rulin 曹汝霖

Caonidun 草泥囤
chang (coffin repository) 廠
chang (prostitute) 娼
chang-san 長三
Changsheng yulanpen hui
長生盂蘭盆會
Changshou hui 長壽會
Changxing hui 長興會
Chao-Hui bang 潮惠幫
Chao-Hui huiguan 潮惠會館
Chaozhou bang 潮州幫
Chaozhou bayi zhiye xuexiao
潮州八邑職業學校
Chaozhou huiguan 潮州會館
Chaozhou shanzhuang 潮州山莊
Chaozhou tang zahuo gonghui
潮州糖雜貨公會
Chaozhou tongxianghui 潮州同鄉會
Chen Duxiu 陳獨秀
Chen Jiongming 陳炯明
Chen Liangyu 陳良玉
Chen Qimei 陳其美
Chengren tang 誠仁堂
Chonghai tongxianghui 崇海同鄉會
choufang 籌防
Cunxintang 存心堂
da tuanti 大團體
dang 党
danghua 党化

Danyang lü Hu tongxianghui
丹陽旅滬同鄉會
Daotai 道太
Daoyin 道尹
Dapu tongxianghui 大埔同鄉會
Daxue 大學
dian 殿
Dianchuntang 點春堂
Dibao 地保
difang zizhi jingshen 地方自治精紳
Ding Richang 丁日昌
Dinghai huiguan 定海會館
dongshi 董事
dongshihui 董事會
Dongting dongshan tongxianghui
洞庭東山同鄉會
Du Yuesheng 杜月笙
Duan Qirui 段祺瑞
Dunrentang 敦仁堂
Dunzitang 敦梓堂
er-san 二三
Fang Jiaobo 方椒伯
Feng Guifen 馮桂芬
Feng Junguang 馮俊光
Feng Shaoshan 馮少山
Fujian bang 福建幫
gai e cong shan 改惡從善
ge 閣
ge huiguan dongshi 個會館董事
ge jie 各界
Ge Pengyun 戈朋云
gesheng shangdong 各省商董
gong 宮
gonggong shiye 公共事業
gonghui 工會
gongju 公舉
gongshi 公事
gongsuo 公所
gongyi lianhehui 公益聯合會
Gongzhong yanshuohui 公忠演説會
Gu Xinyi 顧馨一
Gu Zhuxuan 顧竹軒
guan 官
Guan-Shandong gongsuo
關山東公所
Guancha 觀察
Guandi 關帝

guandu shangban 官督商辦
Guang-Zhao gongsuo 廣肇公所
Guang-Zhao shanzhuang 廣肇山莊
Guang'an huiguan 廣安會館
Guangdong bang 廣東幫
Guangdong guang-yanghuo ye
廣東廣洋貨業
Guangdong julebu 廣東俱樂部
Guangdong lü Hu tongxianghui
廣東旅滬同鄉會
guangfu 光復
Guangfu hui 光復會
Guangshi fangwu 廣式房屋
Guo hong tai 郭鴻泰
Guo Zibin 郭子彬
Guomin dahui 國民大會
guxiang 故鄉
Haichang gongsuo 海昌公所
Haichang lü Hu tongxianghu
海昌旅滬同鄉會
Haining huiguan 海寧會館
Haiyan lü Hu tongxianghui
海鹽旅滬同鄉會
Hangchou gongsuo 杭綢公所
Hangzhou lü Hu tongxianghui
杭州旅滬同鄉會
heilao 黑佬
heiyan 黑煙
Henan tongxianghui 河南同鄉會
hongbang 紅幫
Hongkou 虹口
Hong men 紅門
Hu bei shangye gongsuo
滬北商業公所
Hu nan xue-shanghui 滬南學商會
Hu-Shao shuimuye gongsuo
滬紹水木業公所
Hu she 滬社
Hu xuehui 滬學會
Hu Yongshi kai 滬甬市開
huahui 花會
Huang Yanpei 黃炎培
Huang Zunxian 黃遵憲
Huashang ticaohui 華商體操會
Huatang yanghuobang dianchun-
tang 花糖洋貨幫點春堂
Huaxing hui 華興會

Hubei lü Hu tongxianghui
　湖北旅滬同鄉會
Hubei xuesheng jie　湖北學生界
hui　會
Hui-Ning huiguan　徽寧會館
Huibao　匯報
huidang　會党
huiguan　會館
Huiguo wengong zhuzi shenzhu
　徽國文公朱子神主
hun gui gutu　魂歸故土
Hunan shanhou xiehui
　湖南善後協會
jia-er-jia-da　加爾加答
Jiading tongxianghui　嘉定同鄉會
Jiang-Zhe bang　江浙幫
Jiangbei bang　江北幫
Jiangbei lü Hu weichihui
　江北旅滬維持會
Jianghuai lü Hu tongxianghui
　江淮旅滬同鄉會
Jiangning gongsuo　江寧公所
Jiangning tongxianghui　江寧同鄉會
Jiangsu　江蘇
Jiangxi lü Hu tongxianghui
　江西旅滬同鄉會
Jiangyin huiguan　江陰會館
Jianye gongsuo　蠶業公所
jiao　醮
Jiaying huiguan　嘉應會館
Jiaying tongxianghui　嘉應同鄉會
Jiaying wushu lü Hu tongxianghui
　嘉應五屬旅滬同鄉會
Jie-Pu-Feng bang　揭普丰幫
Jie-Pu-Feng huiguan　揭普丰會館
jiguan　籍貫
Jing Yuanshan　經元善
Jingbang zhuyu ye　京幫珠玉業
Jingye xiang　靜夜想
Jingzhong ribao　警鍾日報
jisi xiqu　祭祀戲曲
jiu shi guxiang de hao, yue shi
　guxiang de yuan
　酒是故鄉的好　月是故鄉的圓
ju yi yu bu yi san yu fan ze bu fu
　ye　舉一隅不以三隅反則不復也
Jun'an she　均安社

kanlou　看樓
kantai　看台
kebang　客幫
kenqinhui　懇親會
Kong Xiangxi　孔祥熙
kunqu　昆曲
Lan Meixian　籃梅先
Lan Weiwen　藍蔚雯
laojia　老家
Li Hongzhang　李鴻章
Li Pingshu/Li Zhongjue
　李平書/李鍾珏
Li Xianyun　李仙云
Li Xiehe　李燮和
Li Yuanhong　李元洪
Liang Qichao　梁啟超
lianghu　糧戶
lijin　釐金
lilong　里弄
Lin Gui　麟桂
Lin Sen　林森
Lingnan huiguan　嶺南會館
Lingnan shanzhuang　嶺南山莊
Liu Hongsheng　劉鴻生
longyin　龍銀
lou　樓
Lu Ban dian　魯班殿
lü chen　旅櫬
Lü Hu Dapu tongxianghui
　旅滬大埔同鄉會
lü Hu gonghui　旅滬公會
Lü Hu Guangdong shanhou xiehui
　旅滬廣東善後協會
Lü Hu Hubei gongren lianhehui
　旅滬湖北工人聯合會
lü Hu Ningbo ren　旅滬寧波人
lü Hu tongxiang gejie　旅滬同鄉各界
lü Hu tongxianghui　旅滬同鄉會
Lü Hu Wanshang miye gonghui
　旅滬皖商米業公會
lü Hu xueshenghui　旅滬學生會
Lü Hu Yueshang zaliang bang
　旅滬粵商雜糧幫
Lu Zongyu　陸宗輿
Lunchuan zhaoshang ju　輪船找商局
Luohan dang　羅漢党
luoye guigen　落葉歸根

lüwai shangmin 旅外商民

mantou 饅頭

miao 廟

Miao bang 廟幫

minjian tuanti 民間團體

Minlibao 民立報

minzhong de da lianhe
　民眾的大聯合

minzhong de xiao lianhe
　民眾的小聯合

minzhong tuanti 民眾團體

Miye gongsuo 米業公所

mujuan tuan 募捐團

nan bang 南幫

Nanhai huiguan 南海會館

Nanhuo hui 南貨會

Nanjing bang zhubaoye gongsuo
　南京幫珠寶業公所

Nianqing hui 年慶會

Niao dang 鳥党

Ningbang 寧幫

Ningbo baihua bao 寧波白話報

Ningbo bang 寧波幫

Ningbo lü Hu tongxianghui
　寧波旅滬同鄉會

Ningbo shuizai jizhenhui
　寧波水災濟振會

Ningshang zonghui 寧商總會

nüdong shenkan 女董神龕

Pan Gongzhan 潘公展

Pinghu lü Hu tongxianghui
　平湖旅滬同鄉會

Pudong tongrenhui 浦東同人會

Pudong tongxianghui 浦東同鄉會

Qianjiang huiguan 錢江會館

Qianye gonghui 錢業公會

Qing bang 青幫

Qingjin hui 青巾會

Quan Hui xiehui 全徽協會

Quan Zhe gonghui 全浙公會

Quan Zhe lü Hu tongxianghui
　全浙旅滬同鄉會

quanshi getuanti daibiao dahui
　全市各團體代表大會

Quan-Zhang huiguan 泉漳會館

renmin tuanti 人民團體

rong gui guxiang 榮歸故鄉

Rong Hong (Yung Wing) 容閎

Rui Cheng 瑞澂

San Shan huiguan 三山會館

San sheng lianhehui 三省聯合會

Sandian hui 三點會

sang guowei 喪國威

sangzi 桑梓

Sanhe hui 三合會

Shandong huiguan 山東會館

Shandong lü Hu tongxianghui
　山東旅滬同鄉會

Shandong xiehui 山東協會

shang 商

shang-xue-gong-bao jie 商學工報界

Shangbu yamen 商部衙門

Shangchuan huiguan 商船會館

Shangda Shaanxi tongxianghui
　上大陝西同鄉會

Shanghai Chaozhou minsheng
　xiehui 上海潮州民生協會

Shanghai daxue 上海大學

Shanghai douye cuixiutang
　上海豆業萃秀堂

Shanghai ge malu shangjie
　lianhehui 上海個馬路商界聯合會

Shanghai qianye gongsuo
　上海錢業公所

Shanghai shangye gongtuan
　lianhehui 上海商業公團聯合會

Shanghai tebie shi chouduan ye
　tongye gonghui
　上海特別市綢緞業同業公會

Shanghai xuesheng lianhehui
　上海學生聯合會

Shanghai Zhe-Hu zhouye gongsuo
　上海浙湖綢業公所

Shanghai zhinan 上海指南

Shanghai zong shanghui
　上海總商會

shangjie 商界

shangtuan 商團

Shangtuan gonghui 商團公會

Shangxue buxihui 商學補習會

Shangxue hui 商學會

Shangye huiyi gongsuo
　商業會議公所

shangye lianhehui 商業聯合會

Shangye qiujinhui 商業求進會

Shangyu tongxianghui 上虞同鄉會

shangzhan 商戰
shantang 善堂
Shantou liuyi huiguan 山頭六邑會館
shanzhang 山莊
Shao Qintao 邵琴濤
Shaoxing huiguan 紹興會館
Shaoxing lü Hu tongxianghui
　　紹興旅滬同鄉會
Shaoxing wanguo gailianghui
　　紹興萬國改良會
she 社
shehui gongtuan 社會公團
shehui tuanti 社會團體
Shen Bingcheng 沈秉成
Shen Dunhe/Shen Zhongli
　　沈敦和/沈仲禮
Shen Enfu 沈恩孚
Shen Honglai 沈洪賚
Shen Manyun 沈縵云
Shenbao 申報
Sheng Xuanhuai 盛宣懷
shenkan 神龕
shenshang 紳商
Shi Liangcai 史量才
Shibao 時報
shoutang 壽堂
Shuangdao hui 雙刀會
Shuangguan 雙官
Shuishou jun'an hui 水手均安會
Shunde huiguan 順德會館
Shushang gongsuo 蜀商公所
Sichuan lü Hu tongxianghui
　　四川旅滬同鄉會
Sichuan qingnian huzhuhui
　　四川青年互助會
Sigongtang 思恭堂
Siming diyi yiwu xuexiao
　　四明第一義務學校
Siming gongsuo 四明公所
Siming lü Hu tongxianghui
　　四明旅滬同鄉會
Siye huiguan 絲業會館
Su bang zhubaoye gongsuo
　　蘇幫珠寶業公所
Subei lü Hu tongxiang lianhehui
　　蘇北同鄉聯合會
Subei nanmin jiuji weiyuanhui
　　蘇北難民救濟委員會

Subei ren 蘇北人
Sun Fo (Sun Ke) 孫科
Sun Yatsen 孫中山
Su-Song-Tai daotai 蘇淞太道台
Suzhou tongxianghui 蘇州同鄉會
ta bang 他幫
tang 堂
Tang dun 糖囤
Tang Jiezhi 湯節之
Tang Jingxing/Tang Tingshu
　　唐景星／唐廷樞
Tang Maozhi 唐茂枝
Tangqiao bang 糖橋幫
Tangye yangguang haiwei nanbei-
　　huo ye 糖業洋廣海味南北貨業
Tao Chengzhang 陶成章
Tianhou 天后
tichang guohuo hui 提倡國貨會
Tingzhou huiguan 汀州會館
Tongwen shuju 同文書局
tongxiang 同鄉
tongxianghui 同鄉會
tongye gonghui 同業公會
tongzhi hui 同志會
Tongzhi Shanghai xianzhi
　　同治上海縣志
tuanbai 團拜
tuanti 團體
tudi 土地
wai bang 外幫
Waiwubu 外務部
Wan Shi Feng 萬世丰
Wang Xiaolai 王曉籟
Wang Yiting 王一亭
Wen Zongyao 溫宗堯
weng 翁
Wenming juyue she 文明據約社
Wenzhou tongxianghui 溫州同鄉會
wo bang 我幫
wu Hui bu cheng dian 無徽不成典
Wu Jianzhang 吳健漳
Wu Tiecheng 吳鐵成
Wu Tingfang 吳廷芳
wujin gonghui 五金公會
wuru Hua guan 侮辱華官
xiandong shenwei 先董神位
Xianggang bayi shanghui
　　香港八邑商會

xiangqing 鄉情
xiangyi 鄉誼
xianshui mei 鹹水妹
xiao tuanti 小團體
Xiaodaohui 小刀會
xiehui 協會
Xijin huiguan 錫金會館
Xin wenhua yuekan 新文化月刊
Xing Zhong hui 興中會
Xing'an huiguan 興安會館
Xinghua huiguan 興華會館
Xingjiang chaye gongsuo
    星江茶業公所
Xu Gongruo 許公若
Xu Run 徐潤
Xu Yuting 徐玉亭
xue-shang-gong jie 學商工界
xunbufang luyijuan 巡捕房綠衣捐
yamen 衙門
Yan Chengye 嚴承業
Yan Xinhou/Yan Xiaofang
    嚴信厚/嚴筱舫
Yang Fang 楊坊
yang huiguan 陽會館
Yang Xinzhi 楊信之
Yang Yuelou 揚月樓
Yanghang jie 洋行街
yanghuo bang 洋貨幫
Yangwu ju 洋務局
Yangyao juanju 洋藥捐局
Yangyao renjuan gongsuo
    洋藥任捐公所
Yangzhou tongxianghui 揚州同鄉會
yao-er 么二
Ye Chengzhong 葉澄衷
Ye Tingjuan 葉廷眷
yifen 義憤
yimu 義墓
yin huiguan 陰會館
yishihui 議事會
yiyan 義演
yizhang 議長
yizhi duiwai aixiang aiguo
    一致對外愛鄉愛國
youzi 游子
Youzi yin 游子吟

yu Hu geshenshi 寓滬各紳士
yu Hu Guangdong quansheng
    shen-shang 寓滬廣東全省紳商
yu Hu Guangdong ren 寓滬廣東人
yu ren tianxia shi; bi zi benxiang
    shi 欲任天下事必自本鄉始
yu tongxiang qingyi you guanxi
    與同鄉情誼有關係
Yu Xiaqing 虞洽卿
Yuan Shuxun 袁樹勛
yuanji 原籍
Yuedong gongsuo 粵東公所
Yueji 粵妓
Yueqiao shangye lianhehui
    粵僑商業聯合會
yulanpenhui 盂蘭盆會
Yung Wing (Rong Hong) 容閎
zai shen qian qing xin 在神前清心
Zeng Shaoqing/Zeng Zhu
    曾少卿/曾鑄
Zhang Jia'ao 張嘉璈
Zhang Jingsheng 張竟生
Zhang Qun 張群
Zhang Zongxiang 章宗祥
Zhaoqing tongxianghui 肇慶同鄉會
Zhe-Hu zhouye gongsuo
    浙滬綢業公所
Zhe-Ning huiguan 浙寧會館
Zhe-Shao huiguan 浙紹會館
Zhejiang chao 浙江潮
Zhejiang lü Hu gonghui
    浙江旅滬公會
Zhejiang lü Hu tongxianghui
    浙江旅滬同鄉會
Zhejiang lü Hu zizhi xiehui
    浙江旅滬自治協會
Zhen bang 鎮幫
Zheng Guanying 鄭觀應
Zheng Zhengqiu 鄭正秋
Zheng Ziliang 鄭子良
zhengxinlu 征信錄
Zhiye gongsuo 紙業公所
Zhongguo furu jiuji zonghui
    中國婦孺救濟總會
Zhongguo tongmeng hui
    中國同盟會

zhongyuanjie 中元詳
Zhou Jinbiao/Zhou Jinzhen
　周晉鑣／周金箴
Zhou Shengyou 周生有
Zhou Xisan 周錫三
Zhu Baosan 朱保三
zhu Hu laogong hui 駐滬勞工會

Zhu Lanfang 祝蘭舫
zhuzhici 竹枝詞
ziqiang 自強
ziyi 梓誼
Zizhi gongsuo 自治公所
zongzi 粽子

Bibliography

All About Shanghai: A Standard Guidebook. Shanghai, 1934; reprint Hong Kong, 1983.

Anderson, Benedict. *Imagined Communities: Reflections on the Origin and Spread of Nationalism.* Rev. ed. New York, 1992.

Applegate, Celia. *A Nation of Provincials: The German Idea of Heimat.* Berkeley, Calif., 1990.

Arnold, Julean, ed. *China: A Commercial and Industrial Handbook.* Washington, D. C., 1926.

————. *Commercial Handbook of China.* 2 vols. Washington D. C., 1919–20.

Ashton, T. H., and C. H. E. Philipin, eds. *The Brenner Debate: Agrarian Class Structure and Economic Development in Pre-Industrial Europe.* Cambridge, Mass., 1985.

Barton, Joseph. *Peasants and Strangers: Italians, Rumanians and Slovaks in an American City, 1890–1950.* Cambridge, Mass., 1975.

Bastid-Brugière, Marianne. "Currents of Social Change." In *The Cambridge History of China,* edited by John K. Fairbank and K. C. Liu, vol. 11, pt. 2, 535–602. Cambridge, England, 1980.

Belsky, R. D. "Bones of Contention: The Siming Gongsuo Riots of 1874 and 1898." *Papers on Chinese History* 1 (Spring 1992):56–73.

Benedict, Carol. "Bubonic Plague in Nineteenth Century China." *Modern China* 14 (April 1988):107–55.

Bergère, Marie-Claire. *L'âge d'or de la bourgeoisie chinoise.* Paris, 1986.

————. "The Chinese Bourgeoisie, 1911–37." In *The Cambridge History of China,* edited by John K. Fairbank, vol. 12, pt. 1, 721–825. Cambridge, England, 1983.

————. *The Golden Age of the Chinese Bourgeoisie.* Cambridge, England, 1989.

————. "The Other China: Shanghai from 1919–1949." In *Shanghai: Revolution and Development in an Asian Metropolis,* edited by Christopher Howe, 1–34. Cambridge, England, 1981.

———. "The Role of the Bourgeoisie." In *China in Revolution,* edited by Mary C. Wright, 229–95. New Haven, Conn., 1968.

———. "The Shanghai Bankers' Association (1915–1927): Modernization and the Institutionalization of Local Solidarities." Paper presented at the International Symposium on Modern Shanghai, Shanghai, September 7–14, 1988.

———, Noël Castelino, Christian Henriot and Pu-yin Ho. "Essai de prosopographie des élites Shanghaïennes a l'époque republicaine, 1911–1949." *Annales: Economies, Sociétés, Civilisations* 4 (July-August 1985):901–30.

Bodnar, John. *Workers' World: Kinship, Community and Protest in an Industrial Society, 1900–1940.* Baltimore, Md., 1982.

Bradstock, Timothy. "Craft Guilds in Ch'ing Dynasty China." Ph.D. diss., Harvard University, 1984.

Britton, Roswell. *The Chinese Periodical Press, 1800–1912.* Shanghai, 1933.

Burgess, John Stewart. *The Guilds of Peking.* New York, 1928.

Cai Xiaoqing. *Zhongguo jindai huidang shi yanjiu* (Research on secret societies and gangs in modern Chinese history). Beijing, 1987.

Cai Xiyao and Wang Jiagui, eds. *Shanghai daxue* (Shanghai University). Shanghai, 1986.

Chai Degeng, ed. *Xinhai geming* (The Revolution of 1911). 8 vols. Shanghai, 1957; reprint, 1981.

———, trans. *Reflections on Things at Hand: The Neo-Confucian Anthology.* New York, 1967.

Chan, Wing-tsit, trans. *A Source Book in Chinese Philosophy.* Princeton, N.J., 1963.

Chang, Hao. *Liang Ch'i-Ch'ao and Intellectual Transition in China, 1890–1907.* Cambridge, Mass., 1971.

Chang Peng. "Distribution of Provincial Merchant Groups in China." Ph.D. diss., University of Washington, 1958.

"Chaozhou huiguan yi'an beicha" (Meeting notes of the Chaozhou Huiguan). Manuscript series. 1913–39 (some years missing).

Chaozhou lü Hu tongxianghui niankan (Annual of the Association of Chaozhou Sojourners in Shanghai). Shanghai, 1934.

Chaozhou lü Hu tongxianghui tekan, jiuguo hao (Special issue of the Association of Chaozhou Sojourners in Shanghai, National Salvation Edition). Shanghai, 1932.

Chen Boxi, ed. *Shanghai yishi daguan* (Anecdotal survey of Shanghai). Shanghai, 1924.

Chen Congzhou and Zhang Ming, eds. *Shanghai jindai jianzhu shigao* (Draft history of modern Shanghai architecture). Shanghai, 1988.

Chen Dingshan. *Chunshen jiuwen* (Old tales of Shanghai's spring). 2 vols. Shanghai, n.d.

Chen, Joseph. *The May Fourth Movement in Shanghai.* Leiden, 1971.

Chen Laixin. *Yu Xiaqing ni tsuite* (Regarding Yu Xiaqing). Kyoto, 1983.

Chen Lizhi. *Hu She cangsang lu* (Record of the vicissitudes of the Hu She). Taipei, 1969.

Chen Weimin. "Zhonggong chengli chuqi Shanghai gongren yundong shuping" (The Shanghai workers' movement in the first years of the CCP). In *Shanghai: tongwang shijie zhiqiao* (Shanghai: Gateway to the world). *Shanghai yanjiu luncong* (Papers on Shanghai), vol. 4, edited by Shanghai shi difangzhi bangongshi (Shanghai local gazetteer office), 8–37. Shanghai, 1989.

Cheng Renjie. "Yingmei yan gongsi maiban Zheng Bozhao" (The comprador of the British American Tobacco Company, Zheng Bozhao). *Shanghai wenshi ziliao xuanji* (Selected materials on Shanghai history and culture) 1 (1978):130–54.

Chesneaux, Jean, ed. *Popular Movements and Secret Societies in China, 1840–1950.* Stanford, Calif., 1972.

Ch'i, Hsi-sheng. *Warlord Politics in China, 1916–1928.* Stanford, Calif., 1976.

China. Imperial Maritime Customs. *Reports on Trade at the Treaty Ports in China.* 1866–1912.

————. Inspectorate General of Customs. *Decennial Reports,* 1882–1891; 1892–1901.

Chinese Repository. Monthly. Canton, 1837–1850.

"Chongjian Guang-Zhao huiguan dongshi" (Huiguan directors at the rebuilding of the Guangzhao Huiguan). Undated, hand-copied document. Courtesy of Du Li, Shanghai Museum.

Clifford, Nicholas. *Shanghai, 1925: Urban Nationalism and the Defense of Foreign Privilege.* Ann Arbor, Mich., 1979.

Coble, Parks. *The Shanghai Capitalists and the Nationalist Government, 1927–1937.* Cambridge, Mass., 1980.

Cochran, Sherman. "Three Roads into Shanghai's Market: Japanese, Western, and Chinese Companies in the Match Trade, 1895–1937." In *Shanghai Sojourners,* edited by Frederic Wakeman and Wen-hsin Yeh, 35–75. Berkeley, Calif., 1992.

Cole, James. *Shaohsing: Competition and Cooperation in Nineteenth-Century China.* Tucson, Ariz., 1986.

Corbin, Alain. *The Foul and the Fragrant.* Cambridge, Mass., 1986.

Courant, Maurice. "Les associations en Chine." *Annales des sciences politiques* 14 (January 1899):68–94.

Darwent, C. E. *Shanghai: A Handbook for Travellers and Residents.* Shanghai, 1920.

Davidson-Houston, J. V. *Yellow Creek: The Story of Shanghai.* London, 1962.

Davis, Natalie Zemon. *Society and Culture in Early Modern France.* Stanford, Calif., 1965.

de Groot, J. J. M. *The Religious System of China.* 6 vols. Leyden, 1892–1910; reprint Taipei, 1964.

Deng Zhongxia. *Deng Zhongxia wenji* (Collected works of Deng Zhongxia). Beijing, 1983.

Dianshizhai huabao (Dianshi Studio pictorial newspaper). 1884–1898; reprint Guangzhou, 1983.

Dillon, Maureen. "The Triads in Shanghai: The Small Sword Uprising, 1853–1855." *Papers on China* 23 (1970):67–86.

Ding Richu. "Xinhai geming qian de Shanghai zibenjia jieji" (Shanghai capitalists prior to the Revolution of 1911). In *Jinian xinhai geming qishizhounian xueshu taolunhui lunwenji* (Collected papers from the conference to commemorate the 70th anniversary of the 1911 Revolution), edited by Zhonghua shuju, 1 (1982):281–321.

——. "Xinhai geming qian Shanghai zibenjia de zhengzhi huodong" (The political activities of Shanghai capitalists before the Revolution of 1911). *Jindaishi yanjiu* (Modern history research) 2 (1982):219–41.

—— and Du Xuncheng. "Yu Xiaqing jianlun" (On the subject of Yu Xiaqing). *Lishi yanjiu* (History research) 3 (1981):145–66.

Ding Shouhe, ed. *Xinhai geming shiqi qikan jieshao* (Introduction to periodicals of the 1911 revolutionary period). 4 vols. Beijing, 1982–83.

Dirlik, Arif. "Ideology and Organization in the May Fourth Movement: Some Problems in the Intellectual Historiography of the May Fourth Period." *Republican China* 12 (November 1986):3–19.

Dong Shu. "Shanghai fazujie de fazhan shiqi" (The period of development of the Shanghai French Concession) *Shanghai tongzhiguan qikan* (Journal of the Shanghai gazetteer office) 1 (1933):701–59.

Dongfang zazhi (Eastern miscellany), 2:11; 2:12 (1905).

Dongting dongshan lü Hu tongxianghui sanshizhou jinian tekan (Thirty-year commemorative issue of the Dongting Dongshan Tongxianghui). Shanghai, 1944.

Dou Jiliang. *Tongxiang zuzhi zhi yanjiu* (Research on native-place associations). Chongqing, 1943.

Du Li. "Yapian zhanzheng qian Shanghai hanghui xingzhi zhi shanbian" (Changes in the character of Shanghai trade associations before the Opium War). In *Zhongguo zibenzhuyi mengya wenti lunwenji* (Compilation of papers concerning the sprouts of capitalism in China), edited by Nanjing daxue lishixi Ming-Qing shi yanjiushi (Nanjing University, Ming-Qing research office), 141–71. Nanjing, 1983.

——. "Yapian zhanzheng qian Shanghai hangyunye de fazhan" (The development of Shanghai shipping trade before the Opium War). *Xueshu yuekan* 4 (1964).

Duara, Prasenjit. *Culture, Power and the State*. Stanford, Calif., 1988.

——. "De-Constructing the Chinese Nation." *Australian Journal of Chinese Affairs* 30 (July 1993):1–26.

——. "Knowledge and Power in the Discourse of Modernity: Campaigns against Popular Religion in Early Twentieth-Century China." *Journal of Asian Studies* 50 (February 1991):67–83.

——. *Rescuing History from the Nation: Questioning Narratives of Modern China*. Chicago, 1995.

——. "Superscribing Symbols: The Myth of Guandi, Chinese God of War." *Journal of Asian Studies* 47 (November 1988):778–95.

Eastman, Lloyd. "The Kwangtung Anti-Foreign Disturbances During the Sino-French War." *Papers on China* 13 (1959):1–31.

Ebrey, Patricia Buckley, and James L. Watson, eds. *Kinship Organization in Late Imperial China*. Berkeley, Calif., 1986.

Elvin, Mark. "The Administration of Shanghai, 1905–1914." In *The Chinese City between Two Worlds,* edited by Mark Elvin and G. William Skinner, 239–62. Stanford, Calif., 1974.

———. "The Gentry Democracy in Chinese Shanghai, 1905–1914." In *Modern China's Search for a Political Form,* edited by Jack Gray, 41–61. London, 1969.

———. "The Gentry Democracy in Shanghai, 1905–1914." D.Phil. diss., University of Cambridge, 1967.

———. "The Mixed Court of the International Settlement at Shanghai (until 1911)." *Papers on China* 17 (December 1963):131–59.

———. "The Revolution of 1911 in Shanghai." *Papers on Far Eastern History* (Canberra) 29 (March 1984):119–61.

———, and G. William Skinner, eds. *The Chinese City between Two Worlds.* Stanford, Calif., 1974.

Er Dingqi, elderly resident of the former French Concession area of Shanghai, native place Ningbo. Interview with the author, Shanghai, March 1983.

Esherick, Joseph, and Mary Rankin, eds. *Chinese Local Elites and Patterns of Dominance.* Berkeley, Calif., 1990.

Evans, Richard. *Death in Hamburg: Society and Politics in the Cholera Years, 1830–1910.* Oxford, 1987.

Fairbank, John K. "The Creation of the Treaty System." In *The Cambridge History of China,* edited by John K. Fairbank, vol. 10, pt. 1, 213–63. Cambridge, England, 1978.

———. *Trade and Diplomacy on the China Coast.* Stanford, Calif., 1953; reprint, 1969.

Fan I-chun. "Duiwai maoyi yu hanjiang liuyu de jingji bianqian, 1867–1931" (Foreign trade and the economic development of the Han River basin). Master's thesis, Taiwan Normal University, 1981.

———. "Guangdong han-mei liuyu de tangye jingji" (The sugar economy of the Han and Mei river basins in Guangdong). *Zhongyang yanjiuyuan jindaishi yanjiusuo jikan* 12 (1983):127–61.

Fan Jiping. "Wo suo zhidao de Zhang Jingshen" (What I know of Zhang Jingshen), *Daren* 11 (March 15, 1971):23–27.

Fang Yinchao. "Guangdong lü Hu tongxianghui gongzuo zhuiji" (Remembrance of the work of the Association of Guangdong Sojourners in Shanghai), *Dacheng* 45 (August 1977):26–27.

Farquhar, Judith, and James Hevia. "Culture and Postwar American Historiography of China," *positions* 1 (April 1993):486–525.

Fass, Joseph. "L'insurrection du Xiaodaohui à Shanghai." In *Mouvements populaires et sociétés secrètes en Chine aux XIXe et XXe siècles,* edited by Jean Chesneaux, 178–95. Paris, 1970.

Feetham, Richard. *Report of the Hon. Richard Feetham to the Shanghai Municipal Council.* 2 vols. Shanghai, 1931.

Fei, Xiaotong. *From the Soil: The Foundations of Chinese Society,* translated by Gary Hamilton and Wang Zheng. Berkeley, Calif., 1992. (A translation of *Xiangtu Zhongguo.*)

Feng Yi. "Le problème des réfugiés à Shanghai, 1937–40." Memoire de DEA, Université Lumière-Lyon 2, September 1993.

Feuchtwang, Stephan. "City Temples in Taipei under Three Regimes." In *The*

Chinese City between Two Worlds, edited by Mark Elvin and G. William Skinner, 263–301. Stanford, Calif., 1974.

Fewsmith, Joseph. "From Guild to Interest Group: The Transformation of Public and Private in Late Qing China." *Comparative Studies in Society and History* 25 (October 1985):617–40.

———. *Party, State and Local Elites in Republican China: Merchant Organizations and Politics in Shanghai, 1890–1930.* Honolulu, 1985.

Field, Margaret. "The Chinese Boycott of 1905." *Papers on China* 11 (December 1957):63–98.

Fong, Hsien Ding. "Chinese Guilds: Old and New." *The Chinese Students' Monthly* 22 (April 1928):14–19.

Fortune, Robert. *A Residence among the Chinese.* London, 1857.

———. *Two Visits to the Tea Countries of China.* London, 1853.

Foucault, Michel. "The Politics of Health in the Eighteenth Century." In *Power/Knowledge: Selected Interviews and Other Writings, 1972–1977,* edited and translated by Colin Gordon, 166–82. New York, 1972.

France. Archives, Ministère des Relations Extérieures. Chine. Correspondance Consulaire. 1847–51.

———. Chine. Politique Étrangère. Concession Française de Changhai. Compte Rendu de la Gestion pour l'exercise. 1897.

———. Chine. Politique Étrangère. Concession Française de Changhai. Vol. 277. 1911–12.

———. Chine. Supplément NS 613. Concession Internationale de Changhai. 1911–16.

———. Série Asie. Chine 31. Shanghai, 1918–22.

———. Série Chine. Correspondance Politique. Shanghai. 1871–81.

Gamble, Sidney. *Peking: A Social Survey.* New York, 1921.

Gao Zhenxiao. *Shanghai Siming Gongsuo dashiji* (Chronology of major events of the Shanghai Siming Gongsuo). Shanghai, 1920.

Garrett, Shirley S. "The Chambers of Commerce and the YMCA." In *The Chinese City between Two Worlds,* edited by Mark Elvin and G. William Skinner, 213–38. Stanford, Calif., 1974.

Gasster, Michael. "The Republican Revolutionary Movement." In *The Cambridge History of China,* edited by John K. Fairbank and K. C. Liu, vol. 11, pt. 2, 463–534. Cambridge, England, 1980.

Ge Gongzhen. *Zhongguo baoxueshi* (History of Chinese newspapers). Hong Kong, 1964.

General Description of Shanghae and Its Environs. Shanghai, 1850.

Giles, Herbert. *Chinese Sketches.* London, 1876.

Golas, Peter J. "Early Ch'ing Guilds." In *The City in Late Imperial China,* edited by G. William Skinner, 555–80. Stanford, Calif., 1977.

Goodman, Bryna. "The Native Place and the City: Immigrant Consciousness and Organization in Shanghai, 1853–1927." Ph.D. diss., Stanford University, 1990.

———. "New Culture, Old Habits: Native-Place Organization and the May Fourth Movement." In *Shanghai Sojourners,* edited by Frederic Wakeman and Wen-hsin Yeh, 76–107. Berkeley, Calif., 1992.

————. "The Politics of Public Health: Sanitation in Shanghai in the late Nineteenth Century." *Modern Asian Studies* 23 (October 1989):816–20.
Great Britain. House of Commons. British Parliamentary Papers. "Commercial Reports." Shanghai, 1879.
————. Public Record Office. FO 228.1256; FO 228.1293; FO 228.162; FO 228.163; FO 228.2512; FO 228.274; FO 228.903; FO 228.2516; FO 228.1634; FO 228.3291; FO 233.96; FO 405.201; FO 680.1992.
Gu Bingquan and Zhang Yingen. "Pudong tongxianghui ji qi dui Pudong de xianqi kaifa" (The Pudong Tongxianghui and its early development of Pudong), *Chuansha wenshi ziliao* (Materials on Chuansha culture and history) 2 (1990):73–87.
Gu Shuping. "Wo liyong Gu Zhuxuan de yanhu jinxing geming huodong" (I used the cover of Gu Zhuxuan to carry out revolutionary activities). In *Jiu Shanghai de banghui* (The gangs of old Shanghai), edited by Zhu Xuefan, 360–66. Shanghai, 1986.
Gu Tinglong. *Shanghai fengwu zhi* (Shanghai landscape gazetteer). Shanghai, 1982.
Guangdong lü Hu tongxianghui disijie huiyuanlu (Fourth anniversary membership record of the Guangdong Tongxianghui). Shanghai, 1937.
Guangdong lü Hu tongxianghui jiuji nanmin weiyuanhui baogaoshu (Report of the Refugee Relief Committee of the Guangdong Tongxianghui). Shanghai, 1938.
Guangdong lü Hu tongxianghui yue'kan (Monthly publication of the Guangdong Sojourners' Association in Shanghai). Shanghai, 1933.
Guangdong xiaoxuexiao jiniance (Guangdong Elementary School yearbook). Shanghai, 1920.
"Guang-Zhao gongsuo guanyu juanjian Guang-Zhao huiguan shixiang" (Guang-Zhao Gongsuo matters relating to fundraising to build the Guang-Zhao Huiguan). 1972. Hand-copied manuscript. Courtesy of Chikong Lai.
"Guang-Zhao gongsuo yi'an bu" (Register of Guang-Zhao Gongsuo meetings), 1912–14, 1920–22, 1930. Manuscript, Shanghai Municipal Archives.
"Guang-Zhao gongsuo yishi bu" (Register of Guang-Zhao Gongsuo meetings), 1891–1911. Manuscript, Shanghai Municipal Archives.
Guang-Zhao gongsuo zhengxinlu (Account-book of the Guangzhao Gongsuo). "Linian jinzhi shumu" (Record of yearly income and expenditures), Guangxu period (1873–1908). Hand-copied manuscript. Courtesy of Du Li, Shanghai Museum.
"Guang-Zhao huiguan guitiao" (Guang-Zhao Huiguan rules). Hand-copied document. Courtesy of Du Li, Shanghai Museum.
Guo Yuming. "Xinhai geming qijian de Shanghai qunzhong yundong" (Mass movements in the Shanghai 1911 Revolution). In *Jinian xinhai geming qishi zhounian xueshu taolunhui lunwenji* (Collected papers from the conference to commemorate the 70th anniversary of the 1911 Revolution), edited by Zhonghua shuju, vol. 2, 935–56. Beijing, 1982.
Habermas, Jürgen. *The Structural Transformation of the Public Sphere.* 1962; reprint Cambridge, Mass., 1989.

Hahn, Steven, and J. Prude, eds. *The Countryside in the Age of Capitalist Transformation: Essays in the Social History of Rural America.* Chapel Hill, N. C., 1985.

Hamilton, Gary. "Nineteenth Century Chinese Merchant Associations: Conspiracy or Combination?" *Ch'ing-shi wen-t'i* 3 (December 1977):50–71.

———. "Regional Associations in the Chinese City: A Comparative Perspective." *Comparative Studies in Society and History* 21 (July 1979):346–61.

Hao, Yen-p'ing. "Changing Chinese Views of Western Relations, 1840–95." In *The Cambridge History of China,* edited by John K. Fairbank and K. C. Liu, vol. 11, pt. 2, 142–201. Cambridge, England, 1980.

———. *The Commercial Revolution in Nineteenth-Century China.* Berkeley, Calif., 1986.

———. *The Comprador in Nineteenth-Century China: Bridge between East and West.* Cambridge, Mass., 1970.

Hauser, Ernest. *Shanghai: City for Sale.* Shanghai, 1940.

Henan lü Hu tongxianghui gongzuo baogao (Report on the work of the Association of Henan Sojourners in Shanghai). Shanghai, 1936.

Henderson, James Joseph. *An International Court for China.* Shanghai, 1879. Pamphlet.

Henriot, Christian. "Bureaucratie locale et modernisation sous le Guomindang." Unpublished paper.

———. "Le gouvernement municipal de Shanghai, 1927–37." Ph.D. diss., University of Paris III, 1983.

———. "La prostitution à Shanghai aux XIXe–XXe siècles (1849–1958)." 3 vols. Thèse d'Etat, Paris, Ecole des Hautes Etudes en Sciences Sociales, 1992.

———. *Shanghai 1927–1937: Municipal Power, Locality and Modernization,* translated by Noel Castelino. Berkeley, Calif., 1993.

Hershatter, Gail. "The Hierarchy of Shanghai Prostitution, 1870–1949." *Modern China* 15 (October 1989):463–98.

———. *Shanghai Prostitution: Sex, Gender and Modernity.* Tentative title, forthcoming.

Hickmott, A. G. *Guide to Shanghai.* Shanghai, 1921.

Hirsch, Eric L. *Urban Revolt: Ethnic Politics in the Nineteenth-Century Chicago Labor Movement.* Berkeley, Calif., 1990.

Ho Ping-ti. "The Geographic Distribution of Hui-kuan (*Landsmannschaften*) in Central and Upper Yangtze Provinces," *Tsinghua Journal of Chinese Studies* n.s. 5 (December 1966):120–52.

———. *Zhongguo huiguan shilun* (On the history of *Landsmannschaften* in China). Taipei, 1966.

Hobsbawm, E. J. *Nations and Nationalism since 1780: Programme, Myth, Reality.* Cambridge, England, 1990.

Hokari Hiroyuki. "Kindai shanhai ni okeru itai shori mondai to shimei kōshō—dōkyō girudo to Chūgoku no toshika" (The management of human remains in modern Shanghai and the Siming Gongsuo—Native-place guilds and China's urbanization). *Shigaku Zasshi* 103 (February 1994):67–93.

———. "Shanghai Siming Gongsuo de 'yun guan wang' de xingcheng—Shanghai Ningbo shangren de tongxiang yishi de beijing" (Coffin-shipment network of the Shanghai Siming Gongsuo — Background for the native-place consciousness of Shanghai Ningbo merchants). Paper presented at the International Conference on Urbanism and Shanghai, Shanghai, October 1991.

Honig, Emily. *Creating Chinese Ethnicity: Subei People in Shanghai, 1850–1980.* New Haven, Conn., 1992.

———. "The Politics of Prejudice: Subei People in Republican-Era Shanghai." *Modern China* 15 (July 1989):243–74.

———. *Sisters and Strangers: Women in the Shanghai Cotton Mills, 1919–1949.* Stanford, Calif., 1986.

Hu She dishisanjie sheyuan dahui tekan (Special issue on the 13th general members' meeting of the Huzhou Association). Shanghai, 1937.

Hu Xianghan. *Shanghai xiaozhi* (Little Shanghai gazetteer). Shanghai, 1930; reprint Shanghai, 1989.

Hu Xunmin and He Jian. *Shanghai banghui jianshi* (Short history of Shanghai gangs). Shanghai, 1991.

Huang, Philip. *The Peasant Family and Rural Development in the Yangzi Delta, 1350–1988.* Stanford, Calif., 1990.

Huang Yanpei. "Pudong lü Hu tongxianghui xuanyan" (Declaration of the Pudong Sojourners' Association in Shanghai). 1931. Unpublished document. Courtesy of Gu Bingquan, Chuansha Gazetteer Office.

———. "Shanghai Pudong tongxianghui mujin goudi jianzhu xuanyan" (Manifesto for Shanghai Pudong Tongxianghui land purchase and building construction fundraising). Pamphlet. Pudong Tongxianghui Archives, Shanghai Archives, 117-1-44.

Huang Zepan. "Shanghai Quanzhang huiguan yange ji kangzhan shiqi de huodong" (The evolution of the Shanghai Quan-zhang Huiguan and its activities during the War of Resistance). *Quanzhou wenshi ziliao* (Quanzhou cultural and historical materials) 13 (1965?):63–67.

Huda liangguang tongxuehui shiwu zhounian jinian te'kan (Special 15th anniversary publication of the Liangguang Students' Association of Shanghai University). Shanghai, 1932.

Hui-Ning huiguan te'kan (Special publication of the Hui-Ning Huiguan). Shanghai, 1932.

Hui-Ning sigongtang chajuan zhengxinlu (Tea-tax Record-book of the Hui-Ning Hall of Thoughtful Reverence) (1875–1934). Hand-copied manuscript. Courtesy of Du Li, Shanghai Museum.

Huitu Shanghai zazhi (Shanghai pictorial miscellany), Shanghai, 1905.

Jaschok, Maria. *Concubines and Bondservants: The Social History of a Chinese Custom.* London, 1988.

Jernigan, T. R. *China in Law and Commerce.* New York, 1905.

Jiang Hao. "Hongmen lishi chutan" (Preliminary examination of the history of the triads). In *Jiu Shanghai de banghui* (Gangs of old Shanghai), edited by Zhu Xuefan, 68–86. Shanghai, 1986.

Jiangning liuxian lü Hu tongxianghui huikan (Journal of the Association of Sojourners from Six Counties of Jiangning in Shanghai). Shanghai, 1935.

Jiangsu 1 (1903). Reprinted in *Zhonghua minguo shiliao congbian jieshao* (Intro-

duction to historical materials from the Chinese Republic), edited by Luo
Jialun, vol. 1, 119–32. Taipei, 1968.

Jiang-Zhe tielu fengchao (Railway agitation in Jiangsu and Zhejiang). 1907; reprint Taipei, 1968.

Jiaqing Shanghai xian zhi (Jiaqing-reign-period Shanghai county gazetteer).
Shanghai, 1814.

Jingzhong ribao (Tocsin), 1904–5. (The English title, "Alarming Bell," appears
on the masthead.) Reprinted in *Zhonghua minguo shiliao congbian jieshao* (Introduction to historical materials from the Chinese Republic), edited by
Luo Jialun, vol. 1, 163–64. Taipei, 1968.

Johnson, Linda Cooke. "The Decline of Soochow and the Rise of Shanghai: A
Study in the Economic Morphology of Urban Change, 1756–1894." Ph.D.
diss., University of California, Santa Cruz, 1980.

———. *Shanghai: From Market Town to Treaty Port, 1074–1858.* Unpublished
manuscript, tentative title.

———, ed. *Cities of Jiangnan in Late Imperial China.* Albany, N. Y., 1993.

Jones, Susan Mann. "Finance in Ningbo: The Ch'ien Chuang, 1750–1880." In
Economic Organization in Chinese Society, edited by W. E. Willmott, 47–77.
Stanford, Calif., 1972.

———. "The Ningbo *Pang* and Financial Power at Shanghai." In *The Chinese
City between Two Worlds,* edited by Mark Elvin and G. William Skinner, 73–
96. Stanford, Calif., 1974.

———. "The Organization of Trade at the County Level: Brokerage and Tax
Farming in the Republican Period." In *Political Leadership and Social Change
at the Local Level in China from 1850 to the Present,* edited by S. M. Jones, 70–
100. Chicago, 1979.

Kōhama Masuko. "Nankin kokumin seifu ka ni okeru Shanhai burujoa dantai no
saihen ni tsuite" (The reorganization of bourgeois groups in Shanghai under
the Nanjing Nationalist government). *Chikai ni arite* 13 (May 1988):33–51.

Kotenev, Anatol M. *Shanghai: Its Mixed Court and Council.* Shanghai, 1925.

———. *Shanghai, Its Municipality and the Chinese.* Shanghai, 1927.

Kraus, Richard. *Brushes with Power.* Berkeley, Calif., 1991.

Kuhn, Philip A. "Local Self-Government under the Republic: Problems of
Control, Autonomy and Mobilization." In *Conflict and Control in Late Imperial China,* edited by Frederic Wakeman and Carolyn Grant, 257–98. Berkeley, Calif., 1975.

Lai Chi-kong. "Cantonese Business Networks in Late Nineteenth Century
Shanghai: The Case of the Kwang-Chao Kung-So." In *Essays in Economic
and Business History,* edited by Edwin J. Perkins, vol. 12, 145–54. Los
Angeles, 1994.

———. "Lunchuan zhaoshangju guoyou wenti, 1878–1881" (Nationalization
problems of the China Merchants' Steam Navigation Company). *Jindaishi
yanjiusuo jikan* 17 (1988):15–40.

———. "Lunchuan zhaoshangju jingying guanli wenti, 1872–1901" (Management problems of the China Merchants' Steam Navigation Company). *Jindaishi yanjiusuo jikan* 19 (1990):67–108.

———. "The Qing State and Merchant Enterprise: Officials, Merchants and

Resource Allocation in the China Merchants' Company, 1872–1902." Paper presented at Symposium on Qing Imperial State and the Economy, University of Akron, February 22–23, 1991.

Lanning, G., and S. Couling. *The History of Shanghai*. Shanghai, 1921.

Lay, William George. *Kung han yi yao: Translations of Official Letters*. Shanghai, 1903.

Lee, K. Y. *Annual Report of the International Relief Committee*. Shanghai, 1938.

Leung, Yuen-sang. "Regional Rivalry in Mid-Nineteenth Century Shanghai: Cantonese vs. Ningbo Men." *Ch'ing-shih wen-t'i* 4 (December 1982): 29–50.

———. "The Shanghai Taotai, 1843–1890." Ph.D. Dissertation, University of California, Santa Barbara, 1980.

———. *The Shanghai Taotai: Linkage Man in a Changing Society, 1843–90*. Honolulu, 1990.

Li Chien-nung. *The Political History of China, 1840–1928*. Stanford, Calif., 1956.

Li Jianmin. *Wusa can'an hou de fanying yundong* (The Anti-British Movement after the May Thirtieth Tragedy). Taipei, 1986.

Li Pingshu. *Li Pingshu qishi zixu* (Li Pingshu's autobiography at 70). Shanghai, 1923; reprint, 1989.

Li Qiao. *Zhongguo hangye shen chongbai* (The worship of gods in Chinese trades). Beijing, 1990.

Li Weiqing. *Shanghai xiangtu zhi* (Shanghai local gazetteer). 1907.

Li Zongwu. "Shanghai Daotai he shangtuan guanxi" (The connections between the Shanghai Daotai and the merchant militia). In *Xinhai geming huiyilu* (Compilation of memoirs of the 1911 Revolution), edited by Wenshi ziliao weiyuanhui (Committee on cultural and historical materials), vol. 7, 526–30. Beijing, 1981.

Lian Kang. "Ji aiguo shiyejia Lan Meixian" (Remembrance of the patriotic entrepreneur Lan Meixian). In *Kangri fengyun lu* (Record of the War of Resistance Against Japan), edited by Wenshi ziliao weiyuanhui (Committee on cultural and historical materials), 309–12. Shanghai, 1985.

Liang Jialu. *Zhongguo xinwenye shi* (History of Chinese journalism). Nanning, 1984.

Lin Man-houng. "Qingmo shehui liudong xishi yapian yanjiu — gonggei mian zhi fenxi (1773–1906)" (A supply-side analysis of the prevalence of opium smoking in late Qing China, 1773–1906). Ph.D. diss., Taiwan Normal University, 1985.

Lin Youren, elderly male resident of the old south city area of Shanghai, former Chaozhou Huiguan janitor. Interview with the author, Shanghai, November 1983.

Liu Huiwu, ed. *Shanghai jindaishi* (Modern Shanghai history). Vol. 1. Shanghai, 1985.

Liu, Kwang-ching. *Anglo-American Steamship Rivalry in China*. Cambridge, Mass., 1962.

———. "British-Chinese Steamship Rivalry in China, 1873–85." In *The Economic Development of China and Japan*, edited by C. D. Cowan, 49–78. London, 1964.

———. "Steamship Enterprise in Nineteenth-Century China." *Journal of Asian Studies* 18 (August 1959):435–55.

Liu Shih Shun, ed. and trans. *One Hundred and One Chinese Poems, with English Translations and Preface.* Hong Kong, 1967.

Lo, Wan. "Communal Strife in Mid-Nineteenth Century Kwangtung: The Establishment of Ch'ih-ch'i." *Papers on China* 19 (December 1965):85–119.

Lu Dafang. *Shanghai tan yi jiu lu* (Record of reminiscences of the Shanghai Bund). Taipei, 1980.

Lu Shiqiang. *Ding Richang yu ziqiang yundong* (Ding Richang and the self-strengthening movement). Zhongyang yanjiu yuan jindai shi yanjiu suo (Academia Sinica, Modern History Institute), 30. Taipei, 1972.

Lu Yaohua. "Shanghai xiaodaohui de yuanliu" (Origins of the Shanghai Small Sword Society), *Shihuo yuekan* 3 (August 1973):9–21.

Luo Suwen. "Cong xiqu yanchu zai jindai Shanghai de qubian kan dushi jumin de yule xiaofei ji shenmei qingqu" (Looking at urban residents' entertainment consumption and tastes through opera performance trends in modern Shanghai). Paper presented at the University of California, Berkeley, March 7, 1992.

Luo Xianglin. "Guangdong minzu gailun" (Discussion of Guangdong nationalities), *Minsu* 63 (June 5, 1933):1–48.

Luo Yudong. *Zhongguo lijin shi* (History of the Chinese *lijin* tax). Shanghai, 1936.

Ma Chaojun. *Zhongguo laogong yundong shi* (History of the Chinese labor movement). Vol. 1. Taipei, 1959.

McElderry, Andrea Lee. *Shanghai Old-Style Banks (Ch'ien-chuang), 1800–1935.* Ann Arbor, Mich., 1976.

MacGowan, D. J. "Chinese Guilds or Chambers of Commerce and Trades Unions." *Journal of the North China Branch of the Royal Asiatic Society* 21 (1886–87):133–92.

MacPherson, Kerrie L. *A Wilderness of Marshes: The Origins of Public Health in Shanghai.* Hong Kong, 1987.

Mann, Susan. *Local Merchants and the Chinese Bureaucracy, 1750–1950.* Stanford, Calif., 1987.

———. "Urbanization and Historical Change in Modern China," *Modern China* 10 (January 1984):79–113.

Mao Dun. "Wenti zhong de dazhong wenyi" (Problems for art and literature for the masses). Originally published in *Wenxue yuebao* (Literature monthly) 2 (July 1932). Reprinted in *Zhongguo xiandai wenxue shi cankao ziliao* (Research materials for the history of modern Chinese literature), 335–37. Beijing, 1959.

Mao Zedong. "Minzhong de da lianhe" (Great union of the popular masses). In *Mao Zedong ji* (Collected works of Mao), 57–69. Tokyo, 1974. Originally published in serial format in *Xiangjiang pinglun* (Xiang River review), July 21, July 28 and August 4, 1919.

Martin, Brian. "The Green Gang and the Guomindang Government: The Role of Du Yuesheng in the Politics of Shanghai." Paper presented at the International Conference on Urban and Shanghai Studies, Shanghai, October 20–24, 1991.

————. "The Green Gang in Shanghai, 1920–1937: The Rise of Du Yuesheng." Ph.D. diss., Australian National University, 1991.

————. "Warlords and Gangsters: The Opium Traffic in Shanghai and the Creation of the Three Prosperities Company to 1926." In *The Nationalists and Chinese Society, 1927–1937,* edited by John Fitzgerald, 44–71. Melbourne, 1989.

Maybon, Ch. B., and Jean Fredet. *Histoire de la Concession Française de Changhai.* Paris, 1929.

Mizoguchi Yūzō. "Chūgoku ni okeru kō, shi gainen no tenkai" (The evolution of the concepts of *gong* and *si* in China). *Shisō* 669 (1980):19–38.

Montalto de Jesus, C. A. *Historic Shanghai.* Shanghai, 1909.

Morse, H. B. *The Gilds of China.* London, 1909; reprint Taipei, 1972.

————. *The International Relations of the Chinese Empire.* Vol. 2. London, 1918.

Mote, F. W. "The Transformation of Nanjing." In *The City in Late Imperial China,* edited by G. William Skinner, 114–17. Stanford, Calif., 1977.

The Municipal Gazette, Being the Organ of the Executive Council for the Foreign Settlement of Shanghai, 1912–1916, 1918–20.

Murphey, Rhoads. *The Outsiders: The Western Experience in India and China.* Ann Arbor, Mich., 1977.

————. *Shanghai: Key to Modern China.* Cambridge, Mass., 1953.

————. "The Treaty Ports and China's Modernization." In *The Chinese City between Two Worlds,* edited by Mark Elvin and G. William Skinner, 17–71. Stanford, Calif., 1974.

Nanjing daxue lishixi Ming-Qing shi yanjiushi (Nanjing University History Department, Ming-Qing History Division), ed. *Zhongguo zibenzhuyi mengya wenti lunwenji* (Collection of papers concerning the sprouts of capitalism in China). Nanjing, 1983.

Negishi Tadashi. *Chūgoku girudo* (Chinese guilds). Tokyo, 1932.

————. *Chūgoku no girudo* (The guilds of China). Tokyo, 1953.

————. *Shanhai no girudo* (The guilds of Shanghai). Tokyo, 1951.

Ningbo lü Hu tongxianghui dibajie zhengqiu jiniankan (Commemorative publication of the eighth membership drive of the Ningbo Tongxianghui). Shanghai, 1933.

Ningbo lü Hu tongxianghui dishiyijie zhengqiu huiyuan dahui jiniankan (Commemorative publication of the eleventh membership drive meeting of the Ningbo Tongxianghui). Shanghai, 1939.

Ningbo lü Hu tongxianghui jiuji beinan tongxiang zhengxinlu (Record-book of the assistance provided to fellow-provincial refugees by the Association of Ningbo Sojourners in Shanghai). Shanghai, 1939.

Ningbo lü Hu tongxianghui linian shouzhi zhengxinlu (Yearly account-book of the Ningbo Sojourners' Association in Shanghai). Shanghai, 1922.

Ningbo lü Hu tongxianghui yuebao (Monthly journal of the Ningbo Sojourners' Association in Shanghai). Shanghai, 1921.

Noboru, Niida. "The Industrial and Commercial Guilds of Peking and Religion and Fellowcountrymanship as Elements of Their Coherence." *Folklore Studies* (Peking) 9 (1950):179–206.

North China Herald. Weekly. 1852–1927.

Ōtani Kōtarō. "Shanhai ni okeru dōkyō dantai oyobi dōgyō dantai" (Native-place and trade groups in Shanghai). *Shina kenkyu* (China research) 18 (1928):255–89; 19 (1929):108–56.

Pan Mingxin. "Shanghai wanguo shangtuan ji qi zhonghua dui" (The Shanghai merchant volunteers and the Chinese Brigade). *Shanghai wenshi ziliao xuanji* (Selected materials on Shanghai history and culture) (Shanghai) 39 (May 1982):103–17.

Peng Zeyi. "Shijiu shiji houqi zhongguo chengshi shougongye shangye hanghui de chongjian he zuoyong" (The reestablishment and function of late-nineteenth-century Chinese urban handicraft and commercial associations). *Lishi yanjiu* (History research) 91 (February 1965):71–102.

———. *Zhongguo jindai shougongye shi ziliao, 1840–1949* (Materials on the history of modern Chinese handicrafts, 1840–1949). Beijing, 1957.

Perdue, Peter. "Insiders and Outsiders." *Modern China* 12 (April 1986):166–201.

Perry, Elizabeth J. "Labor's Battle for Political Space, The Role of Worker Associations in Contemporary China." In *Urban Spaces: Autonomy and Community in Contemporary China,* edited by Deborah Davis, Richard Kraus, Barry Naughton and Elizabeth Perry. Cambridge, England, 1995.

———. "Shanghai gongren bagong yu wuchan jieji de zhengzhi qianli" (Shanghai on strike: Work and politics in the making of a Chinese proletariat). In *Shanghai: tongwang shijie zhiqiao* (Shanghai: Gateway to the world). *Shanghai yanjiu luncong* (Papers on Shanghai), vol. 4, edited by Shanghaishi difangzhi bangongshi (Shanghai local gazetteer office), 38–86. Shanghai, 1989.

———. *Shanghai on Strike: The Politics of Chinese Labor.* Stanford, Calif., 1993.

———. "Tax Revolt in Late Qing China: The Small Swords of Shanghai and Liu Depei of Shandong." *Late Imperial China* 6 (1985):83–111.

Pott, F. L. Hawks. *A Short History of Shanghai.* Shanghai, 1928.

Potter, David. "The Historian's Use of Nationalism and Vice Versa." In *The South and Sectional Conflict,* by David Potter, 34–83. Baton Rouge, La., 1968.

Pudong tongxianghui huisuo luocheng jinian tekan (Special commemorative publication for the inauguration of the Pudong Tongxianghui building). Shanghai, 1939.

Pudong tongxianghui nianbao (Yearly report of the Pudong Tongxianghui). Shanghai, 1933–38.

Qian Shengke. *Shanghai hei mu bian* (Compilation of Shanghai's dark secrets). Shanghai, 1917.

Quan Hansheng. *Zhongguo hanghui zhidu shi* (History of the system of trade organization in China). Shanghai, 1933.

Quan Zhe gonghui huiwu baogao (Report of the work of the All-Zhejiang Association). Shanghai, 1931–32.

Rankin, Mary Backus. *Early Chinese Revolutionaries: Radical Intellectuals in Shanghai and Chekiang, 1902–1911.* Cambridge, Mass., 1971.

———. *Elite Activism and Political Transformation in China: Zhejiang Province, 1865–1911.* Stanford, Calif., 1986.

———. "The Origins of a Chinese Public Sphere: Local Elites and Community Affairs in the Late-Imperial Period." *Etudes Chinoises* 9 (Fall 1990):13–60.

————. "Some Observations on a Chinese Public Sphere." *Modern China* 19 (April 1993):158–82.

Reed, Christopher. "Steam Whistles and Fire-Wheels: Lithographic Printing and the Origins of Shanghai's Printing Factory System, 1876–1898." Paper presented at the conference on Urban Progress, Business Development and Modernization in China, Shanghai, August 17–20, 1993.

Remer, C. F. *A Study of Chinese Boycotts.* Baltimore, Md., 1933.

Ren Jianshu and Zhang Quan. *Wusa yundong jianshi* (Short history of the May Thirtieth Movement). Shanghai, 1985.

Renmin ribao (domestic edition). "Hexu chengli tongxianghui" (Why establish tongxianghui?). September 5, 1985.

Renmin ribao (overseas edition). "Huashengdun Fujian tongxianghui zhuxi Ren Lizeng" (Ren Lizeng, Chairman of the Washington Fujian Tongxianghui). December 9, 1985.

Renmin ribao (overseas edition). "Ningbo he Ningbo bang" (Ningbo and the Ningbo *bang*). November 15, 1985.

Rigby, Richard W. *The May 30 Movement: Events and Themes.* Canberra, 1980.

Rosaldo, Renato. *Culture and Truth: The Remaking of Social Analysis.* Boston, 1989.

Rowe, William. *Hankow: Commerce and Society in a Chinese City, 1796–1889.* Stanford, Calif., 1984.

————. *Hankow: Conflict and Community in a Chinese City, 1796–1895.* Stanford, Calif., 1989.

————. "Ming-Qing Guilds." *Encyclopedia of Chinese History and Culture.* Naples, Italy, forthcoming.

————. "The Problem of 'Civil Society' in Late Imperial China." *Modern China* 19 (April 1993):139–57.

————. "The Public Sphere in Modern China." *Modern China* 16 (July 1990):309–29.

Sanford, James Coates. "Chinese Commercial Organization and Behavior in Shanghai of the Late Nineteenth and Early Twentieth Century." Ph.D. diss., Harvard University, 1976.

Sangren, P. Steven. "Orthodoxy, Heterodoxy, and the Structure of Value in Chinese Rituals." *Modern China* 13 (January 1987):63–89.

Scarth, John. *Twelve Years in China: The People, the Rebels and the Mandarins.* Edinburgh, 1860.

Scherer, Renate. "Das System der chinesichen Prostitution dargestellt am Beispiel Shanghais in der Zeit von 1840 bis 1949." Ph.D. diss., Free University of Berlin, 1981).

Schipper, Kristofer. Conversations with the author, Stanford University, November 19–20, 1985.

Schram, Stuart, trans. Mao Zedong. "Minzhong de da lianhe" (Great alliance of the masses). *China Quarterly* 49 (January-March 1972): 76–87.

Schwintzer, Ernst. "Education to Save the Nation: Huang Yanpei and the Educational Reform Movement in Early Twentieth Century China." Ph.D. diss., University of Washington, 1992.

Shanghae Almanac for 1855 and Miscellany. Shanghai, 1854.

Shanghai bowuguan (Shanghai Museum). Unpublished survey conducted in 1984 of *huiguan* buildings still in existence in Shanghai. Unedited notes on index cards.

————, ed. *Shanghai beike ziliao xuanji* (Compilation of materials from Shanghai stone inscriptions). Shanghai, 1980.

Shanghai cishan tuanti baogaoce (Statistical report of Shanghai charitable groups). Shanghai, 1915.

Shanghai cishan tuanti lianhe jiuzai hui jiuji zhanqu nanmin weiyuanhui bannian gongzuo baogao (Report of the Disaster Relief and War Refugee Assistance Committee of Federated Shanghai Charitable Organizations). Shanghai, 1938.

"Shanghai douye gongsuo cuixiutang ji lüe" (Record of the Shanghai Bean Gongsuo, Cuixiutang). Hand-copied manuscript dated 1924. Courtesy of Du Li, Shanghai Museum.

Shanghai gonggong zujie shigao (Draft history of the International Settlement of Shanghai). Shanghai, 1980.

Shanghai Guangdong gongxue shiwunianzhou jiniankan (Fifteenth anniversary publication of the Shanghai Guangdong Public School). Shanghai, 1926.

Shanghai Guangdong zhongxue xinxiao luocheng jinian ce (Publication commemorating the completion of the new Guangdong Middle School). Shanghai, 1935.

"Shanghai Guang-Zhao huiguan yuanqi" (The origin of the Shanghai Guang-Zhao Huiguan). Undated, hand-copied document, probably dating from the Tongzhi period (1862–74). Courtesy of Du Li, Shanghai Museum.

Shanghai huabao (Shanghai pictorial magazine). Bimonthly. 6 (November 1985).

Shanghai minjian wenyijia xiehui (Shanghai popular culture committee), ed. *Shanghai minsu yanjiu* (Research on Shanghai customs), *Zhongguo minjian wenhua* (Chinese popular culture). Vol. 3. Shanghai, 1991. Courtesy of Mary Erbaugh.

Shanghai Municipal Council. *Annual Report of the Shanghai Municipal Council.* Shanghai, 1875–1927.

Shanghai Municipal Police Reports. National Archives, Washington, D.C. D–7758 (April 12, 1937); D–8133 (October 20, 1937); D–8141 (November 15, 1937).

Shanghai shangwu zonghui tongrenlu (Record of members of the Shanghai General Chamber of Commerce). Shanghai, 1906–24.

Shanghai shangye minglu (Commercial directory of Shanghai). Shanghai, 1931.

Shanghai shangye zhuxu yinghang diaochabu (Shanghai Commercial Deposit Bank, Research Section). *Shanghai zhi tang yu tangye* (Shanghai sugar and sugar trade). Shanghai, 1933.

Shanghai shehui kexueyuan, Jingji yanjiusuo (Shanghai Academy of Social Sciences, Institute for Economic Research), ed. *Rongjia qiye shiliao* (Historical materials on the Rong family enterprises). Vol. 1. Shanghai, 1980.

————. *Yingmei yan gongsi zai hua qiye ziliao huibian* (Collected materials on the British and American Tobacco enterprise in China). Beijing, 1983.

Shanghai shehui kexueyuan, Lishi yanjiusuo (Shanghai Academy of Social Sciences, Institute for Historical Research), ed. *Shanghai xiaodaohui qiyi shiliao huibian* (Compilation of historical materials on the Shanghai Small Sword Uprising). Shanghai, 1980.

———. *Wusa yundong shiliao* (Historical materials on the May Thirtieth Movement). Vols. 1–2. Shanghai 1981, 1986.

———. *Wusi yundong zai Shanghai shiliao xuanji* (Compilation of historical materials concerning the May Fourth Movement in Shanghai). Shanghai, 1980.

———. *Xinhai geming zai Shanghai shiliao xuanji* (Compilation of historical materials concerning the Revolution of 1911 in Shanghai). Shanghai, 1981.

Shanghai shi dang'anguan (Shanghai Municipal Archives), ed. *Shanghai shi dang'anguan kaifang dang'an quanzong mulu* (Catalog of the open archives of the Shanghai Municipal Archives). Shanghai, 1991.

Shanghai shi difangzhi bangongshi (Shanghai local gazetteer office), ed. *Shanghai: tongwang shijie zhiqiao* (Shanghai: Gateway to the world). *Shanghai yanjiu luncong* (Papers on Shanghai), vols. 3–4. Shanghai, 1989.

Shanghai shi gongshang xingzheng guanli ju (The Shanghai Management Bureau for the Administration of Industry and Commerce). *Shanghai shi mianbu shangye* (Shanghai's cotton trade). Beijing, 1979.

"Shanghai shi gongsuo huiguan shanzhuang lianhehui diaocha biao" (Survey of the Shanghai Municipal Federation of *Huiguan, Gongsuo* and *Shanzhuang*). 1951. Shanghai Municipal Archives, 118–1–8.

Shanghai shi nianjian weiyuanhui (Shanghai municipal yearbook committee), comp. *Shanghai shi nianjian* (Shanghai municipal yearbook). Shanghai, 1936.

Shanghai shi tongzhiguan (Shanghai City general gazetteer office), ed. *Shanghai shi tongzhiguan qi'kan* (Journal of the Shanghai City gazetteer office). Quarterly. Shanghai, 1933–35.

———. *Shanghai shi zhongyao faling huikan* (Compilation of significant legal regulations for Shanghai municipality). Shanghai, 1946.

Shanghai shi wenshiguan (Shanghai cultural and historical office), ed. *Shanghai difangshi ziliao* (Shanghai local history materials). Vols. 1–5. Shanghai, 1982–86.

Shanghai shi zizhi zhi (Shanghai municipality self-government gazetteer). Shanghai, 1915.

Shanghai Siming Gongsuo si da jianzhu zhengxinlu (Account-book of the four great construction projects of the Shanghai Siming Gongsuo). Shanghai, 1925.

Shanghai Siming Gongsuo zhengxinlu (Account-book of the Shanghai Siming Gongsuo). Shanghai, 1922–25.

Shanghai tongshe (Shanghai municipal gazetteer office), ed. *Shanghai yanjiu ziliao* (Shanghai research materials). Shanghai, 1936; reprint, 1984.

———. *Shanghai yanjiu ziliao xuji* (Shanghai research materials, continuation). Shanghai, 1939; reprint, 1984.

Shanghai wenshi ziliao xuanji (Selected materials on the history and culture of Shanghai). Shanghai, 1977–89.

Shanghai xian xuzhi (Continuation of the Shanghai county gazetteer). Shanghai, 1918; reprint Taipei, 1970.

Shanghai xian zhi (Shanghai county gazetteer). Shanghai, 1935; reprint Taiwan, 1975.

Shanghai xiangtu zhi (Shanghai local gazetteer). Shanghai, 1908.

Shanghai youlan zhinan (Guide to visiting Shanghai). Shanghai, 1919.

Shanghai zhinan (Guide to Shanghai). Shanghai, editions of 1910, 1914, 1916, 1919, 1922, 1930, 1931.

Shaoxing lü Hu tongxianghui tonggao (Report of the Association of Shaoxing Sojourners in Shanghai). Shanghai, editions of 1911–14.

Shaoxing qixian lü Hu tongxianghui ge gong zhangcheng (Regulations of the Association of Sojourners from Seven Counties of Shaoxing in Shanghai). Shanghai, 1920.

Shaoxing Tongxianghui. Archives. Shanghai Municipal Archives, 117–5–1.

Shaw, Tom. "Liumang in Taipei." Paper presented at Stanford University, November 26, 1986.

Shen Weibin and Yang Liqiang. "Shanghai shangtuan yu xinhai geming" (Shanghai merchant militia and the Revolution of 1911). *Lishi yanjiu* (History research) 3 (1980):67–88.

Shen Yinxian (b. approx. 1918), female resident of the old south city area of Shanghai, former Jiangxi Huiguan doorkeeper and daughter of a Jiangxi Huiguan doorkeeper. Interview with the author, Shanghai, October 1983.

Shenbao. Daily. Shanghai, 1872–1937.

Shiba Yoshinobu. "Ningpo and Its Hinterland." In *The City in Late Imperial China,* edited by G. William Skinner, 391–440. Stanford, Calif., 1977.

"Siming gongsuo wen gao di" (Siming Gongsuo draft document file). 1863–1886. Manuscript, incomplete series. Shanghai Municipal Archives.

"Siming gongsuo yi'anlu" (Meeting notes of the Siming Gongsuo). 1915–39. Manuscript, incomplete series. Shanghai Municipal Archives.

Siye huiguan zhengxinlu (Record-book of the Silk Huiguan). Documents dated 1860. Hand-copied manuscript. Courtesy of Du Li, Shanghai Museum.

Skinner, G. William. "Introduction: Urban Social Structure in Ch'ing China." In *The City in Late Imperial China,* edited by G. William Skinner, 521–53. Stanford, Calif., 1977.

———. "Mobility Strategies in Late Imperial China: A Regional Systems Analysis." In *Regional Analysis,* edited by Carol A. Smith, vol. 1, 327–64. New York, 1976.

———, ed. *The City in Late Imperial China.* Stanford, Calif., 1977.

Smith, Judith. *Family Connections: A History of Italian and Jewish Immigrant Lives in Providence, Rhode Island, 1900–1940.* Albany, N. Y., 1985.

Solinger, Dorothy. "The Floating Population in Chinese Cities: Chances for Assimilation?" In *Urban Spaces: Autonomy and Community in Contemporary China,* edited by Deborah Davis, Richard Kraus, Barry Naughton and Elizabeth Perry. Cambridge, England, 1995.

Stott, Richard B. *Workers in the Metropolis: Class, Ethnicity and Youth in Antebellum New York City.* Ithaca, N. Y., 1990.

Strand, David. "An Early Republican Perspective on the Traditional Bases of Civil Society and the Public Sphere in China." Paper presented to the American-European Symposium on State vs. Society in East Asian Traditions, Paris, May 29–31, 1991.

————. *Rickshaw Beijing: City People and Politics in the 1920s*. Berkeley, Calif., 1989.

Sun, E. T. Z. *Chinese Railways and British Interests, 1898–1911*. New York, 1954.

Sun Xiangyun. "Jiefangqian Shanghai de diandangye" (The pawnshop trade in pre-liberation Shanghai). *Shanghai wenshi ziliao xuanji* (Selected materials on Shanghai history and culture) 49 (1985):126–39.

Sun Yat-sen. *Sanmin zhuyi* (The three principles of the people). Shanghai, 1927.

Suzhou lishi bowuguan and Jiangsu shifanxueyuan lishixi (Suzhou History Museum and the History Department of Jiangsu Normal College), eds., *Ming-Qing Suzhou gongshangye beike ji* (Compilation of Ming-Qing commercial stone inscriptions from Suzhou). Nanjing, 1981.

Tan Xiaochuang, elderly male former resident in the Shanghai Quan-Zhang Huiguan. Interview with the author, Quanzhou, Fujian, March 1984.

Tanaka Issei. "Shindai no kaikan engeki ni tsuite" (Regarding *huiguan* theater in modern times), *Toyo bunka kenkyu kiyo* 86 (November 1981):403–65.

————. "The Social and Historical Context of Ming-Ch'ing Local Drama." In *Popular Culture in Late Imperial China*, edited by David Johnson, Andrew Nathan and Evelyn Rawski, 143–60. Berkeley, Calif., 1985.

Tang Youfeng. *Xin Shanghai* (New Shanghai). Shanghai, 1931.

Tang Zhengchang, ed. *Shanghai shi* (Shanghai history). Shanghai, 1989.

———— and Shen Hungchun, eds. *Shanghai shi yanjiu* (Shanghai history research). Shanghai, 1988.

Teiser, Stephen. *The Ghost Festival in Medieval China*. Princeton, N. J., 1988.

Teng, S. Y. *The Nien Army and Their Guerrilla Warfare*. Paris, 1961.

Thompson, Roger. "Local Society, Opera and the State in Late Imperial China." Paper presented at the 39th Annual Meeting of the Association of Asian Studies, April 10–12, 1987.

Tongren fuyuantang zhengxinlu (Record-book of the Tongren Fuyuan Benevolent Association). Document excerpt dated 1861. Hand-copied manuscript. Courtesy of Du Li, Shanghai Museum.

Tongzhi Shanghai xianzhi (Tongzhi-reign Shanghai county gazetteer). Shanghai, 1871.

Tu Shiping, ed. *Shanghai shi daguan* (A survey of Shanghai). Shanghai, 1948.

Tuan de qingkuang (News of the Shanghai CCP Youth League). March 26, 1985.

Van der Sprenkel, Sybille. "Urban Social Control." In *The City in Late Imperial China*, edited by G. William Skinner, 609–32. Stanford, Calif., 1977.

Wakeman, Frederic. "The Civil Society and Public Sphere Debate: Western Reflections on Chinese Political Culture." *Modern China* 19 (April 1993):108–38.

————. "The Secret Societies of Kwangtung." In *Popular Movements and Secret Societies in China*, edited by Jean Chesneaux, 29–47. Stanford, Calif., 1972.

————. "Social Control and Civic Culture in Republican Shanghai." Paper presented at the Shanghai Seminar, University of California, Berkeley, November 2, 1991.

————. *Strangers at the Gate*. Berkeley, Calif., 1966.

————, and Wen-hsin Yeh. "Introduction." In *Shanghai Sojourners*, edited by Frederic Wakeman and Wen-hsin Yeh, 1–14. Berkeley, Calif., 1992.

Wang Dingjiu. *Shanghai menjing* (The key to Shanghai). Shanghai, 1937.

Wang Shulin, elderly male resident of old south city area of Shanghai, former Chaozhou Huiguan watchman. Interview with the author, Shanghai, November 1983.

Wang Tao. "Heng hua guan riji" (Diary from the hall of fragrant splendor). In *Qingdai riji huichao* (Transcriptions of Qing diaries), 248–68. Shanghai, 1982.

Wasserstrom, Jeffrey. "Student Associations and Student Protest in Contemporary China." In *Urban Spaces: Autonomy and Community in Contemporary China,* edited by Deborah Davis, Richard Kraus, Barry Naughton and Evelyn Perry. Cambridge, England, 1995.

———. *Student Protests in Twentieth-Century China: The View from Shanghai.* Stanford, Calif., 1991.

Watson, James. "Standardizing the Gods: The Promotion of T'ien Hou (Empress of Heaven) Along the South China Coast, 960–1960." In *Popular Culture in Late Imperial China,* edited by David Johnson, Andrew Nathan and Evelyn Rawski, 292–324. Berkeley, Calif., 1985.

———, and E. Rawski, eds. *Death Ritual in Late Imperial and Modern China.* Berkeley, Calif., 1988.

Watt, John. "The Yamen and Urban Administration." In *The City in Late Imperial China,* edited by G. William Skinner, 353–90. Stanford, Calif., 1977.

Weber, Max. *General Economic History.* Glencoe, Ill., 1950.

Wei, Betty Peh-T'i. *Shanghai: Crucible of Modern China.* Hong Kong, 1987.

Wei Bozhen. *Yu Xiaqing xiansheng* (Mr. Yu Xiaqing). Shanghai, 1946.

Weller, Robert P. "The Politics of Ritual Disguise." *Modern China* 13 (January 1987):17–39.

Wenshi ziliao yanjiu weiyuanhui (Cultural and historical materials committee), ed. *Xinhai geming huiyilu* (Reminiscences of the 1911 Revolution). Vol. 7. Beijing, 1981.

Will, Pierre-Étienne. "Modernization Less Science? Some Reflections on China and Japan before Westernization." Paper presented at the Seventh International Conference on the History of Science in East Asia, Kyoto, August 5, 1993.

Williams, E. T. *China, Yesterday and Today.* New York, 1923.

Williams, S. W. *The Chinese Commercial Guide.* Hong Kong, 1863.

———. *The Middle Kingdom.* New York, 1849.

Winslow, Cal. "Sussex Smugglers." In *Albion's Fatal Tree,* by Douglas Hay, Peter Linebaugh, John G. Rule, E. P. Thompson and Cal Winslow, 119–66. London, 1975.

Wright, Arnold. *Twentieth Century Impressions of Hong Kong, Shanghai, and other Treaty Ports of China.* London, 1908.

Wu Guifang. "Songgu mantan" (Anecdotes of the Songjiang area). *Dang'an yu lishi* (Archives and history) 1 (December 1985):91–92.

Wu Qiandui. "Shanghai Guangfu he Hujun dudu fu" (The revolution in Shanghai and the Shanghai military government). In *Jinian xinhai geming qishi zhounian xueshu taolunhui lunwenji* (Collected papers from the conference to commemorate the 70th anniversary of the 1911 Revolution), edited by Zhonghua shuju, vol. 1, 815–38. Beijing, 1982.

Wu Zude. "Jiu Shanghai banghui xisu tezheng" (Characteristics of old Shanghai gang culture). In *Shanghai minsu yanjiu* (Research on Shanghai customs), *Zhongguo minjian wenhua* (Chinese popular culture), edited by
Shanghai minjian wenhijia xiehui (Shanghai popular culture committee),
vol. 3, 77–92. Shanghai, 1991.

Xi Dichen. "Danao gongtang'an" (The Mixed Court uproar). *Shanghaishi tongzhiguan qi'kan* (Journal of the Shanghai city gazetteer office) 1
(1933):407–40.

Xia Dongyuan, ed. *Zheng Guanying ji* (Collected works of Zheng Guanying).
Vols. 1–2. Shanghai, 1982, 1988.

Xingjiang dunzitang zhengxinlu (Record-book of the Xingjiang Dunzitang).
Shanghai, 1926. Hand-copied manuscript. Courtesy of Du Li, Shanghai
Museum.

Xiong Yuezhi. "Shanghai ju'e yundong shulun" (A discussion of the Shanghai
Resist Russia Movement). In *Shanghaishi yanjiu* (Shanghai history research),
edited by Tang Zhenchang and Shen Hengchun, 238–52. Shanghai, 1988.

Xu Dingxin. "Jiu Zhongguo shanghui chaoyuan" (Trends in the development
of old China's Chamber of Commerce). *Zhongguo shehui jingjishi yanjiu* (Research on China's social and economic history) 1 (1983):83–96.

———. "Shanghai gongshang tuanti jindaihua" (The modernization of Shanghai industrial and commercial groups). In *Jindai Shanghai chengshi yanjiu*
(Research on modern Shanghai), edited by Zhang Zhongli, 509–91. Shanghai, 1990.

——— and Qian Xiaoming. *Shanghai zongshanghui shi, 1902–1929* (History of
the Shanghai General Chamber of Commerce). Shanghai, 1991.

Xu Ke. *Qing bai lei chao* (Qing unofficial writings). Shanghai, 1916; Shangwu
yinshuguan reprint Taipei, 1983.

Xu Run. *Xu Yuzhai zixu nianpu* (Chronological autobiography of Xu Run).
Shanghai, 1927.

Xue Gengxin. "Wo jiechu guo de Shanghai banghui renwu" (Shanghai gangsters I have encountered). In *Jiu Shanghai de banghui* (Gangs of old Shanghai), edited by Zhu Xuefan, 87–107. Shanghai, 1986.

Xue Gengxin, former detective for the French Settlement and former member
of the Green and Red gangs. Interview with the author, Shanghai, November 17, 1984.

Xue Liyong. *Shanghai diming luming shiqu* (Shanghai place-name and street-
name anecdotes). Shanghai, 1990.

Yan Xianggu (b. approx. 1910), elderly female resident of the former International Settlement area of Shanghai, native place Shaoxing. Interview with
the author, Shanghai, February 1983.

Yang, C. K. *Religion in Chinese Society*. Berkeley, Calif., 1970.

Yang Chengzhi. *Guangdongren yu wenhua* (Guangdong people and culture).
Guangzhou, 1943.

Yang Hao and Ye Lan, eds. *Jiu Shanghai fengyun renwu* (Leading figures of old
Shanghai). Shanghai, 1989.

Yang Jiayou. *Shanghai zhi wu guji de gushi* (Stories about Shanghai things and
historical sites). Shanghai 1957.

Yao Gonghe. *Shanghai xianhua* (Shanghai idle talk). Shanghai, 1917; Shanghai Guji Chubanshe reprint Shanghai, 1989.

Ye Shuping and Zheng Zu'an, eds. *Bainian Shanghai tan* (One hundred years of the Shanghai bund). Shanghai, 1988.

Zhan Xiaoci, son of Quon-Zhang Huiguan director Zhan Ronghui. Interview with the author, Quanzhou, Fujian, March 19, 1984.

Zhang Chengzong. "Kongzhan banian de Shanghai dixia douzheng" (Shanghai underground struggle in eight years of the War of Resistance Against Japan). In *Kangri fengyun lu* (Record of the War of Resistance Against Japan), edited by Wenshi ziliao weiyuanhui (Committee on historical and cultural materials), vol. 1, 1–21. Shanghai, 1985.

Zhang Cunwu. *Guangxu sanshiyi nian Zhong-Mei gongyue fengchao* (The 1905 Chinese–U.S. labor treaty unrest). Taipei, 1965.

Zhang Jingsheng, ed. *Xin wenhua yuekan* (New culture monthly) vol. 1: nos. 4, 6 (April, June 1927).

Zhang Jishun. "Lun Shanghai zhengzhi yundong zhong de xuesheng qunti (1925–27)" (Regarding student formations in Shanghai political movements, 1925–27). In *Shanghai: tongwang shijie zhiqiao* (Shanghai: Gateway to the world), edited by Shanghai shi difangzhi bangongshi (Shanghai local gazetteer office). *Shanghai yanjiu luncong* (Papers on Shanghai), vol. 4, 97–117. Shanghai, 1989.

Zhang Jungu. *Du Yuesheng zhuan* (Biography of Du Yuesheng). 3 vols. Taipei, 1967–69.

Zhang Xiuhua. "Wo he Tianhou gong" (My experiences with the Temple of the Empress of Heaven). *Tianjin wenshi ziliao xuanji* (Selected materials on Tianjin history and culture) 19 (March 1982):158–207.

Zhang Zhongli, ed. *Jindai Shanghai chengshi yanjiu* (Research on modern Shanghai). Shanghai, 1990.

Zhao Puchu. "Kangzhan chuqi Shanghai de nanmin gongzuo" (Shanghai refugee work during the early part of the War of Resistance). *Shanghai wenshi ziliao xuanji* (Selected materials on Shanghai history and culture (Shanghai) 4 (1980):31–50.

Zhejiang chao (Zhejiang tide) 1 (1903). Reprinted in *Zhonghua minguo shiliao congbian jieshao* (Introduction to historical materials from the Chinese Republic), edited by Luo Jialun, vol. 1, 67–102. Taipei, 1968.

Zheng Tuyou, "Chongtu, bingcun, jiaorong, chuangxin: Shanghai minsu de xingcheng yu tedian" (Conflict, coexistence, mixture and new creation: The formation and characteristics of Shanghai popular culture). In *Shanghai minsu yanjiu* (Research on Shanghai customs), *Zhongguo minjian wenhua* (Chinese popular culture), edited by Shanghai minjian wenyijia xiehui (Shanghai popular culture committee), vol. 3, 1–23. Shanghai, 1991.

Zheng Yingshi. "Chaoji yapianyan shang zai Shanghai de huodong ji qi yu Jiang Jieshi zhengquan de guanxi" (The activities of Chaozhou opium merchants in Shanghai and their relation to Chiang Kai-shek's regime). *Guangdong wenshi ziliao xuanji* (Selected materials on Guangdong history and culture) 21 (1977):1–31.

Zhongguo furu jiuji zonghui (Chinese Society for Assistance to Women and Children). Archives. Shanghai Municipal Archives.

Zhongguo guomindang quanguo minzhong yundong gongzuo taolunhui baogaoshu (Report of the Conference on the Guomindang Central All-China Mass-Movement Leadership Committee). Nanjing, 1934.

Zhongguo jindai huidangshi yanjiu (Research on the modern history of Chinese gangs). Beijing, 1987.

Zhongguo shehui kexueyuan, Jingji yanjiusuo (Chinese Academy of Social Sciences, Economic Research Institute). *Shanghai minzu jiqi gongye* (Shanghai's national machine industry). Beijing, 1979.

Zhongguo shehui kexueyuan, Lishi yanjiusuo (Chinese Academy of Social Sciences, History Research Institute). *Wusi aiguo yundong ziliao* (Materials on the May Fourth patriotic movement). Beijing, 1954.

Zhongyang dang'anguan (Party Central Committee Archive), ed. *Zhongguo zhongyang wenjian xuanji* (Collection of documents of the Central Committee of the Chinese Communist party). Vol. 2. Beijing, 1982.

Zhu Bangxing, Hu Lingge and Xu Sheng, eds. *Shanghai chanye yu Shanghai zhigong* (Shanghai industry and workers). Shanghai, 1939; reprint, 1984.

Zhu Yongfang (b. 1899), elderly male resident of the south city area of Shanghai, native place Jiangsu. Interview with the author, Shanghai, October 1982.

Zou Yiren. *Jiu Shanghai renkou bianqian de yanjin* (Research on population change in old Shanghai). Shanghai, 1980.

Index

Acum (Lin Qin), 60
All-Anhui Consultative Committee,
    40n60, 239
All-province associations, 239
All-Shanghai Association for the Support
    of Armed Resistance, 290
All-Zhejiang Association, 40n60, 239
Alum (Guangdong merchant), 60
Anderson, Benedict, 312
Anfu clique, 246
Anhui: merchants, 32–33, 50, 285, 286;
    pawnshops, 30–31, 34n48; restaurants,
    22, 23; sojourners, 22, 198n55, 224
Anhui Consultative Committee, 263
Anhui Tongxianghui, 286–87
Anti-American Boycott of 1905, 178n2,
    183–87, 201n60, 216n98
Antiforeign activity, 2n1, 64n35, 159, 169–
    70, 174, 179, 202–3. *See also* Anti-
    American Boycott of 1905; Ningbo
    cemetery riots; Zhou Shengyou, case
    of
Anti-Japanese activity, 289–90, 301
Anti-Qing mobilization, 198
Architecture. See *Huiguan* architecture
Artisans. *See* Workers
Association of Chaozhou Students So-
    journing in Shanghai, 229
Association of Fujian Students, 232
Association of Guangdong Seamen, 236.
    See also Guangdong, seamen

Association of Ningbo Seamen, 37, 237,
    275
Association of Zhejiang Students So-
    journing in Shanghai, 232, 237
Augustine Heard and Company, 60,
    140n50

Bailong bang. See Hundred Dragon Society
Baishi Shanfang, 138
Bang, 63 233, 234; use of term, 39–40,
    40n59, 233n39. *See also* Trade associa-
    tions; Worker associations
Bangpai (faction), 39
Banks, 71, 121n2, 142n55, 291
Bean trade, 34–35, 45n69, 50, 59
Bean Trade Association, 34–35
Bennertz and Co. vs. the Jiangnan De-
    fense and Pay Department, 126n13
Bergère, Marie-Claire, 43, 219, 261
Bezaure, Compte de, 164
Bird Society, 67n40, 77
Blue Hand Society, 77
Blue Turban Society, 67n40, 77
Boatmen, 62–65. *See also* Seamen
Bombing, by Japanese, 287–88
Boxer Rebellion, 151–52, 176
Boycotts, 165, 170, 178n2, 182; against Ja-
    pan, 264–65, 276. *See also* Anti-
    American Boycott of 1905; Mixed
    Court Riot of December 1905; Ningbo
    cemetery riots

British-American Tobacco Company, 234

British opium trade, 68n42, 70

British Settlement, 147. *See also* International Settlement

Burial grounds, 8, 147, 160, 275; tax-free status of, 160, 163n32. *See also* Cemeteries; Ningbo cemetery riots

Burial services, 6–7, 91, 95, 102. *See also* Cemeteries; Coffin repositories; Coffin shipment

Cai Naihuang, 204

Cai Zaiqian, 249

Caishen, 58

Cake- and Bean-Trade Gongsuo, 238

Canals, and coffin transport, 252n81, 253

Cantonese. *See* Guangdong

Cantonese Provincials' Guild, 153

Cao Muguan, 265

Cao Rulin, 266

Caonidun. *See* Straw and Mud Gang

Capitalism, 44. *See also* Economic development

Capitalists. *See* Liu Hongsheng; Yu Xiaqing; Zheng Bozhao; Zhu Baosan

Carpenters. *See* Guangdong, carpenters; Ningbo, carpenters

Cemeteries, 6n6, 26, 90, 96n23, 159–60, 251n79, 253. *See also* Burial grounds; Coffin repositories; Ningbo cemetery riots

Chambers of Commerce, 176–77, 240, 267, 277, 283, 285, 303, 309. *See also* Shanghai Chamber of Commerce

Changsheng Hui, 37, 102, 168, 171, 173

Changsheng Yulanpenhui, 102

Changxing Hui, 102

Changzhou native-place associations, 223n13

Chao-Hui *bang*, 58

Chao-Hui Elementary School, 254

Chao-Hui Huiguan, 10, 236, 238, 254, 262; and the opium trade, 41n62, 58, 131–33, 254n89

Chao-Hui Industrial School, 254

Chao-Hui Third-Class Pawnshop Association, 236

Chaoyang county (Guangdong): merchants from, 35, 57–58; vagabonds, 64–65. *See also* Chaozhou

Chaozhou (Guangdong), 55n12, 212n89, 244–48; dialect of, 55; sojourners, 256; students, 229–31, 274

Chaozhou Huiguan, 12, 135n40, 186, 191, 236, 255n91, 256; and business matters, 250–51; and Chaozhou Sugar and Miscellaneous Goods Trade Association, 34, 44–45; decision making in, 228–31; in eighteenth and nineteenth centuries, 50n7, 56–57, 65; and family matters, 249–50; in Guangdong province, 212n89, 244–45, 246–47; as object of extortion, 247–48; during the Republican period, 228–29, 240–42, 274

Chaozhou merchants, 55–57; and the opium trade, 69, 70–72, 131–33, 137, 257n98; and the sugar trade, 30, 34n48, 50, 133–34. *See also* Chaozhou Huiguan

Chaozhou native-place associations, 56, 56–57n16, 77, 293. *See also* Chao-Hui Huiguan; Chaozhou Huiguan; Chaozhou Tongxianghui

Chaozhou Shanzhuang, 253

Chaozhou Sugar and Miscellaneous Goods Trade Association, 34, 44–45, 236

Chaozhou Tongxianghui, 135n40, 231, 285, 286n60, 296, 298. *See also* Zheng Ziliang

Charitable activities, 85n2, 110, 121–25, 144, 253–55. *See also* Disaster relief

Chen Alin, 78, 80

Chen Aliu, 78

Chen Duxiu, 268

Chen Geliang, 61

Chen Jianye, 57

Chen Jiongming, 247–48

Chen Liangyu, 265, 266n16

Chen Qikang, 189

Chen Qimei, 207–8, 211–13, 215

Chen Weihan, 189

Chen Yizhai, 156

Chenghai county (Guangdong), merchants from, 57–58

Chengrentang, 36

Chengxiang neiwai zong gongcheng ju (Chinese Municipal Council), 200–201n59

Cheong Chi-pio, 157

Chiang Kai-shek, 213n90, 239, 277, 301

China Merchants' Steam Navigation Company, 139–42, 145, 288

Chinese Company of Settlement Volunteers, 205

Chinese identity, 13–14, 26–27, 28, 192. *See*

also National identity; Native-place identity; Shanghai identity; Urban identity

Chinese Merchants' Exercise Association, 199

Chinese Municipal Council, 200–201n59, 201, 203, 204, 205, 214, 216

Chinese Ratepayers' Association, 272n36

Chinese Restriction Act of 1882, 184n14

Chinese Society for Assistance to Women and Children, 249n73, 254–55, 283

Chinese Vocational Education Association, 299

Chinese Volunteer Corps, 199

Chinese walled city, 72, 76; map of, 149

Cholera epidemics (1890), 163. *See also* Coffin repositories

Chong-Hai Fellow-Provincials' Association, 190

Chongdehui, 36

Chongming county (Jiangsu), 190n32; island, 49

Chongqing Basheng Huiguan, 158n21

Chun Bing-him, 157

Ciqi (Ningbo) sojourners, 36

City-god procession, 28

City God Temple, 50

Citywide organization, 176–77, 192, 216, 284–85. *See also* Shanghai Chamber of Commerce; Shanghai Federation of Street Unions

Civic activity, 299–303

Civil society, 302. *See also* "Public sphere"

Civilized Treaty Resistance Society, 190

Cixi, Empress Dowager, 171–72n48; "New Policies" of, 176

Class identity, 29, 273, 276–77. *See also* Workers

Cocoon and Silk Guild, 156

Coffin repositories, 6n6, 7, 90–91, 92, 102, 147, 251–53. *See also* Ningbo cemetery riots; Siming Gongsuo, coffin repositories and shipment

Coffin shipment, 91, 164, 225n17, 253. *See also* Siming Gongsuo, coffin repositories and shipment

Commercial Directory of Shanghai, 223

Commercial Education Society, 190, 190n33

Commercial Strive for Progress Society, 190, 191

Commercial Studies Continuation Society, 190

Communications. *See* Transportation and communication technologies

Communist party, 235, 272–73, 303n97

Compradors, 60–62, 121, 127, 138–39, 144

Confucian governance, 111, 116–17

Constitutional preparation societies, 214

Constitutionalist movement, 215

Construction workers, 211n86, 264, 276

Corruption, 196, 197, 303

Cosmopolitanism, 12, 23, 28n40, 122, 125, 127n16, 144–46. *See also* Urban identity

Cotton Transportation and Sales Society, 289

Cotton Yarn Guild, 156

Courts, 256. See also *Huiguan,* mediating role of; Mixed Court

Crepe Trade Association, 287

Culture (as explanatory category), 306–11

Cunxintang, 244

Customs Bureau, 49

Dalai Bank, 291

Dan Gui Chayuan, 112n57

Dang, 40n59. *See also* Secret societies

Danyang Lü Hu Tongxianghui, 262

Daotai, 68n42. *See also* Cai Naihuang; Ding Richang; Feng Junguang; Lan Weiwen; Liang Ruhao; Liu Yanyi; Rui Cheng; Shao Youlian; Shen Bingcheng; Wu Jianzhang; Wu Xu; Ying Baoshi; Yuan Shuxun

Dapu Tongxianghui, 246, 262

David Sassoon, Sons and Company, 131

Daxue ("The Great Learning"), 13, 117

Death ritual, 6, 10, 102, 158–61

Defense tax, 133, 134

Deng Xiaoping, 306, 311

Deng Zhongxia, 233

Dialects, 9, 15–16

Dianchuntang, 77–78, 78n66, 186n20, 185, 190n32, 210

Dianshi Studio, 138

Dibao (constables), 64n34, 97

Dike and Bridge Gang, 72, 77

Ding Richang, 96, 97, 98, 99, 106n47, 139

Ding Richu, 214–15

Dinghai Huiguan, 237

Dinghai Shangchang Huiguan, 237

Dinghai (Ningbo) sojourners, 36, 218, 218n2

Dinghai Tongxianghui, 302n96

Disaster relief, 122, 123–24, 125, 218, 244–45, 291n74. *See also* Floods; War relief

Dongting Dongshan Tongxianghui, 219n5, 289
Double Sword Society, 67n40, 77
Du Li, 43
Du Yuesheng, 284, 302; and Pudong Tongxianghui, 278, 280–81, 298, 300
Duan Qirui, 246, 246n67
Duara, Prasenjit, 312
Duff and David vs. the Swatow Opium Guild, 132
Dunrentang, 36
Dunzitang, 32

Earth god rituals, 92
Economic development, 42, 43–45, 219, 299
Economic nationalism, 119. See also Self-strengthening movement
Economic rights, 198. See also Railway rights
Education, 22, 299. See also Schools
Elites, 12n18, 14–15, 27, 120; interactions with non-elites, 46, 84–85
Elvin, Mark, 86n3, 203, 213, 215
Ever Victorious Army, 127
Exchange Bankers' Guild, 153
Export Trade Association, 26n8
Extraterritoriality, 119

"Face," 190, 195, 256, 282, 302
Fairbank, John, 62
Famine, 111, 123–24, 125, 212n89, 291
Fan Gaotou, 213
Fang Huichang, 189
Fang Jiaobo, 209, 275–76
Fang Mingshan, 165n37
Fang Yizhang, 161n29
Farnham, Boyd and Company, 89
Federated Committee of Sojourning Tongxianghui, 284
Federation of Jiangsu Public Groups, 40n60
Fei Xiaotong, 92
Feng Guifen, 198
Feng Junguang, 85n2, 115n65, 134
Feng Shaoshan, 208
Fenghua county (Ningbo), 36, 245
Fengshun county (Guangdong), merchants from, 57–58
Ferryworkers' union, 284
Floods: in Guangdong, 99, 110, 124n9, 244; of 1905, 122

Flour mills, 234
Foreign concessions, 28, 30–31, 147, 150, 151–52, 153. See also French Concession; International Settlement
Foreign Merchandise Association, 156n15
Foreign Piece Goods Dealers' Guild, 153, 156
Foreign trade: opening of Shanghai to, 48–49; prominence of Guangdong people in, 53, 54, 62
Foreign Trade Lane, 17, 56, 64
Foreigners: and Chinese identity, 27; and May Fourth Movement, 266–67; official functions involving, 125–26; and the opium trade, 68n42, 69n43, 70, 131–32, 136. See also Antiforeign activity; Foreign concessions; Huiguan, and foreigners
Foreign-Goods Trade Association, 26n8
Fortune, Robert, 69
French Concession, 147, 171–72; map of, 149; Ningbo cemetery land in, 159–60, 164; Ningbo residents of, 16, 165
French Convention (1914), 194
French Municipal Council, 160–62
Fudan Chaozhou Students' Association, 232, 236
Fudan Shaoxing Student Association, 237
Fudan University, 263
Fudan University Students' Association, 232
Fudan Zhejiang Student Association, 237
Fujian: boatmen, 62–65; merchants, 30, 34, 50, 133–34, 185, 186n20; neighborhoods, 17; sojourners, 25, 55, 93, 232; trade associations, 34, 50
Fujian bang (Fujian Clique), 77, 184
Fujian native-place associations, 9, 77, 81. See also Dianchuntang; Li Xianyun; Quan-Zhang Huiguan; Xing'an Huiguan; Zeng Shaoqing
Fujian Reconstruction Committee, 263, 268
Fujian secret societies, 77, 79, 80. See also Small Sword Uprising
Fujian Student Association, 238
Fujian Tingzhou Huiguan, 186
Funeral ceremonies, 92n16, 212n90. See also Death ritual
Fuzhou, 59n23

Fuzhou Huiguan, 232. *See also* San Shan Huiguan

Gambling, 256
Gangs, 20, 39, 63–66, 72, 278, 298–99. *See also* Green Gang; Red Gang; Secret societies
Gansu sojourners, 212n89, 224
Gaoqiao, 6
Ge Gongzhen, 143
Ge Pengyun, 184, 189, 191, 192, 192n40
Ge Shengxiao, 161n29
Gender hierarchy, 14, 117
General Works Board, 199–200
Gentry. *See* Elites; Merchants
Ghost Festival. *See* Hungry ghosts; *Yulanpen*
Gold Guild, 153
Gong (public) and *guan* (official), 124
Gong Mujiu, 61
Gongsuo, 39, 40. See also *Huiguan*
Gongzhong yanshuohui. *See* Patriotic Oratorical Society
Government, overlap with, 295–96
"The Great Learning," 13, 117
Green Gang, 67, 278n47, 298. *See also* Du Yuesheng
Gu Xinyi, 208, 214
Gu Zhenghong, 273n37
Gu Zhuxuan, 20, 298
Guan Jiongzhi, 187–88
Guan-Shandong Gongsuo, 49
Guandi, 58, 105n46, 109
Guandong, 49
Guandu shangban, 139
Guang-Zhao Gongsuo, 84n1, 105n46, 185, 236, 241, 255n91, 262, 288; assistance to Guangdong, 90, 110, 244; and carpenters' strike, 89, 153n8; facility of, 85, 126n13; and foreign authorities, 151, 157; and Guangdong events, 207, 212n89, 246, 247–48n70; and May Fourth Movement, 265, 266–67; merchant leadership of, 61, 85, 140; and Mixed Court Riot of December 1905, 188, 190, 191; provided return transport, 91, 128; and religious processions, 98, 99, 129; role in politics, 209–10, 261, 272, 272n36; rules and protocols of, 86, 86n5, 87–88, 89; and Yang Yuelou case, 113, 114, 115. *See also* Tang Maozhi; Wen Zongyao; Xu Run;

Ye Tingjuan; Zheng Guanying; Zhong Ziyuan
Guang-Zhao Hospital, 186
Guang-Zhao Huiguan, 13, 55n11, 59
Guang-Zhao middle school, 254n89
Guang'an Huiguan, 55n11, 74n59, 77
Guangbang Guangyanghuo ye (Guangdong and Foreign Goods Trade), 185
Guangdong, 90, 110, 124n9, 246–47; activists, 196; boatmen, 62–65; carpenters, 63, 88–89, 153n8; dialect, 15, 16; elementary school, 254n89; gangs, 6, 20; neighborhoods, 16, 17; prostitutes, 8, 24, 91, 161–62, 169–70; public school, 254n89; restaurants, 22, 23, 191, 288; revolutionary organizations, 206–7; seamen, 236, 275, 276; trade associations, 50; workers, 62–63
Guangdong and Foreign Goods Trade, 185
Guangdong Army, 247
Guangdong *bang*, 54–62, 138, 184, 233. *See also* Guangdong, gangs; Guangdong native-place associations
Guangdong Club, 236
Guangdong compradors, 60–62, 121. *See also* Compradors; Xu Run
Guangdong *huiguan*, in Zhenjiang, 131, 133
Guangdong Mechanics' Association, 196
Guangdong merchants, 14, 22, 84, 139n49, 193, 207; and the Anti-American Boycott of 1905, 185, 186n23; charitable activities of, 122, 124; and China Merchants' Steam Navigation Company, 140; and gangs, 20, 67; as *huiguan* directors, 85; and the May Fourth Movement, 266, 267, 268; and militia, 127; rice, 285; in trade and foreign relations, 53, 61–62, 145n60; tea, 143. *See also* Chaozhou merchants
Guangdong Merchants' Association of Shanghai, 241
Guangdong Merchants' Miscellaneous Grain and Oilcake Association, 286
Guangdong native-place associations: assistance to Guangdong province, 244–45; before the Opium War, 54–55; forbidden after Small Sword Uprising, 81; in 1919, 236–37; and plague-prevention measures, 157. *See also* Chaozhou Huiguan; Guang-Zhao Huiguan

Guangdong-Ningbo rivalry, 127n16, 141–42, 255
Guangdong province, 243–45, 246n66, 247–48. *See also* Chaozhou
Guangdong regional reputation, 107, 107n48, 113–14, 115–16, 256. *See also* Yang Yuelou, case of
Guangdong secret societies, 67n40, 76, 77, 79, 80. *See also* Small Sword Uprising
Guangdong sojourners: businesses of, 87n6; charitable activities of, 123–24; elite, 107; and the 1937 bombing, 287–88, 291n74; number of, 101n38; in regional hierarchy, 14; religious practices of, 25, 93; revolutionary activities of, 206–7, 211; in Suzhou, 10
Guangdong Sojourners' Commercial Association, 262
Guangdong Sojourners' Reconstruction Association, 236
Guangdong-style residences, 17–18
Guangdong Tongxianghui, 287–88, 295n83, 296
Guangfu Hui, 196, 196n48
Guangxi sojourners, in Suzhou, 10
Guangxu Emperor, 171
Guangzhou (Guangdong), 59; compradors, 60, 62; sojourners, 30, 54, 50n7
Guangzhou Chamber of Commerce, 207
Guangzhou Military Government, 246n67, 262n9
Guangzhou native-place associations, 59–60n23, 77. *See also* Guang-Zhao Huiguan
Guild of the Chihli Provincials and Eight Banner Corps, 153
Guilds, 42–44, 157
Guo Guangshan, 249
Guo Hong Tai establishment, 71
Guo Weiyi, 247
Guo Wenzhi, 74n59
Guo Zibin, 71, 257
Guomindang, 286, 299, 303–4; Shanghai branch office, 292–93, 296. *See also* Nanjing government
Guxiang, as term for native place, 4

Habermas, Jürgen. *See* "Public sphere"
Haichang Gongsuo, 237
Haichang Lü Hu Tongxianghui, 237
Haimen county (Jiangsu), 190n32
Haining (Zhejiang), native-place associations, 224, 237

Haining Huiguan, 237
Haiyan, native-place associations, 224n14, 237
Haiyan Lü Hu Tongxianghui, 237
Hakkas, 80
Han ethnicity, 208, 210
Hang Chou Gongsuo, 34
Hangzhou native place associations, 224n14, 237, 238
Hangzhou silk merchants, 34
Hangzhou Tongxianghui, 237, 238
Hankou, 7n8, 45n70, 125n12, 142n56, 145; identity, 45; merchants in, 120, 121, 268. *See also* Rowe, William
Hankou Lingnan Huiguan, 140
Hao Yen-p'ing, 69, 144
He Suitang, 180n4
He Weisheng, 233n36
He Ying, 189
Henan Northern Expeditionary Army, 208
Henan silk trade, 210n86
Henan Tongxianghui, 263, 270, 295
Henriot, Christian, 24
Ho Ping-ti, 42–43, 44
Hong Kong Chaozhou Commercial Association, 244
Hong Kong Chaozhou Merchants' Association, 242
Hong Kong currency, 242
Hong Kong–Guangzhou railway, 207
Hongkou, 89n9, 218; architecture of, 18; as Cantonese neighborhood, 17, 81n76, 87n6, 127; 1937 bombing of, 287, 288; as plague district, 154
Honig, Emily, 15, 307n6
Hu bei shangye gongsuo (North Shanghai Commercial Association), 182
Hu nan xue-shang hui (South Shanghai Educational and Commercial Association), 185
Hu Ning-Shao Shuimu Gongye Gongsuo, 211n86
Hu She, 12, 45, 284, 287, 295
Hu Xianghan, 17
Hu xuehui. See Shanghai Educational Association
Huaishu tongxiang youyihui, 40n60
Huang Fu, 208n78
Huang Shaoyan, 247
Huang Yanpei, 202, 299–301
Huang Yiquan, 189
Huang Zunxian, 198

Huatang yanghuohang dianchun tang (Peanuts, Sugar and Foreign Goods Association), 34
Huaxing Hui, 196
Hubei activists, 196
Hubei *bang,* 234
Hubei Lü Hu Tongxianghui, 262
Hubei Reconstruction Committee, 264
Hubei sojourners, in regional hierarchy, 15
Hui-Ning Huiguan, 33
Hui-Ning Tongxianghui, 286
Huibao, 142–43, 145–46
Huiguan: burial services of, 8, 90–91, 158, 252n82; business handled by, 85–88; charitable activities of, 110–11, 121–25; and community hierarchy, 86, 88–89, 91, 106, 172, 255; competition for resources of, 228–29; elite and non-elite elements in, 101–3, 105, 172–73, 232; and foreigners, 89, 147–50, 154–58; as lineage or kin network, 111, 115, 117; mediating role of, 87, 89–90, 151, 174–75, 250; after 1949, 305; opera performances in, 25, 103–6, 109; order-keeping role of, 65, 73, 92, 126, 128–29, 150–69; and other native-place associations, 225, 238; public image of, 109, 115, 123–24; relationship with officials, 126n13, 129, 150–51, 294n81; and secret societies, 40n59, 66–67, 73–75, 77–78, 81–83; sponsorship of religious festivals, 92–103, 128–29, 274; support for uprisings, 66–67, 129; as symbols of community, 9, 18; tax collection by, 129–30; temple function of, 91–92; vs. *tongxianghui,* 220–22, 223, 251, 271, 274; urban management activities of, 136–37; use of term, 38–40; women and, 116–17, 251n78. *See also* Burial services; Names of individual *huiguan;* Native-place associations; *Yin huiguan*
Huiguan architecture, 18–21, 85, 104
Huiguan directors, 103, 106, 112, 161; and community interests, 90, 137, 173, 193–94; of the 1860s and 1870s, 84–85; as exemplars of Confucian virtue, 109, 111; merchants as, 121, 144; on national stage, 118, 146, 180; and secret societies, 73–75, 77, 81–83; worship of, 10, 87, 308n7. See also *Huiguan* oligarchy
Huiguan gods, 87, 104, 305. *See also* Tianhou
Huiguan halls, 125–26

Huiguan militia, 126
Huiguan oligarchy, 85–88, 91, 117–18, 166–68, 224, 230
Huilai county (Guangdong), merchants from, 35, 57–58. *See also* Chaozhou
Huizhou (Anhui) sojourners: and pawnshops, 30–31, 34n48; tea merchants, 33
Huju (Shanghai opera), 28n40
Hunan activists, 196
Hunan Affairs Preservation Society, 263
Hunan Reconstruction Association, 259
Hunan Sojourners' Northern Expedition Army, 208
Hundred Dragon Society, 77
Hungry ghosts, 96, 97, 102
Huzhou Huiguan, 211n88, 237
Huzhou Silk Association, 156
Huzhou Silk Cocoon Gongsuo, 211
Huzhou Silk Cocoon Merchants' Guild, 153
Huzhou Silk Gongsuo, 45
Huzhou (Zhejiang) sojourners: benevolent activities of, 35–36, 212n89; silk merchants, 34, 35, 134, 153, 156, 211; ties to Chen Qimei, 211, 213; *tongxianghui,* 224. *See also* Hu She
Huzhou Student Commercial Sojourners' Association, 237

Immigration, 2–4, 5–6, 53–54, 62–64, 218; in post–Cultural Revolution China, 306, 311. *See also* Sojourning
Imperial Bank of China, 156
Imperialism. *See* Antiforeign activity
Intellectuals, 195. *See also* Students
International Settlement, 206, 284; Chinese representation in, 152–58; Chinese residents of, 16, 151–52, 315; legal jurisdiction in, 164n36, 187; map of, 149; parades in, 30–31; plague measures in, 154–55; taxation in, 130, 191, 192, 271. *See also* Hongkou; Mixed Court Riot of December 1905; Shanghai Municipal Council
International Settlement archives, 188n27
International Settlement police, 63n32, 97, 192

Jade Gongsuo, 191n36
Japan: demands of, 220, 261, 263n10, 264; as model, 176, 177; students and radicals in, 195–96, 196n50
Japanese historiography, 42, 43

Jardine, Matheson and Company, 142; compradors of, 60, 127n16, 144; and opium trade, 69, 70
Jewelry trade, 33
Jiading, 78n68, 79, 224n14, 238
Jiading Tongxianghui, 238
Jiang Shaofeng, 247
Jiangbei sojourners, 16, 197n53, 224n14, 263, 268. See also Subei sojourners
Jiangbei Sojourners' Preservation Society, 263, 268
Jianghuai Tongxianghui, 262, 298
Jiangnan Arsenal, 85n2, 201, 208
Jiangning Gongsuo, 186, 238
Jiangning Huiguan, 265
Jiangning Qiyi Lühu Gongsuo. See Jiangning Gongsuo
Jiangning Tongxianghui, 222, 262, 284, 298, 302n96, 308n7
Jiangsu capitalists, 214. See also Shen Manyun
Jiangsu dialect, 15
Jiangsu Financial Bureau, 243
Jiangsu food, 23
Jiangsu gongtuan lianhehui, 40n60
Jiangsu magazine, 196n50, 197, 197n53, 270
Jiangsu merchants, 30, 31, 33, 35, 121, 193, 214; and Chinese Municipal Council, 201, 203; sugar, 133–34
Jiangsu Pottery Trade Association, 262
Jiangsu Provincial Education Association, 263, 299
Jiangsu sojourners, 14, 121n2, 218n1. See also Subei sojourners
Jiangsu–Zhejiang railway, 214
Jiangxi Huiguan, 25, 37n54; in Xiangtan, 103n41
Jiangxi Lü Hu Tongxianghui, 262
Jiangxi merchants, 50
Jiangxi Northern Expeditionary Army Branch Headquarters, 208
Jiangxi Self-Government Comrades' Association, 40n60
Jiangxi sojourners, 16
Jiangyin Huiguan, 269
Ji'anhui, 36
Jiao rituals, 92–93, 95, 96n23, 98, 100, 124, 222
Jiaying Huiguan, 55n11, 62
Jiaying (Guangdong) sojourners, 77. See also Li Shaoqing; Li Shaoxi
Jiaying Tongxianghui, 246, 262

Jiaying Wushu Lü Hu Tongxianghui, 236
Jie (social circles), 238, 273
Jie-Pu-Feng Huiguan, 58, 236, 262
Jieyang county (Guangdong), merchants from, 57–58
Jiguan, as term for native place, 4
Jin Jiuling, 20
Jin Shaocheng, 188
Jing Yuanshan, 122
Jingzhou ribao, 181
Jiyitang, 251n77
Johnson, Linda Cooke, 39n58
Jun'an She, 237, 275. See also Ningbo, seamen

Kaiping Mining Company, 139n49
Kebang (outsider merchant group), 39
Kidnapping, 213, 255, 283
Kunqu (style of opera), 105

Labor movement, 235, 273n37, 277. See also Workers
Lai, Chi-kong, 141
Lan Meixian, 291
Lan Weiwen, 61n28, 81
Landsmannschaften 41, 43
Laojia, as term for native place, 4
Leung Yuen-sang, 124
Li Bai, 7–8
Li Hongzhang, 119–20, 122, 124–25, 126n13, 137, 139, 178n1
Li Houyu, 214
Li Pingshu, 201–3, 204, 205, 207–8, 211n88, 214, 308
Li Shaoqing, 62, 74, 75n59, 77, 78, 82. See also Li Shaoxi
Li Shaoxi, 74n59, 78n68, 79. See also Li Shaoqing
Li Tingyu, 188
Li Weizhuang, 214
Li Xianyun, 62n29, 74, 74n59, 77, 78, 82–83
Li Xiehe, 215
Li Yuanhong, 215
Li Zhengwu, 214
Li Zhisheng, 188
Li Zhongjue. See Li Pingshu
Li Zhongjun, 189
Liang Qichao, 171n47, 206
Liang Ruhao, 85n2
Liangguang native-place associations, 10
Lijin (transit taxes), 130, 133, 134, 136

Lilong housing, 17–18
Lin Afu, 78, 80
Lin Qin, 60
Lin Sen, 278
Lin Youren, 135n40
Lin Yunqiu, 250
Lingnan Middle School, 218
Lingnan Shanzhuang, 253n87
Lingui, 61
Liu Hongsheng, 218, 218n2, 302
Liu Kunyi, 168
Liu Lichuan, 62n29, 78, 79, 80, 81
Liu Rushi, 114n62
Liu Shaozong, 140
Liu Yanyi, 155n12
Lo Chongling, 189
Lo King-sou, 157
Local self-government, 198, 202–3, 226, 297–98, 304. *See also* Chinese Municipal Council
Lu Ban, 63n32
Lu Ban Dian, 88
Lü Hu Dapu Tongxianghui, 236
Lü Hu Haichang Gongsuo, 267
Lü Hu tongxianghui, 41. See also *Tongxianghui*
Lu Qinghua, 189
Lu Zongyu, 266, 267
Lunchuan zhaoshang ju. See China Merchants' Steam Navigation Company
Luohan Society, 77

Ma Chaojun, 196
Ma Zhanshan, 290
Macao, 60
Machine workers, Guangdong, 62–63
Magistrates, 57, 74
Major, Frederick, 138
Manchuria, 290
Mann, Susan, 43, 135n39, 261
Mao Dun, 15–16
Mao Zedong, 258–59
Mao Zumo, 178n1
Marriage, 5, 297n89
May Fourth Movement (1919), 21, 220, 238, 259, 260–69, 270–71, 308
May Thirtieth Movement (1925), 21, 272–73, 273n37
Meng Jiao, "Youzi Yin" by, 5n4
Merchant militia, 127, 204–5
Merchants: elite status of, 50, 83, 119–20,

125; and foreign competition, 131, 139; May Fourth mobilization of, 261, 264, 265–68; nationalism and politicization of, 119, 139, 169, 198–99; relationship to secret societies, 67, 73, 81; and tax collection, 130. *See also* Compradors; Merchant militia
Miao bang. See Temple Gang
Militia organization, 73–75, 76, 126–27, 127–28n18, 199, 204–5
Mingxing Film Studio, 228
Mining-rights recovery movement, 198
Ministry of Foreign Affairs, 189, 190
Minlibao, 208, 209
Mixed Court, 89, 89n10, 111, 113, 136, 151, 250
Mixed Court jail, 187n25, 188, 190, 193n43
Mixed Court Riot of December 1905, 187–95, 199
Miye Gongsuo, 31
Modernity, 46, 123, 144, 177, 307, 309–10
Modernization, 43, 123, 138, 257
Montmorand, Viscount Bernier de, 162n32
Multicity sojourner networks, 12, 119, 123, 146, 244
Multiple-trade associations, 34
Multiprovince associations, 239
Municipal Shanghai Opera Research Society, 28n40

Nanhai Huiguan, 236
Nanhuohui, 36
Nanjing decade, 2, 277–78, 280–87, 291–99
Nanjing government, 212, 273, 292–95
Nanjingbang Zhubaoye Gongsuo, 33
Nanking Guild, 153
Nantian (Ningbo) sojourners, 36
Nation building, 258–60
National Constitutional Assembly, 308
National Federation of Merchant Militia, 205
National identity, 2, 46, 123, 146, 195, 312. *See also* Chinese identity; Nationalism
National Salvation Workers' Training Institute, 290n71
National sovereignty, 183, 187. *See* Mixed Court Riot of December 1905; Nationalism
Nationalism, 169, 174, 179, 183, 271n35, 312; anti-Japanese, 289–90; in early Republican period, 257, 299; and native-place

Nationalism (continued)
    identity, 14, 215–16, 269–70, 312–13;
    and the Ningbo cemetery riots, 158–59,
    169–72; and radicalism, 196, 276
Native Bankers' Association, 156, 185n18
Native banks, 71, 121n2
Native place, 4–7; Chinese terms for, 4,
    5n4
Native-place associations: admission of
    women, 308, 308n7; in business, 141–
    42, 193n42, 250–51; charitable institu-
    tions of, 253–55; and class conscious-
    ness, 276–77; after Cultural
    Revolution, 305–6, 311; decision mak-
    ing in, 299; displacement of, 272–73,
    305; early Republican period, 208,
    222–23, 257; and economic develop-
    ment, 43; and gangs, 76–77, 309; "gov-
    ernmentality" of, 297–98, 314; involve-
    ment with personal problems, 248–50;
    and labor disputes, 275; legitimacy of,
    297, 298, 303; during May Fourth pe-
    riod, 260–77; as mediators between ur-
    ban and rural China, 219–20; member-
    ship of, 276, 295; names for, 38–41; in
    Nanjing decade, 277–78, 280, 291–99;
    and nationalism, 174–75, 269–71, 276–
    77, 300–301; in native-place affairs,
    240–48; and pauper burial grounds,
    6n6; penetration of, by state, 292–96;
    role in mediating disputes, 256; and
    Small Sword Uprising, 76–77; and so-
    cial control, 21–22, 73, 283; sponsors
    of, 302; strength and connections of,
    248–49, 290, 298–99; subdivided by
    trade, 36–37; and urban organization,
    2–3, 10, 46, 119, 177; during war with
    Japan, 287–91; and worker associa-
    tions, 101. See also Huiguan; Tong-
    xianghui; Trade associations
Native-place bang, 130, 133–35
Native-place communities: cooperation
    between, 125, 127; geographic subdivi-
    sion in, 238; hierarchy of, 14, 85, 88,
    116–17, 183, 276, 282; multiport, 11–12,
    123; and social organization, 10–11, 159
Native-place identity, 4–6, 13, 46, 307–8;
    and Chinese identity, 13–14; and cui-
    sine, 8, 22–23; and economic tensions,
    20; in Hankou, 45; and local customs,
    4–5, 26–27, 92; and multiport net-
    works, 146; and nationalism, 196, 208,
    271n35, 313; and Shanghai identity, 146;

and the Small Sword Uprising, 83; in
    time of crisis, 290. See also National
    identity; Native-place sentiment;
    Shanghai identity
Native-place networks, 121; in Hankou,
    53n9, 125n12; and the Revolution of
    1911, 213, 215–16; and the Shanghai
    bourgeoisie, 219; and technological in-
    novation, 138. See also Multicity so-
    journer networks
Native-place rivalries, 123–24, 144, 145;
    Guangdong-Zhejiang, 107, 108–9n49,
    127n16, 141–42; Subei-Jiangnan,
    108n49
Native-place sentiment, 2–3, 7, 12, 281; and
    economic models, 44; egalitarian lan-
    guage of, 274; as "morally excellent,"
    2, 12–13; and nationalism, 14, 222, 259,
    269, 270n33; and radical reform,
    195–98; reformulation of, 217, 220
Native-place trade associations. See Trade
    associations
Negishi Tadashi, 171
Neighborhoods, 16–17, 29
New Culture Monthly, 229–30n27
New Culture Movement, 229, 260
New Life Movement, 304
New Policies, 176
New Year celebrations, 294
Newspapers, 120, 143, 146. See also Hui-
    bao; North China Herald; Shenbao
Niaodang. See Bird Society
Ning-Shao Cotton-Trade Welfare Associa-
    tion, 237
Ning-Shao Lacquerers' Association, 237
Ning-Shao Philanthropic Association,
    229n23
Ning-Shao Shipping Company, 225n17
Ning-Shao Shipping Protection Associa-
    tion, 142
Ning-Shao Steamboat Company, 142, 291
Ningbo: bankers, 50, 142n55; carpenters,
    63n32, 102; construction workers,
    211n86; dialect, 15; food, 22, 23; neigh-
    borhoods, 16, 17n25; prostitutes, 23,
    24; seamen, 37, 237, 275–76
Ningbo baihua bao (Ningbo vernacular),
    196
Ningbo (Zhejiang) bang (Ningbo
    Clique), 77, 138, 233, 234
Ningbo capitalists, 219. See also Liu Hong-
    sheng; Yu Xiaqing; Zhu Baosan
Ningbo cemetery riots, 21, 53n9, 188n26;

and politicization of Ningbo community, 224; and popular nationalism, 169–72, 174–75, 183; Yu Xiaqing in, 193

Ningbo Chamber of Commerce, 212, 267

Ningbo Changsheng Hui, 168, 171, 173. *See also* Changsheng Hui

Ningbo Flood Disaster Collection Committee, 245

Ningbo Gongsuo, 74n59

Ningbo-Guangdong rivalries, 127n16, 141–42, 255

Ningbo Huiguan, 36

Ningbo Lü Hu Tongxianghui. *See* Ningbo Tongxianghui

Ningbo merchants: and Anti-American Boycott of 1905, 186; and the May Fourth Movement, 266, 267, 268; in pre–Opium War Shanghai, 50; and Shanghai General Chamber of Commerce, 177, 178; shipping company of, 141–42; sugar, 30, 34n48; tea, 33. *See also* Yang Fang; Yu Xiaqing

Ningbo Merchants' General Assembly, 206

Ningbo native-place associations, 77, 157, 206, 293. *See also* Ningbo Tongxianghui; Siming Gongsuo

Ningbo sojourners, 16, 22, 53, 98, 162; and the Anti-American Boycott of 1905, 185; number of, in Shanghai, 226n19; politicization of, 175, 196, 224; and the Zhou Shengyou case, 179–83. *See also* Siming Gongsuo

Ningbo Sojourners' Association, 212

Ningbo Student Association, 237

Ningbo Tongxianghui, 224–28, 237, 262, 272n36, 287; and charitable schools, 254n88; disaster and war relief activities of, 245, 288, 291n74; displaced *huiguan* during Republican period, 239–40; involvement in trade, 251, 285; and the May Fourth Movement, 261, 265–66, 267, 268; mediating role of, 249, 256, 284; membership of, 281; as model, 230, 300; and nationalism, 269, 291, 298; and Ningbo affairs, 242–43; photograph of, 227; social program of, 227–28. *See also* Yu Xiaqing

Ningbo workers, 37, 101–2, 168; and the case of Zhou Shengyou, 179, 182; mutual-aid associations of, 101, 238

North China Herald, 74–75, 88, 130; on gangs, 6, 64, 66; on the Mixed Court Riot of December 1905, 191n35,

192–93; on plague prevention, 154–55; on religious processions, 98; reporting on *Shenbao* and Guangdong community, 114–15, 141, 143; and the "Swatow Opium Guild" case, 132

North Shanghai Commercial Association, 182

North-South civil war, 261, 262n9

Northern dialects, 15, 16

Northern Expedition, 208, 239

Official titles, purchase of, 57, 119

Opera performances, 25, 28, 67, 93, 103–6, 109

Opium: dens, 128; runners, 135–36, 136n42; smuggling, 53, 68–70, 135–36; taxation, 130–33, 136, 137

Opium Tax Bureau, 132, 133, 135–36

Opium trade, 53n9, 69, 84, 125, 204; Chaozhou, 41n62, 58, 70–72, 254n89, 257, 257n98; foreigners and, 41n62, 68n42, 69n43, 131–32, 136; and secret societies, 53, 68–69, 78. *See also* Opium, smuggling

Opium War, 68

Overseas Chinese, 184

Pan Gongzhan, 278

Pan Yiguo, 74n59, 77

Paper Trade Militia, 208

Parades. *See* Processions

"Particularism," 122, 123, 276, 297, 307, 313. *See also* Cosmopolitanism

Patriotic Oratorical Society, 189, 190, 191, 192n40

Pawn Brokers' Guild, 153

Pawnshop Gongsuo, 242

Pawnshops, 6, 22, 33–34n48, 71; Anhui, 30–31, 34n48

Peanuts, Sugar and Foreign Goods Association, 34

Perry, Elizabeth, 30, 261

Philanthropy. *See* Charitable activities

Pinghu Lü Hu Tongxianghui, 262

Pirates, 63, 82

Plague-prevention measures, 154–57

Plague Riots of November 1910, 154–56

Police, 191n36, 228n23, 283n53, 294n81, 295; British, 188; foreign, 151, 152; French, 162, 285; Ningbo, 246; and opium runners, 135, 136; Sikh, 95. *See also Dibao;* International Settlement police

Popular festivals. *See* Processions; Religious festivals

Poverty. *See* Vagrancy

Press, 107. *See also* Newspapers

Print lithography, 138

Prisons, 187n25, 188, 190. *See also* Mixed Court jail

Processions, 28, 30–31, 92, 128–29

Prostitution, 5n5, 23–24, 114, 114n62, 188n26. *See also* Guangdong, prostitutes

Provisional Constitution of the Republic of China, 246n67

Public health, 154–57, 163

Public Security Bureau, 283n53, 295, 296. *See also* Police

"Public sphere" (Habermas), 99n33, 120, 146, 299, 302, 303, 304, 311

Public theaters, 106

Public works, 199–200

Pudong: defined, 201–2n61; re-created as native place, 280–81

Pudong dialect, 281

Pudong Fellows Association. *See* Pudong Tongren Hui

Pudong Journal, 202

Pudong Tongren Hui, 202, 203, 281, 308

Pudong Tongxianghui, 11, 284, 285n58, 286, 287, 309; anti-Japanese activity of, 290; building of, 279; directors of, 302n96; Huang Yanpei and, 300–301; inauguration of, 278–80, 296; membership of, 281, 282, 295; relief work, 289, 291n74. *See also* Du Yuesheng

Puning county (Guangdong), merchants from, 57–58

Qianjiang Huiguan, 34, 238

Qianye Gonghui, 37

Qingdao, 263

Qingjinhui. See Blue Turban Society

Qingming (day of sweeping graves), 26

Qingpu *tongxianghui,* 224n14

Qingshouhui. See Blue Hand Society

Quan Hui xiehui (All-Anhui Consultative Committee), 40n60, 239

Quan-Zhang Huiguan, 17, 22, 50n7, 74n59, 210, 288. *See also* Li Xianyun

Quan Zhe gonghui (All-Zhejiang Association), 40n60, 239

Quan Zhe Lü Hu Tongxianghui, 237, 264

Quanzhou (Fujian) sojourners, 34, 77

Radicals. *See* Revolutionaries

Railway rights, 195n47, 198, 214–15

Rankin, Mary Backus, 12n18, 46n70, 120, 120n1, 122, 124, 195n47, 196

Raoping county (Guangdong), merchants from, 57–58

Ratepayers' Association, 152–53, 194, 272n36

Red Gang, 66–67, 135n40, 298

Refugee centers, 288–89. *See also* Disaster relief; War relief

Regional: cuisines, 22–23, 26, 29; groups, hierarchy of, 14; operas, 25, 28, 28n40; reputation, 107–9, 115, 123–24, 256

Regional rivalries. *See* Native-place rivalries

Religious festivals: and *huiguan* prestige, 100–101, 103; as political propaganda opportunities, 269; and secret societies, 100; and social control, 96–97, 128–29; sponsored by *huiguan,* 92–103, 129. See also *Jiao* rituals; *Yulanpen*

Religious practices, 25–26, 27–28

Report of the Conference on the Guomidang Central All-China Mass-Movement Leadership Committee (1934), 293

Restaurants, 22, 23, 29, 191, 288

Restoration Society, 196, 215

Revolution of 1911, 21, 125, 195, 217

Revolutionaries, 195–98, 207, 208

Revolutionary Alliance, 196, 206, 207, 213

Revolutionary publications, 196, 208, 209

Rice Trade Gongsuo, 31

Rickshaw pullers, 179

Riots: antiforeign, 169–70; among Guangdong and Fujian vagabonds, 64–66; wheelbarrow pullers, 159. *See also* Mixed Court Riot of December 1905; Ningbo cemetery riots; Plague Riots of November 1910

Road building, 160–61, 164, 200, 252n81

Robberies, 242, 244–45

Rong Chunfu, 143

Rong Hong. *See* Yung Wing

Rowe, William, 53n9, 69–70n46, 102n40, 120, 122, 135n39; discussion of Hankou based on Weber, 42, 44, 45n70; and primacy of native-place ties, 44, 45, 145

Rui Cheng, 204

Russell and Company, 60, 138, 142
Russo-Japanese War (1904–5), 179n3

Salt trade, 69–70n46, 178n1
Samqua merchants, 61
San Shan Huiguan, 232, 238
Sandian hui (Three Dot Society), 69
Sangzi, as term for native place, 4
Sanhehui, 135n40
Sansheng lianhehui (Three Provinces Federation), 239
Schools, 227–28, 232, 254, 263, 264
Seamen: Guangdong, 236, 275, 276; Ningbo, 37, 237, 275–76; strike of 1919, 275. *See also* Boatmen
Secret societies, 40n59, 66–67, 76–79, 81–83, 100, 278; made into defense militia, 73–75, 81; and opium smuggling, 53, 68–69, 78n68. *See also* Guangdong secret societies
Self-Government Office, 201n59. *See also* General Works Board
Self-strengthening movement, 119–20, 137, 201
Shaanxi Huiguan, 126n13
Shandong: Chaozhou *huiguan* in, 56n16; dialect, 16; merchants, 34, 210, 210n86, 266, 267; sojourners, 15, 49, 210
Shandong Association, 259
Shandong Guild, 156
Shandong Huiguan, 127
Shandong Lü Hu Tongxianghui, 263
Shangchuan Huiguan, 49
Shangda, 232–33
Shangda Zhejiang Tongxianghui, 233n36
Shanghai: architecture, 17–19; bourgeoisie, 240n50, 261; frontier aspects of, 53, 82; guidebooks, 22, 23; languages of, 15–16; local native-place associations, 77, 233; maps of, 51, 52, 148; neighborhoods, 16–17, 16n24, 29; occupied by Chen Qimei, 207–8; opera, 28n40; population of, 2, 4n2, 14, 163, 218, 315; street names, 17; as treaty port, 47–49. *See also* Shanghai identity
Shanghai Archives, 45
Shanghai Chamber of Commerce, 183, 216, 261; and the Anti-American Boycott of 1905, 184–85, 186; and Chinese advisors to Municipal Council, 272n36; dominated by Ningbo merchants, 177, 178, 183n11, 184, 214; vs.

Federation of Street Unions, 271, 272; formation and early history of, 177–78; and the May Fourth Movement, 263, 265, 267; membership of, 178n2, 194n44; and Mixed Court Riot of December 1905, 188, 193n42; in Nanjing decade, 280, 286n62; and native-place associations, 157–58, 193n42; and plague measures, 155–57
Shanghai Chaozhou People's Livelihood Consultative Committee, 248
Shanghai Citizens' Committee for Severance of Economic Relations with Japan, 290
Shanghai City God Temple, 50
Shanghai Commercial Consultative Association, 177, 178n1
Shanghai Educational Association, 184n16, 185
Shanghai Federation of Commercial Groups, 261, 262, 263, 267, 267n24, 268
Shanghai Federation of Street Unions, 271–72, 308
Shanghai Fruit Gongsuo, 242
Shanghai General Chamber of Commerce. *See* Shanghai Chamber of Commerce
Shanghai identity, 27–28, 146, 177, 192, 203, 216. *See also* National identity; Native-place identity; Urban identity
Shanghai Journal of Commerce, 272
Shanghai Money Trade Guild, 50
Shanghai Municipal Council, 127, 127–28n18, 150–51, 159, 200; Chinese Advisory Board, 271, 272n36; and the Chinese exodus from the International Settlement, 151–52; Chinese representation on, 193–94; and the Mixed Court Riot of December 1905, 189, 190, 193–94; and plague-prevention measures, 153–57
Shanghai Municipal Government, 27, 239, 283, 284, 304; Social Bureau of, 227n20, 292–94, 296; war-relief efforts of, 287, 290–91
Shanghai Municipal Silk Trade Association, 45
Shanghai Municipality Cooperative Social Circles National Salvation Association, 290n71
Shanghai Municipality Educationalists' Race Salvation Association, 290n71

Shanghai Municipality Students' Wartime Service Group, 290n71

Shanghai-Nanjing railroad, 202

Shanghai Opium Tax Bureau. *See* Opium Tax Bureau

Shanghai qianye gongsuo (Shanghai Money Trade Guild), 50

Shanghai shangye gongtuan lianhehui. See Shanghai Federation of Commercial Groups

Shanghai shangye minglu (Commercial directory of Shanghai), 223

Shanghai shi zizhi zhi (Shanghai municipality self-government gazetteer), 199–200

Shanghai Shippers' Association, 128n18

Shanghai Silk Cocoon Gongsuo, 134

Shanghai Sojourning Anhui Consultative Committee, 268

Shanghai Sojourning Anhui Rice Merchants' Trade Association, 285

Shanghai Sojourning Guangdong Merchants' Miscellaneous Grain Association, 285

Shanghai Steam Navigation Company, 138

Shanghai Student Union, 261, 264

Shanghai suburbs residents' association, 75n59

Shanghai Sugar and Miscellaneous-Goods Association, 242

Shanghai Telegraph Bureau, 185n18

Shanghai Tramway Company, 234

Shanghai University, 232–33

Shanghai Wartime Literature and Art Society, 290

Shanghai Young Writers' National Salvation Propaganda Group, 290n71

Shanghai zhinan (Guide to Shanghai), 222–23, 224n14, 232, 252n81

Shangtuan gonghui, 204–5

Shangxue buxihui. See Commercial Studies Continuation Society

Shangye lianhehui (merchant federations), 40

Shangye qiujinhui (Commercial Strive for Progress Society), 190, 191

Shangyu Tongxianghui, 290

Shanse Bankers' Guild, 153

Shantou, 56n12, 57n16, 71n50, 241–42, 245n62

Shantou Chamber of Commerce, 241, 242, 244

Shantou Cunxin Benevolent Association, 253

Shantou Finance Board, 242

Shantou Liuyi Huiguan, 241

Shantou Military Expenditure Bureau, 247

Shantou Remittance Association, 242

Shantung Provincials' Guild, 153

Shao Qintao, 156

Shao Youlian, 127n17

Shaoxing (Zhejiang): construction workers, 211n86, 264, 276; Shaoxing wine trade, 210n86; sojourners, 22

Shaoxing Huiguan, 212–13n90, 237

Shaoxing International Improvement Society, 237, 264

Shaoxing native-place associations, 213, 224, 233, 261. *See also* Shaoxing Huiguan; Shaoxing Tongxianghui

Shaoxing Sojourners' Association, 213

Shaoxing Sojourners' School, 263

Shaoxing Tongxianghui, 219n5, 221, 237, 262, 267n24, 293, 294. *See also* Wang Xiaolai

Shen Bingcheng, 115, 161

Shen Dunhe, 155, 156, 157, 166, 205, 206. *See also* Shen Zhongli

Shen Enfu, 207

Shen Honglai, 102, 168, 171, 173–74, 175, 224–25, 224–25n15

Shen Manyun, 205, 207, 208, 211n88, 214

Shen Weibin, 204

Shen Zhongli, 165n37, 180n4. *See also* Shen Dunhe

Shenbao, 8, 134, 183, 194, 224, 295, 301; charitable donations in, 122, 124; and China Merchants' Steam Navigation Company, 141, 145; competition with *Huibao*, 143, 145; on Guangdong community, 108n49, 211n87; on the Mixed Court Riot of December 1905, 192; and native-place networks, 120, 123, 124; on Ningbo cemetery riots, 161, 162, 170–71; notices during May Fourth Movement, 264–65, 267; on plague measures, 156; and popular nationalism, 170n46, 171; reformist attacks on *yulanpenhui* in, 98–99; used to shame officials, 286, 287; and the Yang Yuelou case, 113–15, 115n65, 142

Sheng-Jing Chouye Gongsuo, 33

Sheng Xuanhuai, 122n6, 177

Shengxuehui (Commercial Education Society), 190

Shenjiang Zhouye Gongsuo, 34

Shenqu (Shanghai song), 28n40

Shi Liangcai, 298, 301, 302
Shibao, 209
Shipping, 49–50, 241. See also Seamen; Steamships
Shipu Chamber of Commerce, 243
Shipyard workers, 63, 196, 234
Shuangdaohui. See Double Sword Society
Shuishou Jun'anhui, 37. See also Ningbo, seamen
Shunde Huiguan, 236
Sichuan: native-place associations, 224n14, 233, 262, 263; railway struggle, 209n81
Sichuan Army Organization Alliance, 209n81
Sichuan Han Army, 208–9
Sichuan Lü Hu Tongxianghui, 262, 263
Sichuan Merchants' Gongsuo, 186
Sigongtang, 33
Sijiao Island, 243
Silk and Tea Trade Association, 286
Silk Guild, 153
Silk Huiguan, 35–36, 110
Silk trade, 33–34, 59, 60, 134
Siming Changsheng Hui. See Changsheng Hui
Siming Gongsuo, 12, 86n3, 153, 206, 209, 225, 229n23, 237, 238, 289; admission of women, 308n7; and the case of Zhou Shengyou, 179–80, 182–83; cemetery land of, 159, 160, 275; charitable activities of, 124, 253–54, 274; coffin repositories and shipment, 225n17, 249n73, 252–53, 294n81; earth god temple in, 92; and May Fourth Movement, 266; and Mixed Court Riot of December 1905, 190, 191, 193; in the nineteenth century, 50, 61n28, 81, 126, 127n16; and plague-prevention measures, 157; Shen Honglai and, 173–74, 175; subdivided by trade, 36; and worker mutual-aid associations, 101–2; yulanpen sacrifices at, 102. See also Ningbo Tongxianghui; Siming Gongsuo Cemetery Riots; Siming Gongsuo directors
Siming Gongsuo Cemetery Riots, 158–69; and nationalism, 169–72
Siming Gongsuo directors, 161n29, 183n11, 193; and settlement of Ningbo cemetery strike, 165–68. See also Fang Mingshan; Shen Dunhe; Shen Zhongli; Yan Xiaofang; Yan Xinhou; Ye Cheng'ai; Zhou Jinzhen
Siming Hospital, 253

Siming Lü Hu Tongxianghui, 225
Siming Number One Charitable School, 254
Sino-French War (1883–1885), 127, 170n46
Sino-Japanese War (1894–1895), 144n60, 151, 169
Skinner, G. William, 30, 45, 50
Small East Gate, 50
Small Sword museum, 78n66
Small Sword Society, 67n40, 73, 76, 77
Small Sword Uprising of 1853, 40n59, 48, 53n9, 54, 62, 62n29, 72–83; destruction of huiguan cemeteries in, 159, 160n26
Smuggling, 53, 69n46, 130, 286n60; opium, 68–70, 135–36
Social circles, 238, 273
Social control, 21–22, 73, 283, 96–97, 128–29
Society to Prepare for the Establishment of a Constitution, 207n76
Sojourning, 5n4, 5n5, 6–8, 9n13, 96. See also Native-place identity; Native-place sentiment
Sojourning Guangdong Merchants' Federation, 40n60
Sojourning Indigo Dye Trade Association, 284
Song Hanzhang, 213
South City Roadworks Bureau, 199
South Shanghai Educational and Commercial Association, 185
Southeast Asia, sojourners in, 210, 241–42
Southern Railway Protection Association, 207
State, and society, 291–92, 295, 311, 313–14. See also "Public sphere"
Steamships, 63, 121, 123, 138
Straw and Mud Gang, 72, 77
Strikes: and class relations in native-place associations, 88, 172–73; electrical workers, 284; of Guangdong workers, 63n31, 89, 153n8; May Fourth general, 265–68; Ningbo cemetery, 165–69, 170, 175; of Ningbo and Guangdong seamen, 275. See also Mixed Court Riot of December 1905
Student associations, 231–33, 259
Student military corps, 208
Students: and the Anti-American Boycott of 1905, 184n16, 185n19; arrests of, 261, 263, 265, 268; Chaozhou, 229–31, 274;

Students (*continued*)
in Japan, 196; in May Fourth Movement, 261, 263, 265, 268; and the Mixed Court Riot of December 1905, 189–90; and native-place associations, 224, 229–31, 308; after 1949, 306; radical, 195–96, 232–33
Su Baosen, 157n17, 180n4
Su-Song-Tai Daotai. *See* Daotai
Subang Gongsuo, 33
Subang Zhubaoye Gongsuo, 33
Subei gangsters, 20, 298
Subei Refugee Assistance Committee, 298n92
Subei sojourners, 15, 18; stereotype of, 15, 107–8, 107n48; women, 234; workers, 159, 234, 235n43. *See also* Jiangbei sojourners
Subei Sojourners' Federation, 298
Subei Tongxiang Friendly Society, 40n60
Sugar Gang, 72, 77
Sugar trade, 30, 33–34n48, 133–34, 243, 251n77
Sun Fo, 278, 296
Sun Yat-sen, 206, 210n85, 211, 215, 246n67, 247, 248n70, 248n71, 297; views on nation building, 258–60
Suzhou: sojourners, 54, 224n14; sojourners in, 10, 59–60n23; Suzhou prostitutes, 24; trade associations, 33
Suzhou-Hangzhou-Ningbo Railway, 214
Suzhou Tongxianghui, 238, 269, 269n30
Swatow. *See* Shantou
"Swatow Opium Guild," 131–32
Swindlers, claiming native-place ties, 218–19n3

Taiping rebellion, 35, 53–54, 121n2, 126–27, 151
Taishan county (Guangdong), 63
Taixi Shiwu Gonghui, 37
Takee, 84n1. *See also* Yang Fang
Tan Guozhong, 189
Tanaka Issei, 104, 105
Tang dun. See Sugar Gang
Tang Jiezhi, 272, 308
Tang Jingxing, 40, 61, 85n2, 137, 139n49, 143, 193n43
Tang Maozhi, 35, 60, 61, 110, 132n31, 144
Tang Shaoyi, 247
Tangqiao bang. See Dike and Bridge Gang
Tangye Yang-Guang haiwei nanbeihuo ye

(Fujian Sugar Trade and Fujian Foreign, Guangdong, Seafood and North-South Trade), 186n20
Tao Chengzhang, 212–13n90, 215
Taxation, 33, 129–35, 191, 192, 286. See also *Lijin*
Tea merchants, 50, 112, 121; Anhui, 32–33, 286; Guangdong, 59, 60
Tea Traders' Guild, 153
Technological innovation, 144, 310. *See also* Transportation and communication technologies
Temple Gang, 72, 77
Textile merchants, 71
Textile mills, 234
Theatrical performances, 103–4, 106, 107n47. *See also* Opera performances
Three Dot Society, 69
Three People's Principles, 259, 296
Three Provinces Federation, 239
Tian Zhimin, 156
Tianhou, 9, 25, 50, 56, 58, 67, 87n7
Tingzhou (Fujian) merchants, 34
Titles, purchase of, 61
Tobacco and Wine Federation, 265–66
Tobacco merchants, 50
Tocsin, 181
Tongren Fuyuantang, 6n6, 121
Tongshanhui, 36
Tongwen Shuju, 138
Tongxianghui: activities in native place, 286–87; architecture of, 220, 226; and commercial disputes, 283; compared to *huiguan*, 220–21, 222, 251, 271; and democratic political forms, 220–21, 274; growth in, during Republican period, 223, 239–40; membership of, 226n19, 232, 281–82; in Nanjing decade, 278, 280, 281–87; and nationalist sentiment, 221n8, 299–301; origins of, 217, 224; political activities of, 231, 271; to promote investment in the mainland, 305–6; reformist programs of, 226–28, 299; relationship to *huiguan*, 225; relationship with the state, 286, 291–96, 303–4; use of term, 40–41; in wartime Shanghai, 287–91. *See also* Names of individual *tongxianghui*
Tongye gonghui. See Trade associations
Trade associations, 232, 283, 286, 306; before the Opium War, 49–50; multiple-trade associations, 34; and native-place

organization, 29–32, 32n44, 36–38, 39n58, 45, 250–51; nonexclusive, 35–36; single-trade associations, 32–34; subdivided by native place, 34–35. *See also* Worker associations
Tradition and modernity. *See* Modernity
Transportation and communication technologies, 121, 123, 138
Treaty of Nanjing, 68
Triad Society, 69
Tribute rice, 140n50, 141
Tuanbai (ritual greetings), 294
Twenty-One Demands, 220
Twyman, British Assessor, 187n25, 188, 190, 193n43

Unemployment. *See* Vagrancy
Unequal treaties, 119, 138
United States, Chinese labor and immigration in, 183, 185. *See also* Anti-American Boycott of 1905
Universal Salvation Ritual. See *Yulanpen*
Urban identity, 26, 46, 203–4, 302; and cosmopolitanism, 145–46. *See also* Shanghai identity

Vagrancy, 63–65, 73, 96, 191n36
Van der Sprenkel, Sybille, 18
Van Kah-der, 213
Volunteer Corps of the Municipal Settlement, 199

Wan Nian Feng, 57n16
Wan Shi Feng, 56. *See also* Chaozhou Huiguan
Wan Shi Rong, 57n16
Wang Dingjiu, guidebook of, 22, 23
Wang Ruizhi, 156
Wang Shulin, 135n40
Wang Tao, 104n42
Wang Xiaolai, 219, 278, 298, 302
Wang Yiting, 208, 211n88, 213–14, 302
Wang Zhenchang, 161n29
Wangjiangjing (Jiangsu), silk merchants from, 33
War relief, 291n74, 291–92n76
War with Japan, 287–91
Ward, Frederick Townsend, 127n16
Warlord period, 243n58, 246n67, 257
Weber, Max, 42, 43, 46
Wei family of Guangdong, 112–13

Wen Zongyao, 156, 210, 211n87, 213, 215, 272
Wenming juyueshe (Civilized Treaty Resistance Society), 190
Wenzhou (Zhejiang) native-place associations, 223n13, 237, 262
Wenzhou Tongxianghui, 237, 262
Western imperialism, 47. *See also* Antiforeign activity; Foreigners
Westernization, 137, 309
Widows, 251n78, 308n7
Women: governance of, 116–17; property of, 251n78; and *tongxianghui* membership, 221, 221n9, 282, 308n7
Worker associations, 101, 102–3n40, 272, 284. *See also* Trade associations
Workers: mobilization of, 173, 175, 196, 264; native-place associations for, 88–89, 224, 282; native-place organization among, 63, 233–36; rebellion against *tongxiang* hierarchy, 275–76. *See also* Strikes; Worker associations
World Peace Federation, 261n8
World War I, 219
Wu Jianzhang, 53n8, 61–62, 70n48, 73–74; and Small Sword Uprising, 76, 79, 82
Wu Shaoqing, 194n44
Wu Tiecheng, 278, 284, 291n74, 296, 297n89
Wu Tingfang, 207, 211, 211n87, 213, 247
Wu Xu, 2, 126–27
Wu Zhichang, 139n49
Wuchang Uprising (October 1911), 198, 207, 215
Wuhan, worker organization in, 196
Wujin Gonghui, 37
Wuxi, 233, 234, 249n74; Wuxi huiguan, 153
Wuyuan county (Anhui), tea association of, 32–33

Xi family of Suzhou, 121n2, 219
Xiamen, 73
Xiangqing (native-place sentiment), 2
Xiangshan county (Guangdong): compradors, 60–61; regional reputation of, 107; sojourners, 8, 61, 82. *See also* Xu Run
Xiangshan (Zhejiang) sojourners, 36
Xiangtan, 103n41
Xiangyi (native-place sentiment), 2
Xiaodaohui. See Small Sword Society
Xie Lunhui, 185n18, 194n44

Xijin (Wuxi) Huiguan, 156
Xin'an county (Guangzhou), sojourners from, 55n11
Xing Zhong Hui, 196
Xing'an Huiguan, 66, 74. *See also* Li Xianyun
Xinghua (Fujian) native-place associations, 77
Xingjiang Chaye Gongsuo, 32
Xinya Restaurant, 23, 29n42
Xinzha district, 251–52
Xu Baoting, 60, 61, 62
Xu Dingxin, 43, 186
Xu Gongruo, 156
Xu Hongfu, 138n46
Xu Linguang, 189
Xu Rongcun, 60, 61
Xu Run, 11, 60–61, 121, 137, 138n46, 139n49, 193n43; charitable activities of, 85n2, 122; and China Merchants' Steam Navigation Company, 139–40; and the Mixed Court Riot of December 1905, 189
Xu Yunxuan, 60
Xu Yuting, 127, 144n60
Xu Zhejiang, 215

Yamen architecture, 18–19
Yan Chengye, 191, 192n40
Yan Xiaofang, 165n37, 166, 173. *See also* Yan Xinhou
Yan Xinhou, 177, 178n1, 214. *See also* Yan Xiaofang
Yang Fang, 127, 127n16, 144n60
Yang Liqiang, 204
Yang Xinzhi, 156, 213
Yang Yuelou, case of, 111–17, 142
Yanghang Lane. *See* Foreign Trade Lane
Yantai (Shandong), 56n16
Yao Wennan, 201n60
Ye Cheng'ai, 165n37
Ye Chengzhong, 121, 138, 141, 166
Ye Hongtao, 180n4
Ye Huijun, 205
Ye Tingjuan, 85n2, 143; and the Yang Yuelou case, 113, 113n59, 114, 115
Ye Xinhou, 138
Yi (righteous), 111
Yin county (Zhejiang), 36, 245, 246
Yin huiguan, 8, 8n11, 96n23, 253
Ying Baoshi, 160n26
Ying Guixin, 213

Yixing Company, 78
Yong Tai He tobacco company, 218n2
Yong Wing, 142–43
Yong Xi Tang, 221n8
Yong'an department store, 22
Yongjishe, 36
You Binghan, 194n44, 208
Yu Xiaqing, 84n1, 142n55, 180n4, 194n44, 211n88; formed Chinese Merchants' Exercise Association, 199; as local notable, 138, 218, 278, 302; and the Mixed Court Riot, 189, 193, 194–95; and Ningbo cemetery affair, 168, 193; and the Ningbo Tongxianghui, 284n57, 298; picture of, 200; and plague measures, 156; posts of, 208, 267n23; and railway rights, 214; revolutionary mobilization by, 206; as Siming Gongsuo director, 173, 205; and steamship trade, 142
Yuan Hengzhi, 199n56
Yuan Qicun, 189
Yuan Shikai, 198n55, 217, 243n58
Yuan Shuxun, 199–200
Yuan Zude, 74
Yuanji, as term for native place, 4
Yuedong Gongsuo, 131n27
Yueqiao shangye lianehehui, 40n60
Yulanpen: defined, 93n19; processions and ceremonies, 93–99, 128–29, 168, 269
Yung Wing, 139
Yuyitang, 36

Zeng Ajin, 88, 89n9
Zeng Pan, 189
Zeng Shaoqing, 178n2, 184, 189, 201n60, 204, 216n98
Zhabei, 16, 17n25; 1937 bombing of, 287, 288
Zhan Ronghui, 17
Zhan Xiaoci, 17
Zhang-Chao Huiguan, 56n12
Zhang Chongde, 233n36
Zhang Gui, 74n59
Zhang Jia'ao, 278
Zhang Jingsheng, 229
Zhang Qun, 278
Zhang Sichang, 161n29
Zhang Xueliang, 290
Zhang Zhidong, 144n60, 201
Zhang Zongxiang, 266
Zhangzhou (Fujian) merchants, 34

Zhao Licheng, 161n29
Zhaoqing Prefecture (Guangdong), 59; native-place associations, 50n7, 77, 236, 262. *See also* Guang-Zhao Huiguan
Zhaoqing Tongxianghui, 236, 262
Zhaowen xinbao, 142n56
Zhe-Hu Zhouye Gongsuo, 34
Zhe-Ning Huiguan, 81
Zhe-Shao Gongsuo, opera performances at, 104n42, 105n46
Zhe-Shao Huiguan, 221n8, 237
Zhe-Yan Huiguan, 237
Zhejiang Haichang Gongsuo, 186
Zhejiang Lü Hu Tongxianghui, 262
Zhejiang merchants, 34, 35, 50, 81, 121, 134, 214. *See also* Huzhou sojourners, silk merchants; Ningbo merchants; Rankin, Mary Backus; Ye Chengzhong
Zhejiang native-place associations, 224; list of, 237. *See also* Ningbo native-place associations; Shaoxing native-place associations
Zhejiang sojourners: and banking, shipping and silk sectors, 14–15; and Chamber of Commerce, 214; and Guangfu Hui, 196; immigrated in nineteenth century, 53, 54; nationalist organization by, 205–6, 215, 261; number of, 101, 218n1; in regional hierarchy, 14–15; religious rituals of, 93. *See also* Huzhou sojourners; Ningbo sojourners
Zheng (opium merchants), 71
Zheng Bozhao, 218
Zheng Caoru, 85n2
Zheng Guanying, 60–61, 88n8, 99n33, 122, 123, 137, 139
Zheng Qia Ji establishment, 71
Zheng Sitai, 71, 71n50
Zheng Xiancheng, 189
Zheng Zhengqiu, 71n50
Zheng Zijia, 71n50

Zheng Ziliang, 135n40, 284n57, 298
Zhenhai county (Ningbo): Dike Works Bureau, 243; sojourners, 36, 218
Zhenjiang: Guangzhou *huiguan* in, 59n23; opium trade, 131–33; sugar merchants, 34n48
Zhong Fuguang, 233
Zhong Ziyuan, 156, 157n17
Zhongguo furu jiuji zonghui. *See* Chinese Society for Assistance to Women and Children
Zhongguo Tongmeng Hui, 196. *See also* Revolutionary Alliance
Zhongshan (Guangdong), sojourners from, 218
Zhongyang University (Nanjing), 286n62
Zhongyuanjie. *See Yulanpen*
Zhou Dalin, 161n29
Zhou Fu, Governor General, 180
Zhou Jinzhen, 142n55, 155, 156, 180n4, 185n18, 194n44, 211n88, 214; and Shanghai General Chamber of Commerce, 177, 178n2
Zhou Liansheng, 185
Zhou Lichun, 76, 78n68, 79
Zhou Shengyou, case of, 179–83, 185
Zhou Xiaolu, 173
Zhou Xisan, 265
Zhu Baosan, 180n4, 194n44, 201n60, 208, 209n82, 211n88, 245; and Ningbo Tongxianghui, 225, 226; and plague measures, 156
Zhu Lanfang, 156
Zhu Xi, 32n45
Zhu Zhongsan, 221n9
Zhuang Jianren, 161n29
Ziqiang. *See* Self-strengthening movement
Ziyi (native-place sentiment), 2
Zongli Yamen, 139
Zongzi (leaf-wrapped delicacies), 26

Designer: Nola Burger
Compositor: Graphic Composition, Inc., with Asco Trade Typesetting
Text: Galliard
Display: Galliard
Printer: Braun-Brumfield
Binder: Braun-Brumfield